This Land Is Your Land

This Land Is Your Land

THE GEOGRAPHIC EVOLUTION OF THE UNITED STATES

SEYMOUR I. SCHWARTZ

HARRY N. ABRAMS, INC., PUBLISHERS

To Julia, Hunter, Laura, Dana, and Alexis,

who have benefited

by our country's great past,

and who will be part

of its even greater future.

Pages 2–3: Paolo Forlani. "Il disegno del discoperto della nuoa Franza. . . ."
In Antonio Lafreri's composite atlas, Rome, 1566 (detail; see page 27).

Page 6: John Mitchell. "The so-called red-line map." London, 1755
(detail; see page 187).

Project Manager: Nicole Columbus
Editor: Richard Slovak
Designer: Maria Learmonth Miller

Library of Congress Cataloging-in-Publication Data

Schwartz, Seymour I., 1928–
This land is your land : the geographic evolution of the United States /
Seymour I. Schwartz.
p. cm.
Includes bibliographical references (p.) and index.
ISBN 0–8109–6715–4
1. United States—Geography. 2. United States—Maps. 1. Title.
E161.3 .S39 2000

917—dc21   00–031320

Printed and bound in Japan

Harry N. Abrams, Inc.
100 Fifth Avenue
New York, N.Y. 10011
www.abramsbooks.com

Contents

Foreword

SEYMOUR I. SCHWARTZ IS ONE OF AMERICA'S MOST DISTIN-guished surgeons, recognized as such by his patients, medical academics, professional groups, and foreign governments. The nature of his work fills his busy life with tensions. A man of broad interests, he has needed the distraction of a serious hobby. The hobby he has chosen, collecting the earliest maps of North America and elsewhere in the Western Hemisphere, has carried with it a remarkable understanding of both history and geography. It is no surprise to those who know him that he has become a consultant to the Library of Congress on American cartography. He had earlier published a book describing and providing the historical context of the many remarkable maps in his collection, including one actually drawn by George Washington following the route of his trip as a young man to the Ohio Valley, to warn the French, prior to the French and Indian War, that their activity in the area could lead to war with the British. This current book, much broader in its scope, is both a happy product of his leisure and an authoritative conjunction of history and geography.

How, when, and by whom was America explored and put together as a nation? Were its growth and development accidents of history, or manifest destiny? Why, beyond the realities of frontier democracy and the whims of early explorers, do we have such a diversity of place-names, many of them transplanted from elsewhere? What were the impediments to expansion? These are the kinds of questions Dr. Schwartz explores and explains, as this helpful book takes form from his exhaustive research. The answers mark the stages of the evolution of our country.

And the answers come in many forms. Maps are instructive, but they do not explain the processes that bring them into being. The routes of the first Spanish explorers and their motivations are explained here in detail. We follow Lewis and Clark. We travel the Oregon Trail. Until the Civil War, we watch the struggles in Congress between the free-staters and the slave-staters. Territories are turned into states, and disputed boundaries are negotiated. The story Dr. Schwartz puts together is good both for overview and for detail. The inquiring reader can learn the dimensions of his or her own state, and why the state capital is where it is, or oversee the western march of the pioneer, or understand the relations between a declining Spain and an arrogant Napoleon that made the Louisiana Purchase possible. Here, in one place, all kinds of answers are available. Every library in the country, and particularly high school libraries, should have this easily read book, for reference.

I have the suspicion that geography is not now as central a study in our elementary and secondary schools as it was in the early part of the twentieth century. This is regrettable. History remains an important study for young Americans, but Dr. Schwartz, in quoting the seventeenth-century English explorer John Smith, makes the point that "History without Geography wandereth as vagrant without certaine habitation." Both subjects are so closely tied in this book that it must become an easy research tool for those who want to understand the origins and dimensions of our basic Americana.

Fortunately, our country is young enough so that a researcher like the author can put the facts simply before us, uncomplicated by the riddles of antiquity, and without the mysteries implicit in the distant traditions and changing languages of Europe, Asia, and Africa. Our country, unlike many others, was founded in a relatively literate era, and the records are there for those who are willing to avail themselves of the written word.

One area of confusion in American place-names occurs with respect to Native American names. The hundreds of Indian languages, mellifluous and appealing as they are, were not written (with a few latter-day exceptions), and the Yankee ear was not attuned to their music. They are found all over the map, but frequently their meanings are obscure and their pronunciation has been unwittingly vandalized.

Another entertaining variation in the familiar names brought from other countries by nostalgic immigrants is the sometimes subtle changes in pronunciation that took place after their arrival. For instance, in the area of western New York where Dr. Schwartz and I both live, we have such communities as Lima, Avon, Java, Corfu, Castile, Charlotte, Chili, and Bergen. The locals ignore precedent and mispronounce each one of these historical names rather than strictly following the original pronunciation. Cynics say this is a deliberate ploy to identify the outsiders; if someone pronounces the place-name correctly, we know immediately that he's a stranger to our parts, not one of us. In this light, the deviation is more an expression of local gamesmanship than misunderstanding. Of course, it's always possible that illiteracy played a role sometime in the past.

The illustrations in this book are particularly noteworthy. The author knows as much about American mapping as anyone alive. The fruits of exploration unfold before our eyes, and the delineation of territories and ultimately state boundaries are demonstrated in detail. The explorers of terra incognita were prompt in removing doubts and false rumors about what lay beyond the horizon, and illusions about access to the Orient quickly became a New World for settlers seeking remoteness from the strictures of the Old World. To judge from the rapid sequence of maps, our ancestors had a good idea of where they were headed before they started out.

As we enter the twenty-first century, it is obvious that immigration is bringing us increasing diversity as a national characteristic. We do not resist this, as we did at some times in the past, because by now we know that immigrants bring us a renewed vitality. After a few generations in this country, Americans tend to become complacent about the prosperity and entitlements our American system has brought us. The very diversity of our place-names—English, Native American, Spanish, French, classical, and others—carries the implication of hospitality. If American communities are not open to a wide range of people, what communities are?

Barber Conable Jr.
Chairman of the Executive Committee,
Board of Regents, Smithsonian Institution

Introduction

These are the Lines that shew thy Face; but those
That shew thy Grace and Glory, brighter bee:
Thy Faire-Discoueries and Fowle-Overthrowes
Of Salvages, much Civill'zd by thee_
Best shew thy Spirit; and to it Glory Wyn;
So, thou art Braße without, but Golde within.

JOHN SMITH (fig. 1)—ONE OF THE FOUNDERS OF JAMESTOWN, Virginia, which in 1607 became the first permanent English settlement in America—wrote in 1624: "As Geography without History seemeth as carkasse without motion, so History without Geography wandereth as vagrant without certaine habitation." An understanding of our land, the nation in which we live, can be augmented by considering the country's development in terms of the changes that brought the United States of America to its current configuration and dimensions. Almost five hundred years of discoveries, expansions, and settlements led to the present shape and boundaries of the United States and the definition of the fifty individual states. Contemporary maps created to artistically chronicle these events and the consequent geographic changes dramatically reinforce the words that recount the history of the country's evolution. Discovery and expansion also meant the assignment of names to the newly populated lands and newly established communities. Many of these names have historic implications or fascinating associations. Exploring the cartographic history of the United States and the evolution of our geographic lexicon can provide a greater appreciation for the sentiments perhaps best expressed in Woody Guthrie's lyrics: "This land is your land. This land is my land." Through this exploration, we can better understand the ways in which "This land was made for you and me."

1. *Artist unknown. Portrait of Capt. John Smith. 1614. Engraving. Private collection. Inset on a map by Smith (see fig. 43).*

CHAPTER ONE

Earliest European Probes

FIRST VOYAGES TO THE NEW WORLD

Permanent European settlement of the "New World," a term attributed to Italian navigator Amerigo Vespucci and soon applied to all land in the Western Hemisphere, came about as a result of Christopher Columbus's voyages of discovery. An Italian mariner born in Genoa, Columbus was sailing westward under the flag of King Ferdinand and Queen Isabella of Spain, in search of a shorter route to the East Indies and the Orient, when, on October 12, 1492, he made his initial landfall in the New World, on an island in the Bahamas north of the eastern tip of Cuba. The island, which he named San Salvador, is generally believed to be the one that was subsequently known as Watling Island and has now been renamed San Salvador. (Precise identification of the island where Columbus first landed has been a matter of dispute among scholars.) The natives living there became known as Indians because of the mistaken belief that Columbus had reached the East Indies. They referred to the island as Guanahani. On this trip the voyagers also landed on the shore of Cuba, which Columbus named Juana after the daughter of Ferdinand and Isabella. The final landing during the first voyage was made on the island of Hispaniola (in Spanish, Española, now comprising the Dominican Republic and Haiti), where he built a fort and later established a settlement after the fort was destroyed (fig. 2). This became Columbus's base in the Caribbean, to which he returned on each of his four voyages.

The landfalls made by Christopher Columbus and his crews during their four voyages from Spain between 1492 and 1504 did not include any part of what was to become the United States, with the exception of the region around Boquerón Bay and Cape Rojo in southwestern Puerto Rico. In November 1493, during the second voyage, three days were spent on that island. Several of the sailors on that trip elected to stay in Hispaniola (Dominican Republic). Those men later became the first settlers of Puerto Rico, which was subsequently given the name designating it a "rich port." Columbus's third voyage, in 1498, included a landing on the South American continent, at the mouth of the Orinoco River in present-day Venezuela. During the fourth and final voyage, in 1502–3, Columbus's ships traveled along the east coast of Central America. None of Columbus's crews ever set foot on the North American continent.

Juan de la Cosa's 1500 "Portolan World Chart," a manuscript on oxhide, is the earliest map to show Columbus's discoveries in the Caribbean (fig. 3). It is also the only authentic cartographic record of the John Cabot (Giovanni Caboto) expedition of 1497, conducted under a patent from King Henry VII of England, who was seeking to establish an English claim and presence in the New World. This resulted in the first North American landfall, on either Cape Breton Island or Newfoundland. No permanent settlement resulted from that exploration, however; no name exists today from that voyage, and none appears on Juan de la Cosa's map.

2. Artist unknown. Columbus's landing at Hispaniola. In "In lauden Serenissimi Ferdinandi Hispaniarum regis Bethicae & regni Granatae obsidio victoria & triuphus. Et de Insulis in mari Indico nuper inuetis," Basle: J[ohann] B[ergman, de Olpe], 1494. Woodcut, 11.3 x 7.5 cm. Private collection. The first pictorial representation of the New World. On March 15, 1493, Christopher Columbus returned to Spain from his first voyage and sent letters to the court announcing his discoveries. The second issue of a letter to the court was published in Latin in Basle (now Basel, Switzerland), accompanied by this fanciful illustration.

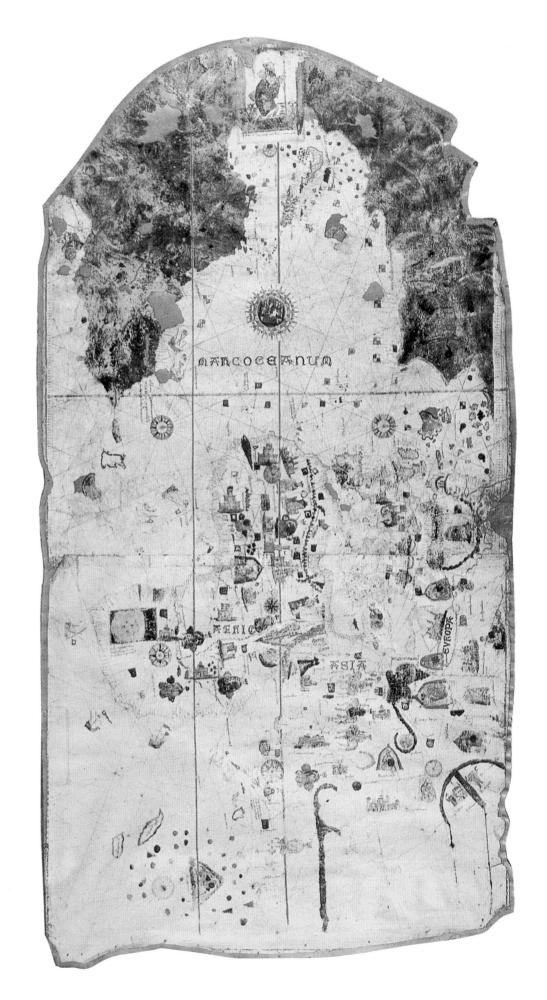

3. *Juan de la Cosa. "Portolan World Chart."*
1500. Illuminated manuscript on oxhide,
96 x 180 cm. Museo Naval, Madrid.
The earliest map showing any part of the
continent of North America. Columbus's
discoveries in the Caribbean are depicted.
The phrases "mar descubierta por yngleses"
(sea discovered by the English) and "cavo de
ynglaterra" (cape of England) indicate evidence
of the Cabot voyages in 1497 and 1498;
the map is the only cartographic evidence of
John Cabot's expedition in 1497, when
he discovered North America.

The first map of the New World to be printed in Spain was produced in 1511 by Peter Martyr (Pietro Martire d'Anghiera), an Italian humanist and historian who was the tutor for the children of King Ferdinand and Queen Isabella. It is also the first printed map to focus on Columbus's discoveries.

An even earlier printed map is historically significant for another reason. It was published in Strasbourg in 1507, and on it is the word "America," the name by which we are recognized (fig. 4). The German geographer-cartographer Martin Waldseemüller actually assigned the name at first only to the South American continent. In the accompanying text, *Cosmographiae Introductio*, Waldseemüller wrote: "Now truly these parts [Europe, Africa, Asia] have been more widely explored, and another, fourth part has been discovered by Americus Vespucius (as will appear in what follows), and I do not see why anyone should rightly forbid naming it Amerige—land of Americus, as it were, after its discoverer Americus, a man of acute

4. *Martin Waldseemüller. "Universalis cosmographia." Strasbourg, 1507. Woodcut, 12 sheets designed to be joined, 137 x 244 cm. Castle Wolfegg, Württemberg. The earliest known map with the name "America" for the New World (labeling what came to be called South America; see the detail above). The Western Hemisphere depicted above the main map shows continuity between the subsequently named North and South America.*

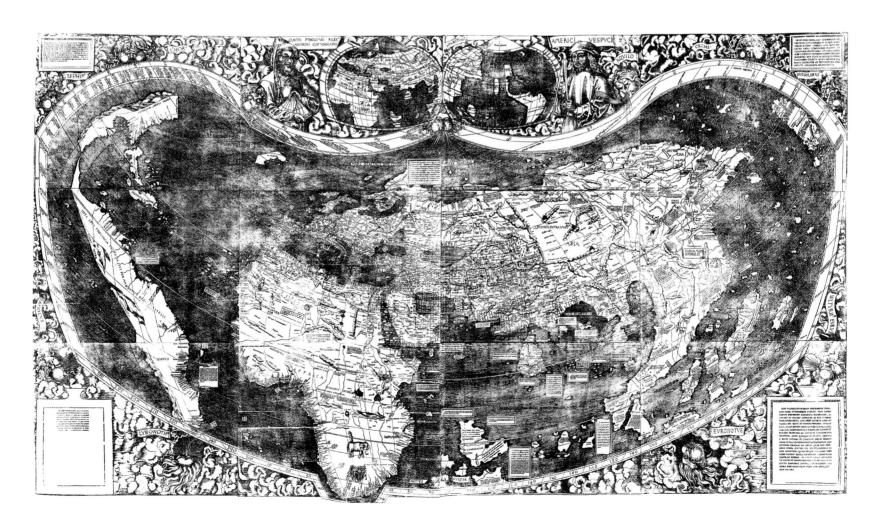

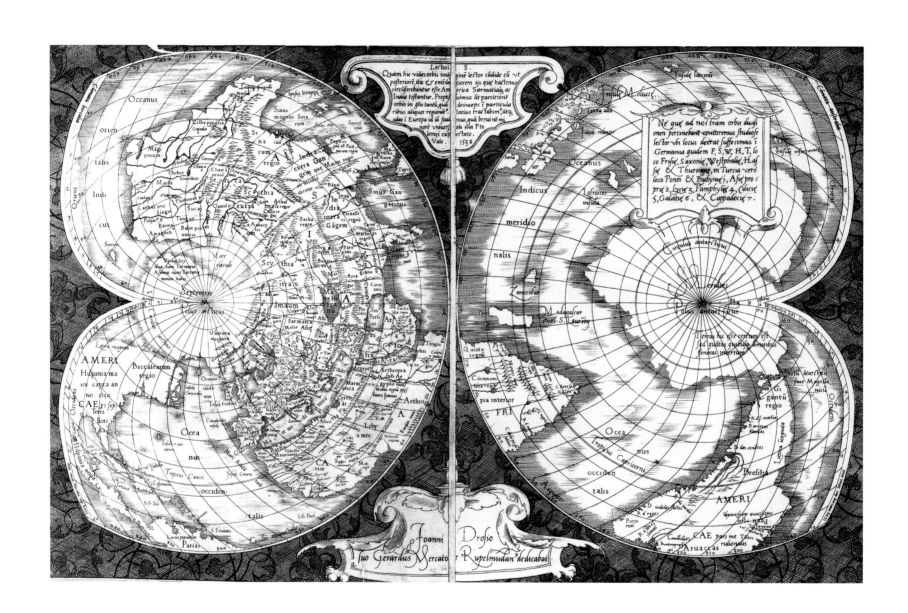

5. *Gerardus Mercator. "A Map of the World in Two Hemispheres." Louvain, 1538.*
Engraved map in a double cordiform projection, 31 x 55 cm.
Rare Books Division, New York Public Library. Astor, Lenox and Tilden
Foundations. The first map to place the name America ("Americae") on both the
North American and South American continents.

genius—or America, since both Europe and Asia have received their names from women." Six years later, in 1513, Waldseemüller acknowledged the primacy of Columbus's discoveries over those of Amerigo Vespucci (who was also known by the Latin name that Waldseemüller used) and dropped the name "America" from his maps and writings. But as is often the case in journalism today, a retraction is rarely noticed.

The name "America" also referred to the North American continent for the first time on the Paris Globe, about 1515, and on a printed map in 1538, when the Flemish cartographer Gerardus Mercator (the Latin name of Gerhard Kremer) published his first world map in Louvain, now in Belgium (fig. 5). But for the first permanent impact on the names in the current continental United States, we must return to the island of Puerto Rico and to the conquistador Juan Ponce de León, who accompanied Columbus on his second voyage.

Ponce de León, the Spanish governor of Puerto Rico from 1509, sailed from the island port of San Germán on March 3, 1513, to explore the landmass that had previously been sighted to the north. About April 2, during the Easter week, known to the Spanish as Pascua Florida, he sighted the continental peninsula to which he assigned the name of the holiday in his writings documenting the journey. Thus, "Florida" became the first European name to be placed on the North American continent. That name designated the entire southeastern part of the continent, encompassing Georgia and the Carolinas in addition to the Florida peninsula, for nearly two hundred years.

During his exploration, Ponce de León passed a cape that he named Cabo de las Corrientes (Cape of the Currents), but shortly thereafter it was renamed Cape Canaveral, which was the Spanish name for canebrake, the thickets of reeds that grow off the coast. Cape Canaveral remains the oldest persistent place-name in the continental United States designating a specific location. With the advent of the United States space program, the name was changed to Cape Kennedy to honor President John F. Kennedy after his assassination in 1963. But as a consequence of a formal petition by a group interested in American history, the historic name Cape Canaveral was reassigned to Cape Kennedy in 1973, while the space center there retained the name of the late president (fig. 6). Continuing his voyage of exploration around the peninsula, Ponce de León sailed west past the Florida Keys and then north, landing around Tampa Bay, or perhaps as far as present-day Pensacola. On a second voyage from Puerto Rico in 1521, he was ambushed by Indians in the vicinity of Tampa Bay and fatally wounded.

In 1519, Alonso Alvarez de Pineda conducted a nine-month exploration of the Gulf of Mexico, which ended in his death but demonstrated that Florida was part of the mainland that extended from Mexico and that there was no passage from the Gulf of Mexico to the Pacific Ocean. The manuscript map from Pineda's exploration bears the name "Florida" for the first time (fig. 7). The first printed map to indicate that name is ascribed to Hernán Cortés,

6. *From the Kennedy Space Center at historic Cape Canaveral, the space shuttle* Columbia *is launched into the night sky for a five-day mission in 1993. Courtesy National Aeronautics and Space Administration, Houston*

7. *Cartographer unknown. "Pineda Chart." c. 1519. Manuscript, pen and ink, 31 x 44 cm. Archivo General de Indias, Seville. This map, describing Alonso Alvarez de Pineda's voyage, is the earliest one to depict the Gulf of Mexico correctly and to assert the absence of a passage from the gulf to the Pacific Ocean. It is also the first dated map to show the name "Florida." In addition, "Corpus Christi" is the name applied to a bay.*

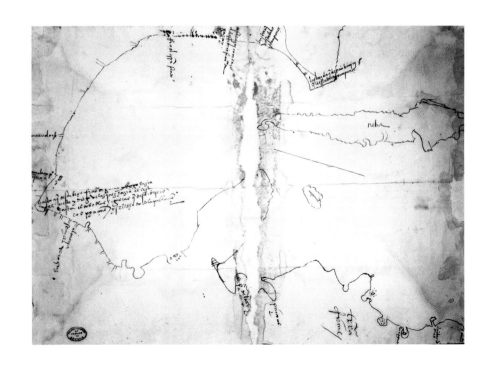

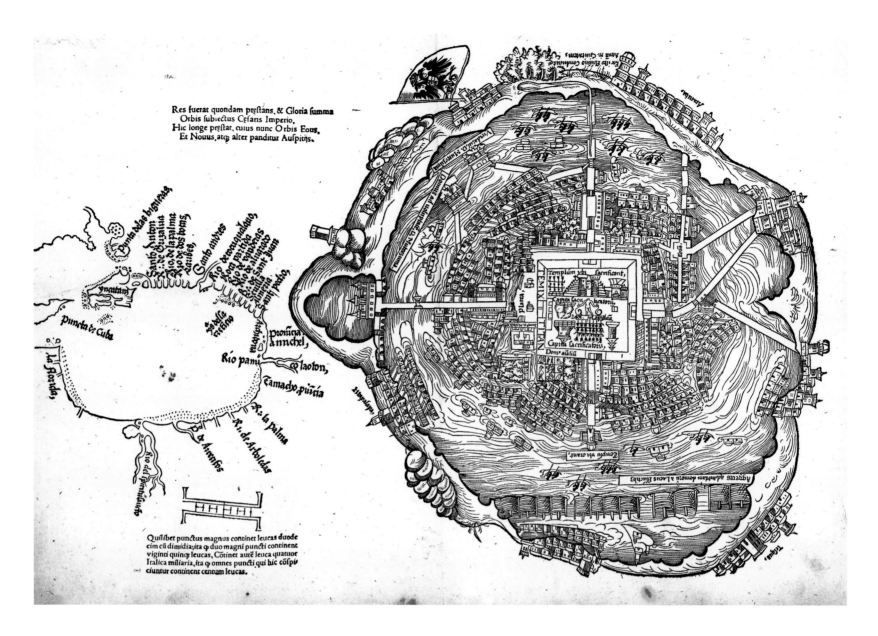

Res fuerat quondam pręstans, & Gloria summa
Orbis subiectus Cęsaris Imperio,
Hic longe pręstat, cuius nunc Orbis Eous,
Et Nouus, atq alter panditur Auspicijs.

Quilibet punctus magnus continet leucas duode
cim cū dimidiā, ita qp duo magni puncti continent
viginti quinqꝫ leucas, Cotinet aurē leuca quatuor
Italica miliaria, ita qp omnes puncti qui hic cōspi
ciuntur continent centum leucas.

8. Hernán Cortés. "Map of Mexico City and the Gulf Coast."
In Cortés's Praeclara Ferdinadi. Cortesi de Nova Maris Oceani Hispania
narratio, *Nuremberg, 1524. Woodcut, 48 x 55 cm. Private collection.*
The first printed map showing the Gulf Coast and the name "Florida," as well as
the earliest plan of a pre-Columbian city.

conqueror of the Aztec emperor Montezuma and of Mexico; it was published in Spain in 1524 (fig. 8).

In 1521, Francisco Gordillo, sailing from Hispaniola, joined up with Pedro de Quexos, who was a slave trader cruising the Caribbean, and proceeded to Winyah Bay (now in South Carolina), where they landed; on a second voyage, they sailed as far north as the Outer Banks (now in North Carolina). Five years later, Lucas Vasquez de Ayllón, a wealthy lawyer and judge, sailed from his home in Hispaniola and landed in the vicinity of what was later called the Cape Fear River, establishing a settlement near present-day Wilmington, North Carolina. That settlement lasted only two years but the area's name,

Chicora, derived from that of a local Indian tribe, survived much longer; it was applied to the coastal region between Charleston, South Carolina, and the Cape Fear River in North Carolina.

The east coast of the North American continent was obviously the most accessible to European mariners, and the geography of that coast was first defined by the voyage of Giovanni da Verrazano (fig. 9). A Florentine navigator sailing for King Francis I of France, Verrazano made landfall on March 1, 1524, near what was later called Cape Fear, North Carolina. He first proceeded southwesterly, then returned north to the Outer Banks separating the Atlantic Ocean from Pamlico and the other Carolina sounds. In the narratives

9. *F. Allegrini. Portrait of Giovanni da Verrazano. 1767. Engraving, after a painting, probably by Giuseppe Zocchi. Courtesy the New-York Historical Society.*
The early-16th-century explorer was the first European to explore the east coast of what would become the United States north of the Florida peninsula. His voyage extended from the northern Florida coast as far north as Newfoundland.

10. *Michael Lok. "North America." In Richard Hakluyt's* Divers voyages touching the discouerie of America and the Islands Adjacent, *London, 1582. Woodcut, 28 x 38 cm. Private collection.*
One of the last representations of the false "Sea of Verrazano." Landmasses are named for Queen Elizabeth I ("R. [Regina] Elizabeth" on the map).

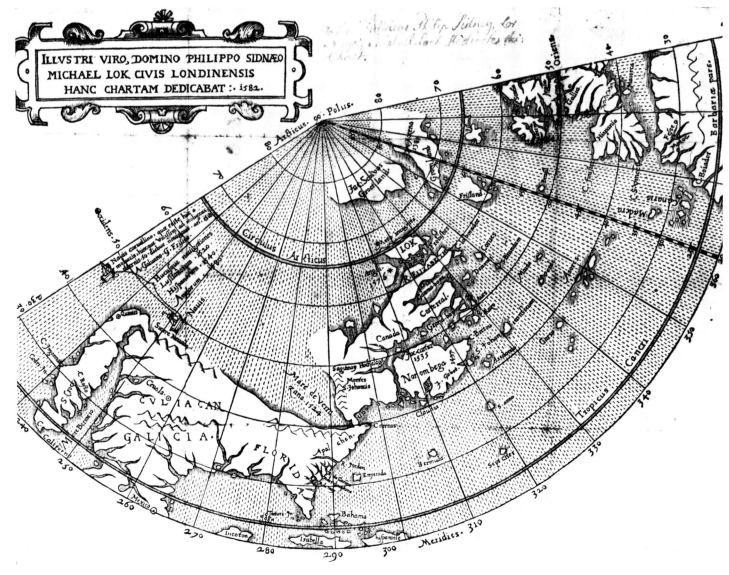

of his voyage, he described the Outer Banks as an isthmus one mile wide and two hundred miles long separating the Atlantic and Pacific oceans. This is the description that resulted in the mistaken "Sea of Verrazano" concept, an attractive suggestion of an easy overland route from the Atlantic Ocean to the Sea of China (Pacific Ocean). This misconception appeared on many maps through the latter half of the sixteenth century (fig. 10).

Verrazano continued north, eventually reaching Newfoundland, before returning to France. On this northern leg of his voyage, Verrazano spent three days anchored along the coast of what became Maryland and Virginia. He named the area Arcadia, because of its similarity to a newly discovered land in the 1504 Italian pastoral poem *Arcadia*. Verrazano missed the opening to Chesapeake Bay, but he became the first European to enter and describe New York Bay and the Hudson River, long before they were so named. He sailed along the waters currently spanned by the modern bridge that bears his name (fig. 11). He then sailed eastward past an island (probably Block Island) that he described as resembling Rhodes, and which he named Aloysia for the mother of the king of France, although it appears as "Luisa" on the maps that chronicled the voyage. Verrazano anchored in Newport Harbor and assigned the name Refugio to Narragansett Bay. But these names, along with the others Verrazano designated in his logs—including Bay Santa Margarita, in honor of the king's sister, for New York Harbor; Vandoma, for a large river, probably the estuary of the Delaware River; and Angoulême, the duchy held by

11. The Verrazano-Narrows Bridge, named in honor of the first European to sail through New York Bay. Courtesy Mayor Rudy Giuliani, New York City. Photograph by Mayor Rudy Giuliani

Francis I before taking the throne, for the land around the bay and river—quickly fell into obscurity.

Also in 1524, Estévan Gomez, after sailing from Spain to Cuba, bypassed the southern and middle Atlantic coast but followed the coast from New England to Nova Scotia in search of a Northwest Passage to the Orient. He explored the Penobscot River in Maine, calling it Río de los Gamos (River of the Deer).

THE INTERIOR OF NORTH AMERICA

Meanwhile, the initial penetrations into the interior of North America were being made at the directive of the Spanish conquistadores, who had established footholds in Mexico and Cuba. By 1521, Cortés had gained control of Tenochtitlán (at what is now Mexico City) and the entire Aztec Empire. The natives there told stories of the legendary Seven Cities of "Cíbola" (a Spanish name derived from the Indian word for buffalo), supposedly laden with gold, in a land to the north. Those tales of wealth served as an impetus for exploration by Spaniards.

The tales were reiterated and reinforced in 1536 by Álvar Núñez Cabeza de Vaca and his three companions. They were the survivors of a group that in 1528 had been shipwrecked on Galveston or San Luis Island off the Gulf Coast of what later became Texas and, during the next eight years, had traveled across present-day Texas, New Mexico, and Arizona before turning south and arriving in Mexico (which by then was the heart of a vast Spanish possession called the viceroyalty of New Spain). Theirs was the first inland journey by Europeans across part of what is now the United States, and during this trip Cabeza de Vaca performed the first chronicled surgical operation in our country; a complete description of the removal of an arrowhead from the chest of an Indian appears in a book that Cabeza de Vaca wrote after he returned to Spain (fig. 12).

Cabeza de Vaca also recorded in his book the second name (after Florida) used to designate a large portion of our country: "Apalachen," derived from the name of a small Indian village in northern Florida. The village had been encountered by Pánfilo de Narváez, who was in charge of the 1527–28 expedition to Florida in which Cabeza de Vaca was second in command. The expedition's goal was to gain control of all the land adjacent to the Gulf of Mexico. After sailing from Spain and landing on the western shore of Florida, Narváez split up his troops, leaving Cabeza de Vaca to lead one group—the one that ended up shipwrecked—while Narváez headed north, ultimately perishing with all his men. "Apalachen" (or a variant) appears on many sixteenth-century maps, referring to a wide expanse of land north of the Florida peninsula (fig. 13). It eventually gave rise to the name assigned to the Appalachian Mountains, which extend along much of the eastern portion of the country. In the early nineteenth century, Washington Irving, the most widely read American author of his time, advocated use of the name Apalachen to designate the entire nation, but the suggestion never gained favor.

12. *De Grazia. "Operation Arrowhead." In* De Grazia
Paints Cabeza de Vaca: The First Non-Indian
in Texas, New Mexico, and Arizona 1527–1536,
Tucson: University of Arizona Press, 1973.
Lithograph, after an oil painting by De Grazia;
17.8 x 20.3 cm. Private collection. This illustration shows
Álvar Núñez Cabeza de Vaca removing an arrowhead from
the chest of an Indian in the 1530s—the first chronicled
surgery in what is now the United States.

13. *Cornely [Cornelis van] Wytfliet. "Florida et Apalche."*
In Wytfliet's Descriptionis Ptolemaicae augmentum
sive Occidentis Notitia, *Louvain, 1597.*
Engraving, 23 x 28 cm. Private collection.
Published in the first atlas devoted solely to the Americas,
this map shows the first ("Florida") and second
("Apalche," or Apalachen) names to be applied to regions
in North America. "Cap de Canaveral" also appears.

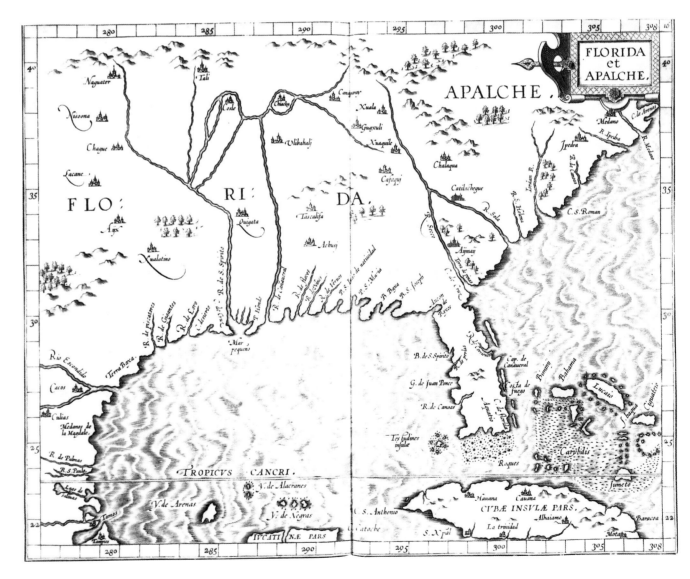

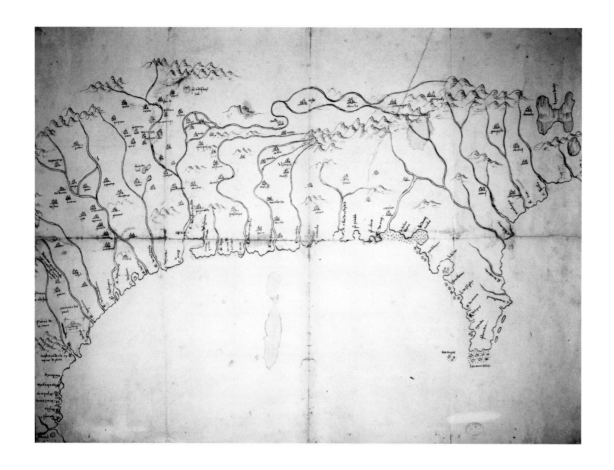

14. *Attributed to Alonso de Santa Cruz.* "Mapa del Golfo y costa del le Nueva España." *c. 1544. Manuscript, ink on paper, 43 x 70 cm. Archivo General de Indias, Seville. The only contemporary map to illustrate the 1539–42 expedition of Hernando De Soto. It shows part of North America extending from Santa Elena (now Port Royal, South Carolina) to the Pánuco River, Mexico.*

15. *[Theodore de Bry?]. A depiction of Hernando De Soto's mistreatment of Florida Indians. In De Bry's Great Voyages, Frankfurt, 1595. Copperplate engraving.*

The prospect of discovering deposits of gold, featured in many native tales, in the interior of the continent inspired Hernando De Soto's quest. De Soto was one of the most successful commanders under the notorious conquistador Francisco Pizarro and had been made governor of Cuba. In 1539, De Soto sailed from Cuba and landed at Tampa Bay. After wintering near what is now Tallahassee, Florida, he led an army of several hundred men across present-day Georgia, the Carolinas, the Great Smoky Mountains, Tennessee, Alabama, and Mississippi. They eventually became the first Europeans to reach the Mississippi River, which they crossed before proceeding through Arkansas and into Oklahoma (fig. 14). They never found gold, however, and in 1542 De Soto died near what is now Ferriday, Louisiana, on the west bank of the Mississippi River. He was buried in the river to prevent desecration of his body by Indians, whom his expedition had mistreated (fig. 15). Despite his extensive travels, no permanent place-names resulted from the De Soto expedition.

Other Spaniards, however, introduced another important name during the first half of the sixteenth century. In the 1530s, one of Cortés's sea captains, sailing off the shore of the peninsula that is now called Baja California, thought that the land he had sighted was an island, and he reported his discovery to Cortés. The conquistador recalled an Indian tale of an island off the west coast that was said to be inhabited and ruled mainly by women and laden with gold and pearls. At the time, there was a well-recognized Spanish romantic poem, *Las sergas del virtuoso cavallero Esplandian* by García Ordoñez Rodríguez

Opposite: 16. *Diego Gutiérrez. "Americae sive quartae obis partis nova et exactissima descriptio." 1562. Engraving, 107 x 104 cm. Library of Congress, Washington, D.C. The first printed map to show the name "California" (as "c. California," on what is now the Baja Peninsula). It also includes the eastern part of North America, and it credits Amerigo Vespucci ("Americo Vespucio") with the discovery of America in 1497.*

de Montalvo, that also told of an island, California, filled with gold and gems and ruled by women under the leadership of their queen, Calafia. According to Antonio de Herrera y Tordesillas, the chronicler of Cortés's accomplishments, Cortés himself designated that the island sighted by the sea captain should be known as California. Diego Gutiérrez's 1562 detailed map of the New World is the first printed one to include the name, as "c. California" (fig. 16).

In 1535, when Cortés himself sailed along the west coast, he thought he sighted another island, which he called Santa Cruz. It was actually part of the Baja California peninsula. Four years later, Francisco de Ulloa sailed up the Gulf of California and proved that Baja California was a peninsula, not an island. Soon after, Hernando de Alarcón confirmed this; he also entered the Colorado River at its mouth, and consequently he is credited with being the first European to reach what is now California.

The Spanish search for gold focused on attempts to find the fabled "Seven Cities of Cíbola." The first viceroy of New Spain, Antonio de Mendoza, sent an expedition north in 1540 under the command of Francisco Vásquez de Coronado, the young governor of Nueva Galicia (now part of western Mexico). Accompanying his expedition was Fray Marcos de Niza, a friar who claimed to have found the golden cities on an expedition a year earlier with one of the four members of the Cabeza de Vaca party. Coronado and his expedition eventually returned to Mexico City, where he reported that the "Seven Cities" were merely Zuni pueblos, which only seemed golden when the bright sun shone on their adobe huts (fig. 17).

17. *Thomas Moran.* Cliff Dwellers. *1899. Oil on canvas, 51 x 76.5 cm. Courtesy Berea College, Berea, Ky. In the bright sun, pueblos seemed golden.*

18. *Thomas Moran.* Grand Canyon. *1912. Oil on composition board,*
40.6 x 61 cm. Nelson-Atkinson Museum of Art, Kansas City, Mo.
Bequest of Katherine Harvey

Nevertheless, Coronado's expedition was successful in exploring much of the current southwestern United States—extending as far northeast as present-day Kansas, a region referred to as Quivira. One of the smaller exploring parties that he sent out reached the rim of the Grand Canyon (fig. 18). His expedition saw the pueblo of Acoma, meaning "white rock people" in Indian, in what is now New Mexico. Acoma, famous for its pottery, was founded sometime between 1100 and 1250 and is the oldest continuously inhabited community in the United States (fig. 19). One of Coronado's lieutenants, Hernando de Alvarado, discovered the Rio Grande, which he named Señora because it was first sighted on the birthday of the Virgin Mary.

While the interior of what would become the United States was being probed in 1540–42, Viceroy Mendoza also sent Juan Rodríguez Cabrillo on a voyage up the western coast. Cabrillo named Cape Mendocino to honor the viceroy. On that voyage of exploration, the ships anchored in San Diego Bay, which Cabrillo named San Miguel. The Cabrillo expedition also anchored in Santa Monica Bay and in a northern bay that a quarter of a century later would be named Drake's Bay. (In 1579, on his westward voyage of navigation, Sir Francis Drake made a landing on the shore of that bay, to which his name was attached. Sixteen years later, Sebastián Rodríguez Cermeño, sailing from Manila in the Philippines, landed in this same inlet northwest of present-day San Francisco and called it San Francisco Bay, because he entered it on the day honoring Saint Francis of Assisi. This was the first use of that name on the North American continent, a name that would later be translocated south to its current location.)

19. *Acoma, founded between 1100 and 1250.*
Photograph © Sarbo®, Albuquerque, N.M.

Opposite, top: 20. *Attributed to Pierre Desceliers. "Harleian mappemonde"*
(detail). c. 1544. Manuscript, pen and ink and watercolor on paper;
entire map, 117 x 249 cm. Department of Manuscripts,
British Library, London. This map shows the discoveries of Jacques Cartier
during his second voyage along the St. Lawrence River, in 1535.
The name "Canada" appears prominently on it.

Opposite, bottom: 21. *Attributed to Giacomo Gastaldi. "La terra de*
Hochelaga nella Nova Francia." In Giovanni Battista Ramusio's
Delle navigationi e viaggi nel quale si contengono le navigatione al
mondo nuovo, *vol. 3, Venice, 1556. Woodcut, 26 x 36 cm. Private collection.*
The first printed plan of a European settlement in North America.
Note the adjacent "Monte Real."

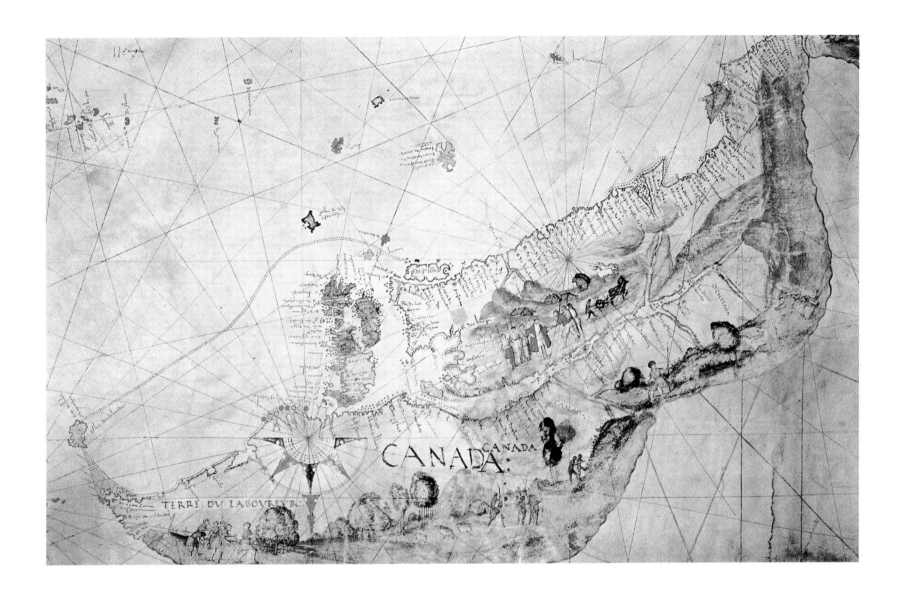

THE FRENCH

On the other side of the continent, the French were also naming bodies of water in the sixteenth century. On August 10, 1535, Jacques Cartier was sailing for the second time for King Francis I of France in search of a Northwest Passage when, in the midst of a storm along the Atlantic coast, he found safe harbor in a vast bay. The day he anchored was the one designated to honor Saint Lawrence, and so the gulf was named. When Cartier entered the river that emptied into that gulf, the same name was applied to it (fig. 20). He then sailed upriver until he was blocked by a series of rapids (which La Salle would sarcastically name La Chine, or China, more than a century later, mocking the belief that the St. Lawrence River offered a gateway to the Orient). Cartier also made reference to the Indian village of Stadacona, at the site of what is now Quebec, and to the larger village of Hochelaga (fig. 21) just before the rapids, at the site of the modern city of Montreal. (He named the adjacent hill overlooking the village Mont Réal, or "Mount

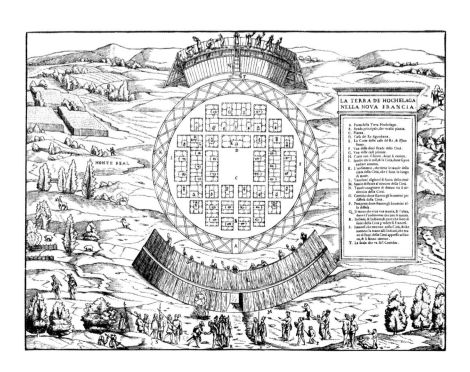

22. Jacques Le Moyne. "R. de Laudonniere and the Timucua." 1564. Gouache on paper. Rare Books Division, New York Public Library. Astor, Lenox and Tilden Foundations. Jean Ribault had the stone column with the French royal coat of arms erected in Florida during his first voyage, in 1562. Another French expedition, two years later, found the Indians worshiping the monument.

Royal." The Indian name of the village would shortly be obscured, while the name of the hill would come to designate a metropolis.) Cartier also applied the name Canada, an Indian word meaning "a collection of homes," to the region between Stadacona and the Saguenay River to the north, closer to the mouth of the St. Lawrence River.

In 1562, continuing the French efforts at colonization in the New World, Huguenot leader Admiral Gaspard de Coligny dispatched a group of the French Protestants under Jean Ribault to establish a colony in the southern part of the continent. After first landing in the vicinity of what is now St. Augustine, Florida, Ribault and his companions sailed into what is now called the St. Johns River, which they named the River of May because they entered it on the first day of that month. The northernmost anchorage during this expedition was in a large inlet that they named Port Royal, a name that persists in that locale in South Carolina. On the banks of the inlet, they built a small wooden structure they called Charlesfort and left thirty men there to establish a colony; it was abandoned not long after, however, when needed aid failed to arrive. In 1564, Coligny sent René de Laudonnière to fortify the area to the south as a buffer

against the Spanish (fig. 22). He built a fort on the south bank of the St. Johns River and named it Fort Caroline in honor of the king of France, Charles IX (Carolus in Latin).

Only a year later, Fort Caroline succumbed to an attack by Spanish forces under the command of Don Pedro Menéndez de Avilés, the newly appointed governor of Florida. In preparing for battle, Menéndez established a base for troops and supplies at a site on Matanzas Inlet, to which he assigned the name St. Augustine because he selected the location on the day that the medievalists had designated to honor that saint. St. Augustine is the oldest continuous European place-name of a settlement in what is now the United States.

In 1566, the first map to be dedicated solely to the North American continent in its entirety was drawn by Paolo Forlani and published in an Italian atlas (fig. 23). The names on that map include Canada, Nova Franza (New France), Civola (Cíbola), Quivira, Apalachen, and Florida. The only inland lake on the map is shown emptying into the "R. S. Lorenzo" (St. Lawrence River). "Sierra Nevada," Spanish for "snowcapped mountains," appears for the first time on a printed map.

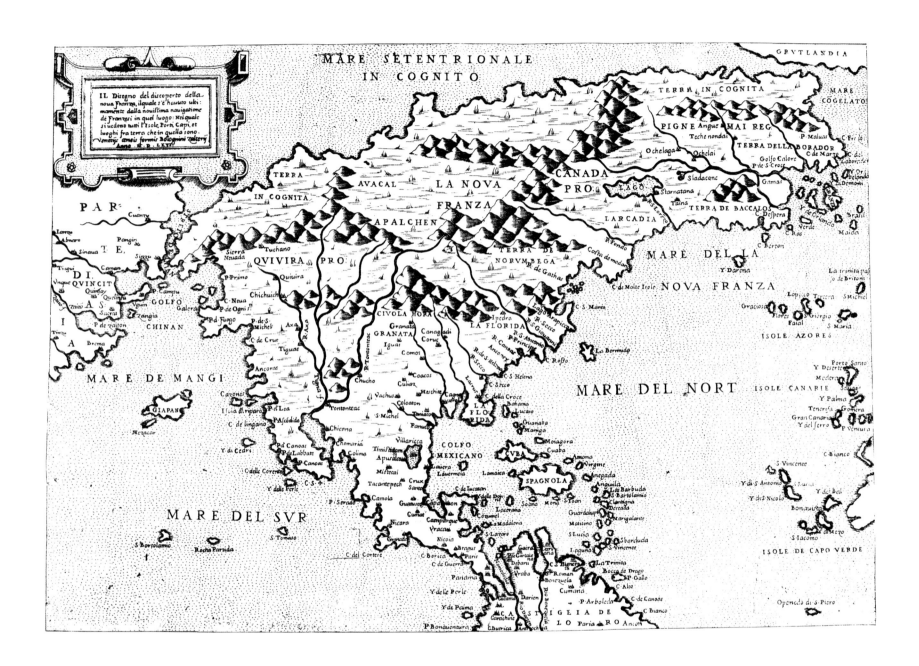

23. Paolo Forlani. "Il disegno del discoperto della nuoa Franza. . . ."
In Antonio Lafreri's composite atlas, Rome, 1566. Engraving, 27 x 40 cm.
Private collection. The first map devoted solely to the entire North American
continent, and the first to show the "Strait of Anian," separating
North America from Asia. This map was attributed to Bolognino Zaltieri
until recently, when it was proved that he had purchased plates from
Forlani and then placed his own imprint on the map.

It was against this background that the English would first establish a temporary presence on the North American continent. After Sir Humphrey Gilbert was lost at sea during an attempt to found a settlement in America and locate the dreamed-of Northwest Passage, his half brother, Walter Raleigh, was granted the privilege of settling the land that had been given to Gilbert, and in 1584 he sent Captains Arthur Barlowe and Philip Amadas to explore the east coast for a suitable site for colonization. Off present-day North Carolina, the captains entered an inlet at the northern end of an island that the Indians called Hatarask, and the explorers landed on an island called Roanoke. Thus, Hatteras, named for a local Indian tribe, and Roanoke, derived from an Algonquian word (Algonquian is a group of languages used by tribes, including the Algonquins, in roughly the eastern half of America) and meaning "white shell place," were the first two Indian place-names to gain permanence in the language of United States geography. Another name resulted from that voyage: during the exploration of the coastline to the south, seamen had panicked about the possibility of a shipwreck near a forbidding promontory, which consequently was named Cape Fear.

In 1585, after Raleigh was knighted, he vowed to establish a colony in the Roanoke region and name it Virginia, to honor Queen Elizabeth, "the Virgin Queen" (fig. 24). In this manner, Virginia became the first English name to be attached to our soil (though it encompassed a larger area than it did later). In 1585, a party of 108 colonists sailed from England to Roanoke Island, with Ralph Lane as governor of this first English colony. During the stay at their settlement, the colonists explored Chesapeake Bay to the north and named that broad expanse of water for a local Indian town that bore the Algonquian terms *che*, meaning "big"; *sepi*, meaning "river"; and *ake*, meaning "at." Some of the Roanoke colonists, including Lane, returned to England with Sir Francis Drake, whose fleet arrived at the area in 1586 on its return voyage from plundering in the West Indies; the few who remained did not survive. This became known as the first "Lost Colony."

Raleigh sent out another group in 1587 under John White, as governor, to establish "the Cittie of Raleigh in Virginea" on the shores of Chesapeake Bay (fig. 25). The 110 colonists were put ashore at Roanoke. At that settlement, on August 18, 1587, Virginia Dare was born to Ananias and Elenor Dare, White's daughter. Thus, Virginia Dare entered the history books as the first child of English parents to be born in the New World. John White returned to England for supplies. When he arrived once again at the settlement on Roanoke Island, in 1590, he found no one still around—including his daughter and young granddaughter—and no definite indication of what had happened to those who disappeared from this second and more famous "Lost Colony."

24. *Attributed to Nicholas Hilliard. Portrait of Queen Elizabeth I, "the Virgin Queen." 1585. Oil on canvas. Hatfield House, Hatfield, England*

25. *John White. "La Virgenia Pars." 1585. Manuscript, pen and ink and watercolor*
on paper, 37 x 47 cm. Department of Manuscripts, British Library, London.
This map shows the southeastern coast from Chesapeake Bay to the tip of Florida.
In August 1587, John White's daughter gave birth to Virginia Dare,
the first child of English parents to be born in the New World.

Cuitas S.AVGVSTINI ligneis ædibus conftructa amæniſſimos habuit hortos, vndiq̃, ſolo fœcundiſſimo, ab Anglis inietto igne deftructa eſt Præſidium hic erat 150 Hiſpanorum, aliutque eodem numero ad 12. verſus Septentrionem leucas in loco S.Helenæ dicto Hæc præſidia autem eo conſilio diſpoſita, vt prohiberent Anglos et Gallos, ne interiectam occuparët regionë.

La cité Sainct Auguſtin toute Baſtie de Maiſons de bois des Jardins tres plaſans et dúnne terre fort ſerile ille a eſté bruſlé par les Angloys il y auoit en ielle vne garniſon de 150 Eſpagnols et vne aultre de pareil nombre a' 12 lieues vers les ſeptentrion au lieu appelle Sanct heleine et ſes garniſons eſtoint pour empeſcher les Angloys et les francois d'entalir le pais giſant au millieu.

26. *Baptista Boazio. "Civitas S. Augustini." In* Voyage des Chev. Fr. Drake aux
Indies occidentales l'an 1585, *Paris, 1588. Engraving, 20 x 28.5 cm.*
Private collection. This first printed map of a city within the present limits of the
United States depicts Sir Francis Drake's defeat of the Spanish fortress
at St. Augustine in 1586.

THE END OF THE SIXTEENTH CENTURY

At the end of the sixteenth century, the only extant European settlement on the Atlantic coast was St. Augustine. Although Drake attacked and ravaged it in 1586, as shown in an engraving that is the first to depict a battle between European powers on the North American continent (fig. 26), remnants of the Spanish settlement persisted.

In about 1595, four prints commemorating the discovery of the New World were published by Johannes Stradanus in Antwerp (fig. 28). They include a map and allegorical representations of Colum-

bus, Vespucci, and Ferdinand Magellan (whose expedition was the first to circumnavigate the globe, in 1519–22, although he was killed in the Philippines). In 1597, the first atlas dedicated solely to the Americas was published by Cornelis van Wytfliet. It includes maps of New Spain (what is now Mexico and the American Southwest), California, Florida "et Apalche" (the Southeast), Norumbega (to become New England) and Virginia, and New France (the name for all the French possessions in North America) and Canada (fig. 27). No other place-names that appear on the maps in the atlas have survived. The land in the northwest of the North American continent bears

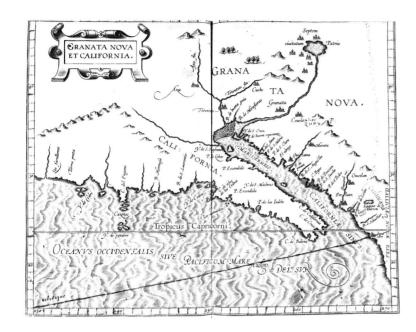

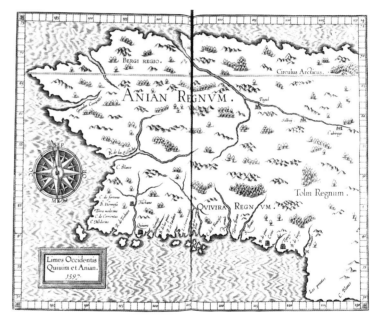

27. *Cornely [Cornelis van] Wytfliet. Five maps in
Wytfliet's* Descriptionis Ptolemaicae augmentum sive
Occidentis Notitia, *Louvain, 1597. Engravings,
each 23 x 29 cm. Private collection. The first atlas devoted
entirely to the New World (see also fig. 13).
Top, left: "Granata Nova et California."
Top, right: "Hispania Nova." Center: "Quivira et Anian."
Bottom, left: "Norumbega et Virginia."
Bottom, right: "Nova Francia et Canada."*

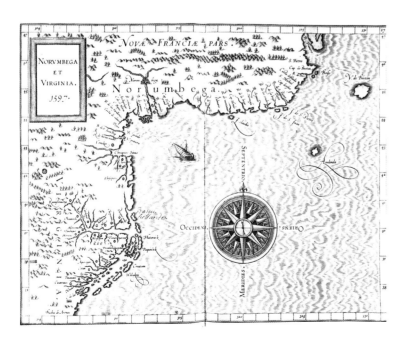

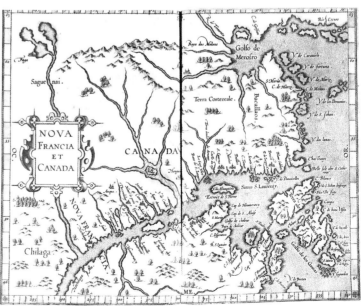

28. Johannes Stradanus.
"Americae Retectio":
four prints commemorating the
discovery of the New World.
Antwerp, c. 1595. Engravings,
each 19.5 x 28 cm.
Private collection.
Top: "Americae Retectio."
Botttom: "Christophorus
Columbus Ligur."
Opposite, top: "Ameri. Vespuc.
[Americus Vespucius
Florent.]"
Opposite, bottom: "Ferdinandes
Magalanes [Magellan]
Lusitanes."

the name Anian, referring to a mythical kingdom that Marco Polo mentioned in the accounts of his travels in the thirteenth century, and which initially appeared on the Asian continent.

In 1598 an expedition was initiated to Tiguex in what is now northern New Mexico. This resulted in the establishment of the second-oldest continuous European settlement in the modern United States, after St. Augustine. Don Juan de Oñate traveled north from Mexico, the area that had taken the name of the local Mexica Indians. The name Mexico, translated from the Indian language, literally means "in the navel of the moon." Oñate crossed the River of the North, which led into a river that the Spaniards called Río Bravo, now known as the Rio Grande. The point at which they forded that river had been previously explored by the Mexican troops of Rodriguez-Chamuscado in 1581, but it was Oñate who named the crossing El Paso del Norte. Over the next several years, Oñate's exploring parties traveled as far northeast as present-day Wichita, Kansas, and then westward to a river that they named the Colorado (Spanish for "colored red") because the water appeared red; then they floated all the way down that river to the Gulf of California. Oñate called the entire region New Mexico, accounting for the introduction of that term. In about 1609, Oñate left some fifty people to establish a settlement approximately 250 miles north of the El Paso del Norte crossing. The community, named La Villa Real de las Santa Fe de San Francisco, became the capital of the region of New Mexico and endured as Santa Fe, meaning "holy faith"—our second-oldest European settlement.

The sixteenth century ended with only a small number of Spanish settlers established on the land that would become the United States of America. There were no settlements from other European countries on North American soil. In Europe, however, the defeat of the Spanish Armada by England's navy in 1588 had resulted in a major shift of power, setting the scene for English colonization and for France's efforts to assert itself on the continent that had just passed the centennial of its European discovery.

The century's ultimate map, the Wright published in 1599–1600, is referred to in Shakespeare's *Twelfth Night* as the "new Mappe with the augmentation of the Indies" (fig. 29). The map depicts the Atlantic coast, the St. Lawrence River, and a single large lake in the region of the Great Lakes, which were yet to be discovered. What the Spanish called Alta (Upper) California—essentially, present-day California—the map labels "New Albion," a name bestowed on the region by Sir Francis Drake, and derived from the mythological term for England.

29. *Edward Wright. "A Chart of the World on Mercator's Projection" (detail).
1599. In Richard Hakluyt's* The Principall Navigations, Voiages, Traffiques, and Discoueries of the English Nation, *London, 1599–1600. Engraving; entire map, 42 x 64 cm.
Private collection. There is a suggestion of a Great Lake ("Lake of Tadouac").
Virginia is noted. The Northwest remains undefined.*

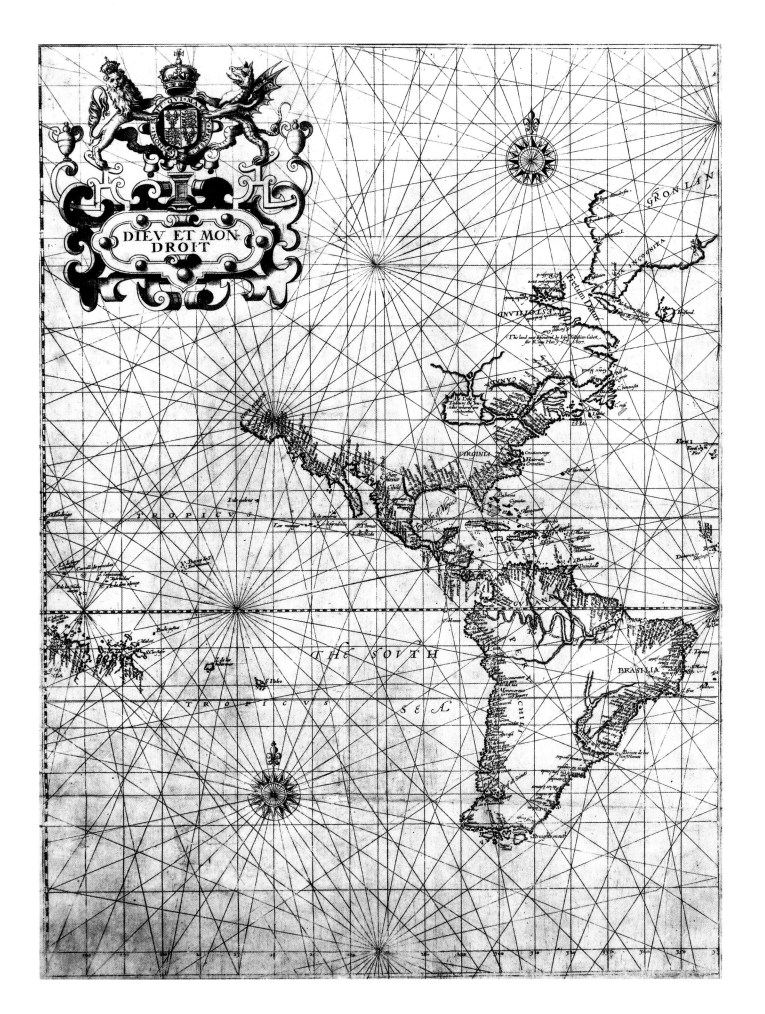

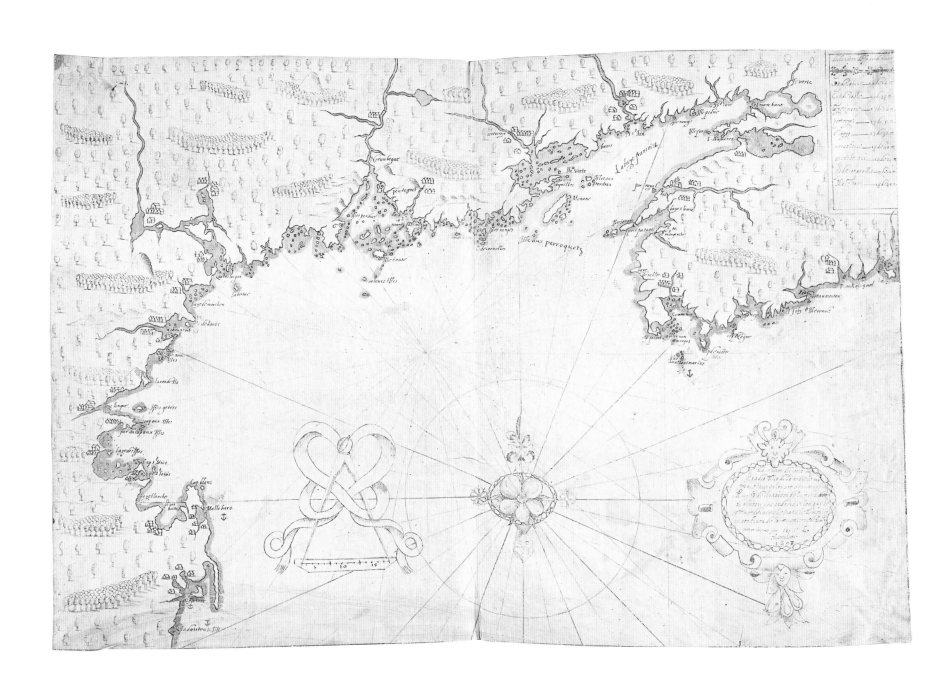

CHAPTER TWO

Early-Seventeenth-Century Sailings and Settlements

EXPANDED INTEREST

At the beginning of the seventeenth century, only Spain had established successful colonies on the North American continent. One was firmly seated in Mexico (the major portion of the possession called New Spain), and the second had a tenuous start in St. Augustine, Florida. In 1602, Sebastián Vizcaíno sailed along the California coast and discovered Monterey Bay, which he named for the man who had sent him, Conde de Monterrey, viceroy of New Spain. By the end of that year, the Pacific coast from the Baja Peninsula as far north as Cap Blanco in present-day Oregon, 43° north latitude, had been viewed by voyagers from New Spain.

The seventeenth century also opened with England's active efforts to colonize the eastern seaboard, particularly because the recent defeat of the Spanish Armada had added to its posture as a major power. In 1602, an important voyage explored the New England coast, which at the time was referred to as the "north part of Virginia." Captains Bartholomew Gosnold and Bartholomew Gilbert, sailing aboard the *Concord* from England, made landfall near Casco Bay, Maine. They proceeded to a headland they named Cape Cod, because it "pestered our ship so with Cod fish," and after rounding the cape, they explored what we know today as Nantucket and Martha's Vineyard. They named the latter for the abundant native grape vines and, perhaps, for Gosnold's daughter. They landed at what is now called Cuttyhunk, which they named Elizabeth's Isle, and then returned home.

The following year, Martin Pring of Bristol sailed along the shores of Massachusetts Bay and stayed almost two months at what would later be named Plymouth Harbor. In 1605–6, George Weymouth sailed to Nantucket and the Maine coast in an abortive attempt to establish a colony for oppressed English Catholics.

THE FRENCH

Meanwhile, France was also stepping up its efforts at colonization. In 1600, Pierre de Chauvin de Tonnetuit and François Gravé du Pont sailed for Canada, where Chauvin established a trading post at Tadoussac, at the mouth of the Saguenay River. The year 1603 marked the first arrival on the North American continent of a towering figure of discovery and cartography: Samuel de Champlain, "the Father of New France." Champlain, a native of Brouage, France, was sailing as an observer with Gravé du Pont in the Tadoussac venture. They ascended the Saguenay River and the St. Lawrence River

30. *Samuel de Champlain. "Description des costs, pts, rades, Illes de la nouuele france facit selon son vray méridien." 1607. Manuscript on vellum, pen and ink and watercolor, 36 x 54 cm. Geography and Map Division, Library of Congress, Washington, D.C. The first delineation of the east coast from Cape Sable, off what is now southwestern Nova Scotia, to south of Cape Cod. Mt. Desert Island ("Isle Mont Deserts") appears for the first time on a map. Present-day Plymouth, Mass., is named "Cap St. Louis," and "La Douteuse Isle" is applied to what is now probably Martha's Vineyard, or possibly Nantucket.*

just beyond the Indian village of Hochelaga to the rapids later called La Chine. In Champlain's narrative, the name Kebec (Quebec), which is Algonquian for "there where the river narrows," appears for the first time. Champlain assigned that name to the bend of the St. Lawrence where Quebec—the first permanent settlement in Canada—was later established, because it had the advantage of being a defensible site. His narrative also refers to Indian tales about what would become known as Niagara Falls, to a great inland lake (one of the Great Lakes), and to the St. Croix River, so named because three streams flowing into it gave it the appearance of a cross.

Champlain sailed in 1604 with Pierre du Gua, sieur de Monts, who had a monopoly for trade in the northeastern region of the continent; this would become a two-year reconnaissance. The journey covered an area from Sable Island, off Cape Breton, to Martha's Vineyard, and it resulted in Champlain's producing the first accurate map of that portion of the coastline. In his first command, aboard an eight-ton pinnace that had been assembled on the Acadian coast, Champlain spent three weeks exploring and charting the Bay of Fundy, which he called La Baye Françoise. After winter quarters were established on the island of St. Croix, Champlain started out on a second voyage of discovery, during which he named Mount Desert Island (off the coast of Maine), because of its absence of trees, and then entered Penobscot Bay and the Kennebec River, to which he attached the Algonquian Indian names Pentagoet and Quinebequy (Kennebec), the latter meaning "long reach." He traveled up the Penobscot River, named for a word meaning "sloping rock," to the site of what is now Bangor, Maine. In 1605, Champlain sailed past Cape Cod, which he named Cap Blanc, and charted Saco Bay, Boston Harbor, and Plymouth Harbor, which he referred to as Port de Cap St. Louis. He entered Nauset Harbor, which he called Port Mallebarre. A distant glimpse of a landmass to the east of that harbor resulted in the naming of an island—either Martha's Vineyard or Nantucket—La Douteuse, or "the doubtful," because of his own doubt about its island status.

The French moved their base camp from St. Croix to Port Royal (now Annapolis Royal) in Nova Scotia, and it was there in 1607 that Champlain drew his first coastal chart, which is now a treasure of the Library of Congress (fig. 30). The manuscript depicts the Atlantic coast from Cape Cod, Massachusetts, to Cape Sable, Nova Scotia. Champlain returned to France that year to replenish supplies. On his return to the New World in 1608, he shifted his attention to the St. Lawrence River, at which time he built the permanent settlement at Quebec. On July 30, 1609, while exploring the interior, Champlain and his men engaged a war party of Mohawk Indians on the eastern shore of Lake Champlain (fig. 31), to which the explorer attached his own name to commemorate his victory and in recognition of the lake's strategic importance.

In 1613, while he was in Paris, Champlain published *Les Voyages*, a narrative of his travels within the North American continent and

31. *[Samuel de Champlain?]. Samuel de Champlain fighting at Lake Champlain in 1609. In Champlain's* Les Voyages de la Nouvelle France Occidentale, *Paris, 1632. Engraving. Private collection*

Opposite, top: 32. *Samuel de Champlain. "Carte geographique de la Nouvelle France." In Champlain's* Les Voyages de Sieur de Champlain, *Paris, 1613. Engraving, 43 x 76 cm. Private collection. The first attempt to show the latitude of New England. The map shows Lake Ontario ("Lac Contenant des canaux des sauuages"), Oneida Lake ("lac des irocois"), Lake Erie ("grand lac contenant 300 Lieux de Long"), and Lake Champlain ("Lac de Champlain").*

Opposite, bottom: 33. *Rowing on the Charles River. Courtesy Greater Boston Convention & Visitor Tourist Bureau, Inc.*

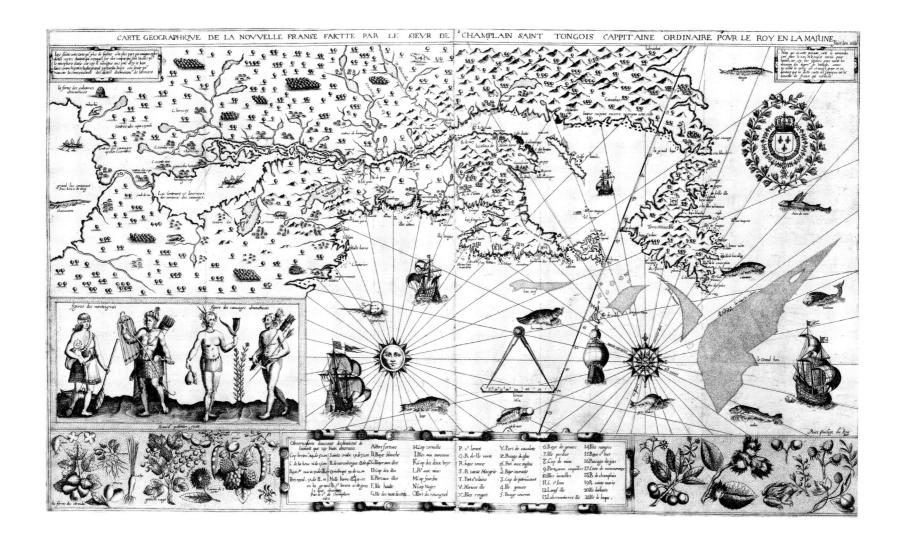

along its coastline. Champlain included with this narrative his first printed map of the region. On the map, a large unnamed lake (later called Ontario) is depicted flowing into the St. Lawrence River, and a "grand lac" is located to the west. Oneida Lake, now named for an Indian tribe, was called "lac des irocois" and oriented incorrectly (fig. 32). The text of *Les Voyages* also includes a reasonably precise description of Boston Harbor and the nearby Charles River (fig. 33).

Two years later, Champlain embarked on a journey that took him to the Georgian Bay area on Lake Huron, and during that trip he became the first European to see Lake Ontario. Pierre Duval's 1653 map of "Le Canada" (fig. 34) used the copperplate of an unpublished 1616 map by Champlain and represents Champlain's personal explorations of the two great lakes that he called Lac St. Louis (now Lake Ontario) and Mer Douce, or "sweet sea" (now Lake Huron). Having heard of a great lake to the west, Champlain incorporated "grand lac" (now Lake Superior) on his final and most extensive map, published in France in 1632 (fig. 35). It was not until 1650 that all five great lakes were represented on a map for the first time (fig. 36). On that map, published in Paris by Nicolas Sanson, the names "Ontario" and "Superieur" (Superior) appear for the first time.

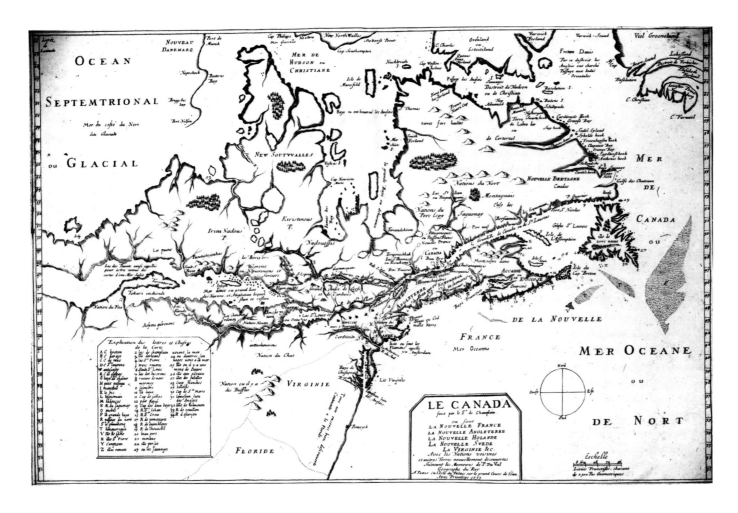

34. *Pierre Duval. "Le Canada." Paris, 1653. Engraving, 36 x 54 cm. Private collection. Using the copperplate of an unpublished 1616 map by Samuel de Champlain, this is the first printed map showing Lake Huron ("Mer Douce") and Lake Ontario ("Lac St. Louis") by a European who personally explored those regions.*

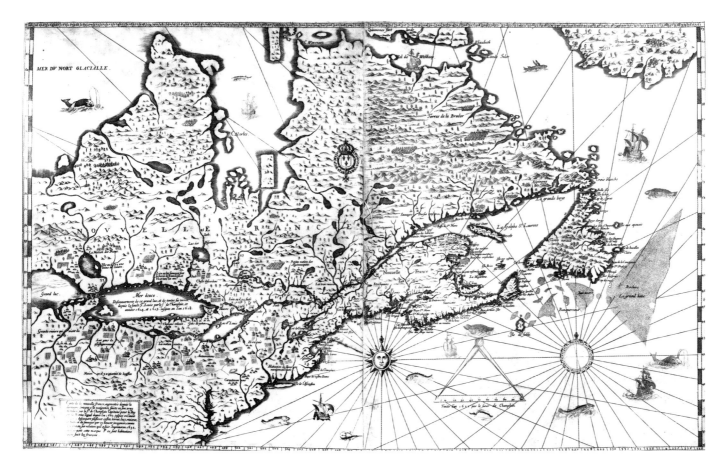

35. *Samuel de Champlain. "Carte de la Nouuelle France." In Champlain's* Les Voyages de la Nouvelle France Occidentale, *Paris, 1632. Engraving, 52 x 86 cm. Private collection. Lake Superior ("grand lac") appears on this map but is based solely on Indian reports. Lakes Erie and Michigan are indistinctly represented.*

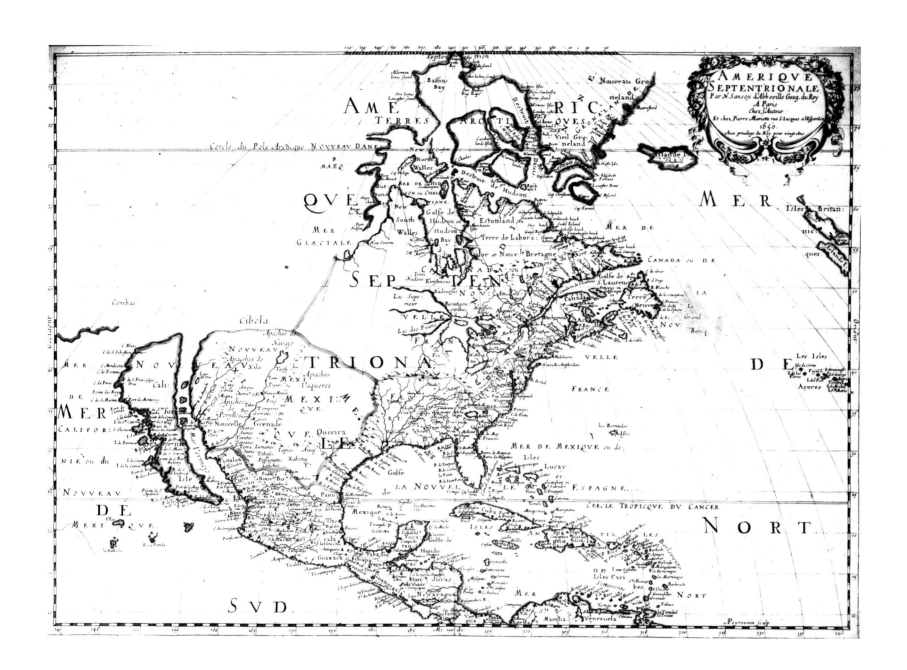

36. *Nicolas Sanson. "Amerique septentrionale." Paris, 1650. Engraving, 38 x 56 cm. Private collection. This depiction of North America is the first printed map to show all five Great Lakes, and the first map to name Lakes Superior ("Lac Superieur") and Ontario. Santa Fe is shown as the capital of New Mexico, but it is located on the west bank of the Rio Grande. California is shown as an island.*

37. *John Smith. "Virginia." 1612. Engraving (6th state, London, 1625), 32 x 41 cm.*
Private collection. The first delineation of Chesapeake Bay. Persisting names include
Capes Henry and Charles, Point Comfort ("Poynt Comfort"), Smith Island
("Smyths Isles"), Appomattox ("Appamatuck"), and Jamestown ("Jamestowne").
Note the inset depicting the council of Chief Wahunsonacock (also known as
Powhatan, the name of the confederacy of tribes in the area that he ruled).

While the French were concentrating on exploring the northern part of the continent during the first half of the seventeenth century, the English were actively settling what would be the beginnings of colonial America. In 1606, several powerful Englishmen with commercial interests received a charter from King James I incorporating the Virginia Company, in two groups: the London Company and the Plymouth Company. On April 10, 1606, a patent was issued to the Virginia Company for the part of America north of Cape Fear, at 34° north latitude, to about the current site of Bangor, Maine, 45° north. These limits were politically motivated and specifically selected so that they would not interfere with the interests of Spain to the south or France to the north.

With the charter for the northern part of this vast area of land, the Plymouth Company sent out a first expedition in August 1606, but it was captured by Spaniards in the West Indies. In May 1607, an expedition outfitted by Sir Ferdinando Gorges, and led by George Popham and Ralegh Gilbert, set out from Plymouth, England, and explored the Maine coast before settling at the mouth of what is now the Kennebec River but was then called the Sagadahoc. The Sagadahoc colony began with the construction of Fort St. George, at what later became Phippsburg. The colony was abandoned the following summer, but the expedition resulted in an accurate description of the coast of Maine, which appeared in the explorers' report of their voyage.

Meanwhile, and far more significant in its long-term impact, the London Company, holding the charter for the southern part of the region, sent out an expedition of three ships under Captain Christopher Newport. The colonists sailed from London on December 20, 1606, and entered Chesapeake Bay on April 26, 1607, first exploring a point of land that comforted them because they observed a channel that was the mouth of a navigable river. They therefore named the land at the mouth Point Comfort. They planted a cross at the southern tip of land at the entrance to the bay and named the area Cape Henry, in honor of the Prince of Wales. Both names have persisted. The explorers then proceeded up the river, which was initially named the King's River but later would become the James River, where in mid-May the 105 Englishmen founded a settlement, which they called Jamestown in honor of King James I. It was the first long-lasting English settlement in the New World.

Twenty-eight-year-old Captain John Smith (see fig. 1), who had been a soldier-of-fortune hero of the Hungarian war against the "infidel" Turks, and who was a catalyst for the expedition, became president of the Jamestown settlement in 1608 (the same year, incidentally, in which Champlain founded Quebec). At that point, Smith began his explorations of Chesapeake Bay. They formed the basis of his 1612 map of Virginia (fig. 37) and also provided the designation of several place-names. To the point of land on the opposite side of Chesapeake Bay from Cape Henry, Smith assigned the name Cape

Charles, honoring Prince Henry's brother. Smith affixed his own name on the map to a group of islands off Cape Henry and used Indian tribal names for the major rivers entering the bay. Thus, Patawomek (Potomac) and Sasqusahanough (Susquehanna) found their way into our current geographic dictionary, but Powhatan, Smith's name for what we call the James River, did not. Smith—who is probably best known today for the tale of his rescue by the Powhatan princess Pocahontas (fig. 38)—left Virginia in 1609, never to return to that region.

In 1610, Thomas West, Baron De La Warr, arrived to serve as the first colonial governor of Virginia. Shortly thereafter, Samuel Argall named a cape to the north Lawar, after the governor. This was transformed into Delaware, a name assigned first to the bay, then to the river that emptied into the northern end of the bay, and eventually to the colony situated on the shore of the bay.

38. Artist unknown. Portrait of Pocahontas. Oil on canvas, after a 1616 engraving by Simon van de Passe; 77 x 64 cm. Courtesy National Portrait Gallery, Smithsonian Institution, Washington, D.C.

Meanwhile, the "second charter" of Virginia was issued in 1609, defining the boundaries as extending from Point Comfort along the seacoast two hundred miles northward and two hundred miles southward, and all "that Space and Circuit of Land, lying from the Sea Coast of the Precinct aforesaid, up into the Land, throughout from Sea to Sea." Also included were all islands within one hundred miles of both seacoasts within those latitudes. (This served as the basis of the "sea-to-sea" claim that the British would make in 1755, at the start of the French and Indian War.) In 1611–12, a third charter expanded the area to include all islands within three hundred leagues of any coastal land within the original charter; this addition encompassed Bermuda.

In Virginia, tobacco—first successfully cultivated and cured for export in 1612 by John Rolfe, the Englishman who married Pocahontas two years later—provided the profits that led to the survival of the settlement after its difficult early years. By 1617, tenant plantations extended twenty miles along the James River. The Virginia Company offered attractive land inducements for settlement. These 1,250-acre tracts were known as "Hundreds," or "Particular Plantations." The Virginia Colony began as a complex of significant plantations, each abutting a navigable river that would allow shipment of tobacco directly to England in return for goods. The plantations were self-contained centers for living and trade; as a consequence, no major community, much less city, developed in the region.

The first major port in the Virginia Colony was established in 1621 at what has become known as Newport News. It was developed initially by the brothers Newce, who named it New Port Newce; as time passed, local settlers considered it more appropriate to honor Captain Newport, who had brought the original colonists from England, and the permanent spelling resulted.

In 1624, five years after America's first representative assembly convened in Jamestown, and during a period of internal turmoil including a devastating Indian attack in 1622 (fig. 39), the Crown annulled the Virginia Company's charter. Formerly a private venture, Virginia became the first English Crown colony, with a governor appointed by the king. Eight years later, when the king granted Maryland's charter, a substantial portion of Virginia's northern boundary was reduced (although vague language in the charter resulted in ongoing disputes over the Maryland–Virginia border, lasting well into the twentieth century). The Connecticut charter of 1662—which, like many charters of the period, extended that colony's land west all the way to what was called the South Sea (Pacific Ocean)—specified 41° north latitude as the northern boundary of Virginia. In 1681, the charter granted to Pennsylvania further reduced Virginia's northern border (as did other changes during the eighteenth century). As for its southern boundary, the charters of Carolina in 1663 and 1665 set that at its current position.

The conception of the geography of the Virginia Colony was influenced by Verrazano's earlier misinterpretation of Pamlico Sound

39. *Richard Schlecht. "Wolstenholme Towne before the 1622 attack." Courtesy National Geographic Society, Washington, D.C. This short-lived Virginia town survived the attack by Indians, only to be abandoned not long afterward.*

as the Sea of China. This is evident on the 1651 "mapp of Virginia . . ." by John Farrer, which depicts a narrow North American continent. A legend on the map indicates that a ten-day march from the head of the James River ends at rivers that empty into the Pacific Ocean (fig. 40). In the early 1650s, colonists in Virginia sought to expand their settlements, and they set their sights on the inland Albemarle region to the northwest, later the center of Thomas Jefferson's activities, as well as on the area to the south that soon became part of Carolina (subsequently North Carolina).

By 1670, the population of Virginia had grown to thirty-five thousand, but the heyday of Jamestown as the first English colonial capital was about to come to an end. During an uprising in 1676 known as Bacon's Rebellion, in which Virginians with land on the western frontier rose up against Governor Sir William Berkeley for refusing to provide them with protection against Indian attacks, the government houses in Jamestown were destroyed by fire—along with much of the rest of the town. Although the town was rebuilt, it began its long decline when the colonial capital was moved in 1699—in part because of dissatisfaction with the swampy environs—a short distance inland to Williamsburg, named for King William III (the word *burg* means "town"). Excavation of the seventeenth-century settlement of Jamestown began in the 1930s, but the most significant discovery, of scattered and subtle remnants of the original fortifications,

40. John Farrer. "A mapp of Virginia discouered to ye Falls." In Edward Williams's
Virgo Triumphans; or Virginia Richly and Truly Valued, 3rd ed.,
London, 1651. Engraving, 27 x 35 cm. Private collection. This map indicates a
narrow isthmus that can be crossed in a 10-day march from the head of
the James and Hudson rivers to reach a lake connected with the Sea of China.
Dutch and Swedish settlements are noted on the map.

came only in the 1990s, stimulating an increased archaeological interest in the site. As for colonial Williamsburg, now a historic restoration (fig. 41), worries about British troops during the American Revolution prompted removal of the capital of Virginia to Richmond, the safest and most central town on a navigable river, in 1779. During the Revolution, Americans also burned Norfolk, which had been founded near Newport News in 1682 and named for the English county, to prevent the British from controlling that strategic port; it was rebuilt in 1805.

In the northeastern part of what remained of Virginia after the Maryland charter, a royal grant of five million acres between the Rappahannock and Potomac rivers was made in 1673 to Thomas Culpeper, who became the colonial governor of Virginia two years later. On Culpeper's death in 1689, the property rights descended to his grandson Thomas Fairfax; thus, one vast land grant would account for two important Virginia place-names, Culpeper and Fairfax.

41. *The Fife and Drum Corps near the magazine at the historic restoration called Colonial Williamsburg. Courtesy Colonial Williamsburg Foundation, Williamsburg, Va.*

Between the lands targeted for colonies by the Plymouth and London companies, the Dutch began their own initial probes of the continent shortly after the founding of Jamestown. In 1609, Henry Hudson, an English mariner sailing under the Dutch flag, entered New York Harbor and sailed up the wide river in search of a shorter passage to the Pacific Ocean. He did not assign a name to the river, which was initially known as the North River; it was only later that the river took Hudson's name. In 1613, the Dutch laid claim to the land flanking the river, which they named New Netherland. A trading post, Fort Nassau, named for Maurice of Nassau (the stadtholder, or chief of state, of the young Dutch republic), was built on Castle Island near what is now Albany. A Dutch navigator named Adriaen Block, sailing for Dutch merchants who hoped to set up a fur-trading business, passed the island that became known as Manhattan, before exploring the New England coast in 1614. He discovered the Housatonic (meaning "beyond mountain at" in Algonquian) and Connecticut rivers and explored Rhode Island, allowing the Dutch to extend their claims. He assigned the name Lange Eylant to the body of land that we still call Long Island. Block also drew a map (fig. 42), which is the first document to show Manhattan as an island and to give the island the name "Manhates," an Indian term meaning either "friendly" or "hilly land," as well as the name of the local tribe. The map was also the first to show Long Island as an island, the first to show the Connecticut River and Narragansett Bay, and the first to assign the name "New Netherland" to the lands between French Canada and English Virginia. Block Island, south of Rhode Island, was named after him.

Another explorer of the New England region, in the same year and for similar fur-trading purposes, was the same John Smith who helped found Jamestown in 1607 and left Virginia two years later. After being treated in England for a gunpowder injury, Smith returned to North America in 1614. During that year, he completed an exploration of the New England coast and incorporated his findings into his second famous map (fig. 43); it was published two years later as part of a small book titled *A Description of New England*. Smith introduced the name "New England," in the title of the book. He also was responsible for placing on the map the word "Massachusetts," meaning "big hill at," and the name of the local Indian tribe. Before publishing his map, Smith invited the fifteen-year-old Prince Charles (later King Charles I) to affix names of his choosing. Prince Charles named Cape Anna (now Cape Cod), for his mother (Queen Anne), and the Charles River, for himself. It was Charles who was also responsible for the insertion of the names of two English towns, Ipswich and Plimouth (later spelled Plymouth).

The second permanent English colony in North America had a religious impetus, sparked by the dissatisfaction of the Puritans with the English church and by their desire to establish a separate community. These religious separatists believed that they were directly

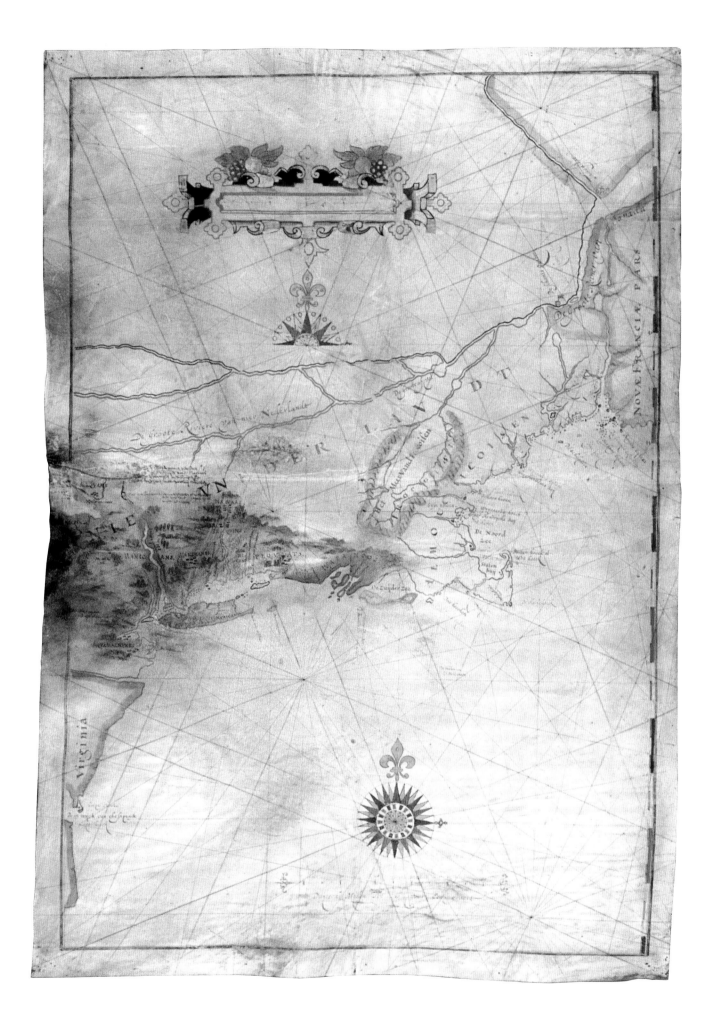

42. Adriaen Block. "Map of the East Coast from Chesapeack to Penobscot Bay." 1614. Manuscript, pen and ink and watercolor, 66 x 47 cm. Map Room, Algameen Rijksarchief, The Hague. The first map to show Manhattan ("Manhates") as a separate island. Lake Champlain ("Meer Vand Irocoisen") is erroneously placed east of the Connecticut River. Long Island and Long Island Sound are also depicted.

THE PORTRAICTURE OF CAPTAYNE IOHN SMITH ADMIRALL OF NEW ENGLAND.

Ætat 37 Aᵒ 1616

These are the Lines that shew thy Face; but those
That shew thy Grace and Glory, brighter bee:
Thy Faire-Discoueries and Fowle-Overthrowes
Of Salvages, much Civilliz'd by thee
Best shew thy Spirit; and to it Glory Wyn;
So, thou art Brasse without, but Golde within.

If so; in Brasse (too soft Smiths Acts to beare)
I fix thy Fame, to make Brasse Steele out weare.
Thine, as thou art Virtues,
Iohn Dauies, Heref:

Simon Passeus sculpsit

NEW ENGLAND

The most remarqueable parts thus named.
by the high and mighty Prince CHARLES,
Prince of great Britaine

HONI SOIT QVI MAL Y PENSE

Aborden

Gunnells Ih

Lowmonds

Edenborough

Cambridg

The Base

St Iohn Towne

Norwich

Fines Ils

Schooters hill

The River Forth

Pembrock Bay

Sandwich

Leth

Gerrards Ils

Dartmouth

Heighton Ils

Willowby Ih

Iorswich

Po: Kent

Harington Bay

Cape ElizAbeth

Barty Ils

Pennis Ih

Snadoun hill

Boston

Hull

Poynt Dauis

Smith Iles

SouthHampton

Cape ANNA

Bristow

Bassable

Talbotts Bay

Fawmouth

Fullerton Ils

The River CHARLES

Cary Ils

Cheuyot hills

P. Murry

London

Poynt Suttliff

Oxford

Poynt Gorge

Cape IAMES

Plimouth

Milford Hauen

STUARDS Bay

Barwick

A Scale of Leagues

2   4   6   8   10

Observed and described by Captavn Iohn Smith.
1614

London
Printed by IamesReeue

316   317   318   319

44½

44

43½

43

42½

42

316   317   318

under the influence of God and were not responsible to the English bishops; individuals had the right to choose their leaders under the guidance of God, and the chosen leaders were then to be obeyed. In 1608, some of the Puritans fled England for the Netherlands, settling first in Amsterdam and then in Leiden. Eventually an English merchant, Thomas Weston, put together funding for a colony in America and provided the vessel to transport the Puritans. The *Mayflower* set sail from Plymouth, England, with 101 colonists (later called Pilgrims), 40 of whom were Puritans; the remainder of the famous voyagers were selected to look after Weston's mercantile interests in the New World. The leaders of the Puritans initially planned to establish a settlement on the shore of the Hudson River near Manhattan, but the ship was blown off course. On November 19, 1620, the voyagers sighted Cape Cod but determined that the region could not support life and consequently continued their quest for a place to settle. Plymouth Harbor offered the most propitious site, and the colony began with the exploratory party's landing on December 21, 1620 (fig. 44). The name Plymouth was assigned because it had appeared on John Smith's map and also was their port of embarkation in England.

Massachusetts land had originally been included in the first charter for the Virginia Company, before its mention in the 1620 charter of New England that led to the landing at Plymouth. After that initial landing, Weston sent out more colonists, who were not Puritans but were concerned with his mercantile interests. This second wave of colonists settled near Boston Harbor to establish a fur trade, but because they were unsuccessful they abandoned the colony after a short period of time. Subsequently, the Plymouth Colony converted what was initially collective farming to individual ownership, thereby creating a more attractive situation for settlers. By 1630, there were about three hundred members in that colony, which had dissolved its partnership with the London merchants by paying off its debts. The Plymouth colonists also set up trading centers along the Kennebec and Connecticut rivers.

Before the next and more significant immigration of English colonists into New England occurred, the Dutch interest intensified. Proceeding from the claim to New Netherland that was made in 1613, the Dutch West India Company was established in 1621 with the priv-

44. *Plimoth Plantation, a re-creation of a period village in the second permanent English colony in North America. Courtesy Plimoth Plantation, Plymouth, Mass. Photograph by Ted Curtin*

ilege of colonizing the New World, as well as the western coast of Africa south of the tropic of Cancer. The first Dutch settlement in America was on Nut Island (Governors Island), off the tip of the Battery at the lower end of the island of Manhattan. Additional trading posts were established at Fort Orange (now Albany), also known by the Dutch name Beverwyck, meaning "beaver town," and at a second Fort Nassau along the Delaware River, near what is now Gloucester, New Jersey. (This was part of an expansion of the Dutch land claim, from the Hudson River region to the area around the lower Delaware River.) The names of the two forts honored the Dutch ruler, who by 1618 had inherited the title of prince of Orange as well as count of Nassau. The settlement was named New Amsterdam (later to become New York) and was the focal point of a relatively small number of immigrants (fig. 45). In 1626, a fort and settlement were established on Manhattan itself, which was reported to have been purchased for the equivalent of twenty-four dollars in goods by Peter Minuit for the Dutch West India Company. The inhabitants erected a wall at the northern end of their settlement, at what was later called

43. *John Smith. "New England." 1614. Engraving (6th state, London, 1625), 30 x 35 cm. Private collection. The earliest accurate map of the Massachusetts Bay Colony. "Plimouth," Cape Cod ("Cape Anna"), and "The River Charles" are located on it. "Boston" also appears but is located at what is now York, Maine. The Pilgrims were cognizant of the map, and when they landed at Plymouth Harbor in 1620, they retained the name.*

t' Fort nieuw Amsterdam op de Manhatans

Wall Street (fig. 46), to keep out Indians and wolves. Peripherally, farms, called *bouweries* in the Netherlands, sprang up.

In 1633, the Dutch bought land from the Pequot Indians on the shore of the Connecticut River, where Hartford later was settled. In 1638, Peter Minuit, now in the employ of Sweden, established the first Swedish community in North America: Fort Christina, named to honor the Swedish queen, was built on the site that later became Wilmington, Delaware. Swedish ownership in America was short-lived, however, ending in 1655 when the Dutch, under Peter Stuyvesant, conquered the Swedish settlement.

The role of the Dutch as a significant factor in the development of our country extended for only a half century; their major legacy was a series of place-names for locales in what is currently New York State. By 1630, New Amsterdam had three hundred inhabitants and Fort Orange was central to the major Dutch interest of establishing a fur trade. Between the two places, feudal domains were developed by proprietors called patroons, each of whom received fifty miles of frontage along the Hudson River in return for bringing

fifty settlers to the region. The names of these major landowners, such as Van Cortlandt, De Lancey, and Rensselaer, were added to maps and have endured.

Other place-names assigned by the Dutch derived from their homeland. For example, the names Brooklyn, Flushing, and Harlem, all now part of New York City, came from the names of towns in the Netherlands and initially appeared as Breukelyn, Vlissingen, and Haerlem. Flatbush, the section of Brooklyn in which the Brooklyn Dodgers' Ebbets Field (fig. 47) was located until the late 1950s, came from the Dutch *vlak-bosch*, meaning "level forest." The "vliet" in Watervliet, along the Hudson River just north of Fort Orange, means "brook."

Many of the additional names that the Dutch assigned, such as Poughkeepsie, were corruptions of Indian names. Poughkeepsie was the Algonquian designation for a local waterfall and translated as "little rock water at." Ossining, which much later became the site of a New York State prison with its famous electric chair, also has an Algonquian derivation, meaning "little stone at." Schenectady, which

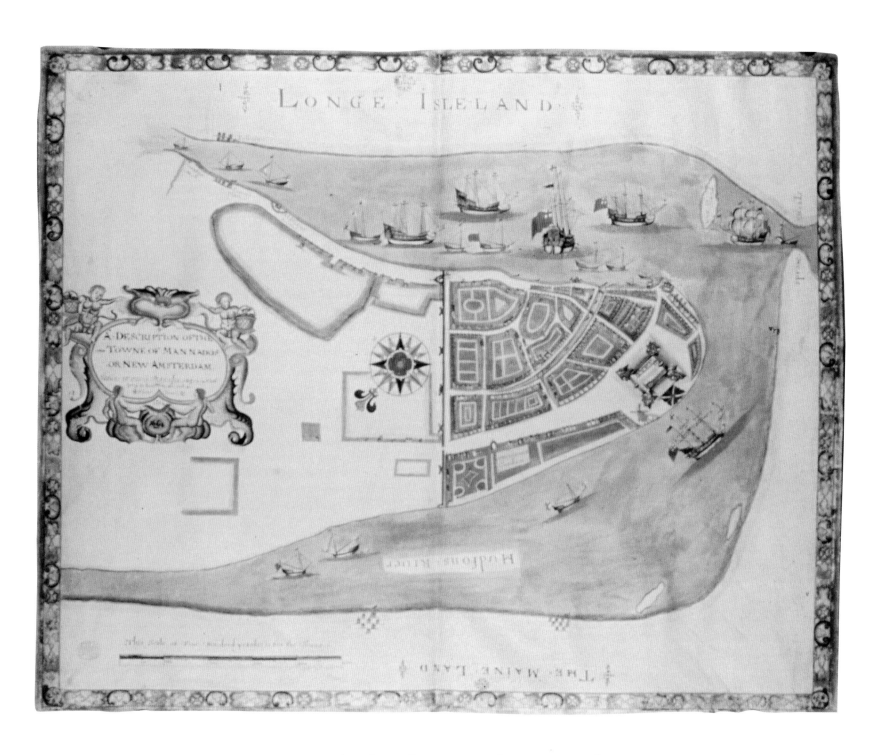

48. *Cartographer unknown. "A Description of the Towne of Mannados:
or New Amsterdam." 1664. Manuscript, pen and ink and watercolor, 56 x 71 cm.
Map Library, British Library, London. Known as the "Duke's Plan,"
this shows Manhattan and the Dutch settlement after the English capture
and renaming of it.*

was founded by the Dutch trader Arent van Curler where he signed a peace treaty with the Indians in 1642 in current upstate New York, derived from Iroquoian, meaning "beyond the pines." Schenectady, not far from the Hudson River, remained the westernmost community in New York until 1712, when settlements sprang up farther west.

The Dutch extended their interests by establishing more settlements in 1641. Tappan Zee combined the name of an Indian tribe, Tappan, and *zee*, the Dutch word meaning "sea." Staten Island was named for the Staaten, the Dutch States-General, the governing body of the Netherlands. Yonkers derived from the Dutch *jonkheer*, meaning "landowner," and it referred to the land of a *jonkheer* named Adriaen Van der Donck. The following year, Jonas Bronck built his house on what would be called the Bronx (derived from Bronck's) River. The name of the river was subsequently attached to the entire area that later became a borough of New York City. In various places, descriptive terms were added to the Dutch word *kill*, meaning "creek," which accounts for such names as Catskill (perhaps because of the presence of a mountain lion); Schuylkill, meaning "hiding creek" (referring to a time when a Swedish vessel concealed itself there); and Peekskill, named for a Dutch trader, Jan Peek.

In 1650, Peter Stuyvesant, the director general of New Netherland since 1645, engineered a short-lived policy of peaceful coexistence with the Indians and also settled a border dispute with the neighboring Connecticut Colony. Meanwhile, the Dutch expansion was continuing; they built Fort Beversede, near what is now Philadelphia, in 1648, and Fort Casimir, at what is now New Castle, Delaware, three years later.

But this relatively brief period of Dutch control in part of North America was about to end. In 1664, King Charles II, having been restored to his throne of England four years earlier, declared war on the Netherlands and granted to his brother, the duke of York (who later became Charles's successor, King James II), the entire region between the Connecticut and Delaware rivers as well as Long Island, Nantucket, Martha's Vineyard, and the portion of Maine that lies east of the Kennebec River. On September 8, 1664, Peter Stuyvesant, unable to confront the superior numbers of the English fleet off the southern end of Manhattan, surrendered the entire Dutch colony without a battle. New Amsterdam was renamed New York (fig. 48), Fort Orange became Albany (the Scottish title of the duke of York), and Fort Casimir became New Castle, in honor of the English earl of Newcastle.

THE MASSACHUSETTS BAY COLONY

As famous and important as New York would become, the first truly successful English colonization in the New World was the Massachusetts Bay Colony, which was already flourishing by the time New Amsterdam changed hands and its name. Massachusetts Bay, which would serve as the nucleus from which other colonies in New England developed, began like the Plymouth Colony with a group of Puritans who felt the need to seek shelter outside England because

49. *Swan boats (owned and operated by the same family since 1877) at the Public Garden in Boston, the oldest public garden in any U.S. city. Courtesy Greater Boston Convention & Visitor Tourist Bureau, Inc.*

of their religious beliefs. Its royal charter was granted in 1629, a year after the council of the Plymouth Colony made a grant of land to the New England Company (renamed the Massachusetts Bay Company in 1629). The new colony defined its territory as including all parts of New England that lay between three miles south of the Charles River at Boston and three miles north of the Merrimack River, named for an Algonquian word meaning "deep place"— roughly the present-day border between northeastern Massachusetts and New Hampshire—as well as land within three miles of the southernmost part of Massachusetts Bay. It was specified in the charter that within these latitudes, the lands extended from the Atlantic Ocean to the South Sea (Pacific Ocean).

The colonists, led by their governor, John Winthrop, arrived in Massachusetts in June 1630, about a year after an advance party had settled at a place they called Salem. Salem was so named because the Puritans thought that the Indian name for the region of their settlement, Naumkeag, had been left by the Ten Lost Tribes of Israel and meant "comfort haven." Therefore, it was deemed appropriate to adopt the anglicized version of the Hebrew word for peace, *shalom* (as in the name of the Holy City of Peace, Jerusalem).

From the beginning, the Massachusetts Bay Colony had more inhabitants than the Plymouth Colony. There were already three hundred by the end of 1630, and they had set up trading posts on Cape Cod and along the Kennebec River. Led by Winthrop, they initially selected a site for the seat of government on a peninsula they called Charlestown. But because the water supply was unreliable, it was soon moved to a nearby peninsula, which was named Boston (fig. 49) after a coastal village in Lincolnshire from which several of the settlers,

The South part of New-England, as it is Planted this yeare, 1634.

A Prospect of the Colledges in Cambridge in New England

including the influential Thomas Leverett, an alderman back in England, had come. (England's Boston, incidentally, was derived from Saint Botolph.)

During the 1630s alone, about twenty thousand English people settled along the shores of Massachusetts Bay. As early as 1634, thirteen towns appear on the first map drawn by a settler in the region, William Wood, which was published in his book *New Englands Prospect* (fig. 50). The settlements are Salem, Meadford, Water Towne, Newtown (now Cambridge), Roxbury, Dorchester, Charles Towne, Winisimet (Chelsea), Sagus (Lynn), Mount Wollaston (Braintree), Wessaguseus, Plimouth, and Boston. Most of the names were taken from English place-names and were authorized by the colony's court. Roxbury was named for the rocky terrain. New Towne (as it was initially spelled) was changed to Cambridge because many of the settlers had come from that part of England; more specifically, it honored the founder of the first college (fig. 51) on North American soil, John Harvard, who had gone to that great English university, Cambridge.

The colony continued to be settled in all directions through the rest of the century. In 1635, a group of settlers led by Simon Willard moved seventeen miles inland from Boston and called their new community Concord, connoting a "peaceful state." At about the same time, Springfield, on the Connecticut River not far north of new settlements in the Connecticut Colony, was founded by William Pynchon, who had been squire of Springfield, England. Worcester, originally settled in 1684 and located halfway between Springfield and Boston, also took its name from an English town. Close to Boston, Marblehead was named for hard rocks in the region. At about the same time, Brookline was known as Muddy River. When it was incorporated in 1705, it adopted its current name because a brook constituted one of its boundary lines. In the southeast part of the colony, just east of Rhode Island, was Fall River, a translation of the Algonquian name for the region, meaning "falling water." The nearby island colonies of Nantucket—a name derived from an Algonquian term meaning "narrow river at," and referring to the channel between it and the adjacent Tuckernut Island—and Martha's Vineyard, which were settled by Massachusetts colonists, had been included in a grant to the New York Colony in 1664; they were permanently added to Massachusetts, however, in 1691, the year in which England combined Massachusetts Bay, Plymouth, and Maine into a single royal colony, Massachusetts.

A MAP of the BRITISH EMPIRE in AMERICA with the FRENCH and SPANISH SETTLEMENTS adjacent thereto by Hen Popple

CHAPTER THREE

Completing the Original Thirteen Colonies

NEW HAMPSHIRE AND MAINE

After the successful establishment of settlements at Jamestown and Plymouth by an England energized for expansion, it was logical to continue efforts at colonization along the Atlantic seacoast. The first phase in the evolution of what was to become the United States of America was the creation and development of the original thirteen English colonies.

The beginnings of the extension of English colonization took place north of the Plymouth Colony and date to August 1622, when John Mason and Sir Ferdinando Gorges were granted all the land between the Merrimack and Kennebec rivers, in what is now south-eastern New Hampshire and southwestern Maine. In 1629 they divided their holdings: Gorges retained the land northeast of the Pis-cataqua River, named after an Algonquian term meaning "fork of river at," and Mason kept the land south and west of it. That same year, the Council for New England made a separate grant to Mason specifying land along the seacoast from the middle of the Merrimack to the Piscataqua, up the Piscataqua to its head and then another sixty miles northward, and sixty miles westward from the middle of the head of the Merrimack.

In 1631, one year after the establishment of the Massachusetts Bay Colony, Mason founded the colony of New Hampshire, to which he had been given a royal patent, and initiated a settlement on the Piscataqua River. The fact that Mason spent most of his life in Hampshire, England, accounts for his designation of the colony's name. In 1635, a supplementary grant to Mason extended the land up to the Naumkeck and Newickwanock (also spelled Newickewanock,

and meaning "between rapids") rivers between Maine and New Hampshire. Not long after Mason died that same year, poor living conditions and a constant fear of Indian attacks led the colonists in New Hampshire to seek the protection of Massachusetts. Forty-five years later, when the attacks ceased and the colonists felt secure, New Hampshire was formally separated from the Massachusetts Bay Colony by royal decree, but New Hampshire continued to share the same governor as Massachusetts until 1741. In 1776, New Hampshire became the first colony to declare its independence from Great Britain, in keeping with the state's motto, "Live Free or Die."

The first settlements in the New Hampshire Colony were established in the tidewater region of the Piscataqua estuary and included Portsmouth and Exeter, each taking the name of an English city. After the local Abenaki Indians were conquered in the late sev-enteenth and early eighteenth centuries, settlement accelerated with an influx of Puritans from Massachusetts and Scotch-Irish from Ulster, in northern Ireland. New Hampshire's capital since 1808, Concord, was not named until 1763, at which time it took the name of the established Massachusetts town, where some of its settlers had lived. Laconia, the name bestowed on a New Hampshire town in the eighteenth century, was the original name given to the entire colony by Sir Ferdinando Gorges in 1629, in reference to the many lakes in the region. The most populous city, Manchester, was not named that until the early nineteenth century; it took its name from the English city, as was the case with Derry, Dover, Durham, Hampton, Milford, and Rochester. Keene honored Sir Benjamin Keene, a friend of the eighteenth-century governor Benning Wentworth. The name Hanover, the home of Dartmouth University, is a reminder that the reigning

52. Henry Popple. "A Map of the British Empire in America with the French and Spanish Settlements adjacent thereto." 1733. Engraving, hand-colored, 239 x 229 cm. Private collection. The first large-scale printed map of North America. Parallel horizontal lines attest to the "sea to sea" concept of land owned by various colonies.

monarchs of England in the eighteenth century came from the House of Hanover.

As for the other portion of the 1622 grant assigning "all that part of the mainland" to Mason and Sir Ferdinando Gorges, it was modified by a royal charter in 1639 formally granting Gorges the right to settle the "Province of Maine," northeast of the Piscataqua River. In 1652, however, five years after the death of Gorges, the Massachusetts Bay Colony claimed jurisdiction over Maine. When Massachusetts was designated a royal colony in 1691, Maine was included within its boundaries, and so it remained—with only gradual settlement— until it became a state in 1820.

CONNECTICUT

At about the same time New Hampshire was first being settled, new settlements were also being established on the other side of Massachusetts. In 1630, the Plymouth Council granted the Connecticut Colony to the council's president, the earl of Warwick. After King Charles I confirmed the grant in 1631, the earl transferred title to the land to Viscount Saye and Sele, Lord Brooke, Sir Richard Saltonstall, and others. Connecticut was initially settled by Pilgrims from Massachusetts, who in 1632 were invited by the Mohegan Indian chief in the region to farm along the shores of the "River Quonehtacut," from which the colonial name derived. The Algonquian name means "long river at," and the colony became the first to be named for a river; Delaware would later follow suit. The move by the Puritans from Massachusetts to Connecticut can be called the first western migration in this country.

A Dutch fort, called Fort Good Hope, had been erected in 1633 along the Connecticut River, but the post was short-lived. Then, in 1636, at the same location, Hartford (fig. 53) became the first significant settlement in the colony of Connecticut. Named for Hartford, England, it was followed to the south and north, respectively, by Wethersfield and Windsor, both also English place-names. Other settlements gradually sprang up from the southwest corner of the colony to the eastern part. In 1640, Greenwich was founded and named for that English town. Nearby Darien, now regarded as a bedroom community for New York City, was settled in 1641 and named for the Isthmus of Darien, later called the Isthmus of Panama, which Vasco Núñez de Balboa crossed before becoming the first European to view the Pacific Ocean. By contrast, Norwalk, settled in 1650, anglicized the Indian term *norwaak*, meaning "at a point of land." Naugatuck, about halfway between Norfolk and Hartford, was taken from an Algonquian term meaning "one lone tree," and Willimantic, halfway between Hartford and the colony's eastern border, means "good cedar swamp." Waterbury, founded in 1674 near Naugatuck, referred to the river running through it, while Danbury, founded in 1685 to the southwest, continued the pattern of adopting English place-names. Stamford, just west of Norwalk, also assumed the name of an English town. Middletown was so named because it was mid-

53. *Hartford, Conn.*
Courtesy the Metro Hartford Chamber of Commerce

way between the towns of Hartford and Old Saybrook; the latter honored two of the colony's original patentees by combining the name of Viscount Saye and Sele with that of Lord Brooke.

In 1638, while Connecticut was first being settled, another company of Puritans, from London, was establishing a trading port at New Haven—named to emphasize that it was a "new harbor"—with the hopes that it would rival Boston and New Amsterdam (still twenty-six years away from being renamed New York). The port of New Haven extended its domain to become a short-lived independent colony, which had a separate constitution and spread to the north shore of Long Island. At the time, both English and Dutch settlements proliferated on Long Island. In 1662, King Charles II combined Connecticut and New Haven to create the single colony of Connecticut. New Haven and Hartford were the joint capitals of Connecticut from 1701 to 1875, when Hartford became the sole state capital.

In the charter granted to Connecticut in 1662, the specified colonial boundaries were "the Narragansett River, commonly called Narragansett Bay," on the east, with "a line extending west to the South Sea from that bay," and the "Line of the Massachusetts plantation" on the north. The eastern boundary was changed by the 1663 charter for Rhode Island. In 1683, an agreement was reached between the governors of New York and Connecticut that established the boundaries between those colonies. The line began at the mouth of the Byram River, extended along a series of straight lines of specified distances, at right angles to one another, to a line running parallel to the Hudson River, "in every place 20 mile distant from that river," north to the Massachusetts border (fig. 54).

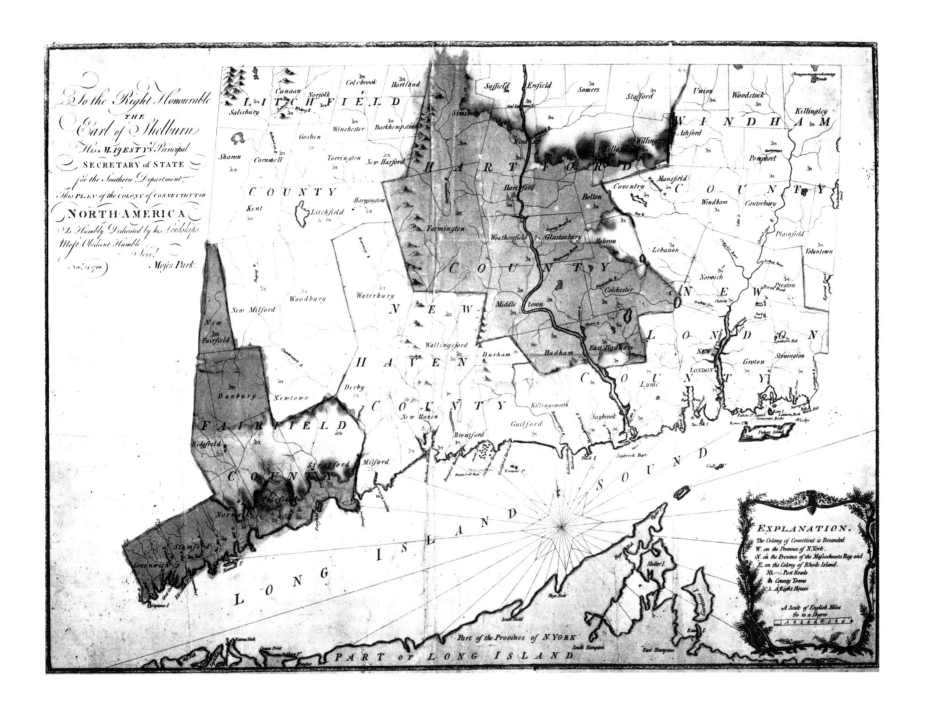

54. Moses Park. "Plan of the Colony of Connecticut in North America." 1766.
Engraving, 53 x 73 cm. Private collection. The first map designed, engraved,
and published in Connecticut. It was requested by the earl of Halifax
to improve postal service.

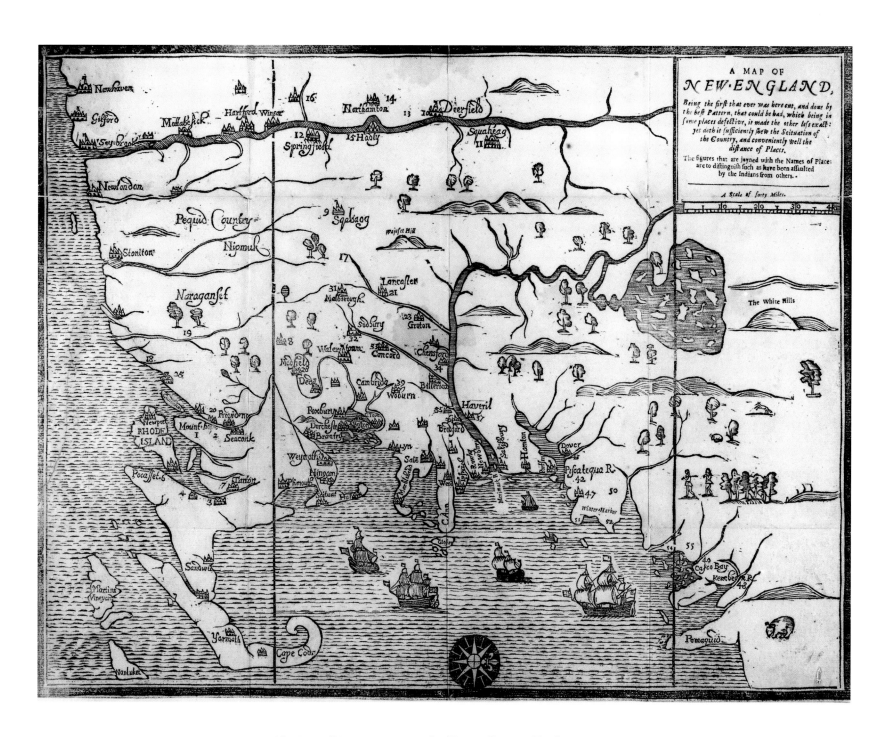

55. *John Foster. "A Map of New-England." In William Hubbard's* A Narrative
of the Troubles with the Indians in New-England . . . , *Boston, 1677.
Woodcut, 30 x 38 cm. Special Collections, Princeton University Library,
Princeton, N.J. The first map engraved and printed in North America, it illustrates
King Philip's War (1675–76). The map is oriented with north to the right;
the river at the top is the Connecticut, and the one at the center is the Merrimack.
The map shows the boundaries of the Massachusetts Bay Colony
according to its 1629 royal charter.*

Another colony began with a migration from Massachusetts, but that was a forced move. In 1635, Salem minister Roger Williams and his followers were banished from the Massachusetts Bay Colony, because they were regarded as too liberal in espousing more complete religious freedom than the Puritans were willing to accept. Williams's group proceeded south to the nearby region populated by the Narragansett Indians, whose name would later be assigned to the local bay, and in 1636 they founded what would later become the colony of Rhode Island, beginning with a settlement at Providence—given its name by Williams for "God's merciful *providence*." Two years later, two other religious exiles from the Massachusetts Bay Colony, William Coddington and Anne Hutchinson, founded Portsmouth, originally known as Pocasset, the Algonquian term for "where the stream changes size." Coddington moved south on the same island to establish Newport in 1639. These three settlements, Providence, Portsmouth, and Newport—along with Warwick, also formed by dissidents from the Massachusetts Bay Colony—were included in a Parliamentary patent that powerful friends in London obtained for Roger Williams in 1644, following an initial grant solely for Providence. Portsmouth, Newport, and Warwick took their names from towns in England.

The grant to what was then called the Providence Plantations included land bordering the Massachusetts Bay Colony to the north and northeast, the Plymouth Patent to the east and southeast, and the Narragansett Indian lands to the west; to the south was the ocean. The land grant extended about twenty-five miles into the Pequot River country. In that year, the Court of Providence Plantations ordered that the "island commonly called Aquethneck [meaning 'island at' in Algonquian] shall be from henceforth called the Isle of Rhodes, or Rhode Island." That name for the island where Portsmouth and Newport were located came from the geographic similarity to the Aegean island that Verrazano had suggested during his voyage of exploration more than a century earlier (although the island he applied the name to was probably Block Island). In 1663, King Charles II granted a royal charter to the colony of Rhode Island and Providence Plantations, having as its southwest corner the mouth of the Pawcatuck River (from an Indian word meaning "falls in river") and along that river until it turns north, at which point the boundary became a straight line to the southern boundary line of Massachusetts. Block Island was also included in the colony.

In the first half of the seventeenth century, the English usually negotiated with Indians for land rights, but conflicts often arose. In 1637, Connecticut colonists almost annihilated the Pequot Indians and thereby secured their settlements. This would be followed by the much larger-scale King Philip's War in 1675–76, which involved tribes and colonists in much of New England and virtually ended an organized Indian presence in the entire region (fig. 55).

While New England was being settled, so were other colonies to the south, beginning with Maryland. In 1632, King Charles I granted George Calvert, the first Lord Baltimore, absolute governing power over a proprietary form of colony, on a large segment of land that had been part of northern Virginia. The boundaries were defined as including all land between the ocean on the east and Chesapeake Bay on the west, divided by the promontory called "Watkins Point" and extending north to 40° north latitude, as well as the land west and south to the uncharted "farther bank of the Potomac River down to Chesapeake Bay."

Lord Baltimore had converted to the Roman Catholic faith and intended to make his colony a refuge for Catholics, who were persecuted in heavily Anglican, anti-Catholic England, while not excluding other religions—unlike the Puritan Plymouth and Massachusetts Bay colonies. Ironically, Anglicans were dominant among the initial settlers of Lord Baltimore's colony, and Puritans immigrated there from Virginia shortly thereafter. The Eastern Shore, the area east of Chesapeake Bay, was eventually dominated by Scotch-Irish Protestants.

The king assigned the colony its name, "Terræ Mariæ, anglice, Maryland," to honor his wife, Queen Henrietta Maria. Lord Baltimore accepted the name because it could also be interpreted as honoring the Virgin Mary. He died before the charter took effect, and it was his son, the second Lord Baltimore, who sent two ships under the leadership of his brother to Chesapeake Bay to establish the first settlement in Maryland. Located just off the bay on the north shore of the Potomac River, it was named St. Marys. Only this first settlement and first capital is noted, as "St. Maries," on the so-called Lord Baltimore's Map, published in 1635 (fig. 56). Although Baltimore County is named on a 1671 map, the town of Baltimore was not founded until 1729, after which it became the center of trade and a major port.

In his new colony, Lord Baltimore applied the "headright system" that had been used in Virginia: for everyone who brought servants over at his own expense, one hundred free acres were allotted for each male servant and fifty acres for each woman or child. If the master brought over enough to rate two thousand acres, he was granted a manor. Tobacco, which was grown successfully on the fertile soil, was the only cash crop. At the end of the seventeenth century the capital was moved to Annapolis, which was more centrally located along the western shore of Chesapeake Bay (fig. 57) and had been named in 1694 for Princess—later Queen—Anne, with *polis*, the Greek word for "city," appended. Well to the northwest, Frederick Calvert, the sixth Lord Baltimore, gave his name to the colonial town of Frederick. In 1762, a German settler named Jonathan Hager founded a town near the northern border that he called Elizabeth-Town, after his wife, but that people insisted be called Hagers Town. Thus, Hagerstown became the official name.

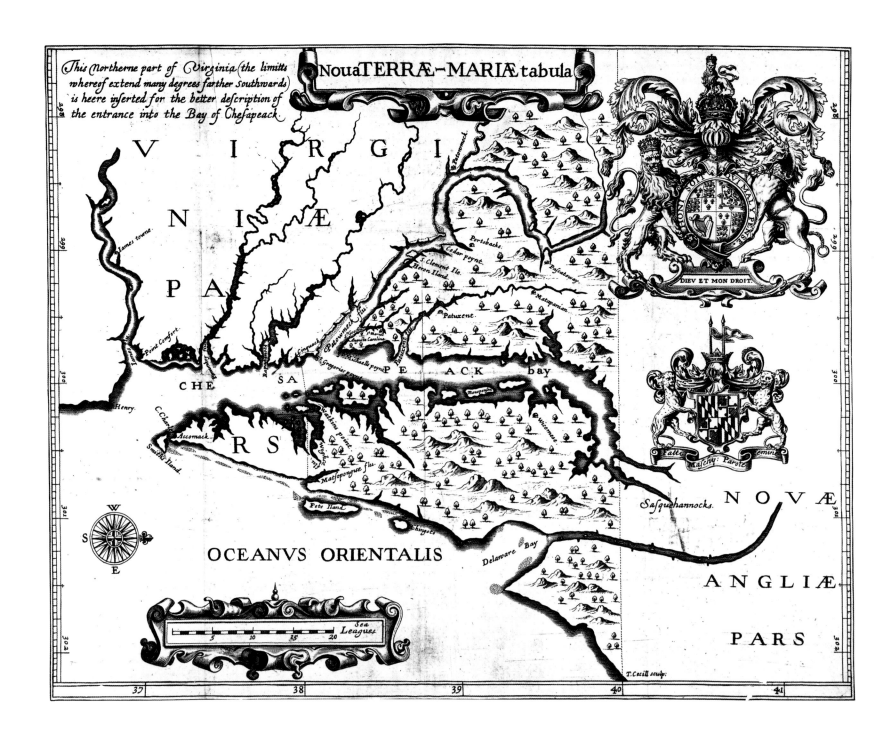

This Northerne part of Virginia (the limitts whereof extend many degrees farther southwards) is heere inserted for the better description of the entrance into the Bay of Chesapeack.

NouaTERRÆ-MARIÆ tabula

DIEV ET MON DROIT.

V I R G I
N I Æ
P A R S

James towne.

Point Comfort.

Henry.

C. Charles.

Accomack.

Smith's Iland.

Portobacke.
Cedar poynt.
S. Clement Ile.
Heron Iland.
Pascatoway.
Matapanian.
Patuxent.

Michaell pynt.
Gregories pynt.

PE ACK bay

Moupanon.

Wicomeco.

Sasquehannocks.

NOVÆ
ANGLIÆ
PARS

Watkins Point.

Matopongue flu.

Pete Iland.

Shivgoes.

Delaware Bay

CHE   SA   RS

OCEANVS ORIENTALIS

Sea Leagues.
5   10   15   20

T. Cecill sculp:

37   38   39   40   41

56. *Cartographer unknown. "Noua Terræ-Mariæ tabula." 1635. Engraving,*
30 x 39 cm. Newberry Library, Chicago. Known as "Lord Baltimore's Map,"
this is the first separate map of Maryland and presents its boundary lines
with Pennsylvania and Virginia.

57. *Chesapeake Bay mosaic. 1976. Copyright Earth Satellite Corporation*

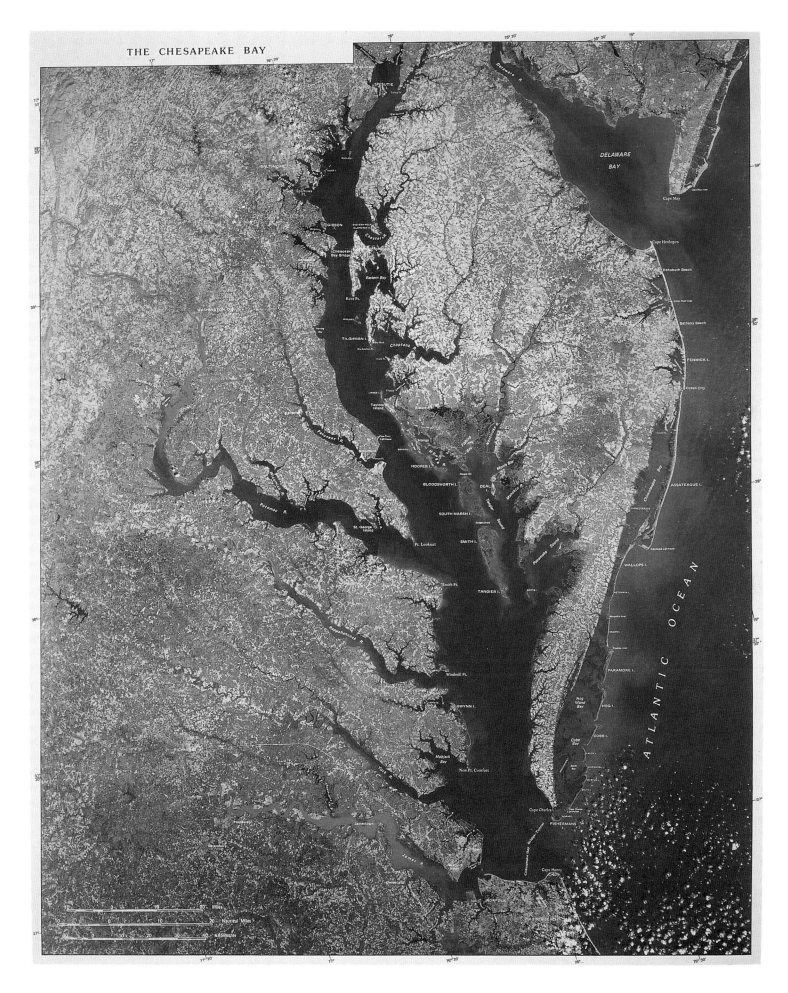

58. *John Seller. "A Mapp of New Jarsey [sic]." 1675. Engraving, hand-colored,
52 x 60 cm. Private collection. The first map to use the name "New Jersey"
(albeit spelled incorrectly), it shows New Jersey as it was in 1664. It is also the first
English map to include a view of New York City that had first appeared on a
Dutch map by Nicolas Visscher, and the earliest view to bear the name "New York."*

As mentioned previously, the duke of York, brother of King Charles II, received title to the land between the Connecticut and Delaware rivers in 1664, most of which had been the Dutch colony of New Netherland. He then apportioned a section known as the Province of New Jersey to two friends, Sir George Carteret and Lord John Berkeley. The boundaries were defined as including all lands adjacent to New England lying west of Long Island and Manhattan Island, and bounded on the east by the Atlantic Ocean and part of the Hudson River. The western boundary was Delaware Bay and the Delaware River, extending south to Cape May at the ocean and north as far as the northernmost part of the Delaware River, at 41°40' north latitude; from that point, the northern boundary crossed in a diagonal line to the Hudson River at 41° north.

The name of the new colony—the charter read "which said tract of land is hereafter to be called by the name or names of Nova Caesarea or New Jersey" (fig. 58)—satisfied two associations. Sir George Carteret was from the island of Jersey, and it was also on that island off the French coast that the duke of York had found asylum during England's Civil War in the 1640s. Cape May, at its southern tip, had already been assigned its name in the early part of the century, changing the spelling of the name of a Dutch captain, Cornelis Mey, who sailed those waters.

Settlement (in addition to Hackensack, which the Dutch had already founded) began soon after the duke of York turned the land over to Carteret and Berkeley. In 1666, Newark was established by a group of Puritan settlers who emigrated from Connecticut and took the name of an English town. Jersey City was chartered in 1668 on land that had been purchased from the Indians in 1630. The first seat of colonial government was at Elizabethtown. That name also had a double origin: Lady Carteret's given name, Elizabeth, and Elizabeth Castle, a fortress on the island of Jersey. A group of Quakers established their first settlement in New Jersey at Salem in 1675, and two thousand Quakers came from England shortly thereafter and settled around that nucleus along the east bank of the Delaware River near the bay.

In 1676, the colony was split into East Jersey, with its assembly at Elizabethtown, and West Jersey, with an assembly at Salem or Burlington, which was farther upriver and inhabited mainly by people from Yorkshire, England; the name Burlington was a corruption of Bridlington in Yorkshire. To the northeast, New Brunswick, around which later followed East, South, and North Brunswick, was called that because elector of the Duchy of Brunswick-Lüneburg was one of the titles of the early-eighteenth-century English king George I, the first king from the German House of Hanover (anglicized from Hannover).

The two Jerseys were united in 1702 as a single royal province, New Jersey, when the proprietors surrendered their powers to the crown. Trenton, which became the capital in 1790, had been called Trent's Town by William Trent, who founded the settlement in 1714. Evidence of the continuing Dutch influence in the region persists in the Oranges (including East, West, and South Orange), initially part of Newark and named for the Dutch prince of Orange. Indian and English languages were combined in the naming of Perth Amboy: the first part, honoring the earl of Perth, was joined with an Algonquian word, *amboy*, meaning "hollow out," referring to the surrounding valley. One of the surviving signs of the Indian presence in the colony, consisting mainly of Lenapes, or Lenni-Lenapes (whom the settlers called Delawares), is the name Hoboken (fig. 59), an Algonquian word meaning "tobacco pipe," because the town's site was near a quarry for stone from which the pipes were made. In addition, Hackensack took the name of an Indian tribe, and the name Passaic derives from an Algonquian term meaning "valley." Nearby Paterson was not named until the end of the eighteenth century, when it took the name of the state's governor, William Paterson, who had been a leader at the 1787 convention that resulted in the U.S. Constitution. Camden, along the Delaware River to the south, was named for Charles Pratt, Lord Camden, a supporter in England of the American cause.

59. *Frank Sinatra, 1944.*
The singer was born in Hoboken in 1915.

PENNSYLVANIA AND DELAWARE

The final chapter in the settlement of what were called the Middle Colonies began in 1681 when William Penn (fig. 60), a Quaker who inherited a claim on a large royal debt owed to his father, received a charter from King Charles II for an area between 42° north latitude and 39° north, running west from the Delaware River through five degrees of longitude. It was originally the homeland of the Lenape (Delaware), Shawnee, and Susquehanna Indians. Before the grant, in 1638, the Swedish West India Company had already established the first permanent settlement in that area, along the west bank of the Delaware River. The Swedes proceeded to purchase the land extending

60. Artist unknown. "William Penn trades with the Indians." Engraving, after a 1771 painting by Benjamin West; 42 x 30 cm. Private collection

61. P. Lindstrom. "Nova Svecia hodie dicta Pennsylvania." 1702. Engraving, 27 x 13 cm. Private collection. This shows the Swedish colony along the Delaware River in 1654. The Dutch captured New Sweden's forts the following year.

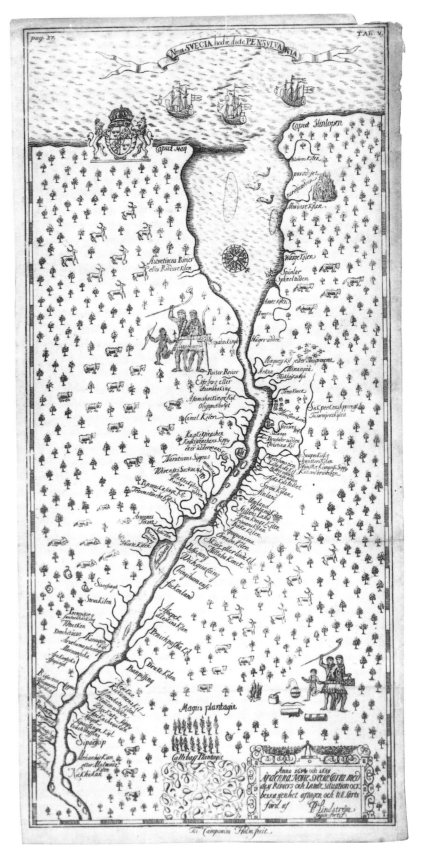

from Cape Henlopen, at the mouth of Delaware Bay, to the falls of the Delaware and called it New Sweden (fig. 61). In 1655 the Dutch captured the territory, and when England seized New Netherland in 1664, this land also was claimed by the duke of York.

Penn wanted his land called New Wales, but the king declared the name to be Pennsylvania, joining *sylvania,* Latin for "forest," to the name of the grantee's father. The colony was to provide a place to which persecuted English and European Quakers could immigrate and a locale in which all religions would be tolerated. Penn himself went to the colony in 1682 and, between the Delaware and Schuylkill rivers (fig. 62), laid out Philadelphia, the first formally planned city in the New World (fig. 63). The name Philadelphia, from the Greek meaning "brotherly love," is mentioned in the New Testament and was assigned to attest to the religious liberty that was to characterize the colony. Swedes and Finns, survivors of the New Sweden colony, were already living in the Philadelphia area. Germans of the Mennonite sect established the settlement in Germantown in 1683. Shortly thereafter, Welsh Quakers founded Radnor and Haverford, named for a Welsh county and a Welsh town, respectively (fig. 64). Almost immediately after Penn's arrival in America he also looked to the Susquehanna Valley, which had first been explored by the French trapper Étienne Brulé in 1616, for future expansion.

When Penn received his original charter, the status of what was then referred to as the Three Lower Counties—the future Delaware—was overlooked. In 1701, Penn issued his Charter of Privileges, calling for a governor and council appointed by the proprietor, and an assembly that included representatives from each county. The settlers in the Three Lower Counties, however, who were unhappy about being made part of the charter issued to a Quaker, were granted some autonomy in 1701, including their own separate assembly, although the Three Lower Counties remained under Penn's proprietary government (fig. 65). In addition to New Castle (renamed from Fort Casimir when the settlement passed from Dutch to English hands), Delaware's early settlements included its later capital city, Dover, which would take its name from the English Channel port, and its largest city, Wilmington, on the site of the Swedish Fort Christina. Initially the settlement was named Willington, for a local developer, but Penn changed the name to honor the earl of Wilmington, who had an expressed enthusiasm for the colonies.

The royal charters granted to Lord Baltimore and William Penn had ill-defined boundaries. In order to resolve the boundary dispute between Pennsylvania and Maryland, a survey was completed in 1767; the result was the 1768 publication of the Mason-Dixon Line, which permitted Pennsylvania to include Philadelphia in its borders and to include land that gave it access to Delaware Bay, while Maryland maintained Baltimore in its province (see figs. 113 and 114).

62. *Thomas Eakins.* The Champion Single Sculls (Max Schmitt in a Single Scull). *1871. Oil on canvas, 82 x 117.5 cm. Courtesy the Metropolitan Museum of Art. Purchase, The Alfred N. Punnett Endowment Fund and George D. Pratt Gift, 1934 (34.92). Copyright 1994. A view of the Schuylkill River.*

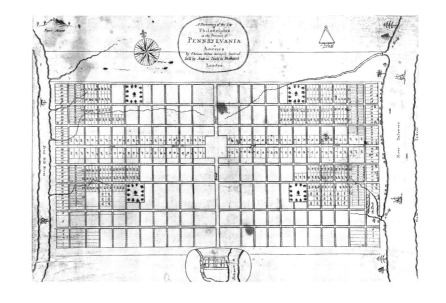

63. *Thomas Holme.* "A Portraiture of the City of Philadelphia." *1683. Engraving, 29 x 44 cm. Courtesy American Philosophical Society, Philadelphia. The first printed plan of a city in what later became the United States. The area is laid out in squares between the Delaware and Schuylkill rivers. High Street and Broad Street intersect at a central square. North–south streets are numbered, while east–west streets are named for trees.*

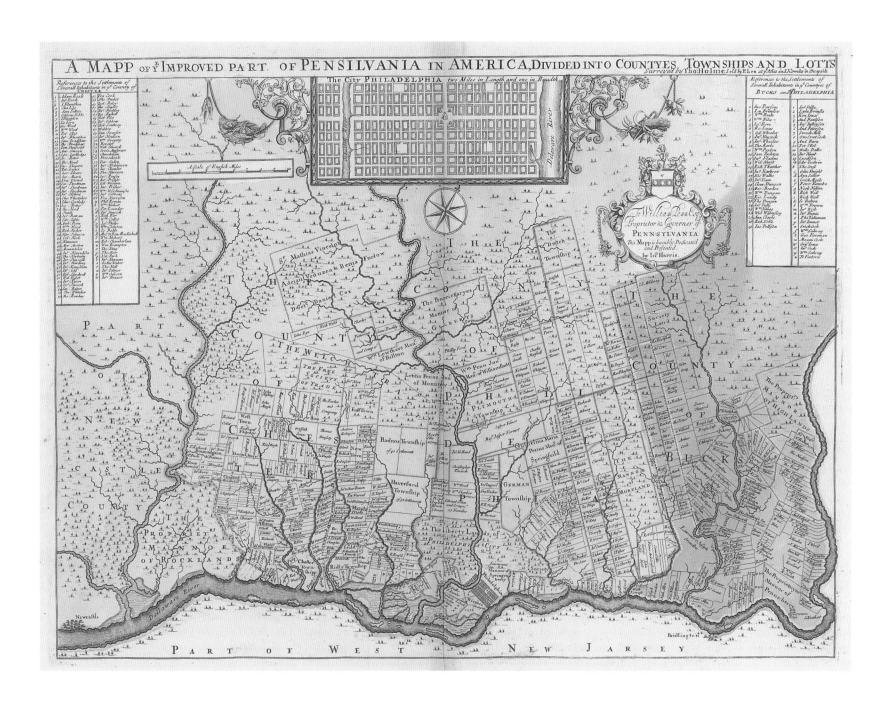

64. Thomas Holme. "A Mapp of ye Improved part of Pensilvania in America, Divided into Countyes Townships and Lotts." 1687. Engraving, hand-colored, 40 x 54 cm. Private collection, Philadelphia. An early map of grants made to William Penn. Settlements west of the Delaware River are shown, and landowners in Chester, Bucks, and Philadelphia counties are listed in the legend. The inset is a city plan of Philadelphia.

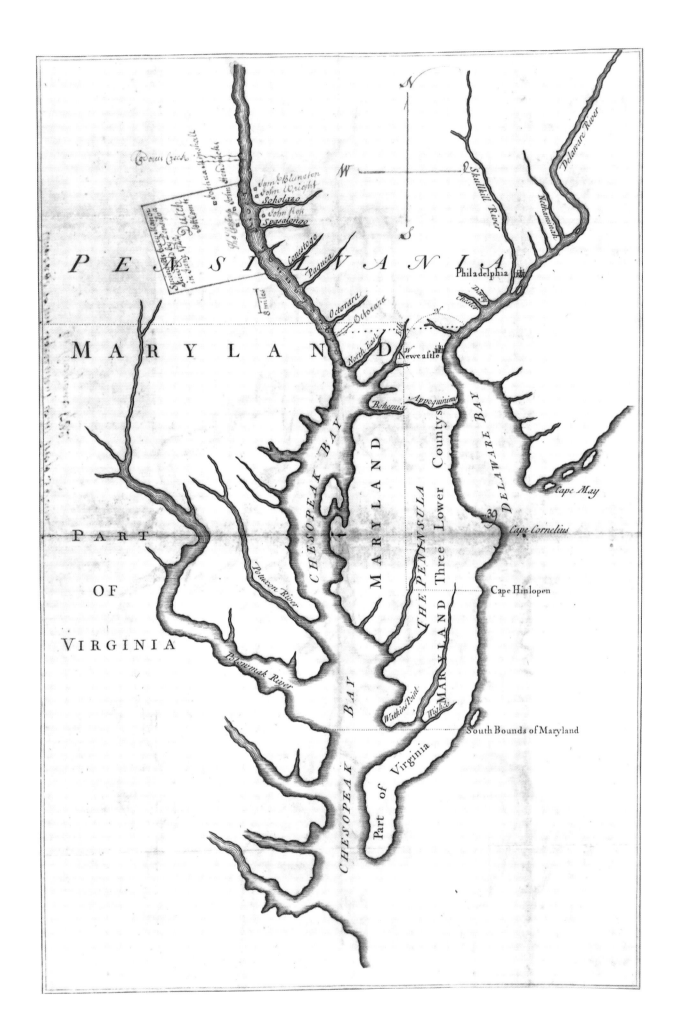

Cedons Creek

Sam. Blunston
John Wright
Soholazo
John flos
Spasalongo

Conestogo
Paqueca

PENSILVANIA

Speechnas besy knor
dent by Benedict
in May 1721 Dutch
settlement

8 miles

Octorara
Octorara

Skullkill River

Delaware River

Nahaninah

Philadelphia

Derby
Chester

MARYLAND

North East
Elk
Newcastle

Appoquinimy

Bohemia

Three Lower Countys

DELAWARE BAY

Cape May

CHESOPEAK BAY

MARYLAND

THE PENINSULA

39
Cape Cornelius

PART

OF

VIRGINIA

Patuxen River

MARYLAND

Cape Hinlopen

Potowmak River

Watkins Point
Wighco

South Bounds of Maryland

CHESOPEAK BAY

Part of Virginia

CHESOPEAK BAY

65. *John Senex. Untitled map
of Pennsylvania. 1732.
Engraving, 36 x 24 cm.
Private collection. The first
printed map to show an early
boundary settlement between
Pennsylvania and Maryland.
It also shows the
Three Lower Counties,
the part of Pennsylvania that
later became Delaware.*

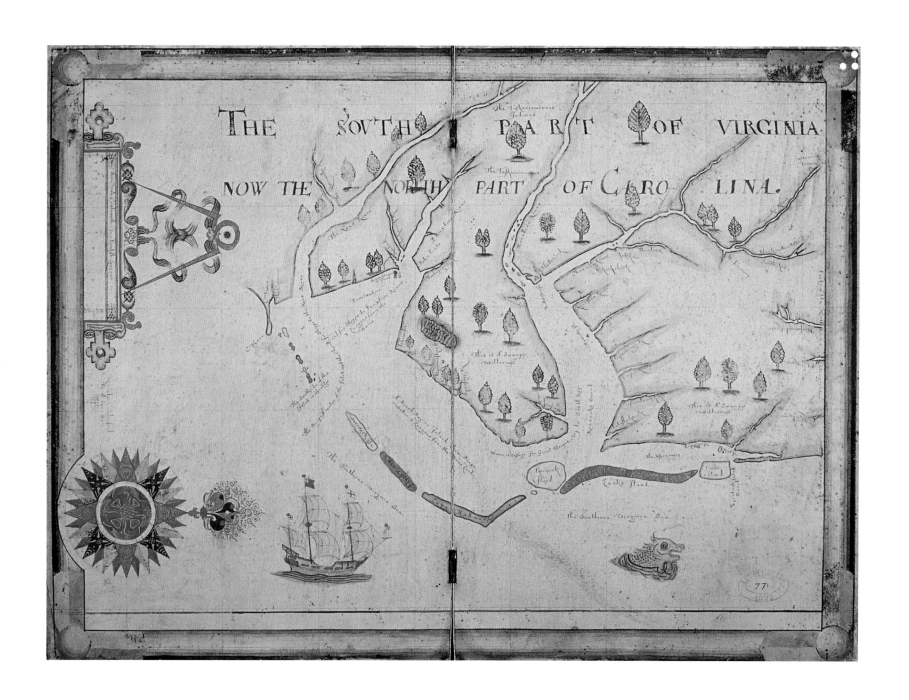

66. *Nicholas Cumberford. "The South Part of Virginia Now the North Part of Carolina." 1657. Manuscript on vellum, pen and ink and watercolor with gilt, 35 x 47 cm. Rare Books Division, New York Public Library. Astor, Lenox and Tilden Foundations. This map of the area around the Pamlico and Albemarle sounds identifies what was probably the first permanent settlement in North Carolina.*

67. *Bishop Roberts. Charleston, S.C. Before 1739. Watercolor on paper, 38 x 111 cm.*
Courtesy Colonial Williamsburg Foundation, Williamsburg, Va.

THE CAROLINAS

To the south, the history of the Carolinas—the homelands of the Cherokee, Catawba, Tuscarora, and Yamasee Indians, and the site of the Lost Colonies of Roanoke in the 1580s—dates to 1629, when King Charles I of England granted Sir Robert Heath, the attorney general, land to the south of the Virginia settlements in order to establish a new province, which Heath suggested be named for the king; he thus called it Carolina, after Carolus, the Latin equivalent of Charles. The name appeared on a map for the first time in 1651, as "Carolana" within "Ould Virginia." The genesis of the colony as formerly a part of Virginia is also attested to by a 1657 manuscript map labeled "The South Part of Virginia Now the North Part of Carolina" (fig. 66). Heath did not attempt any settlements, and the land within the grant was first settled by farmers from neighboring Virginia. The colony of Carolina was not formally established until 1663, when King Charles II reassigned the land extending from the southern border of Virginia south to the Florida peninsula, at about the latitude of what is now Daytona Beach, to a group of eight promoters and politicians spearheaded by Anthony Ashley Cooper (then called Lord Ashley), chancellor of the exchequer of England, and Sir John Colleton, a wealthy planter living in Barbados.

The 1663 charter defined the boundaries as extending from the north end of Lucke Island, in the southern Virginia seas at about 36° north latitude, south as far as the mouth of the St. Mathias River on the Florida coast, with two east–west parallels extending from the Atlantic Ocean to the South Sea (Pacific Ocean). A second charter, in 1665, extended the northern boundary to the north end of the Cuttihuck River or inlet, at 36°30' north latitude. This is approximately the current northern boundary of North Carolina.

Even before those charters were granted, in 1660, the Massachusetts Bay Colony had sent Captain William Hilton to determine the feasibility of developing a colony at Cape Fear. The first attempt at settlement occurred at the mouth of the Cape Fear River. These Puritans from Massachusetts soon returned home, disappointed with the potential of the area. A second trip by Hilton was underwritten by several proprietors from Barbados. On this voyage, Hilton anchored farther south at Port Royal, which had been named one hundred years earlier by Jean Ribault, during his abortive attempt to establish a French colony there. Hilton assigned his own name to an island in the area, which thus became Hilton Head Island. In 1664, a settlement was established on the Cape Fear River and named Charles Town; it did not persist and should not be confused with the present Charleston, South Carolina, which did not come into being until 1670, when William Sayle, the first governor, founded what he also named Charles Town (fig. 67). At that time, Sayle named the Ashley and Cooper rivers for one man, his sponsor, Lord Ashley (who in 1672 became the first earl of Shaftesbury).

Meanwhile, in a series of three inland journeys conducted in 1669 and 1670, John Lederer, a surgeon from Germany in the employ of Governor William Berkeley of Virginia, set out from the region of what is now Charlottesville and explored and mapped the Piedmont and

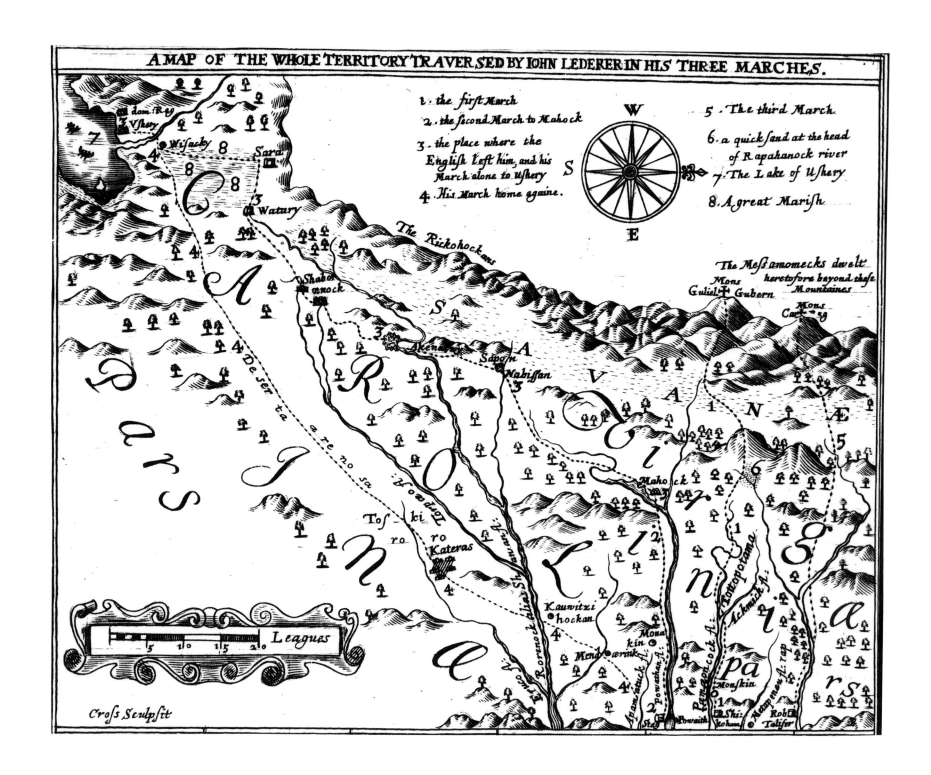

A MAP OF THE WHOLE TERRITORY TRAVERSED BY IOHN LEDERER IN HIS THREE MARCHES.

1. the first March
2. the second March to Mahock
3. the place where the English Left him, and his March alone to Ushery
4. His March home againe.

5. The third March.
6. a quick sand at the head of Rapahanock river
7. The Lake of Ushery
8. A great Marish

W S E

The Rickohocans

The Messamomecks dwelt heretofore bevond these Mountaines

Mons Guliel Gubern

Mons Cart

dom Reg
Ushery

Wisacky   Sara
Watary

C

A

R

O

L

I

N

A

Desert a renosa

Shabosmenock

Akenatzy
Sapon
Nahissan

V

I

R

G

I

n

I

A

Æ

Mahock

Toskiroro Kateras

Kauwitzi hockan

Mona kin

Mendoerink

pars

Leagues
5 10 15 20

Cross Sculpsit

68. *John Lederer. "A Map of the Whole Territory Traversed by John Lederer in his Three Marches." In Sir William Talbot's* The Discoveries of John Lederer *in Three Several Marches from Virginia to the West of Carolina, London, 1672. Engraving, 17 x 21 cm. Courtesy Tracy W. McGregor Library of American History, Special Collections Department, University of Virginia, Charlottesville. This map aided in opening up fur trading between Virginia colonists and Indians in the Carolinas.*

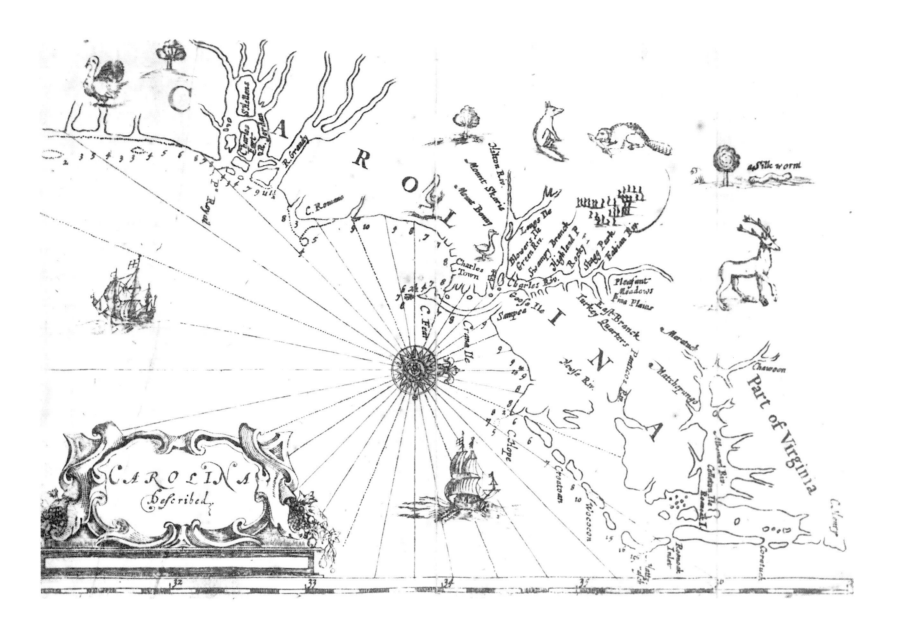

69. *Cartographer unknown. "Carolina described." In Robert Horne's*
A Brief Description of The Province of Carolina . . . , *London, 1666.*
Engraving, 14.5 x 22 cm. Private collection. This map shows a silkworm
and the 1664 settlement of Charles Town near Cape Fear, in what later became
North Carolina (not to be confused with Charles Town, later Charleston,
in what subsequently became South Carolina).

pine barrens of Carolina. Lederer skirted the southern end of the Appalachian Mountains, traveled across the Piedmont region of what became North Carolina, and continued into present-day South Carolina (fig. 68). Lederer's efforts helped set up fur trading with the Indians. Also in 1671, another physician, Henry Woodward, considered to have been the first English settler in South Carolina, defined a land route from Charles Town to Virginia. In 1673, James Needham and Gabriel Arthur, in the employ of the trader Abraham Wood, explored western Carolina, in the neighborhood of what is now Asheville, during a mission to establish relations with the local Indians.

Most of the early settlers in the southern part of the Carolinas were poor whites from Barbados. In 1680, some French Huguenots settled near Charles Town (in what is now North Carolina), for the specific purpose of establishing the cultivation of silkworms. The first map (fig. 69) that focuses specifically on Carolina, dated 1666, depicts a silkworm and a mulberry bush in the region. Neither the silkworms nor the mulberry bushes that were imported flourished, however, and the plans to create a source of silk in the New World failed. At about the same time, a group of Scottish émigrés settled in Port Royal but were driven out by Spaniards, who claimed the rights to that land. Nevertheless, more French immigrants arrived in the southern part of the colony and successfully established rice farming and an active trade with the Caribbean islands.

In the northern part of Carolina, originally settled by French Huguenots who moved from adjacent Virginia to farm, the first actual community, founded in 1706 on the lower Pamlico River, was named Bath in honor of the English city. This was followed, in 1710, by New Bern to the south. That name was assigned by Baron de Graffenried of Bern, Switzerland, who brought over German and Swiss settlers. That settlement was almost wiped out by the Tuscarora Indians.

In 1728, a boundary line was established between Virginia and Carolina. William Byrd was one of the Virginia commissioners assigned to delineate the line, and his description of the expedition provides a vivid picture of the Great Dismal Swamp near the coast of the two colonies. Because of the marked schism in the development of the northern and southern parts of the province, the proprietors of Carolina sold out to the Crown, which split it into the two royal provinces of North and South Carolina in 1729.

Columbia was the name given to the South Carolina capital in 1786. It stemmed from a name for the United States, in honor of Columbus, that appeared in 1775 in Philip Freneau's poem "American Liberty." Greenville—like the city of the same name in North Carolina—took its name from the Revolutionary War hero Nathanael Greene. Beaufort was named for the duke of Beaufort, one of the aristocratic proprietors of the colony. Spartanburg was named for the colony's Spartan Regiment, which reached heroic heights during the American Revolution, and Sumter was named for General Thomas Sumter, who also played an important role in that war. Berea was the name of a town in Macedonia, Greece, that is mentioned in the Bible.

GEORGIA

The thirteenth English colony, Georgia, was not established until well into the eighteenth century, and its inception followed the original Carolina grant by more than a century. By the beginning of the eighteenth century, the estimated population in the English colonies in what would become the United States had already reached 250,900, distributed as follows: Virginia, 58,600; Massachusetts, 55,900; Maryland, 29,600; Connecticut, 26,000; Pennsylvania and Delaware, 20,500; New York, 19,100; New Jersey, 14,000; North Carolina, 10,700; Rhode Island, 5,900; South Carolina, 5,700; New Hampshire, 5,000. Spanish settlers were insignificant in numbers, and the entire French population was estimated to be approximately 6,000.

During the first half of the eighteenth century, the population of the English continental colonies quadrupled, and at the onset of the French and Indian War in 1754 it would reach 1.2 million. This was brought about by large-scale immigration of Scotch-Irish, Germans, and French. They settled the frontiers from Maine to Georgia. Newly arrived settlers migrated to the western parts of Virginia and Maryland, as well as to the southern Piedmont of North Carolina.

In 1716, at the insistence of Governor Alexander Spotswood of Virginia, the formalized settlement of the Piedmont in that colony was begun. Thomas Fairfax, proprietor of the Northern Neck of Virginia, sold land he had inherited from his grandfather Thomas Culpeper to immigrants from Pennsylvania, who then populated the Shenandoah Valley as well as the Piedmont.

By the 1730s, the Spanish had established forts in western Florida and in Louisiana along the frontier to the south of the English settlements. At that time, England (or Great Britain, as it was officially known by then) acknowledged its error in having only passively supported the settlers in the South Carolina region during Queen Anne's War, the American portion of what was called in Europe the War of the Spanish Sucession, pitting England, Austria, and the Netherlands against Spain and France in roughly the first decade of the century. In America, the Spanish and French formed an alliance with the Choctaw Indians to counter the Carolinians' alliance with the Yamasee Indians. The Treaty of Utrecht, which ended the war, left an ill-defined border between Carolina and Spanish Florida. The British response to the general threat of the Spanish to the south was the promulgation of a new colony to be situated between South Carolina and Florida.

In 1732, a royal charter for Georgia, which was named for King George II, was granted to General James Oglethorpe and associates, who were motivated by an altruistic desire to provide a refuge for those who were caught up in an archaic penal system or suffered religious persecution. The lands within the grant extended from the northernmost part of the Savannah River along the Atlantic coast south to the Altamaha River, and west from the heads of the two rivers to the South Sea (Pacific Ocean). Georgia initially prohibited alcohol and slavery, but because the former was ineffective and the latter interfered with economic development, both prohibitions were repealed.

Oglethorpe arrived in Georgia in 1733 and founded Savannah, adopting for the settlement the longtime Spanish name of the adjacent river, meaning "treeless" or "barren." The settlement was laid out with a precise plan (fig. 70) on the shore of that river (fig. 71), as was the colony's second-oldest settlement, Ebenezer, a name taken from the Bible by immigrants from Salzburg, Germany. The town of Augusta, named for the Princess of Wales, the daughter-in-law of King George II, evolved in 1735 as a trading post at the head of the navigable part of the Savannah River. In 1738, Mark Carr, who had served with Oglethorpe, developed his plantation; the colony bought the surrounding land in 1779 and laid out the town of Brunswick, naming it for the king's ancestral home, the Hanover Duchy of Brunswick-Lüneburg.

A map by Henry Popple, published in 1733, the year Georgia was first settled as the thirteenth colony, depicts the British colonies in America and their land claims at the time (fig. 52). During the first half of the eighteenth century, the need for land to support a livelihood was the stimulus for expansion. This led to the development of

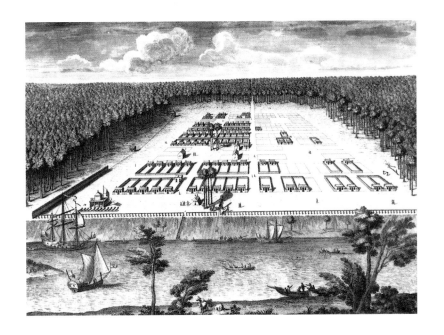

70. *Peter Gordon. "A View of Savannah." 1734.*
Engraving, 40 x 55 cm. Courtesy John D. Duncan.
James Oglethorpe's plan for Savannah, Ga.,
consisting of four wards, each centered around an open
square with lots reserved for official buildings.
Each ward had 40 house lots.

71. *The nuclear ship* Savannah *in the Savannah River;*
this 1962 photograph shows the embankment,
River Street with its cotton warehouses from
the 19th century, Johnson Square, and City Hall.
Courtesy Savannah News Press

new settlements adjacent to the older established communities, as well as a pushing back of the frontier. In 1748, a group of Virginians, including Thomas Jefferson's father, Meriwether Lewis's grandfather, and Dr. Thomas Walker, formed the Loyal Land Company and received a patent for eight hundred thousand acres along the southern border of Virginia, now southeastern Kentucky. The company dispatched Walker to find suitable places on and beyond the frontier for Virginians to settle. He explored what is now Tennessee and, in 1750, discovered the Cumberland Gap. He named that vital mountain pass after the duke of Cumberland, the commander in chief of the British army who had gained fame for his 1746 victory at Culloden Moor in Scotland, thereby precluding the Catholic Stuarts' recapture of the English throne. Walker himself became Kentucky's first permanent settler. Following his lead, through the Cumberland Gap, settlers from Pennsylvania and North Carolina would pass into Kentucky in the second half of the eighteenth century and create a new frontier farther to the west (fig. 72).

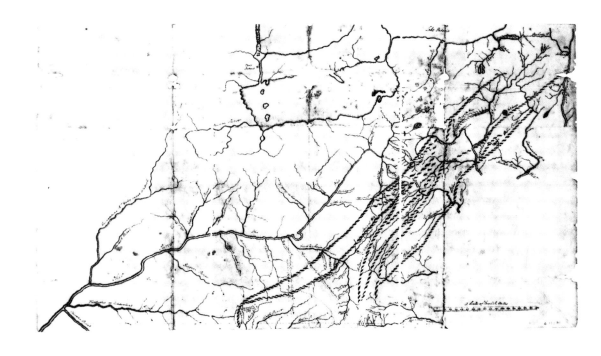

72. *George Washington. "Aligany. Copied from a Map*
of Doctor Walker laid before the Assembly." 1769.
Manuscript on paper, 52 x 97 cm. Manuscript Division,
Library of Congress, Washington, D.C. This map is
based on Dr. Thomas Walker's survey of western Virginia
as far as the Cumberland Gap—the gateway to a new
frontier, which he discovered in 1750.

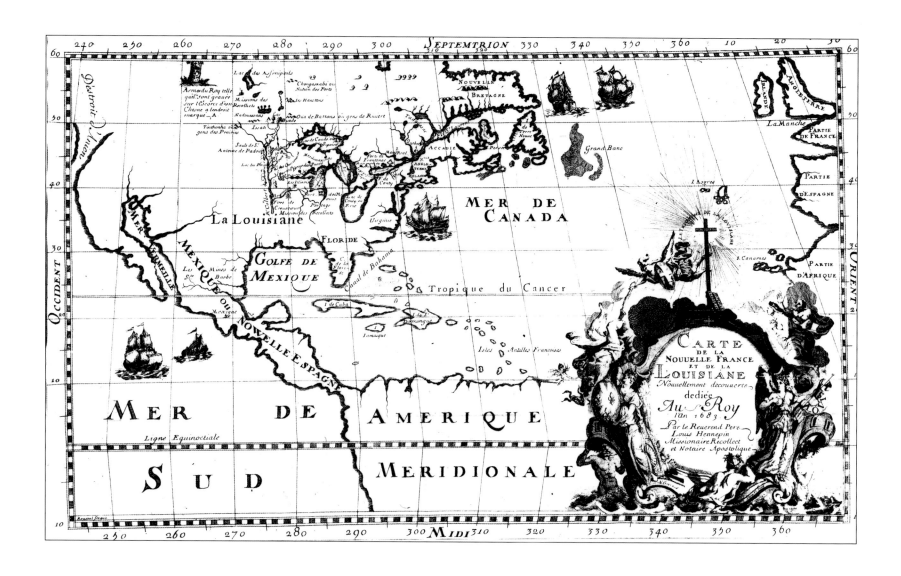

CHAPTER FOUR

Away from the Atlantic Coast
(1600–1750)

THE FRENCH AND THE GREAT LAKES

At the same time that early development of the English settlements was taking place up and down the eastern seaboard, the French Canadians were extending westward along the Great Lakes and, eventually, the Mississippi River. This expansion was stimulated by the commercial enterprise of fur trapping and trading with the Indians, as well as the fervor of the Jesuit priests to spread the Gospel among the natives. In four of five cases, Indian names for the Great Lakes gained permanence. What its discoverer, Samuel de Champlain, had called Lac St. Louis became Lake Ontario, an Iroquoian word meaning "beautiful lake." Champlain's Mer Douce became Lake Huron, taking its name from that of the local Indian tribe. In 1634, Jean Nicolet became the first European to see Lake Michigan, originally called Lac des Illinois, meaning "men," and also named for a local tribe. Michigan derives from the Ojibwa (also spelled Ojibway) tribal name Michiguma, meaning "big waters." Nicolet also reached Green Bay, on the western shore of Lake Michigan, which was originally named Baye des Puans, meaning "bay of bad smells." He trekked throughout the Fox River valley in present-day Wisconsin and, on his return, related Indian tales of a great river in the interior. Thus, Nicolet became the first European to mention what became known as the upper Mississippi River.

A place of portage that led from a river chain to Lake Michigan was given the Algonquian name Chicagou, designating either an "onion place" or a "garlic place," because wild onions or garlic grew there. Settlement on that site, and its permanent name of Chicago, came much later (fig. 74). As for the last of the Great Lakes to be explored—not until 1669—it was initially called Lac du Chat, French for "lake of the cat," referring to a fierce group of Indians who inhabited the southern shore. They called themselves "the panthers or long-tailed" and used the Indian term *yenrish*, which was eventually transformed into Erie. Even before Lake Erie was explored, it appeared with the other four Great Lakes, including "Superieur" (Superior), on a 1650 French map (see fig. 36).

In 1641, the Jesuits set up a mission at Sault Ste. Marie, between Lakes Huron and Superior. "Sault" is the archaic spelling of *saut*, the French word for "waterfall." During the 1660s and early 1670s, the Jesuit religious order annually published its activities on the Great Lakes region, and included maps, in a series of books entitled *Relations*. One of these publications carries the word "messi-sipi," derived from two Algonquian terms, *messi*, meaning "big," and *sipi*, meaning "river." The 1672 *Relations* contains the first large-scale printed map of the biggest Great Lake, Lake Superior, so named by the French because it is the "highest lake" (fig. 75).

73. Father Louis Hennepin. "Carte de la Nouuelle France et de la Louisiane Nouuellement decouuerte." In Hennepin's Description de la Louisiane Nouvellement Decouverte au Sud'Ouest de la Nouvelle France, *Paris, 1683. Engraving, 26 x 44 cm. Private collection. The first map to show the Falls of St. Anthony ("Sault de St. Antoine de Padou"), at the site of present-day Minneapolis, Minn. The surmised lower course of the Mississippi River, indicated by the dotted line, is approximately correct. Louisiana ("Louisiane") is named on a printed map for the first time.*

74. *The skyline of Chicago—a name derived from an Algonquian word meaning an "onion place" or "garlic place." Photograph by Karen Hirsch*

75. *Attributed to Charles Dablon and Claude Allouez. "Lac Svperievr." In* Relation des Missions aux Outaouacs des Annees 1670 et 1672, *Paris, 1672. Engraving, 17 x 23 cm. Private collection. An accurate presentation of Lake Superior and the northern part of Lake Michigan ("Lac des Ilinois"). The first map to distinguish Green Bay ("Baye des Puans") from Lake Michigan. Jesuit missions in the area are also located on the map.*

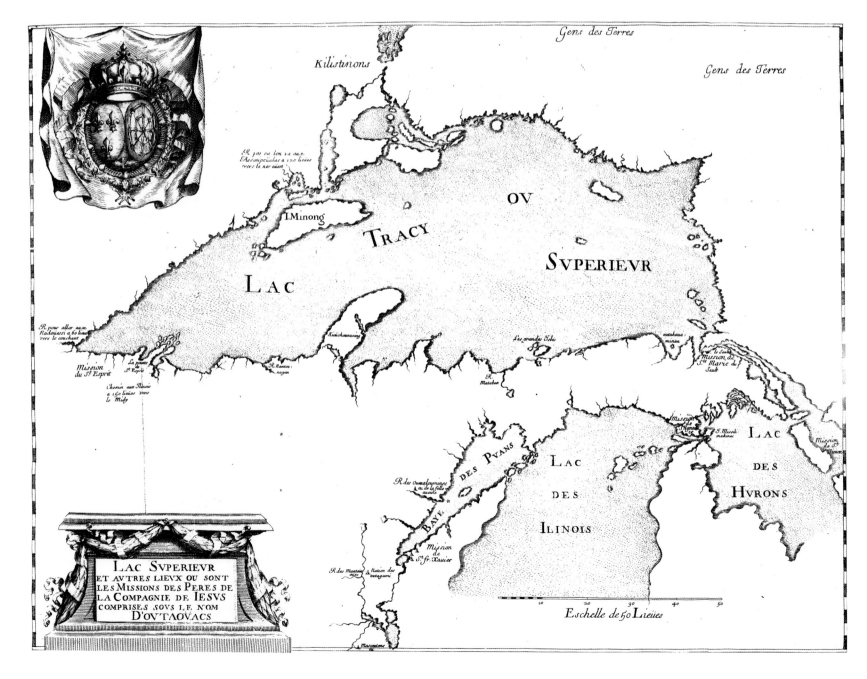

In 1663, the French government in Quebec embarked on an expansionist policy westward in search of furs, minerals, and a shorter route to China. This initially focused on finding the Mississippi River, and the quest began at Green Bay. Louis Jolliet, a fur trader and explorer, was called on to lead the expedition, which was initiated at the mission of St. Ignace, along the Straits of Mackinac between Lakes Michigan and Huron, in May 1673. The name of the straits came from the island of Michilimackinac (now Mackinac), derived from the Ojibwa term for "big turtle at," probably because of its shape. The Jesuits, ever eager to extend their influence over the Indians, sent Father Jacques Marquette, who was born in New France and knew the Algonquian language, along as their emissary.

Accompanied by five woodsmen, Jolliet and Marquette left from Green Bay in two canoes and followed the Fox River to the Mescousing River, known later as the Ouisconsing and finally as the Wisconsin River, into the upper Mississippi River. Continuing south, they came to the entrance of the Missouri River, which they called the Pekittanoui, or "muddy water." Farther south, they encountered the entrance of the Ohio River, flowing from the northeast, and their journey ended at the entrance of a river from the west, the Arkansas River, named for the Indian tribe and settlement of Arkansea at the junction of the Arkansas and Mississippi rivers. The explorers decided to stop about four hundred miles from the mouth of the Mississippi at the Gulf Coast because of fear of the Spaniards along the shores of the southern part of the river.

On the return trip, they found a shortcut to Lake Michigan by following the Illinois and Des Plaines rivers to a portage at Chicago that brought them to the lake. Their findings are preserved on the so-called Marquette Map of 1673–74, now in the Archives de la Compagnie de Jésus in Quebec (fig. 76). The map identifies the Missouri River, which eventually received that name, meaning "place of the big canoes" in Algonquian, and the Ohio, which is the Iroquoian term for "fine river." The name of the Ohio River actually underwent several transformations. Marquette called it the Ouaboukigou, but the French later named it the Oubache, which the English converted to Wabash—a name subsequently given to another river that flows into the Ohio. Well into the eighteenth century, confusion persisted between the current Wabash and Ohio rivers.

Several place-names can be dated from that monumental journey of discovery. Among the tribes along the Mississippi were the Maha, meaning "upstream people," and resulting in the name Omaha; the Kansa, from which Kansas evolved; the vowel-laden Ouaouiatonon, which would be shortened to Iowa; and the Peouarea, which became Peoria. The Rivière des Moingouena was compacted to Des Moings and eventually converted to the similar-sounding French Rivière Des Moines, meaning "river of the monks."

Nine years would pass between the exploration of Jolliet and Marquette and the completion of the discovery of the entire length of

76. Cartographer unknown. "Marquette Map." 1673–74. Manuscript on paper. Courtesy Archives de la Compagnie de Jésus, St. Jérôme, Quebec. The only known extant document from the expedition of Louis Jolliet and Father Jacques Marquette. The Wisconsin and Illinois rivers are identifiable. This map is also the first to show the mouths of the Missouri ("PEKITTANOUI" or "Pekittanoui") and Ohio ("OUABOUSKIGOU" or "Ouaboukigou") rivers.

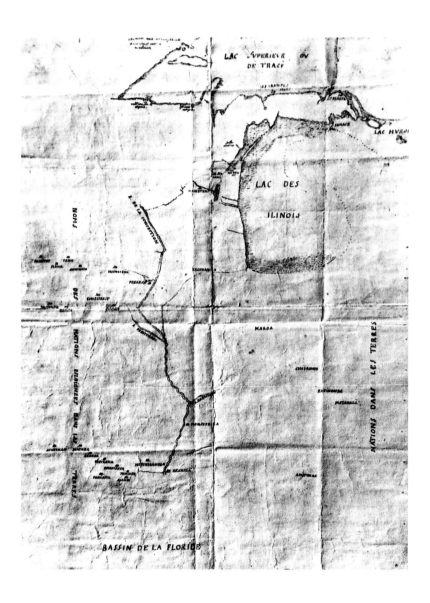

the Mississippi River by identifying its mouth and delta. In the interim, Daniel Greysolon, sieur Dulhut, whose name was anglicized to Duluth, set up camp in 1679 on the western shore of Lake Superior, where the modern city named in honor of his role in pacifying the regional Indians is now located. Dulhut's settlement was the farthest west any French or English colonist had reached by then.

The mission of completing the discovery of the Mississippi River took place under the leadership of René-Robert Cavelier, sieur de La Salle, who envisioned a huge commercial empire extending

77. *Artist unknown. Niagara Falls. In Father Louis Hennepin's* La Nouvelle Decouverte d'un tres grand pays, *Utrecht, 1697. Engraving, 12 x 16.5 cm. Private collection. The first print of the famous falls.*

78. *Artist unknown. Buffalo. In Father Louis Hennepin's* La Nouvelle Decouverte d'un tres grand pays, *Utrecht, 1697. Engraving, 12 x 16.5 cm. Private collection. One of the earliest printed pictures of this animal.*

from the St. Lawrence River to the Gulf of Mexico. In 1678, the adventurous, self-promoting Father Louis Hennepin joined La Salle during his preparations. That year Hennepin visited Niagara Falls, and the following year he named Lake Ste. Clare (now Clair), between Lakes Huron and Erie, for the maiden who established the first Franciscan order of nuns at Assisi and was canonized in 1255. Hennepin published the first description of the natural wonder of Niagara Falls in 1697 (fig. 77). The work in which the description appears was the most widely read contemporary book of French exploration of North America, and it includes one of the earliest printed representations of a buffalo (fig. 78).

Before beginning his own momentous journey, La Salle had Hennepin explore the upper Mississippi River. During that exploration, Hennepin named a widening of the river Lake Pepin, for a French explorer, and at the site of the present-day Twin Cities of Minneapolis and St. Paul he named the Falls of St. Anthony, after Saint Anthony of Padua. (Hennepin's own name is appropriately perpetuated as that of the county in which Minneapolis is located.) The names of these bodies of water appear on his 1683 map (fig. 73), which also contains the name "Louisiane" for the first time on such a document and depicts the course of the Mississippi, shown in what is approximately its correct location. There is no substantiation, however, of Hennepin's claim that he preceded La Salle in traveling all the way down the river to the Gulf of Mexico.

In February 1682, La Salle and the explorer Henry de Tonti, accompanied by twenty Frenchmen and thirty-one Indians, canoed

out of the Illinois River into the Mississippi and headed south. They reached the Gulf of Mexico on April 9 and, in a ceremony upstream, took possession of the land in the name of King Louis XIV of France. They laid claim to all the lands that drained into the great river, and it is contended that La Salle himself assigned the name Louisiane. During his trip, La Salle's troops built a post at the mouth of the Chicago River and another where the St. Joseph River enters Lake Michigan in what is now southwestern Michigan. Along the Illinois River, ninety miles southwest of present-day Chicago, La Salle also built the short-lived Fort St. Louis. In 1684, La Salle was directed to found a colony in the region of Galveston Bay—and he was specifically instructed by the French court to falsify the course of the Mississippi River in his writings and on his maps by moving the mouth to the west, thereby claiming more land for France. This accounts for the geographic misrepresentation of the lower Mississippi on maps of that era (fig. 79).

La Salle returned to France that same year but fell out of favor with the French court. He then set forth without sponsorship to establish an entrepreneurial settlement along the lower Mississippi River. Sailing from France, but mistaking the location of the mouth of the Mississippi River, his group landed at Matagorda Bay, off the shore of what is now Texas—and four hundred miles to the west of the Mississippi. La Salle then began an overland expedition to find the river, but on the way he was murdered by his own mutinous men (fig. 80). The ship that carried the men on their voyage sank off the coast—and, astonishingly, was rediscovered in 1998 (fig. 81).

79. Henri Joutel. "Carte Nouvelle de la Louisiane. . . ." In Journal Historique du Dernier Voyage que feu M. de la Salle fit dans le Golfe de Mexique . . . , Paris: Robinot, 1713. Private collection. *The only roughly contemporary printed map of La Salle's quest for the mouth of the Mississippi River.*

80. *Artist unknown. Two prints of La Salle's final expedition in search of the mouth of the Mississippi River. In Father Louis Hennepin's* Nouveau Voyage d'un pais plus grand que l'Europe, *Utrecht, 1698. Private collection. Left: The arrival of La Salle at Matagorda Bay. Right: The assassination of La Salle.*

The French persisted in their efforts to identify the mouth of the Mississippi River from the Gulf of Mexico, as part of a grand plan to gain control of the vast expanse of the entire Mississippi River valley. In 1699, Pierre le Moyne, sieur d'Iberville, sailing from France, became the first European to enter the Mississippi Delta from the Gulf Coast. He continued upstream until he reached the main channel of the river, proceeded east along a small tributary that would be named for him, and discovered Lakes Maurepas and Pontchartrain, thereby earning for himself the epithet "Founder of Louisiana." The names of the two lakes honored French political figures of the time, Comte de Maurepas and Comte de Pontchartrain. As for the Iberville River, it is now called Bayou Manchac. At one time it was part of a waterway between the Mississippi River and the Gulf of Mexico, creating an Island of New Orleans; landfills ultimately erased its insular condition.

Jean-Baptiste le Moyne, sieur de Bienville, Iberville's eighteen-year-old brother, was made second-in-command when Iberville sailed for France in 1699 to inform the king of his successful discovery of the Mississippi River's point of exit on the Gulf Coast. That year, Bienville encountered an English ship sailing upriver in the region of what later became New Orleans. The ship had been sent by Dr. Daniel Coxe from the Carolina colony to lay claim to his grant of "Carolana" from King Charles II of England. Bienville boarded the ship and convinced its Captain Bond that the French had already established possession. This episode reinforced the French claim; consequently, that portion of the river was called the English Bend.

Also in 1699, French fur trappers built a fort at Biloxi, derived from an Indian tribal name, in order to safeguard the mouth of the Mississippi. The fort was moved eastward, in 1702, to Mobile, that name being a corruption of the Spanish name of the local Mauvila

81. *Experts work to recover the* Belle, La Salle's *last ship, which was rediscovered in 1998—more than 300 years after it sank. Photographs © 1997 Kay Chernush. Top: The central area of the site is pumped dry to permit work on the wreck. Above: A bronze four-pounder taken from the* Belle.

tribe. When Iberville returned the following year, he explored the Mississippi as far north as present-day Natchez, then inhabited by the tribe bearing that name. With the explorer Louis de Saint-Denis, he also traveled along the Red River into the current Texas Panhandle and entered what is now Oklahoma.

Up the Mississippi, meanwhile, near present-day East St. Louis, French fur trappers in 1699 developed a settlement called Cahokia, another name derived from that of an Indian tribe. Around the Great Lakes, the French reinforced their position on the Straits of Mackinac in 1700. The following year, Antoine de La Mothe, sieur de Cadillac, established Fort Pontchartrain du Détroit—later to become simply Detroit—combining the name of an influential French diplomat (who was also honored near New Orleans) with the French words meaning "of the strait." During the first half of the eighteenth century, French traders and missionaries continued to explore the upper Mississippi and the Ohio, Red, and Arkansas rivers. In 1713, Étienne Venyard, sieur de Bourgmont, surveyed the Missouri River from the Platte River, south of present-day Omaha, Nebraska, to its mouth. The French also reached the Rio Grande in 1713 and the Spanish town of Santa Fe in 1739. In that same year, traveling from Canada and the Great Lakes, Pierre Gaultier de Varennes, sieur de La Vérendrye, reached the Mandan Indian villages on the Missouri River.

THE SPANISH AND FRENCH—
AND RUSSIANS

After their initial incursions in the sixteenth century, the Spanish advances from New Spain into what would become the United States were sporadic and relatively inconsequential. By the middle of the eighteenth century, only a few missionaries and small trading expeditions passed from the western part of present-day Mexico into New Mexico and what would become Texas—a name assigned by the Spanish because Indians used *techas,* from the Spanish *tejas,* meaning "friends," as a way to greet early Spanish explorers. That name would not appear on a printed map until 1718, however, when Guillaume Delisle's "Carte de la Louisiane" noted "Mission de los Teijas etablie en 1716" (fig. 83, inset). There were also probes into Texas from the northern area of current Mexico, crossing the Rio Grande. Toward the end of the seventeenth century, the leaders in New Spain became increasingly concerned about the French activities along the Gulf Coast, and in 1698 a fort was erected at the western end of the Florida Panhandle and named Pensacola, for the regional Indian tribe.

In 1701, during a significant journey of exploration, Father Eusebio Kino (fig. 82) crossed the Sonora desert in northwestern Mexico and proved that California was not an island—a matter of some dispute, despite the findings of Ulloa and Alarcón back in about 1540. With rare exceptions—a small map that appears on the title page of a 1622 book entitled *Descriptio Indiae Occidentalis,* by Antonio de Herrera y Tordesillas; a larger map by Abraham Goos that was incorporated into a book, *West-Indishe Spieghel,* published in Amsterdam

82. *Suzanne Silvercruys. Statue of Father Eusebio Kino. Bronze. Photograph by Karsh, Ottawa. This was placed by the state of Arizona in National Statuary Hall, Washington, D.C., on Feb. 14, 1965.*

83. *Guillaume Delisle. "Carte de la Louisiane et du Cours du Mississipi." 1718. Engraving, 50 x 65 cm. Private collection. Generally regarded as the main source for all later maps of the Mississippi River. This is also the first map to mention Texas ("Mission de los Teijas etablie en 1716," in the inset). San Antonio and New Orleans, which were both established in 1718, are not noted on this map.*

84. *Henry Briggs. "The North part of America." In Samuel Purchas's* Purchas his
Pilgrimes, *vol. 3, London, 1625. Engraving, 29 x 36 cm. Private collection.
The first large map to show California as a sizable island rather than part
of the continent. The earliest map with the name "Hudson Bay," applied here to
the southern extension now called James Bay. "Plymouth," "Hudson's River,"
and "James Citti" are also shown on this map.*

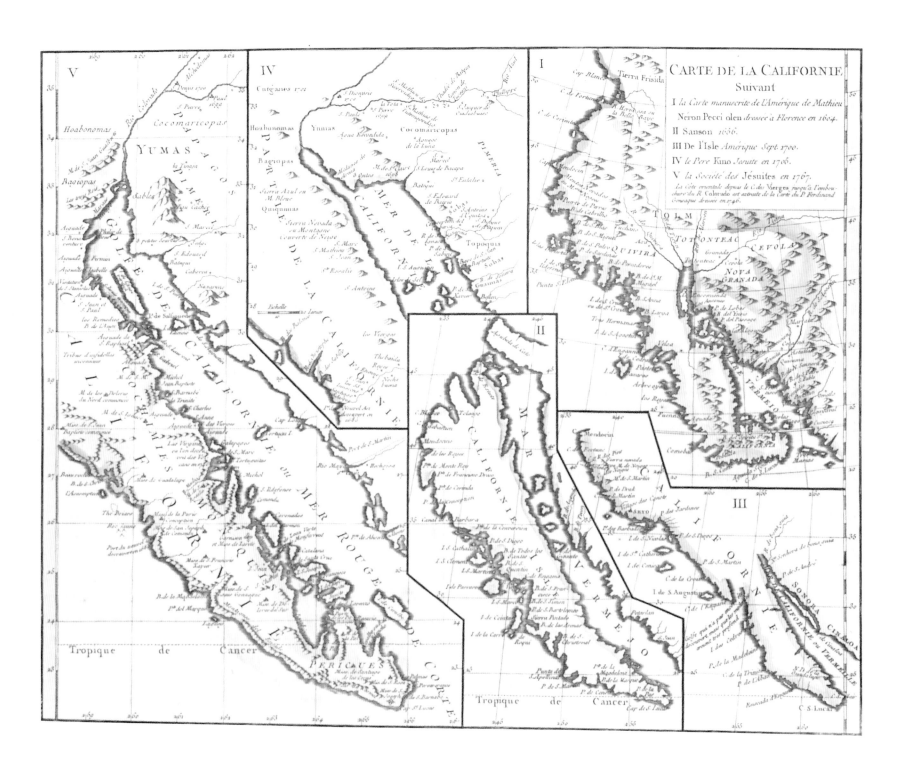

85. *Didier Robert de Vaugondy. "Carte de la Californie." 1779. Engraving, hand-colored, 29 x 38 cm. Private collection. Represents various stages in the mapping of California from 1604 through 1767.*

Béjar were built on land that the Indians called Yanaguana, meaning "refreshing waters," and which would form the nucleus of San Antonio de Bexar, later the most important Spanish post in Texas (fig. 87). The name San Antonio dates from 1691, when Don Domingo Téran de los Rios came upon a river and named it for Saint Anthony of Padua, because the discovery was made on what had been declared that saint's day during medieval times. Also in 1718, well to the east in French-held Louisiana, the sieur de Bienville founded New Orleans (fig. 88), naming the settlement in honor of the duc d'Orléans, the regent at the time, who came from that city on the shore of the great French river the Loire. Incidentally, Delisle's 1718 map (see fig. 83), the first large-scale map to depict the entire course of the Mississippi River, includes neither of these new settlements.

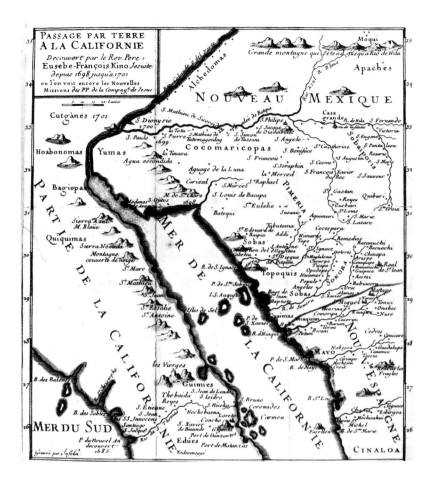

86. *Father Eusebio Kino. "Passage par terre A la Californie." 1705. Engraving, 24 x 21 cm. Private collection. The first engraving of Father Kino's now-lost manuscript map depicting his crossing of the Sonora desert, disproving the widespread notion that California was an island.*

87. San Antonio's River Walk. Courtesy San Antonio Convention & Visitors Bureau

in 1624—all maps depicting the North American continent that were published before 1625 show California with its well-defined peninsula as part of the continent. In 1625, however, Henry Briggs published a map (fig. 84) in London showing California as an island, as the conquistador Hernán Cortés had thought ninety years earlier. Subsequently, throughout the remainder of the seventeenth century, maps presented California as an island. Even after Father Kino published his findings in the Jesuit *Relations* of 1703 (fig. 86), the cartographic error persisted until King Ferdinand VI of Spain issued a royal decree stating that California was not an island (fig. 85).

The year 1718 witnessed the founding of what would become two major American cities, both associated with distinct characteristics and romantic histories. In Texas, Governor Martín de Alarcón and Father Antonio de San Buenaventura y Olivares founded the mission of San Antonio de Valero—which became known as the Alamo, a Spanish word referring to the poplar or cottonwood trees in the area—and the Villa de Béjar (or Bexar). The mission and the Villa de

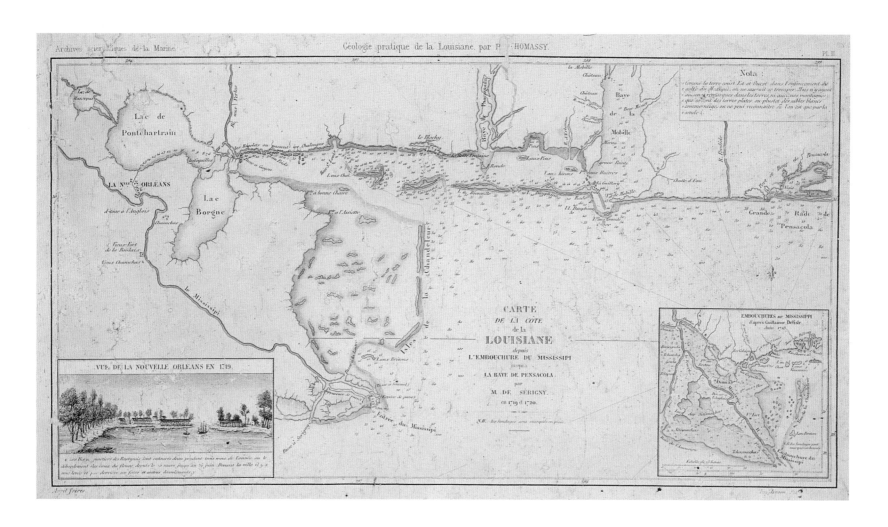

88. Old and new views of New Orleans. Above: M. de Serigny.
"Carte de la Cote de la Louisiane depuis l'Embouchure du Mississipi [sic] jusqu'a
la Baye de Pensacola." 1719. Reprinted in R. Thomassy's Geologie de la
Louisiane, Paris, 1860. Engraving, 19 x 35.6 cm. Historical Museum
of New Orleans. Inset (lower left): "Vue De La Nouvelle Orleans en 1719."
Below: A modern view of Jackson Square near the New Orleans
riverfront. Courtesy Keith Reemtsma

Shortly thereafter, mainly because of the persistent efforts of the sieur de Bourgmont, the French pressed on in their attempt to gain complete control of the Mississippi River and to create buffers against Spanish expansion. During the early part of the eighteenth century, the French carried out repeated explorations of present-day Texas, Oklahoma, Louisiana, and Alabama, resulting in a great increase in knowledge about this segment of our country. In 1719, while following the Red River from western Louisiana to northern Texas and then going into what is now Oklahoma, Bernard de la Harpe also built a fort at Natchitoches, along the Red River. The Spanish countered these French activities in part by building a presidio, or fortified settlement, in western Kansas. The French responded to this by establishing Fort Orleans in the center of the current state of Missouri, along the Missouri River.

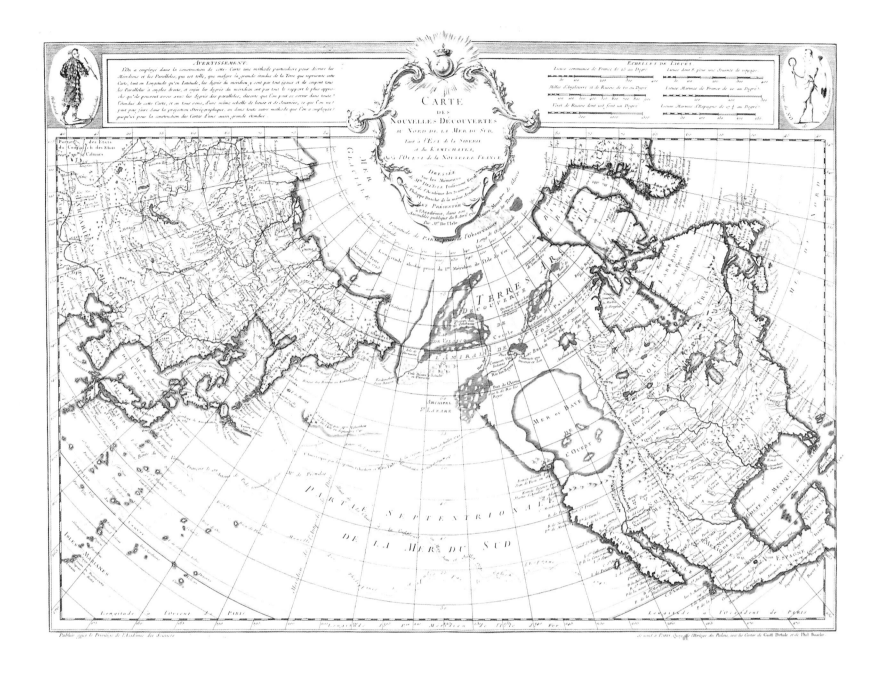

Meanwhile, toward the end of the first half of the eighteenth century, another foreign power was making its first tentative appearance in the Western Hemisphere, from a completely new direction. In 1741, far to the north, the Danish sea captain Vitus Bering, sailing for Russia, passed though the strait that was assigned his name as a consequence of a voyage he had made thirteen years earlier. During his second voyage, he sighted Mount St. Elias, in what is now Alaska, and landed on Kayak Island, but he did not reach the mainland (fig. 89). Russian settlement of the northwestern edge of the continent was still some decades in the future.

89. *Philippe Bauche. "Cartes des Nouvelles Decouvertes au Nord de la Mer du Sud." 1752. Engraving, 46 x 63 cm. Private collection. Cornerstone map of Alaska, depicting Vitus Bering's first (1728–30) and second (1741–42) expeditions for Russia; he died during the second, at the end of 1741. The fictitious 1,200-mile-long "Mer ou Baye de l'Ouest" in the northwestern part of America is shown for the first time.*

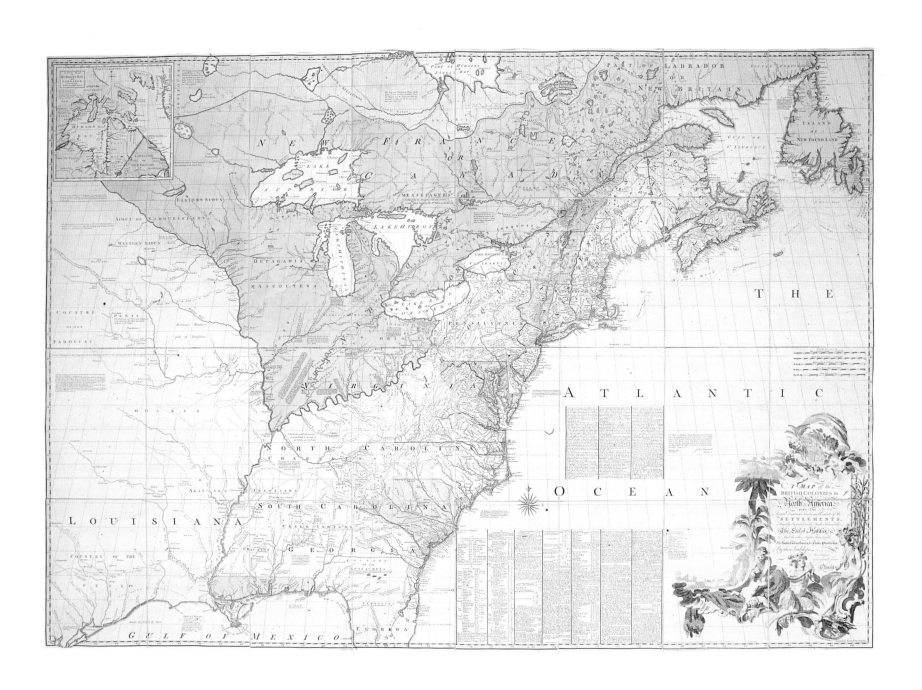

CHAPTER FIVE

Britain Gains Control of the Continent

THE BRITISH AND THE INDIANS

The population in the British colonies had increased to approximately 1.5 million by the middle of the eighteenth century. More people meant a need for more land. Between 1750 and 1775, there was mass emigration from the crowded communities in Massachusetts and Connecticut. In that twenty-five-year span alone, 119 new townships were established in New Hampshire, 94 in Maine, and 74 in what would become Vermont. To the south, a group of Germans belonging to the Moravian religious sect purchased one hundred thousand acres near the Yadkin River in North Carolina, near present-day Winston-Salem, and several brethren of the same sect left Bethlehem, Pennsylvania, to found Betharaba, from a biblical place-name, in North Carolina. In 1751, John Robinson, Speaker of the Virginia House of Burgesses, was granted a large tract of land along the Greenbrier River in current West Virginia. In 1752, at the Treaty of Logstown, consummated on the shore of the Ohio River eighteen miles below what is now Pittsburgh, the Iroquois and Lenape (Delaware) Indians ceded land south of the Ohio River to the Colony of Virginia.

At the midpoint of the century, relations with the Indians, which were integral to the development of the country, were inconsistent. Along the eastern seaboard from Maine to the Florida boundary, the Indians had been subjugated and made to live in small enclaves, and therefore had little impact on the settlers' proposed expansion. Inland in the north, throughout Maine, New Hampshire, Vermont,

and New York, the colonists and the Micmac, Abenaki, Algonquin, and Iroquois Indians lived interdependently with the settlers. The same situation pertained to the Choctaws, Creeks, and Seminoles, who for the most part lived amicably with the settlers of Georgia, Alabama, Mississippi, and Louisiana. But to the west of the Appalachian Mountains and the Mississippi River, warfare among Indian tribes and raids on the spreading settlements were frequent occurrences. There was no cohesive effort, however, on the part of the Indians throughout the country to interfere with colonial expansion.

Throughout history, wars have resulted in expansion of the victor's landholdings at the expense of the vanquished. The result is the establishment of new boundaries. The first conflict to have a significant long-term effect on the North American continent has retained the popular title of the French and Indian War. It was the last and most important of a series of four colonial confrontations between England and France dating back to 1689, and essentially corresponding to wars in Europe between the two great powers. The French and Indian War took place from 1754 to 1763 as an integral part of the first world war of modern times; it was called the Seven Years War in Europe, where it did not begin until 1756. The eighteenth century's longest and bloodiest war in North America, the French and Indian War resulted in British domination of the land, accompanied by changes in property rights and place-names.

The central issue of the French and Indian War was disputed land in the Ohio Valley. Settlers in Pennsylvania and Virginia sought

90. *John Mitchell. "A Map of the British and French Dominions in North America with the Roads, Distances, Limits, and Extent of Settlements." London, 1755. Engraving, hand-colored, 137 x 196 cm. Private collection. Commissioned by the British government to define British claims before the French and Indian War, this map was used after the American Revolution to establish the boundaries of the United States of America under the Treaty of Paris. Each side in the negotiations had its own copy of the map. It was subsequently used to clarify boundary disputes throughout the 19th century and as recently as 1932.*

the land, which both groups laid claim to, for expansion, while France regarded itself as sole possessor of the region, which was vital to its own commercial interests. France had protected its claims by building a series of forts along the Mississippi River and the Great Lakes. Along the Mississippi, for example, Fort de Chartres, named for the French city, was erected near Kaskaskia, a village named for the regional Indian tribe, in southwestern Illinois. Just off Lake Ontario, a fort was built at Niagara, which derived its name from that of the local Indian settlement, Ongniaahra, meaning "point of land cut in two" (fig. 91). American frontiersmen built a rough fort at Sandusky—derived from the Iroquoian name the Indians assigned to the local river, Ot-san doos-ke, meaning "source of pure water"—not that far around the southern shore of Lake Erie from where Cadillac had constructed the fort at Detroit.

In 1753, on the eve of the onset of the war, the location of what was to become a major American city was determined by George Washington, at the time a twenty-one-year-old major in the Virginia militia and surveyor (fig. 92). When Lieutenant Governor Robert Dinwiddie of Virginia learned that the French had built two forts near the southern shore of Lake Erie, in what is currently Waterford, Pennsylvania, he dispatched Washington on a trip of more than five hundred miles to the garrison there called Fort LeBoeuf, to insist that the French troops depart peacefully. Washington left Williamsburg on October 31, 1753, with a seasoned frontiersman, Christopher Gist, as his guide. During the journey, Washington surveyed the confluence of the Allegheny and Monongahela rivers, forming the Ohio River.

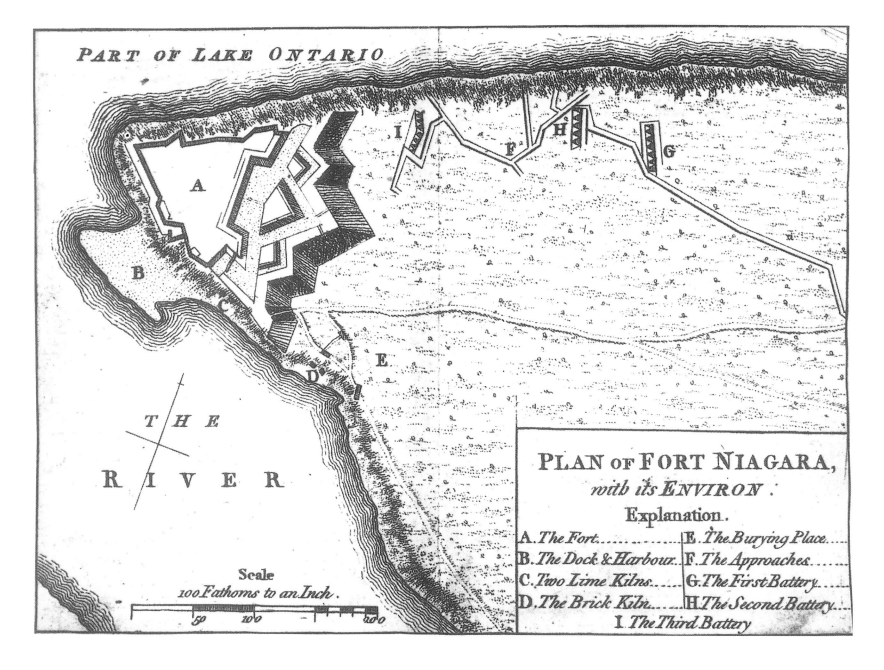

PART OF LAKE ONTARIO

THE
RIVER

Scale
100 Fathoms to an Inch.
50   100   200

PLAN of FORT NIAGARA,
with its ENVIRON.
Explanation.
A. The Fort............   E. The Burying Place....
B. The Dock & Harbour   F. The Approaches......
C. Two Lime Kilns....   G. The First Battery....
D. The Brick Kiln....   H. The Second Battery..
            I. The Third Battery

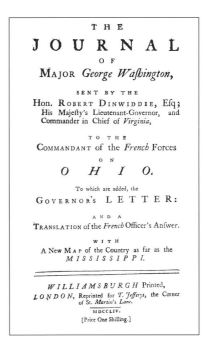

THE

JOURNAL

OF

MAJOR *George Washington*,

SENT BY THE

Hon. ROBERT DINWIDDIE, Efq;
His Majefty's Lieutenant-Governor, and
Commander in Chief of *Virginia*,

TO THE

COMMANDANT of the *French* Forces

ON

O H I O.

To which are added, the

GOVERNOR'S LETTER:

AND A

TRANSLATION of the *French* Officer's Anfwer.

WITH

A New MAP of the Country as far as the
MISSISSIPPI.

WILLIAMSBURGH Printed,
LONDON, Reprinted for *T. Jefferys*, the Corner
of St. *Martin's Lane*.
MDCCLIV.
[Price One Shilling.]

Opposite: 91. *John Rocque. "Plan of Fort Niagara
with its Environ." In Rocque's* A Set of Plans and Forts
in America. Reduced from Actual Surveys, *London,
1763. Engraving, 12 x 17 cm. Private collection.
This shows the fort built at the point where the Niagara
River empties into Lake Ontario.*

92. *Charles Willson Peale. Portrait of George Washington.
1772. Oil on canvas, 128 x 103 cm. Courtesy
Washington-Custis-Lee Collection, Washington and Lee
University, Lexington, Va. The earliest portrait of
Washington painted from life shows him in the uniform
of a colonel in the Virginia militia.*

93. *George Washington. Title page from* The Journal
of Major George Washington, *Williamsburg, Va.,
and London, 1754. Private collection. This records
Washington's mission to Ft. LeBoeuf on the eve of
the French and Indian War.*

As specified in the text of Washington's journal, which he
wrote on his return to Williamsburg and published in January 1754
(fig. 93), and also penned in the inset on his manuscript map (fig. 94),
Washington suggested a location for a British fort at the junction of
those rivers. He emphasized its strategic advantage in protecting
British settlements in the region against incursions by the French. On
February 17, 1754, Virginians began building the fort at that location
and proposed naming it Fort Prince George, in honor of the heir to
the British throne (the future King George III). Two months later, the
French captured the site and finished building the structure, which
they named Fort Duquesne in honor of the governor of New France
(fig. 95). Four years later, as the British were nearing victory in the
war, the French abandoned and blew up the fortifications on November 24, 1758. The next day, the site was named Fort Pitt, honoring the
secretary of state in Great Britain, William Pitt (fig. 96), whose ministry was responsible for intensifying British activity in the French
and Indian War.

Around the nucleus of Fort Pitt, the city of Pittsburgh would
develop, but a controversy surrounded the name into the twentieth
century. Since the fort's original naming by Brigadier General John
Forbes, it was a stronghold of Scotch-Irish immigrants, who spelled
the name of the city "Pittsburgh"; later, there was an influx of German settlers, who preferred "Pittsburg." A charter of 1816 listed the
name as "Pittsburg," but even in 1890 some newspapers were using
the "gh" ending while others were using "g." That year, the report of the
federal Board on Geographic Names decided on Pittsburg, but this
was not accepted by the city's major newspaper, the Stock Exchange,
or the University of Pittsburgh. Finally, on July 19, 1911, the U.S.
Department on Geographic Names reversed its original decision,
and "Pittsburgh" became the official name of the city (fig. 97).

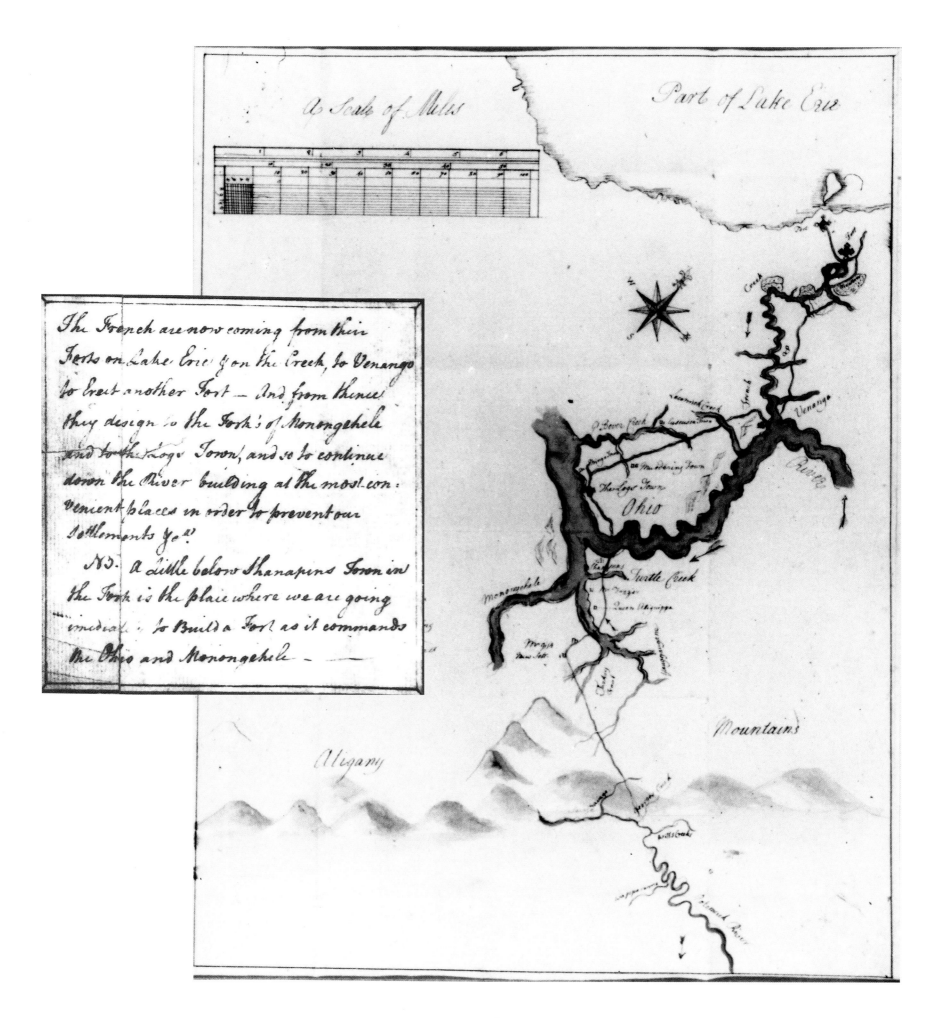

Opposite: 94. *George Washington. Sketch map. Manuscript on paper, 46 x 36 cm. Private collection.*
Here Washington records his journey from Williamsburg, Va., to Ft. LeBoeuf, between Oct. 31, 1753, and Jan. 16, 1754. Text on this map suggests the location for a fort (inset enlargement); it was initially named Ft. Prince George, was completed by the French under the name Ft. Duquesne, and was renamed Ft. Pitt when the British retook it. The site became the nucleus of the city of Pittsburgh.

Right: 95. *[Robert Stobo]. "Plan of Fort le Quesne. Built by the French at the Fork of the Ohio and Monongahela in 1754." London, 1755. Engraving, 33 x 30 cm. Private collection. The first printed map of Ft. Duquesne, which the French abandoned on Nov. 24, 1758; the British renamed it Ft. Pitt the next day. Capt. Stobo was a hostage, imprisoned in the French fort, who smuggled the scale map out of the fort by means of a Mohawk named Moses the Song, who passed it along to the British.*

96. *Richard Brompton. Portrait of William Pitt, first earl of Chatham. 1772. Oil on canvas, 116 x 86 cm. Courtesy National Portrait Gallery, London*

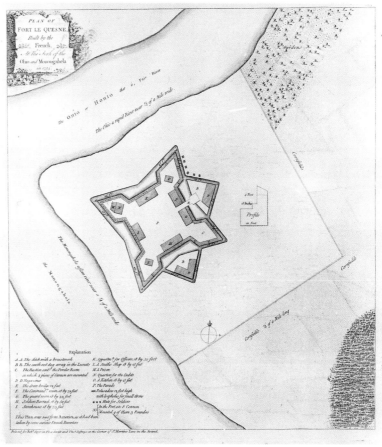

97. *Pittsburgh (or, to many earlier residents, Pittsburg), the modern city that arose at the point where the Monongahela and Allegheny rivers join to form the Ohio River. Courtesy Kirby Hare*

Before full-scale warfare began between the French and English combatants on North American soil, salvos were issued by mapmakers whose charts laid claim to the land for one side or the other. British claims to the continent were based on the fact that it had been discovered in 1497 by John Cabot (Giovanni Caboto), sailing under the flag of England. Enforcing this claim were grants made in the first half of the seventeenth century by King James I of England to the London Company of all the land from approximately Cape Fear, North Carolina, to Liscomb, Nova Scotia. Subsequent grants to the Virginia Company and to the Grand Council of Massachusetts indicated that all colonial lands extended from "sea to sea"—in other words, from the Atlantic Ocean to the Pacific.

98. Jean-Baptiste Bourguignon d'Anville. "Canada Louisiane et Terres Angloises par Sr D'Anville." Paris, 1755. Engraving, hand-colored, 88 x 114 cm. Private collection. This map indicates French claims and locates French forts at the outset of the French and Indian War. The inset shows the St. Lawrence River ("La Fleuve Saint-Laurent").

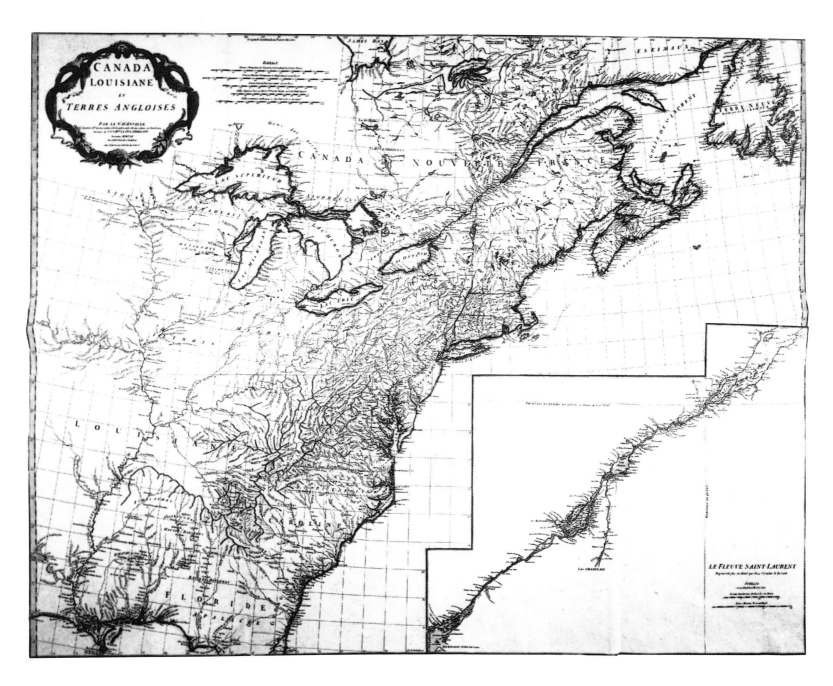

France, on the other hand, regarded itself as possessor of all the lands that drained into the Mississippi River and its branches, based on the discoveries of Jolliet and Marquette, and subsequently La Salle. The French protected their claims with strategically located forts.

The year 1755 witnessed the publication of several maps that depicted the geography, asserted the boundaries, and made graphic statements of claims that would have far-reaching consequences long after the French and Indian War. John Mitchell's map, published in London, indicated that the boundaries of the thirteen English colonies extended westward across the Mississippi River, reflecting their "sea to sea" charters (fig. 90). By contrast, the French maps, as exemplified by that of royal geographer Jean-Baptiste Bourguignon d'Anville, placed the western boundaries of the English colonies at the Allegheny Mountains and laid claim to the land west of that mountain chain (fig. 98). Lewis Evans's map, published in America that year, emphasized the importance of the Ohio Valley as the focus of dispute between the two major European powers (fig. 99).

99. *Lewis Evans. "A General Map of the Middle British Colonies, in America: viz Virginia, Mariland, Delaware, Pensilvania, New-Jersey, New-York, Connecticut, and Rhode Island . . . and of part of New France: wherein is shewn the Antient and Present Seats of the Indian Nations." Philadelphia, 1755. Printed in color on silk, 49 x 64 cm. Private collection. The inset shows the Ohio Valley, which was the center of contention between the British and French interests.*

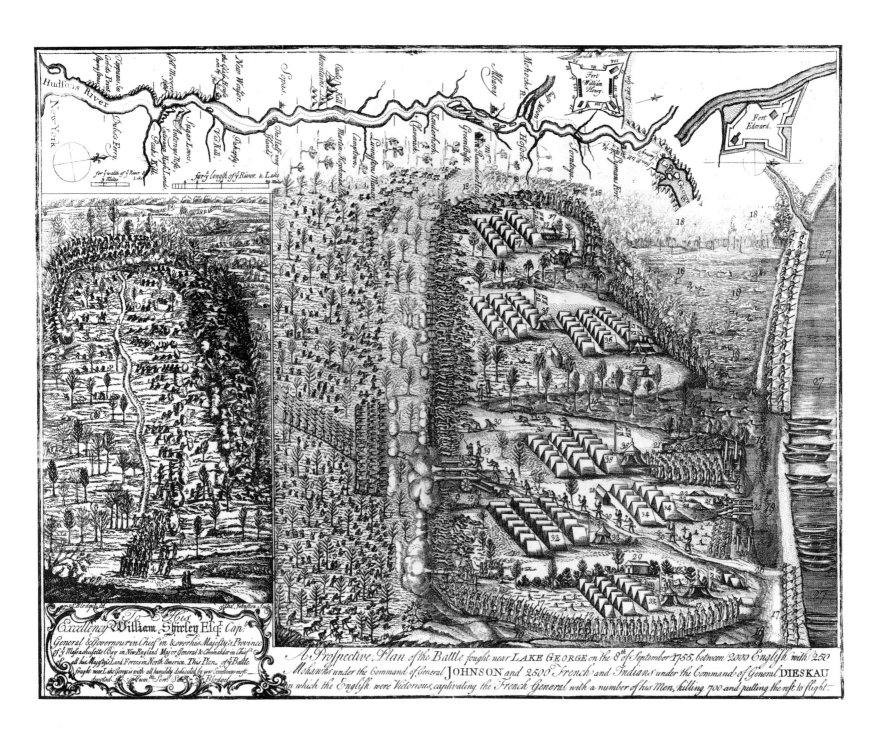

100. *Samuel Blodgett. "A Prospective Plan of the Battle Fought near Lake George on the 8th of September 1755. . . ." Boston and London, 1755. Engraving, 35 x 45 cm. Private collection. The first print to show a battle on the North American continent. The plan is in two parts: to the left is the first engagement, to the right is the second.*

Military actions by a force under the command of George Washington resulted in the outbreak of the French and Indian War in 1754. The first British triumph took place the following year at Fort Beauséjour, in the easternmost portion of what is now Canada, a region the French at the time called Acadia. After that fort fell, the British renamed the region Nova Scotia (including the northern part, which later became the Province of New Brunswick), meaning New Scotland, then rounded up the Acadians and dispersed them throughout the colonies. Some found their way to New Orleans, where their descendants came to be known as Cajuns, a corrupted pronunciation of "Acadian."

Until the climactic battle on the outskirts of Quebec in 1759, most of the military activity of the war focused on forts. The initial British target in 1755 was the capture of Fort Duquesne (see fig. 95). The first British general to set foot on American soil, Major General Edward Braddock, led troops 112 miles from Fort Cumberland, Maryland, to the French fort. Although the route was relatively straight, it passed through wilderness and required the creation of a road, which is depicted on the Mason-Dixon map of 1768 (see fig. 114). Before the British forces actually reached the fort, they were attacked by French troops and Indians allied with the French. The result was a major defeat of the British, including the death of Braddock.

Another significant battle that year took place at Lake George (fig. 100) in New York, just below Lake Champlain. The French called the southern body of water Lac de Sacrament, but on the eve of the battle, William Johnson (fig. 101)—the New York Indian agent known by the Indians as Warraghiyagey, and the most effective British colonial military leader during the war—gave it the name Lake George, "not only to honor his majesty but to ascertain his undoubted dominion there." The strategically located Crown Point, a few miles to the north along Lake Champlain, was previously called Pointe à la Chevelure (Scalp Point) by the French, apparently in relation to a scalping incident that took place there. In the area of Lake George, two recently built British forts, Fort Edward and Fort William Henry, received their names to honor King George II's grandsons. Another name that came out of that battle was that of Colonel Ephraim Williams, who six weeks before had made a will that was to provide funds for the establishment of a men's college in western Massachusetts. Williams died leading troops on the first day of the battle, and his memory is perpetuated by Williams College and Williamstown, Massachusetts.

In 1756, Lieutenant General Louis-Joseph de Montcalm assumed command of all French forces in North America, and the French captured Fort Oswego, another Iroquoian derivative, meaning "flowing out" and referring to the exit from Lake Ontario into the St. Lawrence River to the northeast. In 1757 he led the French and their Indian allies during their infamous capture of Fort William Henry (fig. 102), at the southern end of Lake George. The drama of the

101. *John Wollaston. Portrait of William Johnson.
c. 1750. Oil on canvas, 76 x 63.5 cm.
Courtesy Albany Institute of History and Art,
Albany, N.Y.*

ensuing massacre by Indians, despite a promise of safe conduct to the defeated British, was memorialized in James Fenimore Cooper's novel *The Last of the Mohicans* (fig. 103). Areas of significant battles of the war, and trails in the region, also were often depicted on powder horns (fig. 104).

The tide turned in favor of the British in 1758, and the following year the French were forced to abandon both Fort Carillon, strategically placed between Lakes George and Champlain, and Fort Niagara. The British renamed the former Fort Ticonderoga, an Iroquoian name meaning "between lakes." The decisive battle of the French and Indian War took place shortly afterward, just outside Quebec on the Plains of Abraham, named for Abraham Martin, known as Maitre Abraham, who had originally owned that land. As part of the British preparation for that campaign, Lieutenant James Cook, then a thirty-year-old junior officer but later to become the famous captain who discovered the

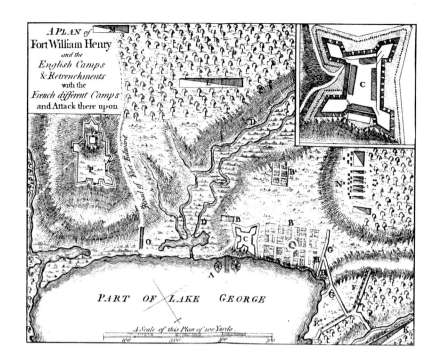

Opposite, top: 102. *John Rocque. "A Plan of Fort William Henry and the English Camps & Retrenchments with the French different Camps and Attack there upon." In Rocque's* A Set of Plans and Forts in America. Reduced from Actual Surveys, *London, 1763. Engraving, 12 x 17 cm. Private collection. The site of the 1757 capture that James Fenimore Cooper described in his novel* The Last of the Mohicans *(1826).*

Opposite, bottom: 103. *Thomas Cole.* Landscape Scene from "The Last of the Mohicans." *1827. Oil on canvas, 63.5 x 79 cm. Courtesy New York State Historical Association, Cooperstown, N.Y. Photograph by Richard Walker*

104. *Right: A carved powder horn, made at the time of the French and Indian War, that shows forts along Lake Ontario. c. 1763. Below: An enlargement of the carving. Both: Courtesy Barry MacLean*

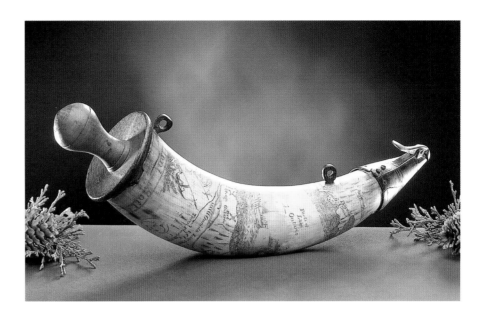

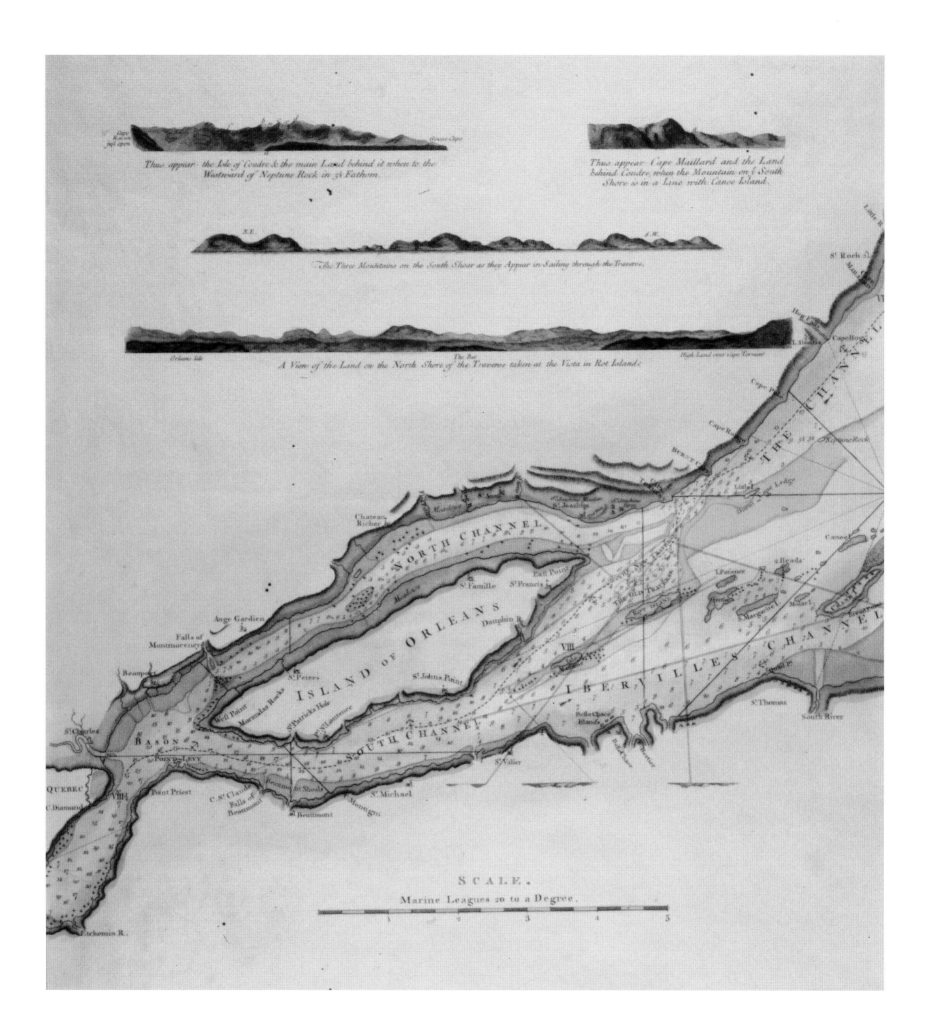

Thus appear the Isle of Coudre & the main Land behind it when to the Westward of Neptune Rock in 3½ Fathom.

Thus appear Cape Maillard and the Land behind Coudre, when the Mountain on ye South Shore is in a Line with Canoe Island.

The Three Mountains on the South Shear as they Appear in Sailing through the Traverse.

A View of the Land on the North Shore of the Traverse taken at the Vista in Rot Island.

NORTH CHANNEL

THE CHANNEL

ISLAND OF ORLEANS

IBERVILLES CHANNEL

SOUTH CHANNEL

BASON

QUEBEC

SCALE.

Marine Leagues 20 to a Degree.

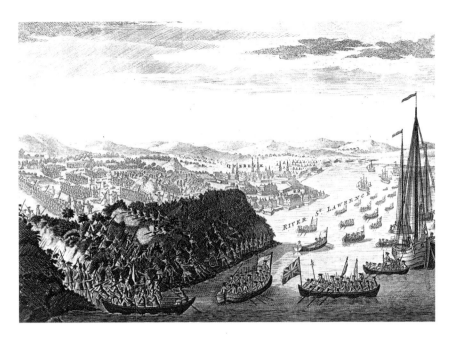

Opposite: 105. *James Cook. "A New Chart of the River St. Laurence" (detail). London, 1760. Engraving, hand-colored; entire map, 172 x 117 cm. National Library of Australia, Canberra. The entire map covers the area from Richelieu Falls to Anticosti Island. Cook executed the map as a junior officer in the British navy.*

106. *Artist unknown. "A View of the Taking of Quebeck by the Englishes Forces Commanded by Genl. Wolfe Sep 13ᵗʰ, 1759." In An Accurate and Authentic Journal of the Siege of Quebec 1759. By a Gentleman in an eminent Station on the Spot,* London: *J. Robinson, 1759. Engraving, 17 x 25.4 cm. Courtesy National Maritime Museum, Greenwich, England*

107. *William Woollet. "The Death of General Wolfe." 1776. Engraving, after a 1771 painting by Benjamin West; 42.5 x 59 cm. Private collection*

108. *Justus Chevillet. "Mort Du Général Mont Calm." N.d. Engraving, after a painting attributed to François-Louis-Joseph Watteau; 42 x 50.8 cm. Private collection*

Hawaiian Islands, took soundings of the St. Lawrence River in 1758 and drew the first accurate map of it (fig. 105).

After moving upriver, setting up camp across the St. Lawrence from the well-fortified French city, and struggling for weeks to find a weak spot in the French defenses, the British secretly ascended the 180-foot precipitous path at L'Anse au Foulon, just south of Quebec, on the night of September 12–13 and formed up on the Plains of Abraham by morning (fig. 106). The startled French then gathered their troops in opposition. With what was later described as "the most perfect volley ever fired on a battlefield," the British routed the French. Both the British general who had masterminded the assault, James Wolfe (fig. 107), and the French general defending the city that was the key to all French possessions in North America, Montcalm (fig. 108), were killed in the battle. One month later, news of the victory reached England and was announced in the *London Gazette* (fig. 109), and the British went on to gain effective control of the continent.

The Siege and Taking of Quebec, with a View of the Battle before the Town.

109. Henry Overton. "The Siege and Taking of Quebec, with a View of the Battle
before the Town." In the London Gazette, Oct. 17, 1759. Engraving, 43 x 47 cm.
Private collection. Beneath the engraving are two letters to William Pitt:
one from Gen. Robert Monckton, dated Sept. 15, 1759,
and the other from Vice Adm. Charles Saunders, dated Sept. 20, 1759.
These are the first reports of the British victory at Quebec.

The fighting in North America ended with the fall of Montreal in 1760, and the full consequences of the British victory in the French and Indian War were spelled out in the Treaty of Paris, signed on February 10, 1763, which formally ended the entire Seven Years War. All of France's possessions on the North American continent east of the Mississippi River, with the exception of New Orleans, became the property of Great Britain. Realizing that this would happen, France in 1762 secretly ceded the vast expanse of land west of the Mississippi to its European ally Spain, which had to surrender Florida to the British under the 1763 treaty; in exchange, Britain returned Havana, Cuba, which the British had seized in 1762, to Spanish control. The British organized Florida into two provinces, East Florida and West Florida, divided by the Apalachicola River in the Panhandle. Among the French living on the eastern shore of the Mississippi River was Pierre Laclède, who moved to the west bank, which was beyond British control. In February 1764, he broke ground for the settlement of St. Louis, which he named in honor of the canonized thirteenth-century French king Louis IX. Shortly thereafter, St. Louis was designated the capital of Upper Louisiana, the land north of the Arkansas River (fig. 110).

110. Gateway Arch (1965), on the banks of the Mississippi River, is symbolic of St. Louis being the gateway to the West during much of the 19th century. Photograph by David Nixon

With the war against the French at an end, Britain turned its attention to the ongoing conflicts between settlers and Indians along the frontier, which flared up soon after the Treaty of Paris was signed. In the spring of 1763, an alliance of hostile Indian tribes under the leadership of Pontiac, chief of the Ottawas, laid siege to Detroit, by then in British hands, and began to attack numerous other British outposts. Despite a major defeat in August by British troops under the command of Colonel Henry Bouquet at the Battle of Bushy Run, southeast of Fort Pitt, Pontiac's Rebellion did not completely end until 1766 (fig. 111). Meanwhile, Britain made an attempt to eliminate the conflicts by separating the settlers and the Indians. In October 1763, King George III (fig. 112) issued a royal proclamation that no colony could grant, and no individual could acquire, land west of the Appalachian Mountains. The remaining Indians in the East were relegated to land west of the mountain barrier, to separate them from the colonists. But settlers simply disregarded the Proclamation Line of 1763. Land speculation continued unabated, including by George Washington, whose Mississippi Company of just fifty investors petitioned for 2.5 million acres at the junction of the Ohio and Mississippi rivers. At the same time, the Creeks and Cherokees in the South and the Iroquois in the North continued to occupy their land east of the line. Nevertheless, the British had signed treaties with various Indian tribes and confederacies by 1766, essentially ending Indian incursions against the settlers for the time being. The continent was able to remain free from major conflict for about a decade.

During this period of relative peace, several colonies acquired land from the Indians, one way or another. (The 1760s had already begun with the Cherokees in South Carolina ceding much of their land in the backcountry to that colony, after suffering a major defeat at the hands of the colonists.) As part of the 1768 Treaty of Fort Stanwix, a large tract of land was secured from the Iroquois in western New York. At the same time, the Indiana Company purchased 1.8 million acres from the Iroquois south of the Ohio River, extending from the southern border of Pennsylvania to the Little Kanawha River in what is now West Virginia. In 1770, a grant was made to the Grand Ohio Company to establish the proprietary colony of Vandalia in the Ohio Valley. The same year, the Treaty of Lochaber added nine thousand square miles to Virginia from Indian cessions. A treaty with the Creek Confederacy in 1773 moved the boundary of Georgia west to the Oconee River.

At the end of the French and Indian War, other adjustments were also taking place around the British colonies. The most densely populated part of colonial America was New England. Growth in that region had taken place both in coastal towns, which concentrated on fishing, and in inland communities, which expanded their farming. Overpopulation of these areas led to the migration of settlers into the relatively underpopulated regions of Maine, New Hampshire,

Vermont, and northern New York. There was also migration from Connecticut to northeastern Pennsylvania's Wyoming Valley, which was named for the Algonquian expression *mechhe-weami-ing*, meaning "big flats at." The nucleus of this Pennsylvania settlement took the name Wilkes-Barre in 1769, to honor John Wilkes and Isaac Barré, two English politicians who were sympathetic to the American cause. The nearby city of Scranton did not develop until the nineteenth century, when coal was discovered; it was named for a leading mining family. Pennsylvanians also spread out, settling the land adjacent to the forks of the Ohio River and the valleys of the Monongahela and Youghiogheny rivers. Both of these rivers were given Algonquian names: Monongahela means "high banks—falling down," while Youghiogheny means "contrary stream," because its waters run north to the Monongahela, rather than to the Atlantic Ocean.

111. *Grignion. "The Indians giving a Talk to Colonel Bouquet in a Conference at a Council Fire near his Camp on the Banks of the Muskingum in North America in Octr. 1764." In [William Smith's]* An Historical Account of the Expedition against the Ohio Indians in the Year MDCCLXIV, *London, 1766. Engraving, after a painting by Benjamin West; 20 x 16 cm. Private collection. Henry Bouquet is the colonel whose British troops handed a major defeat to the Indians taking part in Pontiac's Rebellion in 1763, helping to convince some of the tribes to stop fighting the following year.*

112. *Attributed to school of Allan Ramsay. Coronation portrait of George III. 1760–70. Oil on canvas, 244 x 159 cm. Courtesy Colonial Williamsburg Foundation, Williamsburg, Va.*

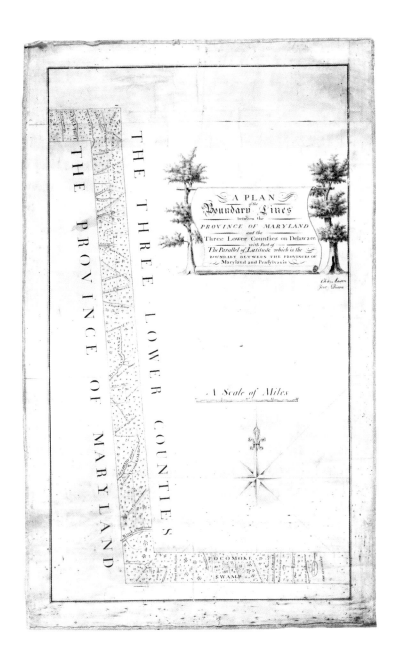

At about this time, Pennsylvania and Maryland finally agreed to settle their boundary dispute. Charles Mason and Jeremiah Dixon, who had established their reputations as surveyors in England, were commissioned to precisely define the boundary line. Their work, carried out from 1763 through 1767, determined the boundary line to be 39°43'17.6" north latitude. This represents the first precise measurement of latitude on the North American continent, and it is depicted on maps published in 1768 (figs. 113 and 114).

During the twelve-year interim between the French and Indian War and the American Revolution, Maryland relied primarily on its wheat crop, while Baltimore became a leading seaport. Philadelphia was the richest and most populated city on the entire continent, and Pennsylvania, including the Germans and the Scotch-Irish on the frontier, was rigidly controlled by urban merchants. Semiautonomous Delaware, on the other hand, was made up of smaller farms. New Jersey colonists also generally farmed. In New York, the large manors along the Hudson River and large parcels of land in Manhattan continued to give testimony to the Dutch influence more than a century in the past. New York City still ranked behind Philadelphia and Boston in population.

This period also saw the economies of the southern colonies improve. At the time, Georgia's economy was based on indigo and rice, and its population was approximately ten thousand, including many black slaves. South Carolina had become a prosperous colony, with more than one hundred thousand people. Charleston, founded a century earlier, was one of America's major urban centers. North Carolina, however, was characterized by little in the way of prosperity. There was expansion of settlement in the Carolina Piedmont.

113. *Cartographer unknown. "A Plan of the Boundary Lines between the Province of Maryland and the Three Lower Counties on Delaware with Part of that Parallel of Latitude which is the Boundary between the Provinces of Maryland and Pennsylvania." Philadelphia, 1768. Engraving, 37 x 67 cm. Private collection. Part of a map drawn as a result of the Mason-Dixon survey, to settle a long-standing boundary dispute between Maryland and Pennsylvania.*

114. *Cartographer unknown. "A Plan of the West Line or Parallel of Latitude, which is the Boundary between the Provinces of Maryland and Pennsylvania." Philadelphia, 1768. Engraving, 50 x 64 cm. Private collection. Continuation of the Mason-Dixon survey. This map was meant to be joined with fig. 113, but the two maps were separate publications.*

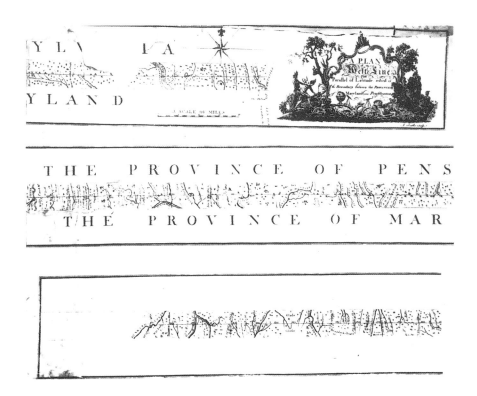

Various religious and ethnic groups, including Quakers, Lutherans, and Moravians, established settlements in western North Carolina. The back-country had an increase in settlement, but there was a distinct schism between the coastal and western populations. In 1763, West Florida, which then included Mobile, Biloxi, and Pensacola, the center of government, was sparsely populated, but it had established friendly relations with the Creek and Choctaw Indians. After the Spanish withdrew from East Florida, the Seminole Indians became dominant there, although a small number of settlers began arriving in that region from South Carolina.

Settlers also began moving through the Cumberland Gap, discovered by Dr. Thomas Walker barely a decade earlier, into the frontier in the western portions of what was then North Carolina and Virginia. In 1765, Lieutenant Henry Timberlake became the first person to use the name "Tennessee" on a map (fig. 115), to identify the local river. The name came from a Cherokee town in the area. In 1769, Daniel Boone began a two-year exploration of a region known as Kentucke, an Iroquoian word meaning "meadowland"; in 1775, in what is now central Kentucky, he erected a fort called Boonesborough (fig. 116). In the same year, James Harrod led a group of settlers who established Kentucky's first permanent community, appropriately named Harrodsburg.

Between 1766 and 1768, there was other important exploration into the interior of the continent. *Travels through the Interior Parts of North America in the Years 1766, 1767, and 1768*, published in London in 1778, chronicles Jonathan Carver's exploration of the Wisconsin and upper Mississippi Rivers (fig. 117). Carver was the first to refer in print to reports of a large mountain range that

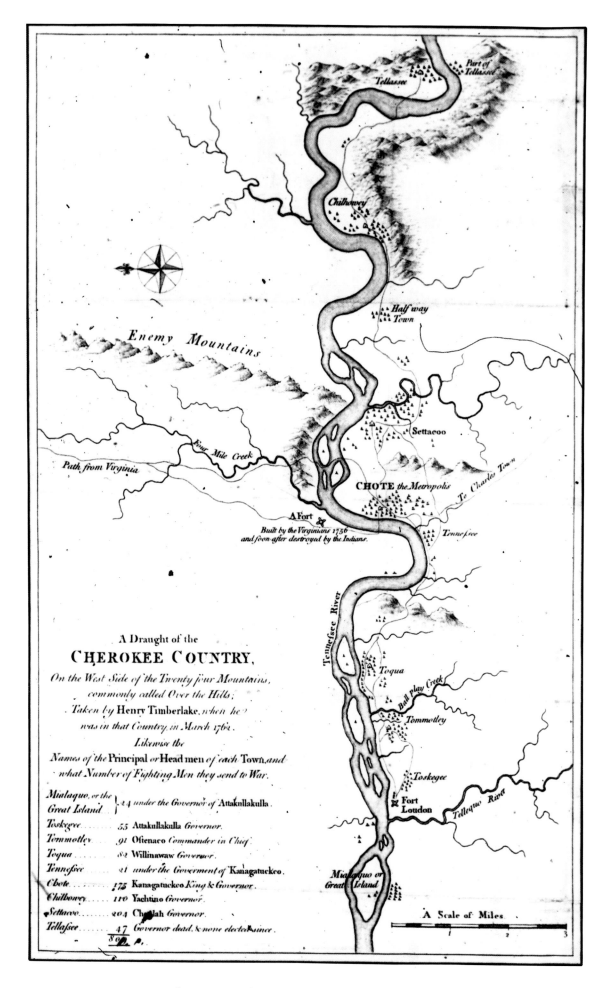

Opposite: 115. *Henry Timberlake. "A Draught of the Cherokee Country." In Timberlake's* Memoirs of Lieut. Henry Timberlake, *London, 1765. Engraving, 39 x 24 cm. Private collection. The first map of the Tennessee region by an observer, who fought there during the French and Indian War. The Tennessee River is followed from the Great Smoky Mountains to Ft. Loudoun and Great Island. It is in part a memorial, naming for each town the Indian chief, and the number of men, who fought in the war.*

Right: 116. *Boonesborough, erected by Daniel Boone in Kentucky in 1775.*

117. *Artist unknown. "Falls of St. Anthony, 1766." In Jonathan Carver's* Travels through the Interior Parts of North America in the Years 1766, 1767, and 1768, *London, 1778. Engraving. Private collection. The site of what would later become Minneapolis, along the Mississippi River.*

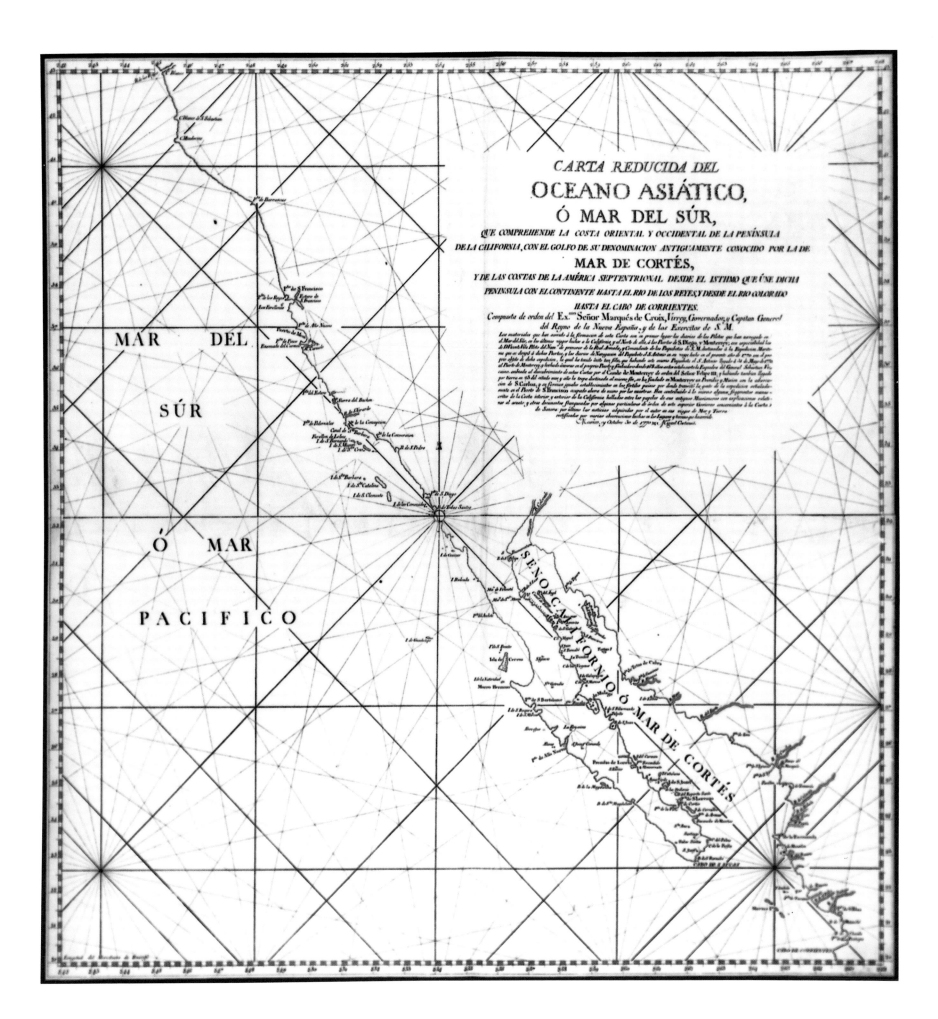

CARTA REDUCIDA DEL
OCEANO ASIÁTICO,
Ó MAR DEL SÚR,
QUE COMPREHENDE LA COSTA ORIENTAL Y OCCIDENTAL DE LA PENÍNSULA
DE LA CALIFORNIA, CON EL GOLFO DE SU DENOMINACION ANTIGUAMENTE CONOCIDO POR LA DE
MAR DE CORTÉS,
Y DE LAS COSTAS DE LA AMÉRICA SEPTENTRIONAL DESDE EL ISTHMO QUE ÚNE DICHA
PENÍNSULA CON EL CONTINENTE HASTA EL RIO DE LOS REYES, Y DESDE EL RIO COLORADO
HASTA EL CABO DE CORRIENTES.

MAR DEL

SÚR

Ó MAR

PACIFICO

SENO CALIFORNIO Ó MAR DE CORTÉS

would serve as a barrier to overland exploration of the Pacific Ocean from the east: the Rocky Mountains. In that book, the name "Oregon" also appears for the first time.

SPANISH MISSIONS AND EXPEDITIONS

On the other side of the Rockies, meanwhile, exploration was continuing in the western portion of the continent. As part of a master plan to prevent the Russians from gaining control along the west coast, the Spanish established a series of missions during a period of more than a decade. In 1769, Captain Gaspar de Portolá and Father Junípero Serra started by founding one in San Diego—the first European settlement in Upper California. On the shore of a river that they named Porciuncula, after the Franciscan shrine near Assisi, they assigned the name Nuestra Señora Reina de los Angeles de la Porciuncula (Our Lady Queen of the Angels of the Little Portion)—what would later become Los Angeles. They traveled through the San Fernando Valley and the Santa Clara Valley and established a mission at Monterey in 1770. During their journey, they reached the lower end of what is now called San Francisco Bay (not the bay given that name in 1595, but now called Drake's Bay), becoming the first Europeans to view that body of water (fig. 118).

In 1771, Father Francisco Garcés passed through the Colorado Desert, in what is now southeastern California, into the San Jacinto Valley and became the first European to enter the Great Basin, the vast area stretching east from the Sierra Nevada to central Utah. He was also second after Coronado's expedition in reaching the Grand Canyon. In 1775, Juan Manuel de Ayala sailed through the Golden Gate and was the first to record passage through that area around what is now San Francisco. During that voyage, Yerba Buena and Alcatraz islands were mapped; the name Alcatraz, meaning "pelican," was assigned to present-day Yerba Buena Island, while the current Alcatraz itself was unnamed (fig. 119).

Opposite: 118. *Miguel Costansó. "Carta reducida del Oceano Asiático, ó Mar del Súr, que comprehende la Costa Oriental y Occidental de la Península de la California. . . ." Madrid, 1771. Engraving, 70 x 72 cm. Private collection. This map shows the west coast of North America from "R. de los Reyes" on the Oregon coast to "Cabo de Corrientes" in Mexico. It also mentions the founding of missions at Monterey and San Francisco. Costansó served as cosmographer on the Portolá expedition in 1769–70.*

119. *Don Davey. Sketch of San Francisco. 1968. Watercolor, 28 x 21 cm. Private collection. The illustration shows San Francisco Bay, including the island of Alcatraz.*

CHAPTER SIX

A Nation Is Born

GROWING TENSIONS

In 1754, the common cause against the French had not been sufficient to break down the rivalries among individual British colonies. Benjamin Franklin's Albany Plan of Union (fig. 121), proposed that year, would have created a president general appointed by the Crown and a council appointed by all the colonies' assemblies in proportion to their contributions to a war chest for use in the British cause. The proposal was not accepted by any of the colonies or by England. In 1763, at the time of the Treaty of Paris, there was no strong colonial sentiment to eliminate the control exerted by England. The colonists did feel, however, that they had won the war themselves, with little help from the British army and navy.

After Parliament in England began to impose a series of taxes on the colonies to help pay for the war and colonial defense, an atmosphere of discontentment expanded rapidly, with each side taking steps that fed the other's growing animosity. There were even outbreaks of violence (fig. 122). Citizens protested a tax on tea (fig. 123); in the Boston Tea Party of December 16, 1773, some activists emptied that cargo from three ships into Boston Harbor. In response, England closed the port of Boston and mandated that the colonists provide for the housing of British troops in Boston, among other measures that together became known in the colonies as the Intolerable Acts. The other colonies agreed that they needed to discuss a common course of action, as they had with the intercolonial Stamp Act Congress of 1765. The result was the First Continental Congress, held in Philadelphia in September 1774. At that point, there was still widespread resistance to any declaration of independence, although a majority of the fifty-six delegates, representing all the colonies except faraway Georgia, supported a dominion type of status: self-government subject only to the king, not Parliament. No further significant action was taken by either Parliament or the colonists until fighting broke out in April 1775. By this time, the colonial population was estimated at 2.5 million.

JOIN, or DIE.

Opposite: 120. *Abel Buell. "A New and correct Map of the United States of North America Layd down from the latest Observations and best Authority agreeable to the Peace of 1783." New Haven, Conn., 1784. Engraving, hand-colored, 109 x 122 cm. Courtesy the New-York Historical Society. Advertised as "the first [map] ever compiled, engraved and finished by one man and an American." The American flag, in the cartouche, appears for the first time on a map printed in the United States.*

121. *Artist unknown. "Join, or Die." c. 1754. Cartoon. Private collection. A motto proposed for the intercolonial government that Benjamin Franklin sought in 1754, without success.*

The Bloody Massacre perpetrated in King-Street Boston on March 5th 1770 by a party of the 29th Regt.

Unhappy Boston! see thy Sons deplore,
Thy hallow'd Walks besmear'd with guiltless Gore
While faithless P—n and his savage Bands,
With murdrous Rancour stretch their bloody Hands
Like fierce Barbarians grinning o'er their Prey,
Approve the Carnage and enjoy the Day.

If scalding drops from Rage from Anguish Wrung
If speechless Sorrows lab'ring for a Tongue
Or if a weeping World can ought appease
The plaintive Ghosts of Victims such as these;
The Patriot's copious Tears for each are shed,
A glorious Tribute which embalms the Dead.

But know, Fate summons to that awful Goal,
Where Justice strips the Murd'rer of his Soul:
Should venal C—ts the scandal of the Land,
Snatch the relentless Villain from her Hand,
Keen Execrations on this Plate inscrib'd,
Shall reach a Judge who never can be brib'd.

The unhappy Sufferers were Mess. Saml Gray, Saml Maverick, Jas Caldwell, Crispus Attucks & Patk Carr
Killed. Six wounded; two of them (Christr Monk & John Clark) Mortally.

Published in 1770 by Paul Revere Boston

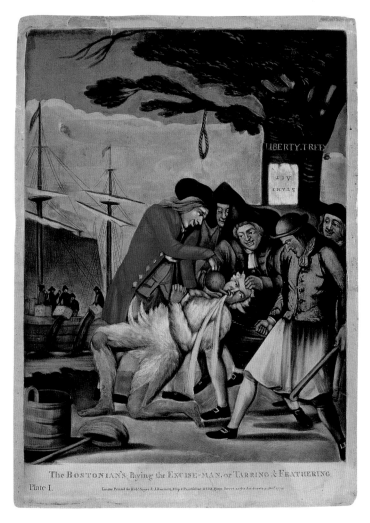

The BOSTONIAN'S Paying the EXCISE-MAN, or TARRING & FEATHERING
Plate I.

THE AMERICAN REVOLUTION

The American Revolution began in the North and was won in the South. As is generally the case, the names of many of the places where battles occurred achieved recognition out of proportion to the intrinsic importance of the locales. The names of the most critical battles offer evidence of the diverse influences that played a role in the development of the country that was about to be established. Native American tribes, the early Dutch settlements, English cities, and individual colonial settlers from England and elsewhere in Europe are all reflected in the names of historically important locations. In addition, the names of numerous military heroes would live on as permanent place-names within the country.

The first armed confrontations, resulting from a British attempt to seize stored military supplies, took place near Boston at Lexington and Concord on April 19, 1775 (fig. 125). Lexington (fig. 124) was named, in 1713, for a village in England; ironically, Concord's name, dating back to 1635, had been selected to indicate a "peaceful" settlement.

On May 10, 1775, the Second Continental Congress convened in Philadelphia. A month later, while engaging in the long debate over whether to reconcile with England—the Declaration of Independence was not adopted until July 4, 1776—the delegates created a Continental Army (and later a navy) and appointed George Washington commander in chief. Meanwhile, colonial militias and smaller, irregular forces were already confronting the British army. In a surprise attack on the very morning that the Continental Congress began meeting, Ethan Allen and his Green Mountain Boys wrested

124. *Amos Doolittle. "The Battle of Lexington" (plate I). New Haven, Conn., 1775. Engraving, 29.5 x 45 cm. Courtesy Chicago Historical Society*

125. *I. DeCosta. "A Plan of the Town and Harbour of Boston." London, 1775. Engraving, 37 x 49 cm. Geography and Map Division, Library of Congress, Washington, D.C. The first printed map of the first battle of the American Revolution. It shows troops fighting at Lexington and Concord, and it also indicates the site of the Battle of Bunker Hill, only six weeks after it was fought.*

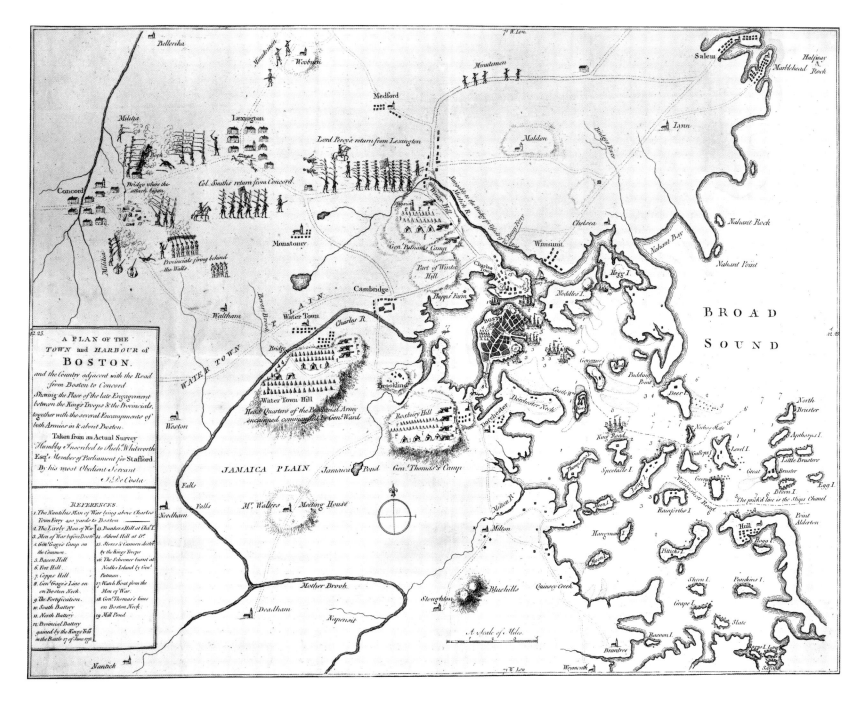

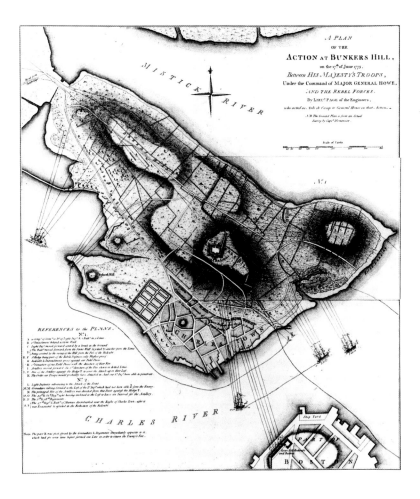

126. *Thomas Hyde Page. "A Plan of the Action at Bunkers Hill on the 17th of June 1775." London, c. 1775–78. Engraving, 49 x 39 cm. Private collection. The most detailed representation of the famous battle. The names of Bunker Hill and Breed's Hill are transposed; the battle actually occurred on Breed's Hill. An overlay lets the viewer follow various phases of the battle.*

control from the British of the strategically important Fort Ticonderoga, between Lakes George and Champlain, along with nearby Crown Point soon afterward. On June 17, on the strategic high ground of Boston's Charlestown peninsula, the British finally managed to push a large force of well-entrenched colonial defenders back from Breed's Hill to Bunker Hill—which became the name of the battle—only at great cost (fig. 126). Dr. Joseph Warren, who died leading colonials in that battle, is honored by the names of cities in Massachusetts, Pennsylvania, and other states. The following March, it was the colonials' surprise emplacement of artillery painstakingly dragged from Fort Ticonderoga over the winter that convinced the British to abandon Boston. That triumph did not take place, however, until after the failure either to win Canada over or to capture Quebec, its most important city. General Richard Montgomery, whose name subsequently became attached to the capital of Alabama and several

other communities, led colonial troops to Canada, where he besieged Montreal into surrender in November 1775 and then joined Benedict Arnold's colonial force outside Quebec. In the assault on December 31, the colonials were defeated and Montgomery was killed.

Another major setback occurred not long after the Americans formally declared their independence from Great Britain. On August 22, 1776, thousands of British troops landed on Long Island below the American position at Brooklyn Heights, and they took possession of the area in a bloody battle five days later. Although about a thousand Americans were captured and a few hundred killed, Washington succeeded in withdrawing most of his troops, first to Manhattan and eventually across the Hudson River to New Jersey, without significant additional losses; a British plan to envelop Washington's forces was dropped after heavy fighting on October 28 at the Battle at White Plains, New York, on the mainland to the northeast. However, on November 16, Washington suffered a defeat at Fort Washington, which he had constructed on the northern end of the island of Manhattan, and about twenty-eight hundred Americans whom he had left behind to hold the fort were captured. It is ironic that the first location in America to be given Washington's name was the site of his first major defeat, and the culmination of his loss of New York City to the British for the remainder of the war. The fort's name was changed to Fort Knyphausen, honoring a Hessian general whose German mercenaries had fought alongside the British in that battle (fig. 127).

On January 3, 1777, barely a week after Washington's famous Christmas attack on Trenton, American soldiers chased away the British at nearby Princeton, which had been incorporated in 1724 and bore the name of a part of the royal family. In 1757, the College of New Jersey had moved to Princeton—which gave its name to the college in 1896—and built Nassau Hall, at the time the largest building in the colonies (fig. 128). Bullet holes from the Revolutionary battle can still be seen in the walls of that building. General Hugh Mercer was mortally wounded during the battle at Princeton (fig. 129), and his name has been attached to cities and counties, including the county where Princeton is located.

During the summer of 1777, attention shifted again to upstate New York, where the British were marching south from Canada toward Albany. The outnumbered Americans evacuated Fort Ticonderoga in New York on the night of July 5–6 and headed south, some of them encountering British fire on the way at the Battle of Hubbardton in Vermont on July 7. On August 16, Americans successfully attacked hundreds of Germans and other troops seeking supplies at Bennington. That Vermont community, chartered in 1749, bears the name of Governor Benning Wentworth of New Hampshire, who had issued the land grants to create Vermont. Not far north of Albany, the entire British campaign ended in decisive defeat at Saratoga, the site of critical battles in September and October and the surrender of that entire British army a few days later. The name

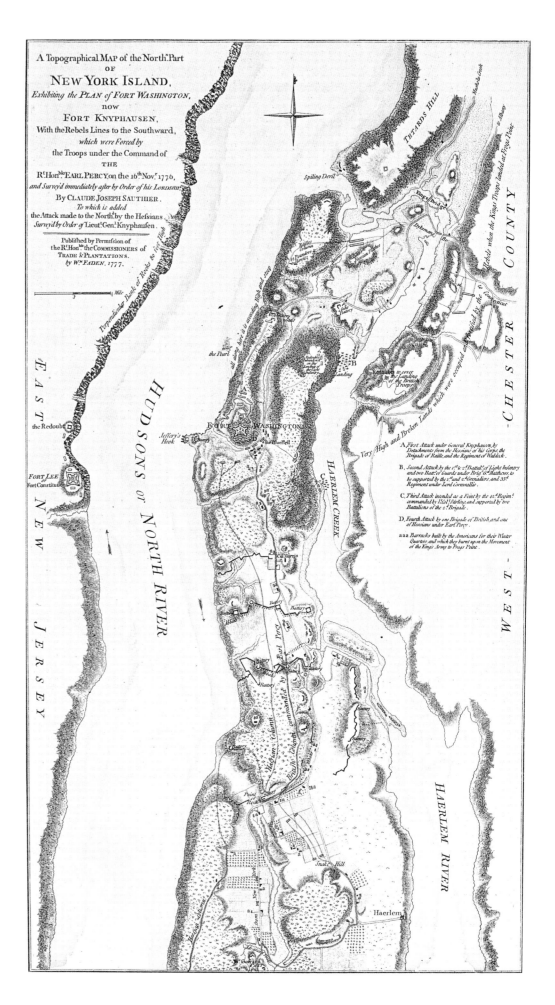

127. *Claude Joseph Sauthier. "A Topographical Map of the North Part of New York Island Exhibiting the Plan of Fort Washington now Fort Knyphausen. . . ." London, 1777. Engraving, 47 x 26 cm. Private collection. George Washington was defeated by mainly Hessian troops fighting for the British. This was his most serious tactical defeat, because about 2,800 Americans could not be withdrawn from Manhattan with the rest of his men and were captured.*

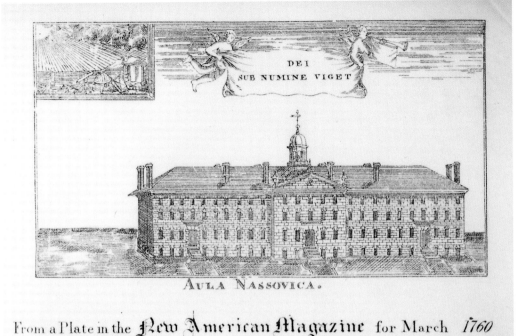

128. *Artist unknown. The earliest view of Nassau Hall. In* New American Magazine *(March 1760). Copperplate engraving, 8 x 16 cm. Courtesy Princeton University, Princeton, N.J.*

129. *John Trumbull. The Death of General Mercer at the Battle of Princeton, 3 January 1777. After 1789. Oil on canvas, 51 x 76 cm. Courtesy Yale University Art Gallery, New Haven, Conn. Trumbull Collection. Mercer County, where Princeton is located, is one of the places named in honor of this general.*

Saratoga is of Iroquoian derivation, but its meaning is unknown; as for the British defeat, it was followed by French entry into the war, all but guaranteeing eventual American victory. One of the American heroes of Saratoga was Colonel Daniel Morgan of Virginia, a captain in the Quebec campaign and later the general who won a decisive battle at Cowpens in South Carolina on January 17, 1781; he is honored with the names of communities in several states.

In Pennsylvania, the British finally caught up to Washington's army on September 11, 1777, at Brandywine Creek, southwest of Philadelphia; the name is derived from the Dutch *brandewijn*, a colonial drink popular in the region. Once again, the Americans were beaten but managed to escape. A sizable American force suffered another serious defeat ten days later at nearby Paoli, which bore the name of a famous Corsican revolutionary, originally applied to a tavern in the vicinity. The British then entered Philadelphia on September 26. Washington unsuccessfully attacked on October 4 at suburban Germantown, a settlement that dated to 1683 and took its name from the settlers' country of origin. Afterward, the American army retired to winter quarters at Valley Forge, a few miles to the west. The last major battle in the North took place on June 29, 1778, in New Jersey at Monmouth, named for an English town. The British commander had decided to abandon Philadelphia, and a large American force sent by Washington inconclusively encountered the enemy army during its march to New York City. The British then withdrew to Manhattan to plan their next moves, while Washington took up positions nearby. Both sides awaited action by America's new ally, the French.

Elsewhere during the war, fighting on the western frontier included the American capture in 1778 of two settlements that had been named for Indian tribes, the Cahokia and Kaskaskia, in what later became southwestern Illinois. (Between 1000 B.C. and A.D. 1500, when the original Mound Builders occupied the region, Cahokia was one of the world's largest settlements.) In the South, most of the fighting consisted of skirmishes, although the British did capture Savannah, Georgia; Charleston, South Carolina; and other key southern cities. Further, the Battle of Camden (fig. 130) in South Carolina, on August 16, 1780, accounted for a greater loss of lives than any other single event and represented one of

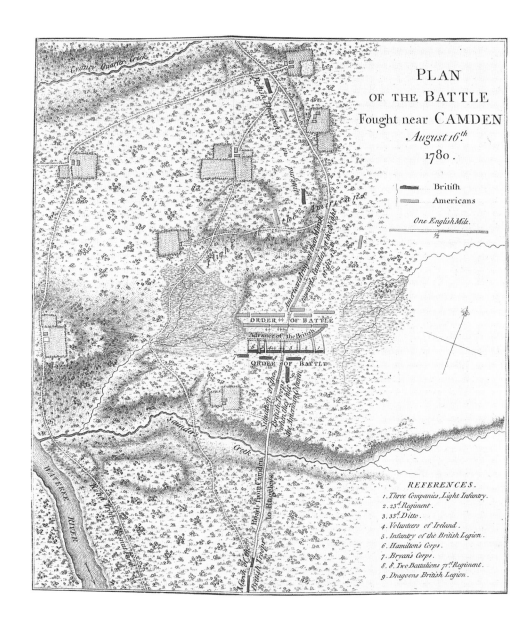

130. *Cartographer unknown. "Plan of the Battle Fought near Camden August 16th 1780." In Banastre Tarleton's* History of the Campaigns of 1780 and 1781, *London, 1787. Engraving, 22 x 19 cm. Private collection. One of the worst defeats suffered by American forces, this battle destroyed the reputation of Gen. Horatio Gates. The self-styled Baron de Kalb, a German-born general who led American troops, was wounded during the battle and died three days later.*

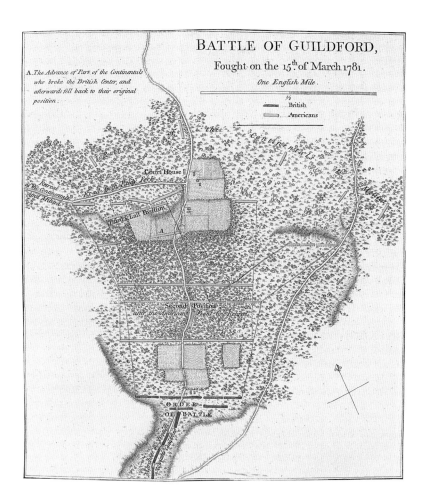

131. *Cartographer unknown. "Battle of Guildford Fought on the 15th of March 1781." In Banastre Tarleton's* History of the Campaigns of 1780 and 1781, *London, 1787. Engraving, 22 x 19 cm. Private collection. Guilford, as it is commonly spelled, was a major turning point of the war. The Americans were led by Gen. Nathanael Greene, a Rhode Islander who would win back the South.*

hero, whose name well deserved the perpetuation it received in various place-names. The British, meanwhile, marched through parts of Virginia before setting up a base at Yorktown, which was named for both the English city and the duke of York. There the British general, Lord Cornwallis, suddenly found himself besieged by Washington's army and French forces, both of which had covertly moved down from New York (fig. 133), as well as by a large French fleet that had sailed from the West Indies (fig. 134). By the time a British fleet left New York to attempt a rescue, the British army at Yorktown had surrendered, on October 20, 1781. It was the last major military action of the American Revolution, although formal peace was still two years away.

Overall, the Revolution was a success thanks in no small part to the efforts of several individual foreign soldiers who joined the American cause, and their names survive on our maps. For example, Baron von Steuben, the Prussian officer who joined Washington at Valley Forge and helped train the American army, left his name on several counties and communities, including Steubenville, Ohio. Casimir Pulaski, the Polish officer in the Revolutionary army who was killed at Savannah, is remembered by towns in Iowa, New York, Tennessee, Virginia, and Wisconsin. The name of the marquis de Lafayette (fig. 132), the important young aide to Washington and a hero of Yorktown, had been bestowed on nineteen communities, as La Fayette or Fayetteville, by 1831.

the worst defeats suffered by the Americans, dimming the luster of General Horatio Gates, one of the heroes of Saratoga. Like the city in New Jersey, the locale of this critical battle had been named in honor of Charles Pratt, Lord Camden, who supported the cause of the American colonists before the Revolution began.

General Daniel Morgan began to turn the tide in the South with his one-sided victory at Cowpens; two months later, on March 15, 1781, the Battle of Guilford Court House (fig. 131), named for the English town and located near present-day Greensboro, North Carolina, dealt the British heavy losses, though the Americans were forced to withdraw. It was a turning point in the war, because it helped convince the British to abandon Georgia and the Carolinas and instead move into Virginia. General Nathanael Greene, Gates's successor as commander in the South, emerged from the southern campaign a major

Opposite: 132. *N. le Mire. Marquis de Lafayette. "Liberté: Conclusion De La Campagne de 1781 En Virginie. To his Excellency General Washington this likeness of his friend The Marquess de la Fayette, is humbly dedicated." 1789. Engraving, 47 x 32.4 cm. Private collection*

133. *Sebastian Bauman. "Plan of the Investment of York and Gloucester." Philadelphia, 1782. Engraving, 65 x 46 cm. Private collection. The first American publication of a map of the final battle of the American Revolution. The map was originally drawn in late 1781, shortly after the battle, at George Washington's request. Successive positions during the battle are detailed.*

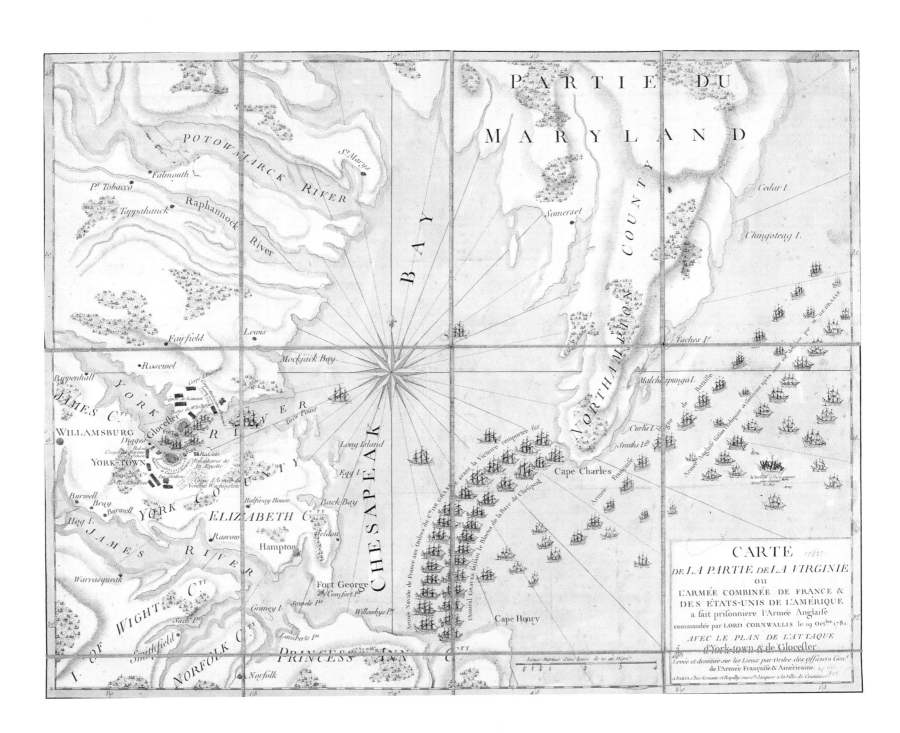

134. *Cartographer unknown. "Carte de La Partie de La Virginie. . . ." Paris, 1782.*
Engraving, hand-colored, 47 x 61 cm. Private collection. This map emphasizes
the crucial role played by the French fleet under the command of Comte de Grasse.

And so the United States of America was born. Great Britain formally accepted its existence with the signing of the Treaty of Paris on September 3, 1783—but the name first appeared on a map five years earlier, albeit translated into the French "Etats Unis" (fig. 135). Its government was based on the Articles of Confederation, which the Continental Congress had adopted on November 15, 1777, but which had not gone into effect until the last of the thirteen new states, Maryland, ratified the document on March 1, 1781.

The 1783 peace treaty established the boundaries of the new nation. Land between the Allegheny Mountains and the Mississippi River was transferred from British sovereignty to the new nation. A line of demarcation between the United States and Canada was defined from east to west by the St. Croix River and the St. Lawrence–Atlantic watershed (an ill-defined boundary line that was disputed until 1842), then the forty-fifth parallel to the St. Lawrence River (the current northern boundaries of New Hampshire, Vermont, and New York), along that river and through the middle of four of the Great Lakes (all except Michigan), and from there to a point west of the Lake of the Woods (in present-day Minnesota and Manitoba), terminating at the as-yet-unknown source of the Mississippi River. A line following the Mississippi River south to the thirty-first parallel became the boundary between the United States and Spanish Louisiana, while that latitude, as well as the Apalachicola (a tribal name) and St. Marys rivers, defined the boundary between the United States and East and West Florida, which Britain returned to the control of Spain (a late and not very important entrant in the war against Britain). Until 1798, Spain also claimed a large area east of the Mississippi River, south of the Tennessee River, and west of the Flint River in western Georgia—somewhat more than what is now Mississippi and Alabama. These boundaries are depicted on the first American map of the United States, published by Abel Buell in New Haven, Connecticut, in 1784 (fig. 120), and on the larger and more precise map by I. Norman, published in 1791 (fig. 136).

The exact wording about the boundaries between the United States and the British possession of Canada, and between the United States and Spanish possessions, first appears in Article II of the provisional treaty between the two nations, dated November 30, 1782:

> From the northwest angle of Nova Scotia, viz, that angle which is formed by a line drawn due north from the source of St. Croix River to the highlands, along the said Highlands which divide those rivers that empty into the river St. Lawrence, from those which fall into the Atlantic Ocean, to the northwesternmost head of Connecticut River; thence down along the middle of that river to the 45th degree of north latitude; from thence by a line due west on said latitude until it strikes the river Iroquois or Cataraquy [St. Lawrence]; then along the middle of said river into Lake Ontario, through the middle of said lake until it strikes the communication by water between that lake and Lake Erie; thence along the middle of said communication into Lake Erie; through the middle of said lake until it arrives at the water communication between that lake and Lake Huron; thence along the middle of said water communication into the Lake Huron; thence through the middle of said lake to the water communication between that lake and Lake Superior; thence through Lake Superior northward of the Isles Royal and Phelippeaux, to the Long Lake; thence through the middle of said Long Lake, and the water communication between it and the Lake of the Woods, to the said Lake of the Woods; thence through the said lake to the most northwestern point thereof, and from thence on a due west course to the river Mississippi; thence by a line to be drawn along the middle of said river Mississippi until it shall intersect the northernmost part of the 31st degree of north latitude. South, by a line to be drawn due east from the determination of the line last mentioned, in the latitude of 31 degrees north of the equator, to the middle of the river Apalachicola or Catahouche; thence along the middle thereof to its junction with the Flint River; thence straight to the head of St. Mary's River to the Atlantic Ocean. East, by a line to be drawn along the middle of the river St. Croix, from its mouth in the bay of Fundy to its source, and from its source directly north to the aforesaid highlands which divide the rivers that fall into the Atlantic Ocean from those which fall into the river St. Lawrence; comprehending all islands within twenty leagues of any part of the shores of the United States, and lying between lines to be drawn due east from the points where the aforesaid boundaries between Nova Scotia on the one part and East Florida on the other, shall respectively touch the Bay of Fundy and the Atlantic Ocean; excepting such islands as now are, or hitherfore have been, within the limits of the said province of Nova Scotia.

Although the Treaty of Paris defined the southern boundary of the United States, Spain did not formally accept it until 1795. At that time, the boundary between the United States and the Spanish colonies of West and East Florida was stated to be a line beginning on the Mississippi River and running due east at 31° north latitude to the Apalachicola River (also known, in Georgia, as the Chattahoochee), then along the middle of that river to the junction with the

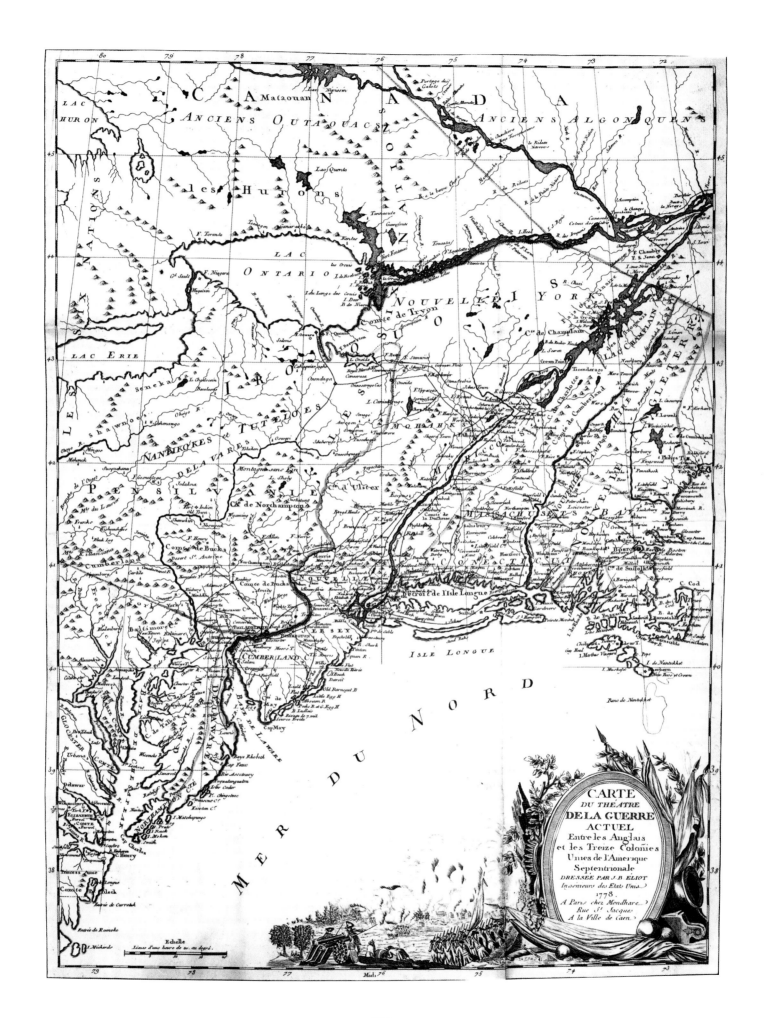

CARTE
DU THEATRE
DE LA GUERRE
ACTUEL
Entre les Anglais
et les Treize Colonies
Unies de l'Amerique
Septentrionale
DRESSÉE PAR J.B.ELIOT
Ingenieurs des Etats Unis
1778.
A Paris chez Mondhare
Rue St Jacques
A la Ville de Caen

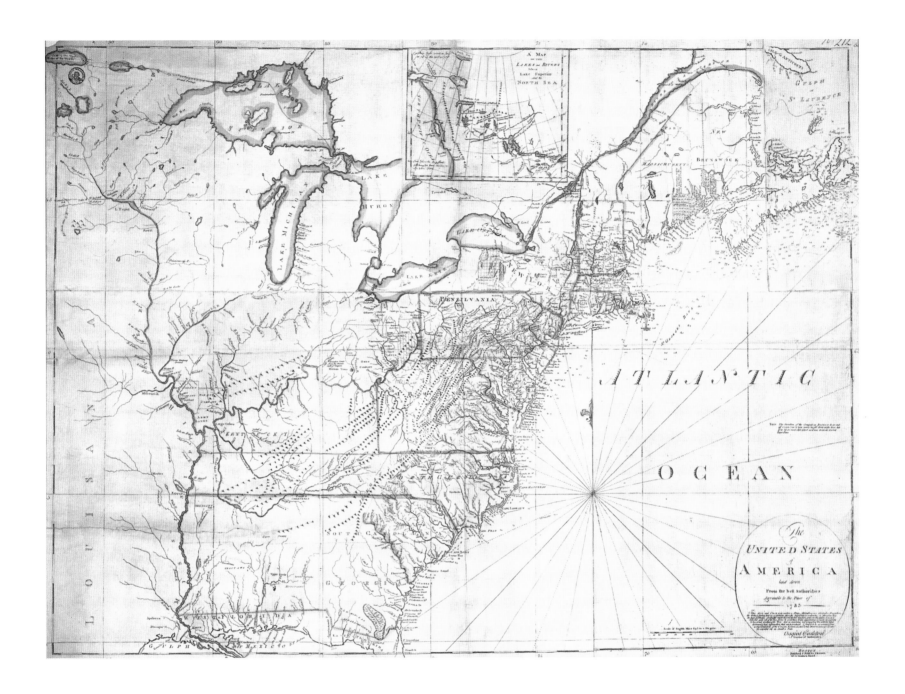

Opposite: 135. *J. B. Eliot. "Carte du théatre de la guerre actuel entre les Anglais
et les Treize Colonies Unies de l'Amerique Septentrionale." Paris, 1778. Engraving,
70 x 51 cm. Private collection. Drawn by an American engineer but published
in Paris, this is the first map to present the name "United States"
(in French—as "Etats Unis"—in the cartouche).*

136. *I. Norman. "The United States of America laid down From the best
Authorities Agreeable to the Peace of 1783." Boston, 1791. Engraving, with outlines
hand-colored, 82 x 114 cm. Private collection. This map shows the boundary lines
established by the Treaty of Paris. Territory acquired in a major land sale in western
New York in 1788, mountains west of the Ohio River, and new townships
from Maine to Ohio are all depicted.*

Flint River, and from there straight to the St. Marys River and down that river to the Atlantic Ocean.

Within the boundaries defined by the Treaty of Paris were thirteen former British colonies, now American states. Two of them, Connecticut and Massachusetts, were named after an Indian term or tribe in that region, respectively; Georgia, the Carolinas, Virginia, Maryland, Delaware, and New York had names connected with the British royalty and aristocracy; New Jersey and New Hampshire had been named for locations in England; Pennsylvania bore the name of the entrepreneur who founded it; Rhode Island was uniquely named for an Aegean island (fig. 137).

The establishment and recognition of the United States of America brought into focus not only the totality of the territory encompassed and the new nation's central government, but also the individuality of each state. In many cases, boundaries still had to be agreed on and disputes resolved, at a time when each state was competitively encouraging internal development and expansion. To consider the original thirteen states as distinct entities necessitates stepping out of a purely chronological mode. In each instance, the geographic assessments are accompanied by the first map of the state published within the United States. Most of these appear in *Carey's American Atlas*, published by Mathew Carey in Philadelphia in 1795.

MASSACHUSETTS

Massachusetts, which was the sixth state to ratify the Constitution, on February 6, 1788, had to settle its boundaries with Vermont and New Hampshire to the north, New York to the west, and Connecticut and Rhode Island to the south (fig. 138). The northern boundary of Massachusetts had been defined in 1740 as following the course of the Merrimack River, at a distance three miles north of that river beginning at the Atlantic Ocean and ending at a point due north of Pautucket (now Pawtucket) Falls (now Lowell, Massachusetts), then a straight line due west from that point to New York. This line also established the boundary between Massachusetts and what soon became the first additional state, Vermont. A dispute between Massachusetts and New Hampshire, over whether "three miles north of the Merrimack River" was to be measured from the mouth of that river or from the northernmost point along its course, was not resolved until 154 years later, in 1894.

The boundary between Massachusetts and New York had also been the subject of a controversy, which began in 1664 and was not resolved for a century. In 1773, the two colonies agreed on a line that began at a monument erected in 1731 by commissioners from Connecticut and New York. The monument was located twenty miles east of the Hudson River. The line then ran slightly northeasterly for 50 miles, 41 chains, and 79 links (the chain used for measurement in surveying has one hundred links and is sixty-six feet in length) to a marked oak tree. In 1786, Massachusetts also gave up its earlier claims to lands in western New York (based on the 1629 charter granting it lands west to the South Sea).

Massachusetts and Connecticut had agreed on a boundary line in 1713, according to which several northern Connecticut towns, including Woodstock and Suffield, were given to Massachusetts. The contract was voided in 1749; the current boundary was not fixed until 1905. The line west of the Connecticut River began at a location 8 rods (132 feet) south of the southwest corner of West Springfield and ran west, with a small jog protruding into Connecticut, to the New York border. East of the Connecticut River, the line began at a monument marking the junction of Massachusetts, Rhode Island, and Connecticut, ran a very short distance north to a monument at the northeast corner of Connecticut, just above 42° north latitude, and then followed a straight line west to the Connecticut River.

137. *Amos Doolittle. "A Display of the United States of America—To the Patrons of Arts and Sciences, in all parts of the World, this plate is most respectfully Dedicated, by their most obedient humble Servant. Amos Doolittle." New Haven, Conn.: A. Doolittle, 1788–89. Engraving, 52 x 42 cm. This is considered one of the most important portraits of Washington.*

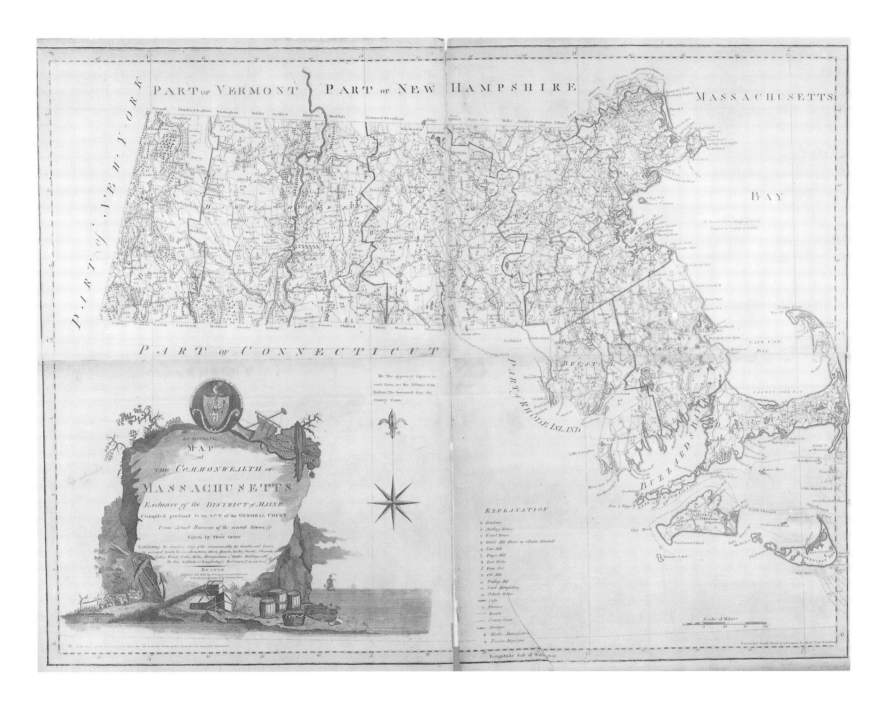

The east–west boundary between Massachusetts and Rhode Island was contested by the two parties for more than two hundred years. It was initially defined in 1642 as running west from a stake three miles south of the southernmost part of the Charles River, at about 42° north latitude. The jagged north–south line between Massachusetts and eastern Rhode Island was initially fixed in 1741 and finally modified in 1898. Massachusetts currently contains more than eight thousand square miles.

The derivations of many place-names in Massachusetts, such as Springfield and Worcester, have been considered previously (see chapter 2). The overwhelming majority of the names of towns in Massachusetts came from the names of cities and towns in England. This was particularly true of towns named in the seventeenth century, such as Attleboro, Barnstable, Beverly, Billerica (Billericay in

138. *Osgood Carleton. "An Accurate Map of the Commonwealth of Massachusetts Exclusive of the District of Maine Compiled Pursuant to an Act of the General Court from Actual Surveys of the Several Towns &C. . . ."* Boston: O. Carleton and I. Norman, 1795. Engraving, 118 x 88 cm. Courtesy Clements Library, University of Michigan, Ann Arbor. The first separately published map of the state of Massachusetts. This detailed map shows counties, townships, rivers, and roads.*

139. *John Singleton Copley. Portrait of Paul Revere. 1768.*
Oil on canvas, 89 x 72 cm. Courtesy Museum of
Fine Arts, Boston. Gift of Joseph W. Revere,
William B. Revere, and Edward H. R. Revere

Colonel John Quincy, a local resident, and Holyoke was named for either an early settler or Edward Holyoke, president of Harvard College. In the eighteenth century, Shirley was named to honor the colonial governor William Shirley. Stoughton was named for Lieutenant Governor William Stoughton, who gained recognition in 1692 by presiding at the witchcraft trials in Salem. Walpole was named for Sir Robert Walpole, the leading British minister in the early eighteenth century. In the 1800s, Somerville honored Captain Richard Somers, a hero at Tripoli. Lowell took its name from Francis Cabot Lowell, who brought cotton manufacturing to the area. Peabody, initially part of Salem, was referred to as Brooksbury Village and later South Danvers; when the city was incorporated in 1868, it adopted the name of the merchant and philanthropist George Peabody, who was born there.

Duxbury and Wellesley were both named for family seats. Duxbury was named in 1635 for Duxbury Hall, the seat of the Standish family, thereby honoring a leader of the Plymouth Colony. Wellesley took its name from the nineteenth-century estate of the financier-philanthropist H. H. Hunnewell. Wellesley was his wife's family name.

The Native American input is evident is several place-names. Agawam translates as "overflow land" and Chicopee means "swift water" in the Algonquian language. Hyannis took its name from a seventeenth-century Indian chief, while Natick was the name of a local tribe. Saugus and Seekonk are related Algonquian words, the former meaning "small outlet" and the latter "outlet at." Swampscott translates as "red rock at."

NEW HAMPSHIRE

New Hampshire, which on June 21, 1788, became the ninth state to ratify the Constitution, had boundary lines established between it and Vermont, Canada, and Maine, as well as Massachusetts (fig. 140). The western boundary of New Hampshire, separating it from what soon evolved into Vermont, was first defined in 1764, when it represented the boundary between New Hampshire and New York. That boundary consisted almost entirely of the western banks of the Connecticut River, from where it enters Massachusetts to as far north as 45° north latitude. The northern boundary of New Hampshire was not set until a treaty with Great Britain in 1842, which also finally defined the boundary between Canada and Maine. The New Hampshire boundary began at the junction of that state with Maine and the Province of Quebec, at 45°18'20" north latitude and 71°05'04" longitude; then it proceeded by an irregular line, along the divide between the waterways flowing into the St. Lawrence River and the rivers running south, to the head of Halls Stream and down that stream to the Connecticut River at the forty-fifth parallel.

The boundary between New Hampshire, with its more than nine thousand square miles (making it larger than Massachusetts), and Maine was essentially defined in 1740. The dividing line passed through the mouth of Piscataqua Harbor; up the middle of the

England), Braintree, Dartmouth, Dedham, Falmouth, Framingham, Gloucester, Haverhill, Hingham, Ipswich, Lynn, Malden, Marlborough, Medford, Milford, Milton, Newport, Northampton, Sandwich, Sudbury, Swansea (Wales), Taunton, Weymouth, and Yarmouth. The adoption of English place-names continued into the eighteenth century, as evidenced by Acton, Andover, Chelsea (a London district), Grafton, Leominster, Ludlow, Needham, New Bedford, Shrewsbury, Stoneham, Tewksbury, Waltham, and Wareham. Melrose, incorporated in 1850, was named for a town in Scotland popularized by the writings of Sir Walter Scott.

Several communities took their names from people. Pittsfield honored William Pitt, Britain's secretary of state during the French and Indian War; Amherst took the name of Lord Jeffrey Amherst, Britain's victorious general at the end of that war. Revere was named for the famous Bostonian Paul Revere (fig. 139), silversmith and night rider at the onset of the American Revolution. Quincy was named for

140. Col. Joseph Blanchard and the Rev. L. Langdon. "An Accurate Map of the State and Province of New-Hampshire in New England. . . ." Boston, 1784. Engraving, 76 x 69 cm. Geography and Map Division, Library of Congress, Washington, D.C. The plate of this map was originally engraved in England but then brought to the United States and partially reengraved. The area depicted on the map extends from Quebec south to Boston and from Montreal and Albany east to Penobscot Bay and the Atlantic Ocean.

Newickwanock River, including Salmon Falls, to the farthest head of that river and East Pond; then almost due north, using a series of stone markers, to Kimball's Pond; and beyond to the border with Canada.

As has been noted previously the majority of placenames in New Hampshire derived from English towns. Bedford, however, specifically honored the duke of Bedford. Lebanon came from the name of a biblical mountain. The Algonquian language is represented in Merrimack, meaning "deep place," and Nashua, meaning "deep water."

RHODE ISLAND

Rhode Island has the distinction of being the last of the original thirteen states to ratify the Constitution, on May 29, 1790—about thirteen months after George Washington began serving as the first president of the United States. The complexity of Rhode Island's northern and eastern boundaries with Massachusetts, described above, are offset by the relatively simple boundary with Connecticut, which was essentially adopted in 1703 and never subsequently modified (fig. 141). That boundary line ran from the mouth of the Ashawaug (later Ashaway) River, from the Algonquian word for "middle," where it empties into the Pawcatuck River, to the southwest corner of the Warwick purchase, and then almost straight north to Massachusetts. Rhode Island was and still is the smallest state, with just over twelve hundred square miles.

The derivation of the names of the smaller cities in Rhode Island followed the pattern previously described for the major cities. Bristol, Coventry, Cumberland, and Smithfield came from place-names in England. Cranston was named for Samuel Cranston, governor of Rhode Island from 1698 to 1727. Barrington honored Viscount Barrington, a lawyer and theologian, while Johnston was named for Augustus Johnston, an eighteenth-century politician. The Algonquian language is represented in Pawtucket, meaning "open-divided stream," and Woonsocket, meaning "deep descent at." Westerly was appropriately named—it is located at the western extreme of the state.

CONNECTICUT

On January 9, 1788, Connecticut became the fifth state to ratify the Constitution. Its boundaries with Massachusetts to the north and Rhode Island to the east are described above. The remaining Connecticut boundary, with New York, was agreed on by the two colonies in 1683 and has been only minimally modified. That line began at the mouth of the Byram Brooke or River, between Rye and Greenwich, at a point called Lyon's Point (Byram Point);

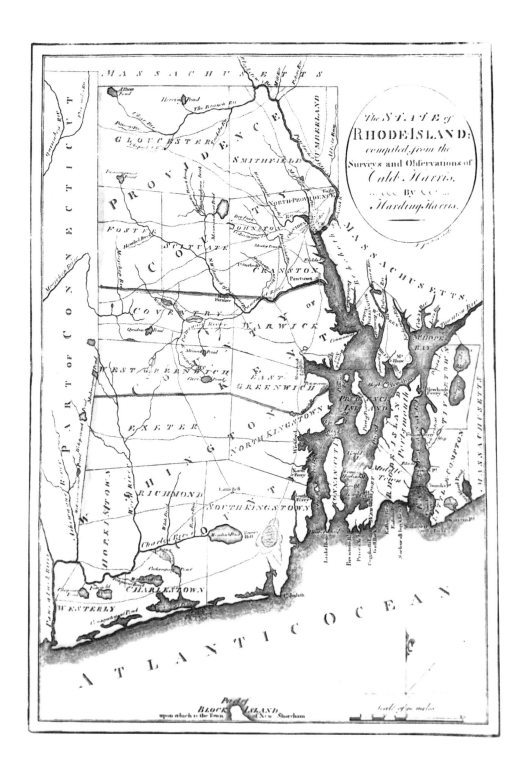

141. *Harding Harris. "The State of Rhode-Island; Compiled from the Surveys and Observations of Caleb Harris. . . ." In Mathew Carey's* Carey's American Atlas, *Philadelphia, 1795. Engraving, 34 x 24 cm. Private collection. This map shows townships and county boundaries, main roads, principal hills, and towns, as well as a college in Providence.*

followed the river to a place where the "Common Road" or "Wading place" crossed it; from that point ran north-northwest to a point eight miles from Lyon's Point; turned at approximately a right angle and ran along a twelve-mile line paralleling the Long Island Sound; turned at another right angle and ran north-northwest again, to a point along a line parallel to and twenty miles east of the Hudson River; and finally ran north along that line to the southern boundary line of Massachusetts (fig. 142).

    After the Revolution, between 1786 and 1800, Connecticut gave up all lands to the west that it had claimed based on its original 1662 charter (extending the colony to the South Sea, or Pacific Ocean), but

142. *A[mos] Doolittle. "Connecticut From the best Authorities." In Mathew Carey's* Carey's American Atlas, *Philadelphia, 1795. Engraving, 40 x 50 cm. Private collection. This map shows counties, cities, courthouses, churches, and roads.*

which were located outside its defined immediate boundaries. The state of Connecticut now contains about five thousand square miles.

Because many Connecticut settlements began early in the history of the colonies, English place-names took root in North American soil on a large scale for the first time in that colony. Early examples include Colchester, Enfield, Guilford, (New) London, Norwich, (Old) Lyme, and Wallingford. Also appearing in America for the first time were the names of Connecticut settlements with simplifications of the spelling of English place-names. Examples of this include Branford for Brentford, Simsbury for Simondsbury, and Windham for Wymondham. Other Connecticut cities with English place-names are Avon, Bristol, Cheshire, Fairfield, Farmington, Groton, Manchester, Meriden, Milford, New Britain, Newington, and Torrington.

In the eighteenth century, Berlin took the name of the German city, while Bethel was named for the town referred to in the Old Testament. New Canaan also came from the Old Testament. Killingly adopted the name of an English manor. Several individuals were honored by having their names bestowed on Connecticut communities. Ansonia was named for a financier, Anson Phelps; Cromwell had been the name of a privateer during the Revolution; Hamden dropped the "p" from the name of its honoree, the settler John Hampden; Ledyard honored Colonel William Ledyard, who was killed in the final year of the Revolution; and Mansfield took the name of a local landowner, Major Moses Mansfield. The naming of Shelton took a circuitous route. In 1717, the parish around which that city would develop was called Ripton for the ancestral English home of its leading citizen, Daniel Shelton. After the Revolution, the name was changed first to Huntington and then, when it was incorporated as a borough, to Shelton—this time honoring another family member, Edward N. Shelton. The name of Bridgeport, which was developed in 1800, is a compound based on its position as a port and the fact that the first drawbridge across the local river had just been completed at the time of its naming. Storrs was named for the brothers Charles and Augustus Storrs, who in 1881 started the Storrs Agricultural School for Boys—which later evolved into the University of Connecticut—at that locale.

NEW YORK

The boundaries of New York, the largest of the Middle Atlantic states with more than forty-nine thousand square miles, were established with Canada and five states: Massachusetts, Connecticut, Vermont, New Jersey, and Pennsylvania (fig. 143). New York was the eleventh state to ratify the Constitution, on July 26, 1788, nine years before Albany succeeded New York City as the state capital. The boundaries between New York and Massachusetts and Connecticut have already been described. New York's other eastern boundary, with Vermont, was not surveyed until 1814. The boundary began at the southwest corner of Vermont and ran north to a lot in the town of Pownal, then to a monument on the west side of the Hosick (later

renamed Hoosic) River, north and east to the southwest corner of Bennington, north to the Poultney River, down the channel of that river to East Bay, through the deepest channel of that bay, and north through the deepest channel of Lake Champlain, east of the Four Brothers Islands and west of Grand Isle and Long Isle (Two Heroes) and of Isle La Motte, to the Canadian border at 45° north latitude. The line was changed slightly in 1876 by cession of some land west of Fair Haven, near the Poultney River, to New York.

The northern and western boundaries of New York, separating it from Canada, were defined by the 1783 Treaty of Paris. The line began in the northeast at the forty-fifth parallel, ran west to the middle of the St. Lawrence River, and then followed the channel of that river to Lake Ontario; then it ran through the middle of Lake Ontario, the middle of the Niagara River to Lake Erie, and the middle of Lake Erie to the longitude separating New York from Pennsylvania. The short western boundary of New York separating it from northwestern Pennsylvania was established to provide the latter state with access to Lake Erie. That line was drawn in 1790, with its northern starting point lying on the meridian that passes through the westernmost point of Lake Ontario; the boundary then continued south to the northern border of Pennsylvania. That boundary between New York and Pennsylvania ran along 42° north latitude between its western point of origin and a marker on a small island in the Delaware River, then down that river to the entrance of the stream called the Mahackamack.

The boundary between New York and New Jersey was defined in the original grant that established the colony of New Jersey, but the line was not officially accepted by either colony until 1772. A diagonal line was drawn from the junction of the Mahackamack with the Delaware River to the west side of the Hudson River at 41° north latitude. The boundary continued down the middle of the Hudson River to the Atlantic Ocean, passing through New York Bay between Staten Island and New Jersey and Raritan Bay. Ellis Island, where millions of immigrants were processed in the late nineteenth and early twentieth centuries, and Bedloe's (now Liberty) Island, the home of the Statue of Liberty, are on the New Jersey side of the boundary line, although ownership disputes involving Ellis Island were not settled by the courts until the late 1990s.

The derivations of the names of the many cities and towns in New York with a population greater than five thousand are varied. Albion adopted the mythological name of England, while Rye transported an actual English place-name, as did Scarsdale, established in 1701 by Caleb Heathcote from Scarsdale, England. Geographic descriptions are evident in such names as Glen Cove, Glens Falls, Watertown, and White Plains. The Dutch heritage is represented by, among many other places, Cortland, derived from the landowner named Van Cortlandt, and Cobleskill, named for Jacob Cobel, who had a mill on the local *kill*, or creek. Hempstead reminds us of the passage of control of New York from the Dutch to the English:

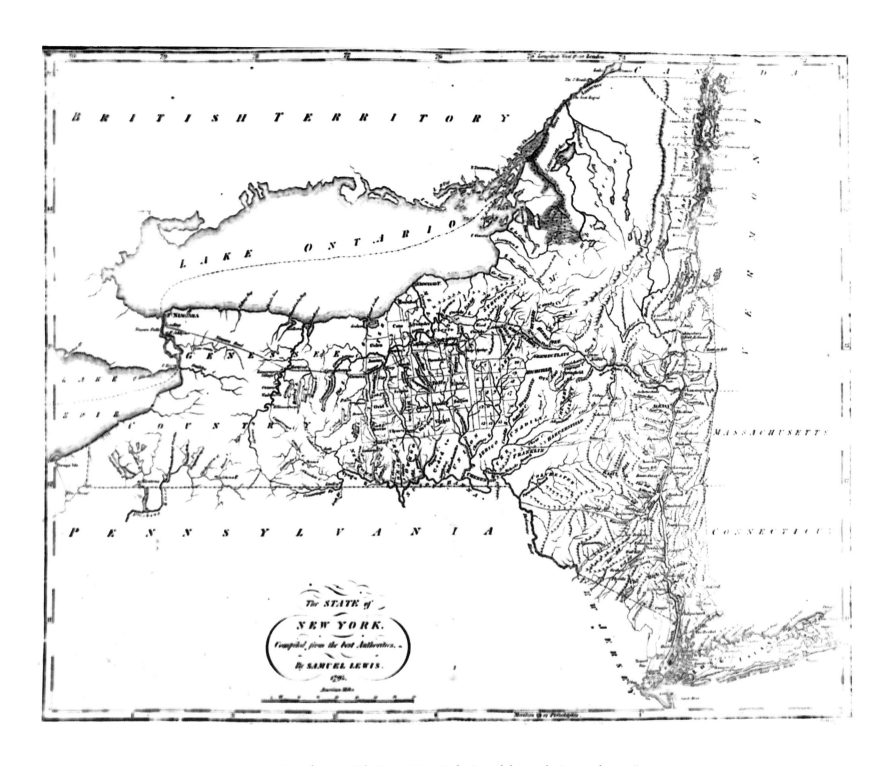

143. *Samuel Lewis. "The State of New York. Compiled from the Best Authorities."*
In Mathew Carey's Carey's American Atlas, *Philadelphia, 1795. Engraving,*
40 x 50 cm. Private collection. The western limit of the state is shown,
incorporating the land adjustment with Pennsylvania. The map also shows the
major road from the Hudson River to Niagara, and many of the towns
with names from classical times are depicted.

originally the settlement was called Heemstede, for a town in the Netherlands; in 1664 the name was changed to the anglicized form. Goshen, where the Hambletonian trotting and pacing race takes place, bears the biblical name of the land in Egypt that the Israelites inhabited. Bethpage also derives from a biblical name.

Indian terms and names identify many current places throughout New York. These include Cheektowaga, meaning "crab apple place"; Cohoes, meaning "pine tree"; Coram, meaning "valley"; Genesee and its variant Geneseo, meaning "beautiful valley"; Hauppauge, meaning "overflowed land"; Irondequoit, meaning "bay"; Lackawanna, meaning "at fork stream"; Mastic, meaning "big stream"; Nyack, meaning "point of land"; Oneonta, meaning "stony place"; and Tonawonda, meaning "swift water." In addition, Commack is a compaction of *winne-commac*, meaning "pleasant land," while Ronkonkoma incorporates *oma*, meaning "fishing place." Oneida and Patchogue were names of Indian tribes; the latter translates as "turning place." Merrick is the contraction of another tribal name, Merricoke. Mamaroneck and Nanuet were named for Indian chiefs, as was Wantagh, which is a variant of Wyandance.

Other individuals' names are perpetuated by several communities. Pelham took the name of the manor that John Pell built. Olean was named in 1807 for Olean Shephard, the first non–Native American boy born in the area. Elmira, where Mark Twain lived and wrote, took the name of a local child for whom her mother shouted loudly and repeatedly. Binghamton was named in 1835 for its developer, William Bingham. Similarly, Corning was named fifteen years later for its developer, Erastus Corning. Fulton honored Robert Fulton, who invented the steamboat. Dobbs Ferry was named for Jeremiah Dobbs, who ran a ferry across the Hudson River from 1730 to 1759; Martha Washington was his most distinguished passenger. Johnson City took the name of George Johnson, the president of Endicott-Johnson Corporation, which also contributed to the naming of the adjacent community of Endicott. Loudonville honored the English earl of Loudon, who participated in the French and Indian War. Massena was named for André Masséna, a French general in the American Revolution. Herkimer honored General Nicholas Herkimer, who led a force of New York State farmers against the British as they moved south from Canada. Herkimer died at the Battle of Oriskany, near the city that bears his name. Ogdensburg was named for Colonel Samuel Ogden, who bought land in the region in 1796. It was originally spelled "Ogdensburgh," but the city dropped the "h" when it was incorporated in 1896. Plattsburgh, where a pivotal sea battle in the War of 1812 took place, was named for its founder, Zephaniah Platt.

Neighboring New Rochelle reflects the French city of origin of its early settlers: Rochelle, the center of the Huguenot movement. Although there is disagreement, it is generally believed the city of Buffalo is derived from the French name for a local creek, Beau Fleuve, meaning "beautiful river," rather than from the animal, which was not in that area; others suggest it was the name of a local Indian.

Toward the end of the eighteenth century, and in the first quarter of the nineteenth century, the classical influence on place-naming in western New York State was apparent in the selection of the names for Troy, Rome, Utica, Syracuse, Ithaca, Ovid, Homer, and other towns. Troy, originally called Vanderheyden's Ferry, initiated the style of using classical names in 1789, when it took its name from the besieged city in Homer's *Iliad*. Rome developed around Fort Stanwix. Utica was named in 1798 for the ancient African city, while Syracuse, which was incorporated in 1825, was named for the Greek city in Sicily.

Other New York place-names had unusual origins. For example, Penn Yan, the name assigned to a village in upstate New York, was the compromise settled on by two groups of settlers, one from Pennsylvania and the other made up of "Yankees" from New England. Another unusual name is Horseheads, named in 1845 to commemorate an event that took place in the American Revolution when the troops killed the horses for food and piled up the heads.

NEW JERSEY

New Jersey, which was the third state to ratify the Constitution, on December 18, 1787, established boundaries with Pennsylvania and Delaware as well as with New York. The boundary with Pennsylvania represented a continuum using the Delaware River as the reference point (fig. 144). The original grant to New Jersey included territory between Delaware Bay, at the latitude of Cape May, and the Delaware River at 41°40' north latitude. That northern point came to constitute the junction with New York and Pennsylvania. The islands within the river were each assigned to whichever state was closer. The line between New Jersey and Delaware was more specifically defined in 1874 as the low-water mark on the eastern shore of the Delaware River, within a twelve-mile radius from New Castle, Delaware, and beyond that the middle of Delaware Bay. Almost eight thousand square miles are contained within these boundaries today.

In addition to previously mentioned place-names, several others were derived from Indian words or names. Absecon comes from the Indian word *absegami*, meaning "small water" or "place of swans." Clifton was originally called Acquackanonk Township, meaning "bush net fishing." Cinnaminson is the Algonquian word for "sugar maple," while Pequannock means "small farm." Secaucus appropriately adopted the Algonquian word meaning "salt marsh" or "snake land." Pennsauken means "tobacco pouch," while Piscataway means "divided river." Several tribal names also persist as New Jersey place-names, including Parsippany and Raritan; the latter, applied to a river and then a town, translates as "stream overflow." Metuchen was named for a seventeenth-century Indian chief.

Other place-names honored European people or places, as well as Americans. Asbury Park was named for the Methodist pioneer Bishop Francis Asbury, and Irvington honored the author Washington Irving. Edison honored its most distinguished citizen, Thomas Alva Edison. Cranford incorporated the name of John Crane, who in 1720

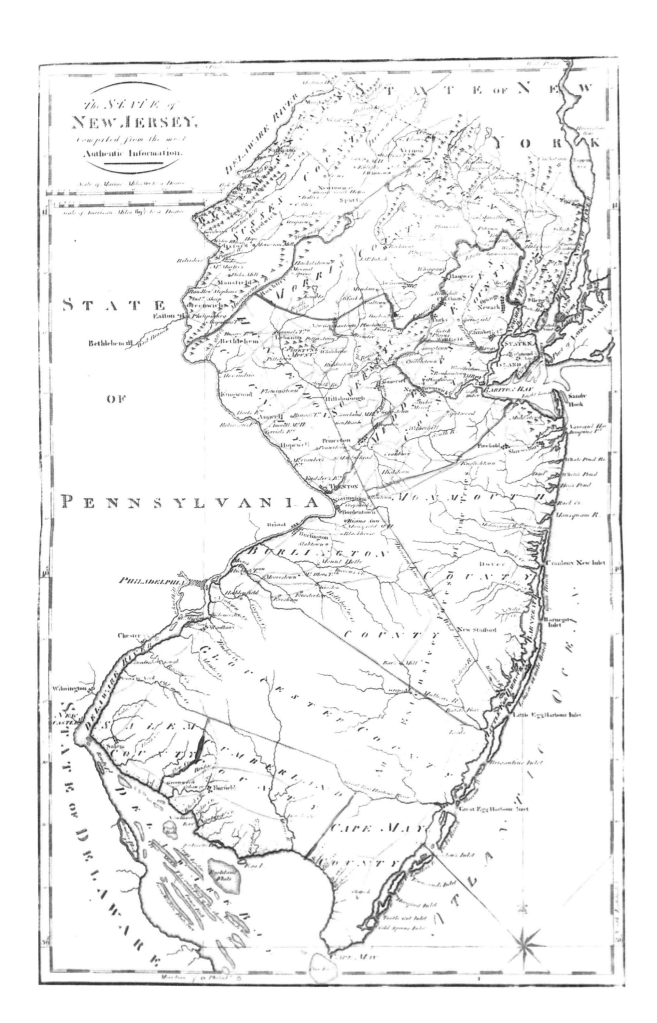

144. Samuel Lewis. "The State of New Jersey, Compiled from the Most Authentic Information." In Mathew Carey's Carey's American Atlas, Philadelphia, 1795. Engraving, 46 x 30 cm. Private collection. This is a topographical map that shows the town, counties, and roads, as well as the historical division line between East and West Jersey.

built a gristmill at a ford of the Rahway River; the mill supplied grain for George Washington's troops during the American Revolution. Bayonne took its name from the French city. Lodi derived from the Italian town, which was the site of one of Napoleon's victories. Bergen is a contraction of the Dutch city Bergen-op-zoom. Teaneck anglicized Teneyck, a local Dutch family name. Tenafly probably derives from two Dutch words, *tuin,* meaning "garden," and *vly,* meaning "valley."

PENNSYLVANIA

Pennsylvania, which on December 12, 1787, became the second state to ratify the Constitution, is bounded by New York, New Jersey, Delaware, Maryland, West Virginia, and Ohio, and currently includes just over forty-five thousand square miles (fig. 145). The New York and New Jersey boundaries with Pennsylvania have been detailed. The triangular piece of land that provided access to Lake Erie was ceded by New York to the United States in 1781 and added to the northwest corner of Pennsylvania in 1792 (fig. 146). The eastern side of the right angle was part of the border between New York and Pennsylvania, its base was an extension of the northern boundary of Pennsylvania west to the state's junction with Ohio, and the hypotenuse was the shore of Lake Erie. At the opposite corner of the state, the short southeastern boundary separating it from Delaware was defined by the 1681 charter to William Penn (when Delaware was the Three Lower Counties of Pennsylvania) as an arc of a circle having a radius of twelve miles with New Castle, Delaware, as the center. As previously mentioned, the border conflict between Pennsylvania and Maryland was resolved by the survey of Charles Mason and Jeremiah Dixon in 1763–67, thus establishing most of the southern boundary of Pennsylvania.

At the time the United States of America was established, there was also a border between Pennsylvania and Virginia, which had been agreed to in 1779. This boundary line was an extension of the

145. *Nicholas Scull. "To the Right Honorable Thomas Penn and Richard Penn Esqrs. True and Absolute Proprietaries & Governours of the Province of Pennsylvania & Counties of New-Castle Kent & Sussex on Delaware This Map of the Improved Part of Pennsylvania is Humbly Dedicated." Philadelphia, 1759. Engraving, 76 x 151 cm. Private collection. The first map of colonial Pennsylvania published in America. The road through "Alleguippy's Gap" and the distance to Ft. Duquesne (later Ft. Pitt, and still later the city of Pittsburgh) are shown.*

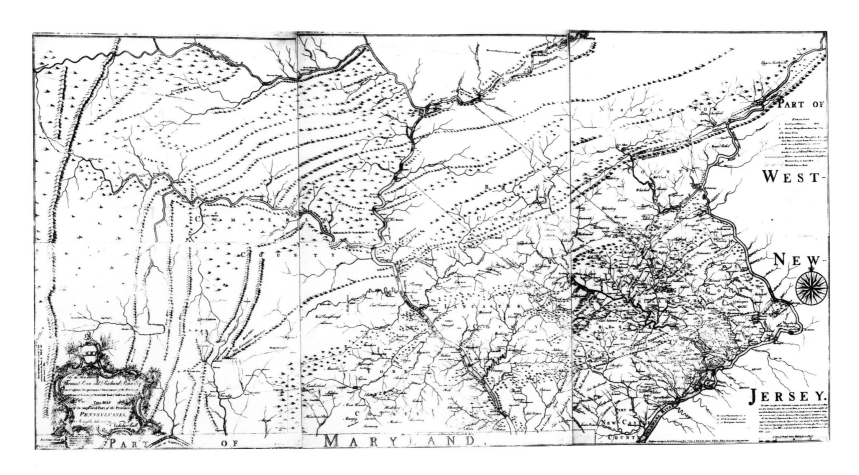

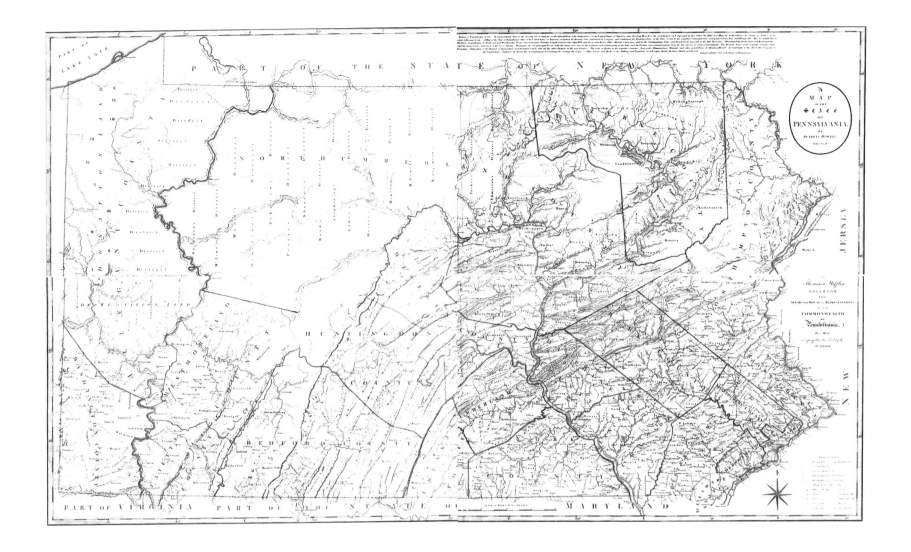

146. *Reading Howell. "A Map of the State of Pennsylvania." Philadelphia, 1792. Engraving, on four plates; entire map, 93 x 160 cm. Private collection. The best 18th-century map of Pennsylvania, and the first detailed map of the state to show exact boundaries. Settlements, towns, and counties are depicted. Each plate was issued in several different states, to reflect changing county and township lines.*

Mason-Dixon Line five degrees of longitude due west, computed from the Delaware River. A meridian drawn north from the western point of that line was defined as the western boundary of Pennsylvania. From the southwest corner of Pennsylvania, the meridian ran to the north side of the Ohio River. The northern part of the boundary line, between the Ohio River and Lake Erie, was surveyed in 1785. The point at the edge of Lake Erie is at 41°58'15" north latitude, 80°31'10" west longitude. Beyond this northern portion of Pennsylvania's western border, the evolution of the Northwest Territory, including the cession of land to the United States by Virginia in 1784 and by Connecticut in 1800, culminated in the formation of the state of Ohio in 1803. The portion of Virginia that lay beyond the southwestern part of Pennsylvania—west of the meridian drawn south of the Ohio River, and south of the extension of the Mason-Dixon Line

west of Maryland—became the state of West Virginia in 1863, two years after pro-Union inhabitants of that part of Virginia rejected the state's secession at the start of the Civil War.

Philadelphia, the site of the Continental Congress in 1774, 1775–1776, 1777, and after 1778 and the birthplace of the Constitution (fig. 147), was the most populous city in the United States during the eighteenth century and the early part of the nineteenth century, until the opening of the Erie Canal in upstate New York catapulted New York City into that position. Philadelphia was the capital of Pennsylvania—both colony and state—from 1683 to 1799 and the nation's capital from 1790 to 1800. From 1800 to 1812, the state capital was Lancaster, which—like Reading and York—had been settled in the first half of the eighteenth century and had been given a place-name from England. That pattern dates back to the very

147. *Nicholas Scull and George Heap. "A Map of Philadelphia, and Parts Adjacent. With a Perspective View of the State-House By. N. Scull and G. Heap."*
Philadelphia, 1752. Engraving, 52 x 30 cm. Geography and Map Division, Library of Congress, Washington, D.C.
This map shows Independence Hall (then called the State House), where the Continental Congress met during most of the American Revolution and afterward, where the United States was born, and where the Constitution was created.

beginning of Pennsylvania; Chester was named in 1682 by its settlers who came from that town in England. Harrisburg became the capital in 1812, though its history goes back to 1753, when John Harris established a ferry service to cross the Susquehanna River; in 1785, the town that bears his name was laid out. Among other eighteenth-century towns, Chambersburg took the name of Benjamin Chambers, who settled the area in 1730 and, after serving as a colonel in the French and Indian War, laid out a town in 1764 that he originally called "Chambers-Town." Allentown was named for William Allen, the holder of an early land grant in the area. Johnstown was named for Joseph Johns, a Swiss immigrant who owned the town site in 1793.

Altoona received its name in the mid-nineteenth century, when one of the town founders bestowed upon it an adaptation of Allatoona, a Cherokee-derived Georgia place-name. Aliquippa was named for a Seneca queen who lived in the first half of the eighteenth century. Erie followed a common progression in naming, from tribe to body of water (Lake Erie) to community. King of Prussia took its name from the sign on a local inn, which depicted King Frederick I of Prussia. Hazleton was named for nearby Hazel Creek. Carbondale's name reflected the coal mining in the region, while Hershey paid homage to Milton S. Hershey, the candymaker who built the town.

DELAWARE

Delaware was the first state to ratify the Constitution, on December 7, 1787, and thereby formally become part of the United States of America. Delaware, which is separated from New Jersey by the Delaware River and Delaware Bay, was initially defined as the Three Lower Counties of Pennsylvania. In 1776, by formal decree, the counties of New Castle, Kent, and Sussex became the state of Delaware (fig. 148). It is the second smallest state, containing about two thousand square miles. As mentioned above, its short northern boundary with Pennsylvania was established in 1681, at the time William Penn received his grant. The southern and western boundaries of Delaware both separated it from Maryland. Those lines began at what was then called Cape Henlopen, after an early Dutch explorer, and now called Cape James or Jonus; the current Cape Henlopen, a little ways to the north, was called Cape Cornelis then. From the current Cape Henlopen, the line ran west about thirty-four miles, and then eighty-one miles slightly northwest until it touched the periphery of the previously described arc of the circle drawn with a radius of twelve miles from the center of the town of New Castle. The line did not stop there, however, but continued a very short distance north (and therefore just to the west of where that arc actually stops as part of the boundary), until it intersected a parallel fifteen miles south of the southernmost part of Philadelphia—an extension of less than twenty acres.

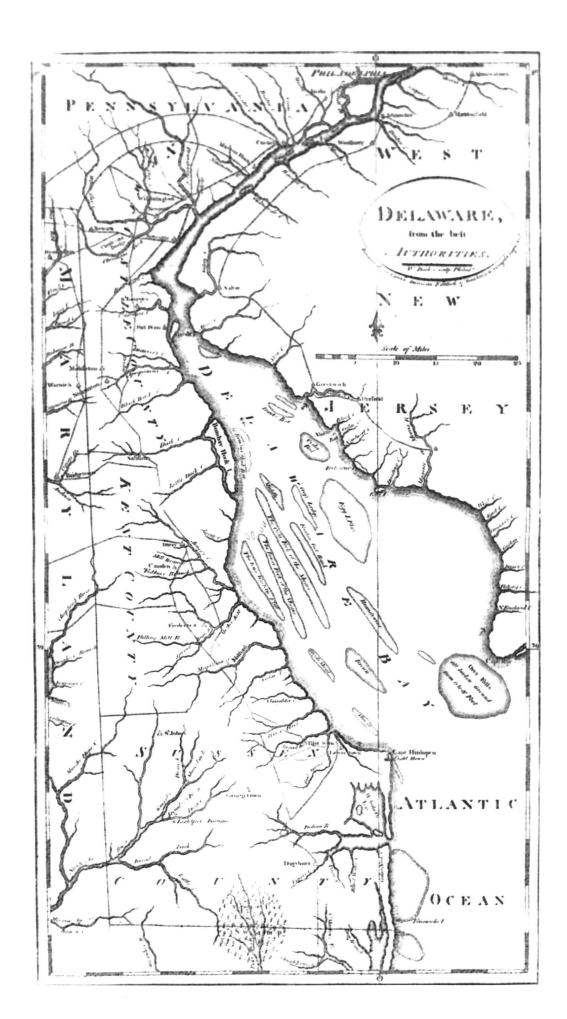

148. *William Barker. "Delaware from the Best Authorities." In Mathew Carey's Carey's American Atlas, Philadelphia, 1795. Engraving, 40 x 23 cm. Private collection. This map shows rivers, towns, principal roads, and boundaries of the three counties.*

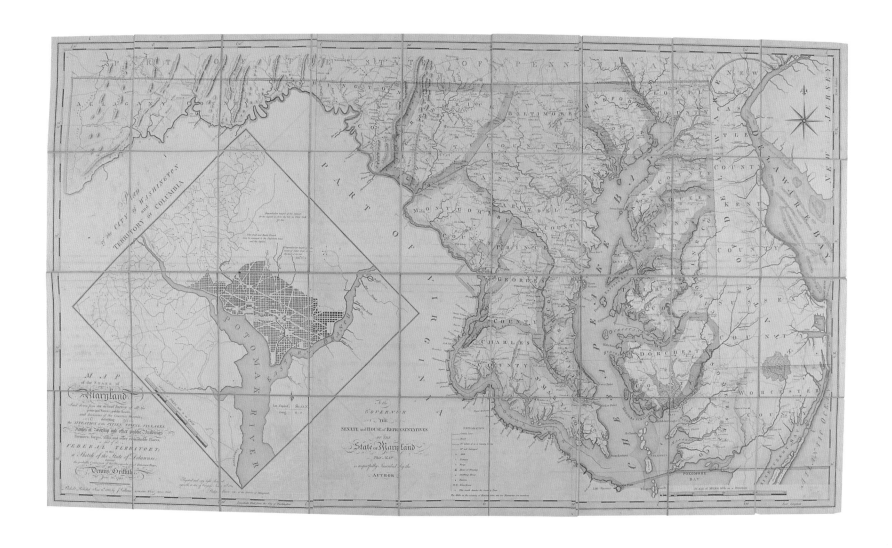

149. *Dennis Griffith. "Map of the State of Maryland . . . ; and of the Federal Territory; as also a sketch of the State of Delaware. . . ." Philadelphia, 1795. Engraving, hand-colored, 75 x 130 cm. Private collection. The best map of Maryland up to then, including political boundaries. The inset is a "Plan of the City of Washington and Territory of Columbia."*

Maryland, the seventh state to ratify the Constitution, on April 28, 1788, initially established boundaries separating it from Pennsylvania, Delaware, and Virginia (fig. 149). The boundary with Pennsylvania was defined by the Mason-Dixon survey of 1763–67. The boundary with Delaware has also been described above. Even after the establishment of Maryland, Virginia retained the southernmost portion of the Eastern Shore, the land east of Chesapeake Bay, ending at Cape Charles (which had been named by John Smith). The boundary between Maryland to the north and Virginia to the south on this narrower portion of the peninsula was determined by drawing a parallel from the southernmost point of the mouth of the Potomac River east across Chesapeake Bay. On the Eastern Shore, the parallel passed through Watkins Point, on the northern shore of the Pocomoke River, and continued eastward to the ocean.

The main boundary line between Maryland and Virginia, to the west of Chesapeake Bay, followed the Potomac River from its mouth northwesterly to the junction with the North Branch of that river, near Fort Cumberland. The line then followed the North Branch of the Potomac River in a southwesterly direction to a marker, which is located at about 79°29' west longitude, and turned north to the southern Pennsylvania border. From the point where that meridian passed through the south bank of the North Branch of the Potomac, Maryland's western border with West Virginia was defined when the latter achieved statehood in 1863. That boundary line extended along the south bank of the river back to the state line between Virginia and West Virginia. Maryland now comprises more than ten thousand square miles.

Annapolis, the city that was named to honor Princess, later Queen, Anne of Great Britain when it became the capital of Maryland in 1694, was the site of many historic events. As the meeting place of Congress under the Articles of Confederation for several months in 1783–84, it was the site of George Washington's resignation as commander in chief of the Continental Army and also the place where Congress ratified the Treaty of Paris, in which Great Britain recognized the independence of the United States of America. It was also in Annapolis that delegates from five states met in 1786 but took no action—except to call a convention in Philadelphia in 1787 to revise the failed Articles of Confederation; that 1787 meeting produced the U.S. Constitution. Baltimore, founded in 1729, was incorporated as a city in 1797. A year later, a new fort was built there overlooking Chesapeake Bay. Constructed on the site of old Fort Whetstone, which was built in 1776, the new fort was named to honor James McHenry, Washington's secretary of war. During the War of 1812, on the night of September 13–14, 1814, the British bombardment of Fort McHenry, witnessed by Francis Scott Key while he was detained aboard a British ship, inspired the young lawyer to compose the poem that later became the lyrics to our national anthem, "The Star-Spangled Banner" (fig. 150).

Bethesda took the name of a biblical location. Bowie replaced Huntington as a name when it incorporated in 1916, thereby honoring Governor Oden Bowie after he obtained rail service from Washington, D.C. Chevy Chase was the name of the land company that began acquiring that property in 1890. Potomac derived from the river that John Smith called Patawomek.

150. *The Star-Spangled Banner, made by Mary Pickersgill. Baltimore, 1813. 9.1 x 12.8 m (when flown). Courtesy National Museum of American History, Smithsonian Institution, Washington, D.C. This is the flag that continued to fly over Ft. McHenry in Baltimore's harbor despite a British bombardment on Sept. 13–14, 1814, during the War of 1812. It inspired Francis Scott Key to write the words that would later become our national anthem. The 30-by-42-foot flag resides in the Smithsonian Institution's National Museum of American History, which began a three-year restoration project in 1999.*

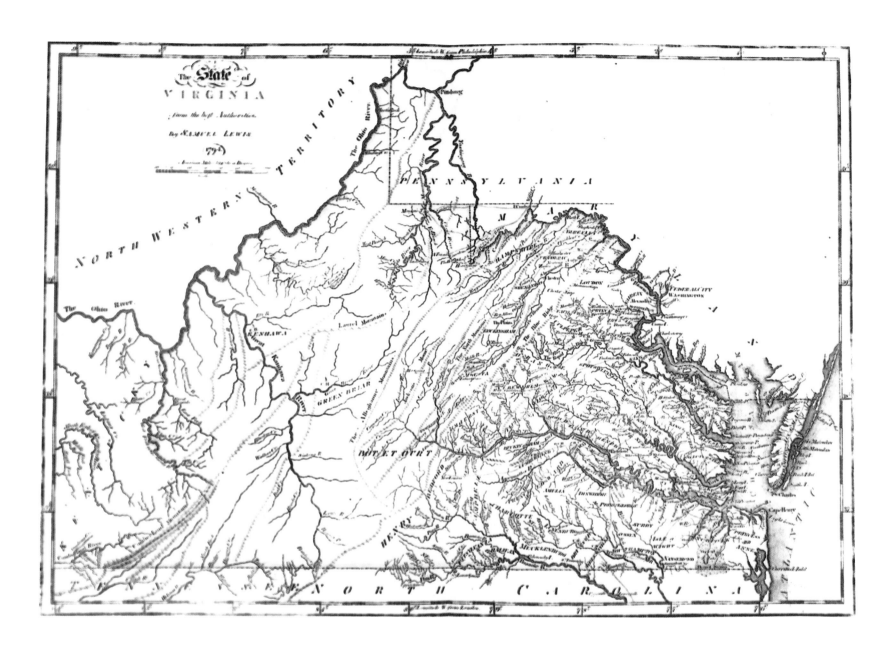

151. *Samuel Lewis. "The State of Virginia from the Best Authorities." In Mathew Carey's Carey's American Atlas, Philadelphia, 1795. Engraving, 34 x 50 cm. Private collection. This map indicates towns and courthouses, and it names counties but does not show their boundaries. The western boundary of the state mistakenly follows the western Levisa Fork on the map, instead of the eastern Tug Fork of the Big Sandy River ("Gr. Sandy R.") to the Cumberland Gap ("Cumberland Divide").*

152. *Henry S. Tanner. The "Lawn" of the University of Virginia, in Charlottesville. Inset on John Wood and Herman Böÿe's "Map of the State of Virginia," New York: Benjamin Tanner, 1826. Engraving, 33 x 67.6 cm. Courtesy Tracy W. McGregor Library of American History, Special Collections Department, University of Virginia, Charlottesville. This was designed by Thomas Jefferson, and the American Institute of Architects has designated it one of the ten best architectural achievements in the United States.*

Virginia was the tenth state to ratify the Constitution, on June 25, 1788. As noted previously, the original grant to Virginia was reduced during the seventeenth century by the charters for Maryland, Connecticut, Pennsylvania, and Carolina. During the eighteenth century, it was additionally reduced, first in 1763, when the Treaty of Paris ending the French and Indian War made the Mississippi River its western boundary, and then again in 1784, when Virginia ceded territory northwest of the Ohio River to the United States. The admission to statehood of Kentucky in 1792 set the boundaries for Virginia at the end of the eighteenth century. These boundaries, as depicted in *Carey's American Atlas*, would be reduced still further, to their present status, by the creation of the state of West Virginia in 1863, during the Civil War. Currently, Virginia contains a little more than forty thousand square miles.

At the end of the eighteenth century, boundaries existed between Virginia and Maryland, Pennsylvania, Kentucky, Tennessee, and North Carolina, as well as the territory west of the Ohio River, called the Northwest Territory (fig. 151). Virginia's boundaries with Maryland and Pennsylvania have been described above. The Ohio River separated Virginia from the western territory, which had been ceded to the United States. The boundary line between Virginia and Kentucky began in southwestern Virginia at the point where the northern border of

Tennessee—the westward extension of the northern border of North Carolina—crossed the top of the Cumberland Mountains near the Cumberland Gap. The line continued in a northeasterly direction along the crests of the mountains to the Tug Fork of the Big Sandy River; headed northwest along the Tug Fork to its junction with the Levisa Fork, forming the Big Sandy; and followed that river north to its confluence with the Ohio River. The southern boundary line of Virginia, with North Carolina to the east and a small section of Tennessee to the west, ran along the parallel of 36°30' north latitude, which had been established by the second charter of Carolina in 1665.

Numerous cities in Virginia were named during the eighteenth century. William Byrd, a colonial writer and member of the Houses of Burgesses and Virginia Council, named Richmond—the state capital during the American Revolution—in 1733 because of the resemblance of its river location to that of the British town of that name on the Thames River. Byrd also assigned Fredericksburg its name, honoring Frederick Louis, Prince of Wales and eldest son of King George II. Petersburg was named at the same time, taking its name either from the local geographic landmark known as Peter's Point or from the city that Czar Peter the Great of Russia built on the shore of the Neva River. Alexandria was named in 1748 for the Alexander family, local landowners. Charlottesville (fig. 152) was settled in 1762, one year after the marriage of King George III to a German princess, Charlotte

Sophia, and it was named to honor the new British queen. Nearby Staunton was dubbed with the maiden name of Governor William Gooch's wife. Portsmouth was named for the English port, while Winchester was named at the time of its founding in 1744 for the English town. Lynchburg took its name from the man who ran a ferry there in 1757. Burke took the name of the great British statesman Edmund Burke. Danville took its name from the Dan River; the word *dan* derives from an Indian term meaning "stream."

Arlington took its name from the plantation of John Custis II, which expanded into the family estate in that locale. The name of a more famous estate just to the south has an ironic twist: Mount Vernon (fig. 153), the home of George Washington (whose wife, Martha, had previously married into the Custis family), had been given its name by its original owner, Washington's older half brother, Lawrence, to honor the British admiral, Edward Vernon, under whom Lawrence had served during a 1741 attack on Cartagena, Colombia; when Lawrence died, the estate was inherited by the younger Washington, who led America to independence from Britain.

153. *Artist unknown.* A View of Mount Vernon The Seat Of General Washington. *1792 or after. Oil on canvas, 58 x 89 cm. Courtesy National Gallery of Art, Washington, D.C. Gift of Edgar William and Bernice Chrysler Garbisch. The home of George and Martha Washington.*

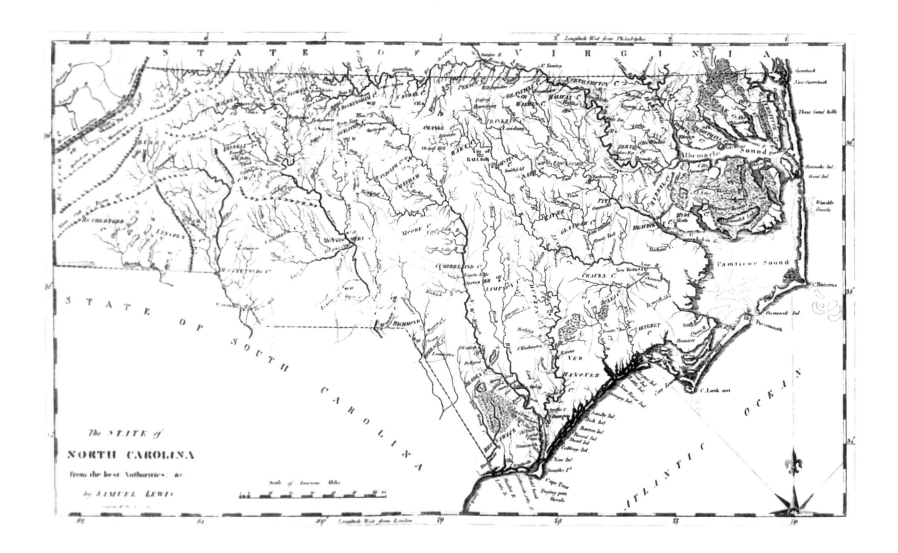

NORTH CAROLINA

When the separate provinces of North and South Carolina were finally established in 1729 from what had been called Carolina, a dividing line was defined, but it remained contested until 1813. North Carolina received more than fifty-two thousand square miles, and South Carolina was left with just over thirty-one thousand square miles. North Carolina was the twelfth state to ratify the Constitution, on November 21, 1789, almost seven months after President George Washington took office. At that time, it had borders to the north with Virginia, to the south with South Carolina and Georgia, and to the west with land that, after North Carolina permanently gave up its claim, was admitted in 1796 as the state of Tennessee (fig. 154). North Carolina's northern border is described above. Its southern boundary, as defined in the state's 1776 constitution, ran from a stake near the mouth of the Little River northwest, through a specifically designated boundary house at 33°56', to 35° north latitude and then west to the Pacific Ocean. As actually surveyed in 1764, the boundary line between North Carolina and South Carolina, as well as part of Georgia, ran from Goat Island on the coast, at 33°51' north latitude, northwest to 35° north latitude (later moved a few miles

154. Samuel Lewis. "The State of North Carolina from the Best Authorities." In Mathew Carey's Carey's American Atlas, Philadelphia, 1795. Engraving, 28 x 47 cm. Private collection. This map shows roads and towns, and gives county names, but it does not show county boundaries. The longitude of the southern state boundary line at Richmond County, where it changes direction from northwest to due west, is mistakenly drawn at 79°12' instead of 79°40' west longitude.

south of there) and due west to within a few miles of the Catawba River, at which point it turned north along the old road between Salisbury and Charleston to the southeast corner of Catawba Indian lands; the boundary line then ran along the eastern and northern borders of the Catawba lands to the point where they intersected the Catawba River, and continued due west to a point near the Blue Ridge Mountains, southwest to the intersection of the Cherokee boundary, and west again on a direct line along the parallel of 35° north latitude, beyond the Chattooga River to the Georgia border with what later became Tennessee. The western boundary of North Carolina with what would soon become Tennessee, as designated by a 1789 act of Congress that took effect the following year, ran along the crest of the Great Smoky Mountains from Virginia to Georgia.

The city named in honor of Sir Walter Raleigh—who established the first English colony in the New World, Roanoke, in what later became North Carolina—was selected as the site of the state's capital in 1788. The largest city in the state, Charlotte, settled by Scotch-Irish in the 1740s and incorporated in 1768, took its name from King George III's queen. Ironically, this community was an early center of rebellion against British rule, and the so-called Mecklenburg Declaration of Independence, purported to be a local expression advocating disassociation from the motherland, was signed there in May 1775. Kinston was originally named Kingston, to honor King George III, in 1762. After the American Revolution, the "g" was dropped to eliminate the connection. Greensboro and Greenville both honored General Nathanael Greene, who had achieved fame for his role in the pivotal Battle of Guilford Court House and other encounters with Lord Cornwallis during the Revolution. Chapel Hill, where the country's first state-sponsored university was chartered in 1789, was named for the small Anglican church called New Hope Chapel Hill that was located at the intersection of the east–west and north–south roads.

Wilmington was named for Spencer Compton, the earl of Wilmington, an English politician with colonial interests in the first half of the eighteenth century. Fayetteville was one of many cities honoring the marquis de Lafayette, the young French hero of the Revolution, while Boone adopted the name of the legendary frontiersman Daniel Boone. Durham, named for Dr. Bartlett Durham, who granted land for development, would evolve in the second half of the nineteenth century. Winston-Salem was a 1913 amalgamation of Winston, established in 1849 and named for General Joseph Winston, a Revolutionary War hero, and Salem, which was settled in 1766 as a Moravian community. Asheville took its name from Samuel Ashe, governor in the 1790s. Concord was a name decided upon for that settlement because it was emblematic of an agreement between two rival factions. Kannapolis was a name coined by J. W. Cannon, president of the Cannon Mills and founder of the town. Gastonia honored William Gaston, a distinguished jurist and composer of North Carolina's state song. Kitty Hawk, the site made famous by the Wright Brothers' landmark flight, was derived from an Indian name, Chickahauk.

SOUTH CAROLINA

South Carolina was the eighth state to ratify the Constitution, on May 23, 1788. The only boundary line for South Carolina, other than the already described one between it and North Carolina, defined the border between South Carolina and Georgia (fig. 155). The 1732 Georgia charter provided that the line between the two provinces would be the Savannah River to its head. A convention between the two states in 1787 fixed the boundary line as running from the mouth of the Savannah River along the northern branch to the confluence of the Tugaloo, the Cherokee word for "fork of a stream," and the Keowee (from a tribal name) rivers, and from there along the northernmost branch or stream of the Tugaloo, also called the Chattooga, until it intersected the northern boundary line of South Carolina.

155. Samuel Lewis. "The State of South Carolina: from the Best Authorities." In Mathew Carey's Carey's American Atlas, *Philadelphia, 1795. Engraving, 44 x 38 cm. Private collection. This map shows the eight precincts, including their names and boundaries, and the principal towns and roads. The northwestern boundary with Georgia includes an error in depicting the northern branch of the Tugaloo (Chattooga) River. In the northeastern part of the state, the longitude of the state border near the Pee Dee River is displaced 20 minutes to the east.*

Georgia was the fourth state to ratify the Constitution, on January 2, 1788. When it received its charter in 1732, its territory consisted of all the land between the northernmost part of the Savannah River and the southernmost part of the Altamaha River, from sea to sea. In 1763, the territory between the Altamaha and St. Marys rivers was added to the colony. When Georgia formally adopted its constitution in 1798, boundary lines were described between the state and South Carolina, North Carolina, Tennessee, and the Spanish possessions of East and West Florida (fig. 156). From the northernmost point of the border with South Carolina at 35° north latitude, the northern boundary line between Georgia and both western North Carolina and Tennessee ran along that parallel all the way to the middle of the Mississippi River (encompassing much of what would later become Alabama and Mississippi). The western boundary line ran down the Mississippi to 31° north latitude and east along that parallel to the middle of the Apalachicola, or Chattahoochee, River, then along the middle of that river to its junction with the Flint River. The boundary followed a line from the Flint to the head of the St. Marys River and continued along the middle of that river to the Atlantic Ocean. All islands within twenty leagues of the coast between the St. Marys and Savannah rivers belonged to Georgia. The state currently comprises almost fifty-nine thousand square miles.

In 1802, when Georgia ceded land to the United States, the state's western boundary was redefined. The line began in the south, on the western bank of the Chattahoochee River, where it crossed the border between the United States and the Spanish possessions to the south. The boundary line ran north along the western bank of the Chattahoochee to the point where Uchee Creek entered the river, then continued in a direct line northwest to Nickajack, on the far side of the Tennessee River, at the Tennessee border.

The cities that evolved in the Georgia colony in the eighteenth century have previously been discussed. In 1801, Athens, the home of the University of Georgia, appropriately took the name of the ancient Greek center of learning. Smyrna was named for the ancient city in Asia Minor. Albany transported its name from upstate New York. Marietta is thought to have been named for the wife of Thomas Willis Cobb, for whom the county was named. Alpharetta used a variant of the spelling of Pennsylvania's Alfarata, which was the name of a fictitious Indian girl in a nineteenth-century song. Columbus, which developed in 1828 as a port on the Chattahoochee, honored the European discoverer of the New World; Americus recognized the early explorer Americus Vespucius (Amerigo Vespucci). Valdosta was derived from the name of the estate of Governor G. M. Troup, which in turn came from the Italian region called Valle d'Aosta. Atlanta, Georgia's most populous city, did not evolve until the nineteenth-century era of railroad expansion, when it was first called Terminus, being the end of a rail line; its current name is derived from the name of the Western and Atlantic Railroad. Macon honored Nathaniel Macon, a prominent southern politician who had fought in the American Revolution. Lawrenceville took the name of naval officer James Lawrence, who uttered the memorable exclamation, "Don't give up the ship!" after being mortally wounded during the War of 1812.

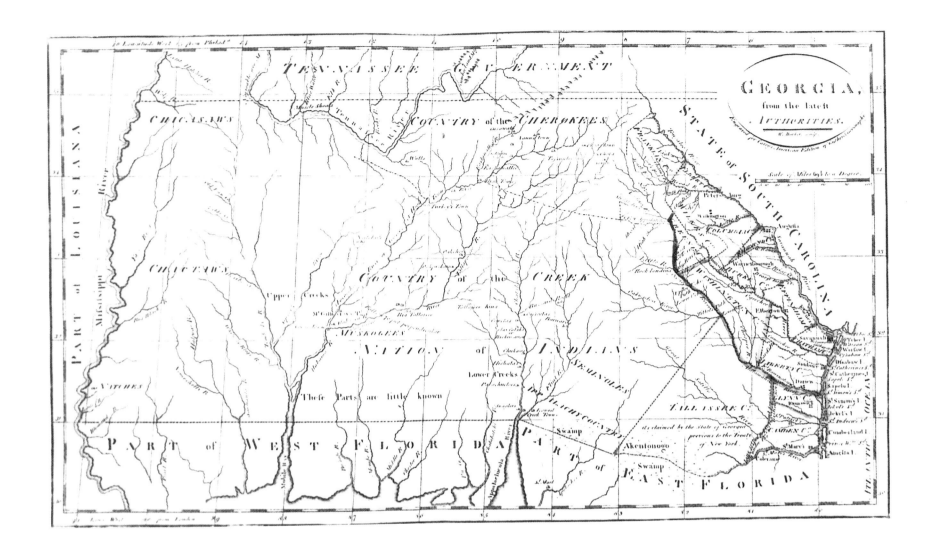

156. *William Barker. "Georgia, from the Latest Authorities." In Mathew Carey's*
Carey's American Atlas, Philadelphia, 1795. Engraving, 23 x 39 cm.
Private collection. This map shows all boundaries and names the counties. Several
Creek and Cherokee towns are located on it.

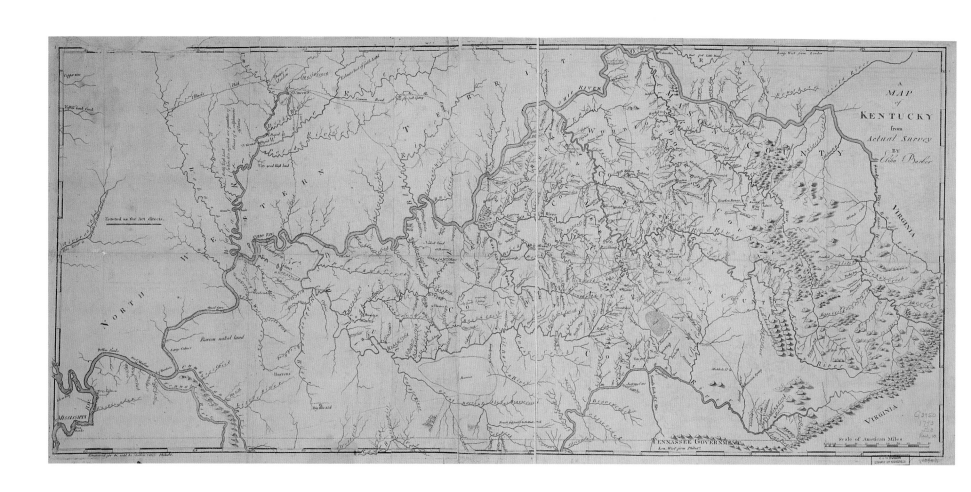

A
MAP
of
KENTUCKY
from
Actual Survey
By
Elihu Barker

CHAPTER SEVEN

Completing the Eighteenth Century

CESSION AND
THE NORTHWEST ORDINANCE

Even before the American Revolution ended, many of the states looked westward for expansion. The settlers in the eastern cities, townships, and rural areas already felt crowded and restricted. By 1780, for example, Virginia had set up a land office in the Kentucky territory, which took its name from an Algonquian word meaning "meadowland." Conflicting claims by individual states, and anticipated rivalries over as-yet-unclaimed lands, had to be addressed. A precedent was established in 1779, when the Continental Congress passed a resolution recommending that Virginia and other states refrain from granting unclaimed lands in the western territories while the Revolution was in process. In 1781, New York ceded to Congress the rights to land west of a line drawn south from the westernmost point of Lake Ontario. Massachusetts followed suit, and it settled its dispute with New York over land east of that boundary line. This led the way for Pennsylvania's purchase of land giving it access to Lake Erie in 1792.

The Treaty of Paris of 1783 greatly increased the amount of unoccupied territory within the boundaries of the new nation. In order to provide land for sale as a source of money for the nation's treasury, more states agreed to cede land to the public domain. In 1784, Virginia formally ceded land northwest of the Ohio River. The following year, Massachusetts ceded land within the limits of the state west of a line passing from the northern boundary to the "most westerly inclination of Lake Ontario and south to Massachusetts's southern boundary providing that the meridian was twenty mile west of the most western part of the Niagara River." In 1786,

Connecticut ceded land west of the western boundary of Pennsylvania, but it retained a tract of land along the southern shore of Lake Erie that was known as the Western Reserve. This land was governed by Connecticut until Ohio became a state in 1803.

South Carolina, in 1787, ceded a strip of land about fourteen miles wide between the Mississippi River and the head of the southern branch of the Tugaloo River. In 1790, North Carolina ceded its lands west of the current western boundary of the state. In 1802, Georgia's cession consisted of land south of Tennessee and west of a line beginning on the western bank of the Chattahoochee River, where that river crossed the border with Spanish Florida, and running north to the Tennessee border.

The various states' withdrawal of claims to the land between the Appalachian Mountains and the Mississippi River and their cessions of land to Congress led to a federal definition for recognizing territories and subsequently forming states within this national land. The initial focus was the land from the Ohio River north to the Great Lakes. In 1784, Thomas Jefferson drafted the Territorial Ordinance, which declared that that land would be divided into ten rectangular territories, each of which would be granted its own territorial government when its population reached twenty thousand inhabitants; statehood would be granted when a territory's population was equivalent to the least populated of the thirteen original states. This measure did not win approval.

But, in its most important action under the Articles of Confederation, Congress adopted the Ordinance of 1787, or Northwest Ordinance, addressing the lands north and west of the Ohio River. This formalized the American system of expansion and subsequent incorporation of land as a territory or state that has persisted

157. *Elihu Barker. "A Map of Kentucky from Actual Survey." Philadelphia,*
[1794]. Engraving, 44 x 98 cm. Geography and Map Division, Library of
Congress, Washington, D.C. A detailed topographical map showing roads and trails,
and part of the Northwest Territory ("North Western Territory") as well.

through the admission into statehood of Alaska and Hawaii. A territory would be recognized as soon as it had a population of five thousand free males, and it could apply for statehood when its population reached sixty thousand. The ordinance also specified that slavery would not be allowed in these particular territories. Ohio, Illinois, Indiana, Michigan, and Wisconsin were eventually created out of the Northwest Territory (which also included the northeastern part of what later became Minnesota). At the time the Northwest Ordinance was passed, Thomas Hutchins, geographer of the United States, conducted a survey of the land, dividing it into townships of six square miles having three sections each, thereby establishing a standard for future land division.

VERMONT

Before the first state to be created out of the Northwest Territory achieved recognition in 1803, three other new states joined the United States. On March 4, 1791, Vermont became the fourteenth state. Its name was adapted from the French words *vert* and *mont*, meaning "green mountain." The land, which was originally the homeland of Iroquois and Algonquin Indians, was included in the charter of the Massachusetts Bay Colony. In 1777, fifty-one towns in a territory known as the "New Hampshire grants" declared themselves an independent state and adopted the name "New Connecticut or Vermont." Four years later, Massachusetts recognized the independence of Vermont, and New Hampshire accepted Vermont's independent status in 1782. New York finally approved of statehood for Vermont in 1790. Vermont's boundaries with its three bordering states are described in chapter 6; the northern boundary with Canada was initially defined in 1783 as being the forty-fifth parallel, which a treaty between Great Britain and the United States reaffirmed in 1842 (fig. 158). Vermont contains almost ten thousand square miles.

The name of Vermont's capital, Montpelier, like that of the state, has a French derivation; it is named for the French city of Montpellier out of appreciation for the role the French played in the American Revolution. The state's largest city, on the other hand, took its name from the English earl of Burlington. Rutland was named because the grantee who received that land parcel came from Rutland, Massachusetts, which in turn took its name from Rutland County in England. Brattleboro honored Colonel William Brattle, who initiated that settlement in 1753. Middlebury was so named because it was geographically the middle of three land grants made during that year in the region. St. Albans took its name from that English town during the eighteenth century, when the Puritans no longer objected to using the names of saints as place-names.

One of the more dramatic selections of a name pertained to Barre. Two local settlers carried out a fistfight to determine which Massachusetts town to name it after: Barre, named for Colonel Isaac Barré, an English supporter of the colonies, or Holden. Barré's champion was victorious. Finally, a domineering political figure

under King George II with the titles of Viscount Tunbridge and Baron Enfield and Colchester was honored by having three towns named after him: Tunbridge and Colchester in Vermont and Enfield in New Hampshire.

KENTUCKY

Kentucky, with its more than forty thousand square miles, was originally included within the limits of the colony and state of Virginia. In 1775, Kentucky frontiersmen organized a government for a proposed state that they named Transylvania, meaning "across the woods"; neither the Continental Congress nor Virginia recognized it, however. In 1789, Virginia gave its consent for the formation of a new state out of the western district of Kentucky, which was then still within Virginia's boundaries. On June 1, 1792, Kentucky was admitted as the fifteenth state. Its eastern border, initially just with Virginia, is described in chapter 6. With the separation of West Virginia from Virginia in 1863, the boundary line between Kentucky and West Virginia would remain the same as the one previously established between Kentucky and that northwestern part of Virginia. Kentucky's northern border, which separated it originally from the Northwest Territory and subsequently from the states of Ohio, Indiana, and Illinois, was the northern shore of the Ohio River as it ran from the northwestern border of Virginia (later, West Virginia) to the point where it entered the Mississippi River; a short segment of the Mississippi River constituted the western boundary of Kentucky (fig. 157).

The boundary between Kentucky and Tennessee stemmed from what had been called Walker's Line, related to a survey done by Dr. Thomas Walker, who defined the parallel of 36°30' north latitude as the border between Virginia and North Carolina. A subsequent survey in 1820 accounts for the break in the western part of the straight line separating Kentucky and Tennessee. The survey indicated that the line ran from the southeast corner of Kentucky to the Tennessee River, then south along that river, which had been surveyed in 1819, to a line west of the river, and from there west to a loop in the Mississippi River.

The territory had become well settled after Walker, who discovered the Cumberland Gap, became its first permanent resident. John Filson's map of "Kentucke" (fig. 159), published in 1784, was the first map published in the United States to depict, in detail, a region west of the Allegheny Mountains. Appearing on that map are Harrodsburg, the oldest settlement; Lexington, probably named for the Massachusetts town where the memorable battle that began the

VERMONT

From actual Survey

159. John Filson. "Map of Kentucke [sic], Drawn from Actual Observations."
Philadelphia, 1784. Engraving, 50 x 45 cm. Private collection.
The first detailed map of an area west of the Appalachian Mountains to be
published in the United States. Eastern and western portions of the map
are distorted, but the central area is accurate. Towns, forts, and trails, as well as
Harrodsburg ("Harrod's Town"), the first settlement in Kentucky, are shown.
The map also locates Daniel Boone's house, southeast of Lexington,
and shows Louisville, with 14 houses, and Clarksville, with 11.

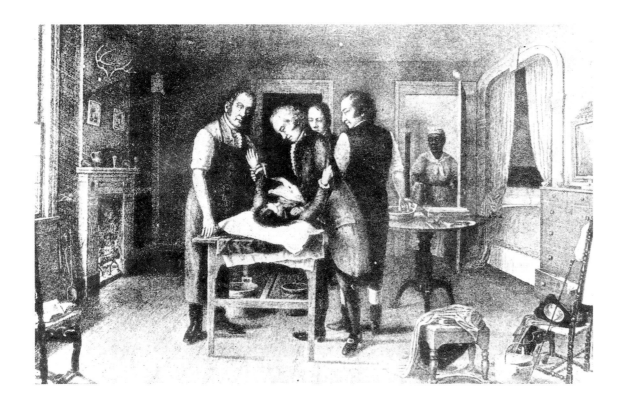

160. *Artist unknown. The first ovariotomy. Lithograph, after an 1877 painting by George K. Knapp; 55 x 70 cm. McDowell House and Apothecary, Danville, Ky. On Christmas Eve of 1809, Ephraim McDowell removed a 22-pound ovarian tumor from Jane Todd Crawford in his home in Danville, Kentucky. This was the first successful elective abdominal operation in the world.*

American Revolution took place in 1775; and Louisville, named in 1780 in honor of King Louis XVI of France, in appreciation of the French alliance. The capital, Frankfort, was originally Frank's Ford, memorializing a man killed by Indians in that region. Danville, the small community in which the world's first successful elective abdominal operation, the removal of a twenty-two-pound ovarian tumor, was performed by Ephraim McDowell in 1809 (fig. 160), had been settled in 1795 and named for its founder, Walker Daniel. In 1800, Bowling Green was settled and named for the lawn bowling that took place there.

Covington would develop later and be named for Leonard Covington, a general in the War of 1812. Fort Knox, the repository of the country's gold bullion, honored General Henry Knox of Revolutionary fame. Hopkinsville honored General Samuel Hopkins when it became a town in 1804, while Colonel Abraham Owen's name was attached in 1816 to a town previously known as Yellow Banks; eventually, the spelling of Owensborough was changed to Owensboro. Erlanger, originally recognized as the settlement of Timberlake, took the name of Baron Frédéric d'Erlanger when it was incorporated in 1882. The Indian presence is also perpetuated in place-names. For example, a local Indian chief was memorialized by the naming of Paducah, while the name of the city of Lone Oak became Okolona; *oko* means "water" in the Choctaw language.

TENNESSEE

On June 1, 1796, Tennessee—named for a regional river, which in turn was named for Tinnasi, an Indian village—became the sixteenth state, the last to be admitted during the eighteenth century. It was also the first state to be admitted in accordance with the rules promulgated by the Northwest Ordinance. The native Cherokees, Chickasaws, and Shawnees had witnessed the building of a fort by La Salle in the area in about 1682 and the early exploration by Daniel Boone in 1769. In 1784, after North Carolina first ceded land to the United States, settlers along the tributaries of the Tennessee River formed the temporary state of Franklin, which persisted through 1788. North Carolina retracted the original cession but reaffirmed it in 1790, setting the stage for the establishment of a new state, which today encompasses more than forty-two thousand square miles.

The jagged eastern boundary line of Tennessee was established by North Carolina's definition of the lands of cession, along the crest of the Great Smoky Mountains from Virginia southwest to Georgia. The northern boundary with Kentucky was essentially defined by the parallel at 36°30' north latitude, as described above. The southern boundary with Georgia and what later became Alabama and Mississippi was along the thirty-fifth parallel. The

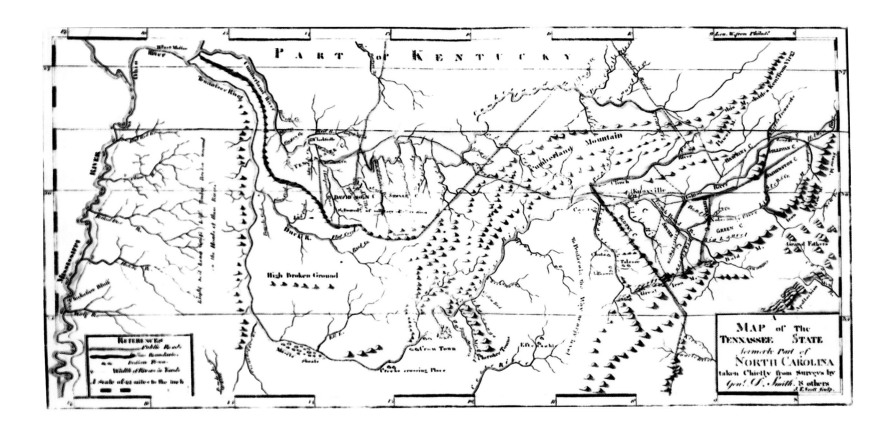

161. *J. T. Scott. "A Map of The Tennassee [sic] State formerly Part of North Carolina taken Chiefly from Surveys by Genl. D. Smith & others." In Mathew Carey's* Carey's American Atlas, *Philadelphia, 1795. Engraving, 25 x 52 cm. Private collection. This topographical map shows settlements, trails, and roads. Knoxville is located on it, and Indian boundaries and towns are depicted.*

162. *Amos Doolittle. Seals of the first sixteen states, surrounding a portrait of John Adams, the second president. 1803.*

western border, defined by the Treaty of Paris in 1783, was set at the middle of the Mississippi River, completing the boundaries of Tennessee (fig. 161).

Among the state's important cities, Knoxville, named for the Revolutionary general Henry Knox, had been settled at the time of statehood. The capital, Nashville, which developed later, also honored a Revolutionary hero, General Francis Nash. Chattanooga came from a Creek term meaning "rock rising to a point" and referring to Lookout Mountain. Memphis, overlooking the Mississippi River, took its name from the ancient Egyptian city at the apex of the delta of the Nile River.

OTHER DEVELOPMENTS

Before the eighteenth century came to a close for the nation and its first sixteen states (fig. 162), other events took place that would have an impact on the settlement of land and development of communities. In 1788, Oliver Phelps and Nathaniel Gorham bought land from Massachusetts and the Seneca Indians that jointly encompassed the western half of New York State. They divided the land into townships and chose a small town on the northern shore of Lake Canandaigua, which in Iroquoian appropriately meant "a place for settlement" or "hilly land," as the principal village of the area (fig. 163). The land office in Canandaigua was the first in the country to be established within the territory to be developed. Phelps and Gorham retained for development the land east of the Genesee River. In 1803, Colonel Nathaniel Rochester purchased one of the parcels; the city that would honor him by assuming his name would develop there. Meanwhile, the land west of the Genesee River reverted to Massachusetts and was purchased by Robert Morris, who sold it to Dutch bankers, leading to the establishment of the Holland Land Company in 1796 (fig. 164). The company's main office was in the New York town of Batavia, a name that was applied to the Netherlands from 1795 to 1806 after the French conquered it.

After the American Revolution, soldiers of the Continental Army, who had been paid in scrip redeemable in land warrants, began to exercise their rights. Many of the soldiers who

163. August Porter. "A Map of Messrs: Gorham & Phelps's Purchase; Now the County of Ontario, in the State of New York; from Actual Survey." New Haven, [1794]. Engraving, 60 x 38 cm. Private collection. The map divides the large purchase into ranges and townships. Rivers, streams, mills, and settlements are shown. Lake Canandaigua ("Canundargua Lake") and the settlement there are identified.

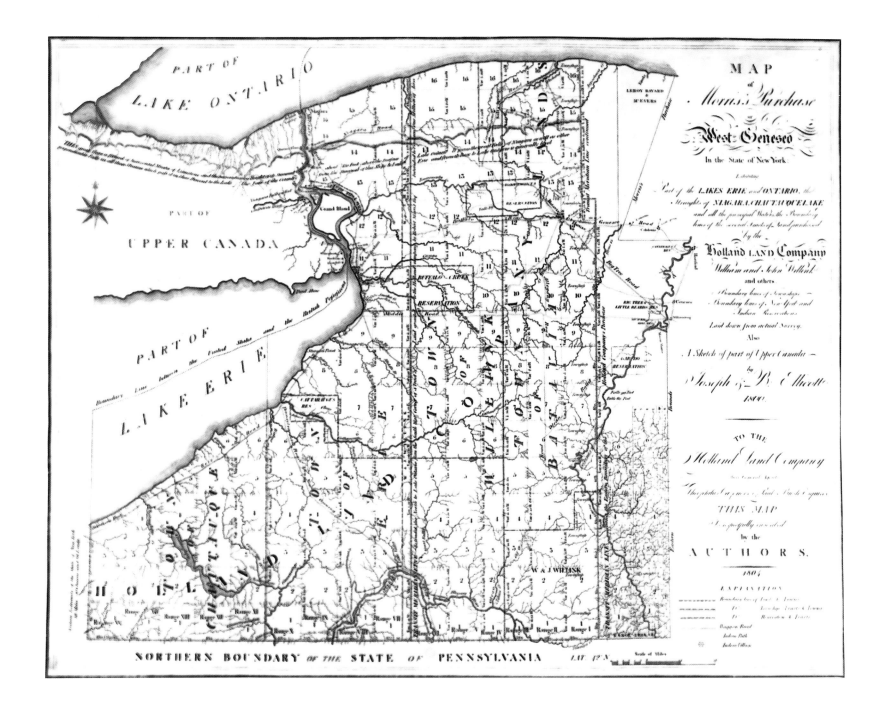

had served under General John Sullivan during his 1779 campaign against the Iroquois in upstate New York were impressed by the fertile land they encountered. With the end of the war, these first American veterans claimed land within designated military districts in New York (fig. 165), Pennsylvania, Maryland, Virginia, Kentucky, the Carolinas, and Georgia. Settlement of the western regions was contingent on the local Indians' ceding or abandoning their lands. In western New York, the Iroquois Confederacy was in total disarray; what had once been a strong alliance of six Indian nations had dissolved into weak, individual tribes. New York and Pennsylvania settlers grabbed most of these lands. To the south, the Cherokees gave up a significant part of their homeland and moved into central Tennessee. Farther south, the Creeks gave up land to Georgia.

164. *Joseph and B. Ellicott. "Map of Morris's Purchase of West Geneseo in the State of New York . . . 1800 / To the Holland Land Company. . . ." 1804. 51 x 67 cm. Private collection. This map shows ranges, parcels, reservations, and townships, particularly Batavia, where the home office of the Holland Land Company was located.*

165. *Cartographer unknown. "A Map of the Military Lands and 20 Townships in the Western Part of the State of New York." [1796]. Engraving, 31 x 29 cm. Private collection. Townships with classical names are noted on this map, along with land purchases and grants for individuals who had participated in the American Revolution.*

A Map of the Military lands and 20 Townships in the Western part of the State of New York

PART OF LAKE ONTARIO

Macombs

Black River

boundary

Adgate

Roosevelts Purchase

ONIEDA LAKE

Wood Creek

Fonda's

Holland

Oswego

Onondaga Falls

Pine River

2 Hanibal
Fish Lake

1 Lysander

3 Cato

Brutus

4 Cayuga Lake

Salt

Mud Creek

Geneva

5 Camillus

6 Cicero

Oneida Reservation

Deep Spring

Road

Onondaga Reservation

7 Manlius

Aurelius

Marcellus

8

9 Skaneateles Lake

10 Pompey

Massachusetts Preemption Line County of Ontario

Seneca or Canandaigua Lake
Robert Morris 64,000 Cls.

11

Romulus

Sipio

12

Milton

CAYUGA County

CAYUGA LAKE

Owasco Lake

13

Tully 14

15 Fabius

Sempronius of

Herkemer

16

17

Ovid

18 Locke

19 Homer

20 Solon

21 Hector

22 Ulysses

Catharines Town

Dryden

23

24 Vergil

25 Cincinatus 64,000 Acres

Watkins & Flint 50,000 d.S

Watkins fluid checked Watkins 25,000

1 2 3 20
19
6 5 4 18
7 8 9 17
12 11 10 16
13 25,000 14 15

Edmonston

Unadilla River

Otsego

County of

County of Ontario

County 7 10 of 11

2 3 6 Watkins & Flint 373,000 d.

Tioga
10 Townships granted to the State of Massachusets

Oweyo Creek

Wm S. Smith

Fayette

Clinton

Otsego

Mohawk Branch

Cook house

Pepackton branch

1 4 5 8 9 12

Chemung line to Oweyo 35.87

Chemung Town

James Watson & Others 14,550

82 Mile Stone being Gorham & Co Corner

Tioga River

Tioga Point

Oweyo Settlement

Hamden

Green

Chenango

Warren

Chenango River

Susquehanna River

80 70 60 50 40 30 20 10 5

PENNSYLVANIA LINE
Scale 10 Miles to an Inch.

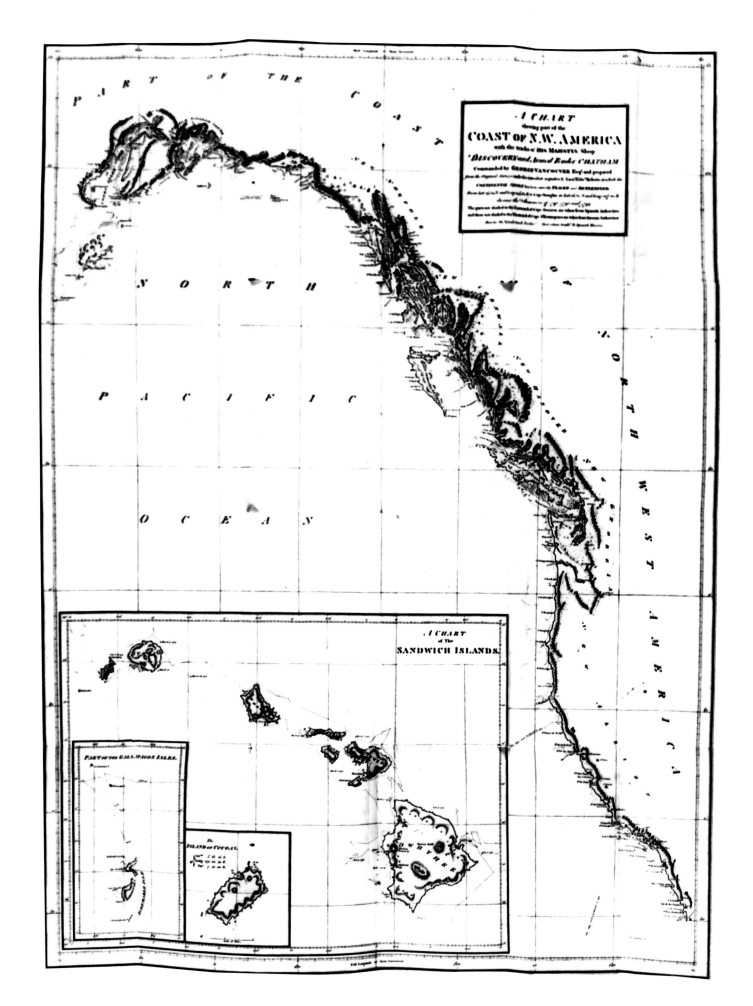

A CHART
shewing part of the
COAST of N.W. AMERICA
with the tracks of His Majesty's Sloop
DISCOVERY and Armed Tender CHATHAM
Commanded by GEORGE VANCOUVER Esq.r and prepared

A CHART
of the
SANDWICH ISLANDS.

PART of the GALLIPAGOS ISLES.

The
ISLAND of COCOS.

At about the same time, there were also developments on the other side of the continent. George Vancouver, an English navigator who had set out from Tahiti and the Hawaiian Islands, was exploring the inlets of the Pacific Northwest in the early 1790s (fig. 166). Even before Vancouver's voyage, in 1778, Captain James Cook (who as a lieutenant had mapped the St. Lawrence River twenty years earlier) had sailed along the west coast of the North American continent, but he had missed the mouth of the Columbia River. Cook did, however, determine the width of the continent by astronomical observations, and he also initiated a sea otter trade. This led to competition in that region involving Great Britain, France, Spain, Russia, and the United States. During his own voyages, in 1792, Vancouver named an island for himself, Mount Rainier for his admiral back home, and Puget Sound for his first lieutenant. That same year, the American captain Robert Gray sailed a ship into the mouth of the Columbia River for the first time, gave the river its name, and staked a claim to the Oregon Country for the United States. The name Columbia had appeared in

Philip Freneau's 1775 patriotic poem, but more pertinently it was the name with which Captain Gray's ship had been christened.

To the northeast at about this time, the North West Company was formed in Canada for fur trading, and Alexander Mackenzie, traveling on behalf of that company, left Fort Chipewyan in Alberta and became the first European north of New Spain to reach the Pacific Ocean by land. Still farther east, the governor of the British province of Upper Canada (equivalent to present-day southern Ontario) proposed that the territory between the Great Lakes and the Ohio River, as well as a portion of New York and Vermont, be made a satellite Indian state. A new Canadian fort was built about one hundred miles southwest of Detroit. To counter these Canadian efforts, Major General Anthony Wayne and two thousand U.S. Army troops built Fort Defiance in 1794, in what is now northwestern Ohio, and then engaged and defeated Indian forces near the newly constructed Canadian fort. That crucial Battle of Fallen Timbers led to the Treaty of Greenville, signed in the fort of that name, in

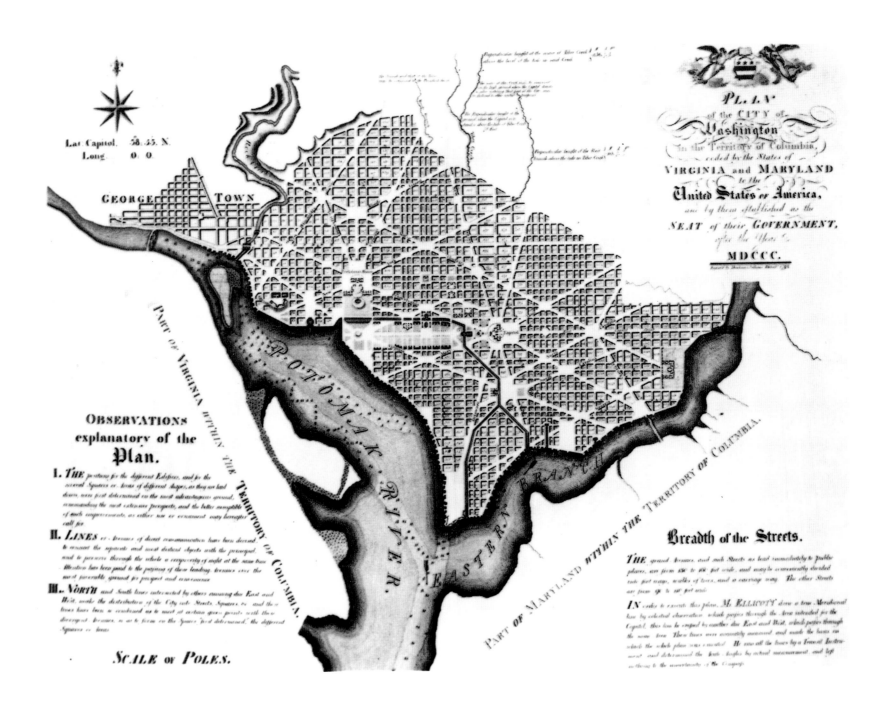

168. *Andrew Ellicott. "Plan of the City of Washington in the Territory of Columbia, ceded by the States of Virginia and Maryland to the United States of America and by them established as the Seat of their Government after the Year* MDCC*." Philadelphia, 1792. Engraving, 51 x 69 cm. Private collection. This plan is based on Pierre Charles L'Enfant's original design. Streets in Washington and Georgetown are depicted.*

present-day western Ohio, on August 3, 1795 (fig. 167). By that treaty, the Indians gave up claims to much of the Northwest Territory, including Vincennes, Detroit, and the site of Chicago, in exchange for what would now be the equivalent of ten thousand dollars. The battle also helped to put into effect a 1794 treaty that Chief Justice John Jay had negotiated in London, extracting a promise from the British to evacuate all of their posts in the Northwest Territory by 1796. All of this permitted expanded American settlement and development of the Ohio Valley. At the same time, the king of Spain granted to the United States the right to navigate the lower Mississippi River, as well as transit rights at New Orleans.

As the century drew to a close, the British explorer and surveyor David Thompson mapped the upper part of the Missouri River for the first time in 1798. In the same year, not long after settlement by treaty of the southern boundary of the United States with West Florida, as well as the Spanish evacuation of Natchez, the Mississippi Territory was established. Comprising the southern part of what later became Mississippi and Alabama, it was initially bounded on the west by the Mississippi River, on the north by the parallel through the mouth of the Yazoo River (named after an Indian tribe), on the east by the Chattahoochee River, and on the south by the thirty-first parallel. The area was later enlarged to include the rest of present-day Mississippi and Alabama, including a strip along the Gulf Coast that Spain had claimed earlier. In 1817 the territory was divided, and the eastern part became Alabama Territory.

One of the most dramatic events of the last decade of the eighteenth century was the creation of the permanent capital of the United States. The exact location of the nation's capital was selected because of President George Washington's personal preference; the shifting of the capital south from New York City and then Philadelphia was also part of a political deal with Virginian Thomas Jefferson and his followers in exchange for support of federal assumption of all state debts from the Revolution. On December 23, 1788, Maryland ceded to the federal government land within the state, "not in excess of ten miles square," to be used for the offices of the national government of the United States. A year later, Virginia passed an identical act, leading to congressional approval in 1790 of the current location of the capital. At that time, Congress indicated that the seat of the federal government was to be located in an area, not exceeding ten miles square, between the mouth of the eastern branch of the Potomac River and the Connogochegue River. In 1791, the area was redefined to include part of the Anacostia River (from a tribal name) and Alexandria, Virginia. The following year, the "Plan of the City of Washington in the Territory of Columbia" was defined on a map (fig. 168) by Andrew Ellicott, which was largely based on the original design in 1791 by Pierre Charles L'Enfant. The seat of the federal government moved to the District of Columbia in 1800. The District of Columbia used only the land provided by the state of Maryland (see fig. 149), and in 1846 the unused land that had been ceded by Virginia was formally relinquished to that state. The national capital city of Washington in the federal District of Columbia (the two have included the same amount of land since the annexation of Georgetown in 1878) was the first of many locations that would honor George Washington.

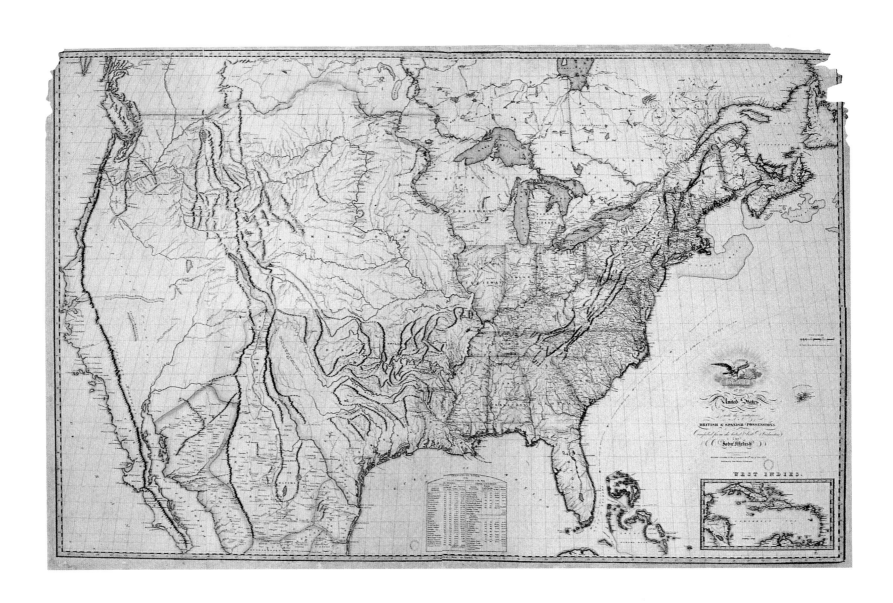

CHAPTER EIGHT

The Nineteenth Century: Early Expansions and Divisions

OHIO

The census of 1800, the second official one under the U.S. Constitution, reported a population of about 5.3 million; in 1790, the first census had counted 3.9 million people. Expansion of settlements occurred in all directions, primarily northward in New England and to the west from the other states. In 1800, the territory northwest of the Ohio River was divided into two parts: the western part became the Indiana Territory and the eastern part became the Ohio Territory, in accordance with the Northwest Ordinance. The Indiana Territory was defined as the land west of a line beginning at the Ohio River opposite the mouth of the Kentucky River, running northward to Fort Recovery, and then continuing north until it intersected the boundary line between the United States and Canada. In the Ohio Enabling Act of 1802, a triangular strip northwest of the Ohio River was added to the eastern portion of the territory. The first capital of the Indiana Territory was Vincennes, named in the first half of the eighteenth century after a Frenchman, François-Marie Bissot, sieur de Vincennes, who had established a fort there in 1732, built a series of forts from Detroit to New Orleans, and later was burned at the stake by Chickasaws near present-day Tupelo, Mississippi.

As for the area east of the Indiana Territory line, the Ohio Company of Associates had purchased a large expanse in present-day southern Ohio in 1787, and the Scioto Company (from a word believed to be Iroquoian for "deer") had bought adjacent land to the west. Marietta, the oldest city in Ohio, was settled by French immigrants in 1788 and named for Marie Antoinette (fig. 170), who was then the queen of France. Two years later, French immigrants also settled Gallipolis; its name is derived from Greek and Latin terms meaning "city of Gaul" (the ancient name for the region of Europe that became France). That same year, General Arthur St. Clair, first governor of the Northwest Territory, gave Cincinnati, site of the first

Opposite: 169. *John Melish. "Map of the United States with the contiguous British and Spanish Possessions Compiled from the latest & best Authorities." Philadelphia, 1816. Engraving, hand-colored, 89 x 142 cm. Geography and Map Division, Library of Congress, Washington, D.C. The first American-produced wall map depicting the country from coast to coast.*

170. *Artist unknown. "Marietta, Ohio, 1847." Engraving. Reprinted in Ephraim G. Squier and E. H. Davis's* Ancient Monuments of the Mississippi Valley, *Washington, D.C.: Smithsonian Contribution to Knowledge, 1948. Smithsonian Institution, Washington, D.C. The oldest city in Ohio, first settled in 1788.*

territorial legislature, its name in honor of the Society of the Cincinnati. That recently formed organization, which consisted of officers who had served in the American Revolution, was named after Cincinnatus, the farmer-soldier hero of ancient Rome. St. Clair was sent to build a fort on the shore of the Maumee River (a variant of the tribal name Miami), to offset British influence with the local Indians. St. Clair's troops were defeated by the Indians, and the Indian threat persisted until General Anthony Wayne's victory at Fallen Timbers in 1794 and the Treaty of Greenville in 1795 brought peace to much of the territory. In 1795, the Connecticut Land Company purchased land in the Western Reserve, in what later became northern Ohio, and Moses Cleaveland, one of the company's directors, took a party of men to the mouth of the Cuyahoga River, from an Iroquoian term meaning "important river," where he planned a settlement. Cleaveland's name was attached to the site, but the first "a" was dropped in 1830, resulting in "Cleveland."

On March 1, 1803, Ohio—named for the river, from the Iroquoian words *oh*, meaning "river," and *io*, meaning "fine or beautiful"—became the seventeenth state, and the first to be carved out of the Northwest Territory. The land had been home to the Erie, Miami, Shawnee, and Ottawa tribes at the time La Salle had claimed to have first explored it in 1669. Fort Industry had been built on the shore of the Ohio River in 1794. After statehood, two other forts, Meigs and Timbers, were the sites of skirmishes during the War of 1812.

The boundaries for the state of Ohio originally were set on the east by the Pennsylvania line north of the Ohio River, and by that river west of Virginia (later, West Virginia); on the south by the Ohio River, to the mouth of the Great Miami River; on the west by a line drawn due north from the mouth of the Great Miami; and on the north by an east–west line drawn from the southernmost part of Lake Michigan and actually running east from the western boundary line with the Indiana Territory, through Lake Erie to the Pennsylvania line. When Michigan was admitted as a state in 1836, the northern boundary of Ohio was altered. It became a line drawn from the southern shore of Lake Michigan, and actually starting at the eastern boundary of Indiana, to the northernmost cape of Maumee Bay. From that point, the line proceeded northeast to the boundary between the United States and Canada in Lake Erie and then to the Pennsylvania line (fig. 171). Currently, the state of Ohio contains more than forty-one thousand square miles.

Ohio's capital city, Columbus, was named in 1812 and was the first city to bear the name of the European discoverer of the New World. Other place-names in the state had diverse origins. Toledo took its name from the Spanish city, Lima from the Peruvian city, Parma from the Italian city, and Lorain from the French province of Lorraine. Akron, which was settled in 1825, named after the Greek word for "summit," because it was located on the top of a divide between two rivers. Dayton, where Wilbur and Orville Wright had a bicycle shop before they made the first sustained manned flight in a gasoline-powered aircraft, was named for its founder, Jonathan Dayton, who began farming the area in 1796. Youngstown similarly took its name from an early settler, John Young, who arrived in 1795. Other Ohio cities named for early settlers include Elyria, which combined the surname of Herman Ely and the last three letters of the name of his wife, Maria; Zanesville, recognizing Ebenezer Zane; and Kent, which adopted the name of several local businessmen. Mansfield was given its name by regional surveyors in order to honor Colonel Jared Mansfield, surveyor general of the United States during the first decade of the nineteenth century.

Oberlin was named for the Alsatian preacher and philanthropist Jean-Frédéric Oberlin. Massillon took its name from Jean-Baptiste Massillon, the bishop of Clermont, France, and a celebrated sermonizer who was a favorite of one of the early settlers. Wooster honored the Revolutionary War general David Wooster. Mentor was named for Hiram Mentor, an early settler. Warren took the name of its surveyor, Moses Warren. Strongsville paid tribute to Caleb Strong, one of the first two U.S. senators from Massachusetts and then governor of that state, and his brother, John. In the twentieth century, Kettering, which was incorporated in 1955, honored Charles F. Kettering, the philanthropist and the inventor of the automobile self-starter.

The classical era is also represented in the lexicon of Ohio city names: Bucyrus took its name from the Persian king Cyrus, preceded by "bu" to indicate "beautiful"; Euclid was named by its surveyors for the famous Greek mathematician; and Xenia is Greek for "hospitality." The Indian influence is evidenced by Ashtabula, an Iroquoian term that means "there are always enough moving," referring to fish; by Conneaut, meaning "mud"; and Gahanna, part of which, *hanna*, means "stream." Chillicothe and Piqua took their names from Indian tribes; the former was also the name of a tribal village.

171. *Rufus Putnam. "Map of the state of Ohio."*
In Thaddeus Mason Harris's The Journal of a
Tour into the Territory Northwest of the
Alleghany Mountains, *Boston, 1805. Engraving,
56 x 48 cm. Geography and Map Division, Library
of Congress, Washington, D.C. The earliest map of
the state of Ohio in the Library of Congress;
it was published two years after Ohio became a state.*

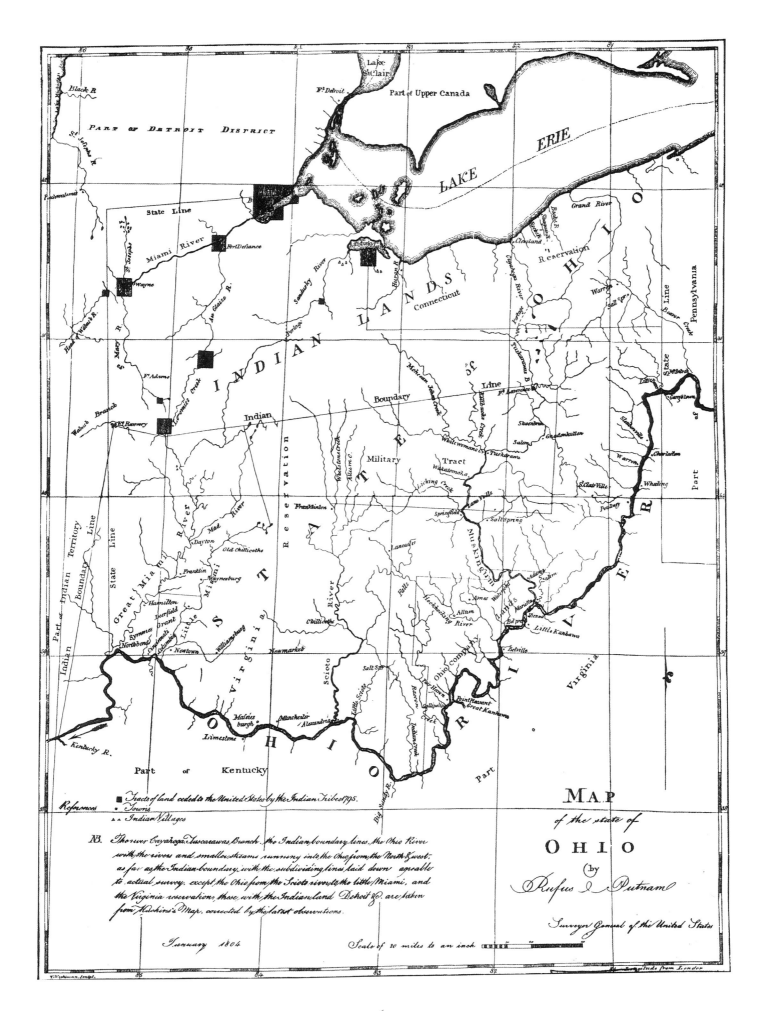

Reference: ◼ Tracts of land ceded to the United States by the Indian Tribes 1795.
• Towns
▲▲ Indian Villages

NB. The river Cuyahoga, Tuscarawas Branch, the Indian boundary lines, the Ohio River
with the rivers and smaller streams running into the Ohio from the North & west,
as far as the Indian boundary, with the subdividing lines laid down agreeable
to actual survey, except the Ohio from the Sciota river to the little Miami, and
the Virginia reservation, those, with the Indian land, Detroit &c. are taken
from Hutchins's Map, corrected by the latest observations.

January 1804

Scale of 20 miles to an inch

MAP
of the state of
OHIO
by
Rufus Putnam
Surveyor General of the United States

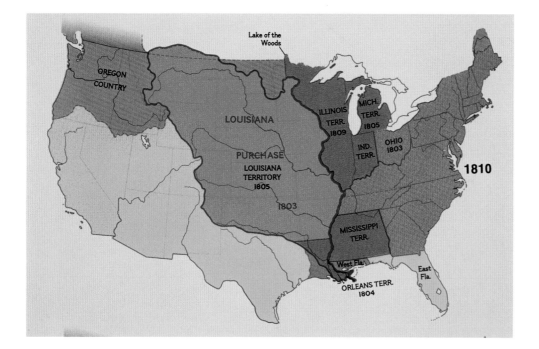

THE LOUISIANA PURCHASE

At the beginning of the nineteenth century, the United States encompassed about nine hundred thousand square miles between the Atlantic seaboard and the Mississippi River. The first major expansion of the United States was the Louisiana Purchase. This refers to the vast territory that La Salle had claimed for France in 1682: the entire Mississippi River Basin, with all its feeding rivers and surrounding lands, and the Gulf Coast, extending as far west as the Rio Grande. France had secretly ceded the "country known by the name of Louisiana" to Spain in 1762, during negotiations to end the French and Indian War, although the relatively small area east of the Mississippi River, except for New Orleans, was transferred to Great Britain under the 1763 Treaty of Paris. That land, north of 31° north latitude, then became part of the United States under the 1783 Treaty of Paris, with Great Britain also ceding the Floridas, south of 31° north latitude, back to Spain at that time.

In 1800, by another secret treaty, a weak Spain returned the area known as Louisiana to France, ruled by the ambitious Napoleon Bonaparte. This left the United States with only restricted use of the Mississippi River and without any land bordering the Gulf of Mexico. In 1802, the Spanish governor of Louisiana, who had not yet been replaced by the French, withdrew American traders' right of transit along the course of the Mississippi River at New Orleans. Concerned about the need for complete American access to the Mississippi River and the Gulf of Mexico, President Thomas Jefferson sent an emissary to France to negotiate with Napoleon for the purchase of New Orleans and West Florida, the strip of Gulf Coast from the Mississippi River east to the Apalachicola. The fact that

Napoleon anticipated a costly war with Great Britain resulted in the surprising French counterproposal, which was finalized by a treaty of cession dated April 30, 1803: the sale of all of Louisiana to the United States for fifteen million dollars.

Jefferson—who decided to ignore his strict-constructionist principles and accept that the federal government had the right to acquire new territory, even though it was not specifically stated in the Constitution—announced the Louisiana Purchase to the public on July 4, 1803, exactly twenty-seven years after the Declaration of Independence. The treaty, which the U.S. Senate ratified in October, doubled the territory under control of the United States. According to the terms of the purchase, the United States acquired all the land that France had laid claim to, from the Mississippi River to the Rocky Mountains and from the Gulf Coast, including New Orleans, to the northern boundary with Canada—the entire drainage basin of the Mississippi to the west of that river (fig. 172). Suddenly the French, Spanish, and Creole inhabitants of Louisiana became American citizens, and the area was guaranteed admission to the Union when the criteria for statehood were achieved.

The Louisiana Purchase was initially divided into two segments at 33° north latitude. North of that parallel, the land was incorporated into the District of Louisiana, under the administration of the Indiana Territory. The land south of that parallel became the Territory of Orleans, inhabited mainly by French and Creoles. From the land acquired by the Louisiana Purchase, the following states eventually would evolve: all of Arkansas, Missouri, Iowa, Oklahoma, Kansas, and Nebraska; most of South Dakota, Montana, Wyoming, and Colorado; and parts of Minnesota, North Dakota, New Mexico, Louisiana, and Texas.

Jefferson's expressed desire to "find the shortest & most convenient route of communication between the United States and the Pacific Ocean, within the temperate latitudes," antedated his presidency. In 1793, as secretary of state, Jefferson had hoped to send the French botanist André Michaux on a mission that would lead to exploration for a route to the Pacific, but the mission was aborted. As president, Jefferson commissioned Captains Meriwether Lewis, his private secretary, and William Clark to carry out an exploration of the vast new territory, which lasted from May 1804 to September 1806.

The leaders began with the preconception, based on a contemporary map by Nicholas King, that there was a waterway connecting the Missouri and Columbia river systems. Lewis and Clark were accompanied by a party of three sergeants and twenty-two other white men; Clark's slave, named York; Drouillard, a part-Indian scout who could interpret Indian languages; and Lewis's dog, Seaman. At the Mandan Indian villages, they would be joined by Toussaint Charbonneau, a French-Canadian trapper who would serve as interpreter, and his teenage, pregnant wife, Sacagawea (also spelled Sacajawea), who was also able to interpret several Indian languages.

During this period in the nineteenth century, St. Louis, which became part of the United States with the Louisiana Purchase, stood out as the gateway to the West. In 1804, the town had only about a thousand inhabitants, but it was the nucleus for trade up the Missouri River. Beginning at Camp Wood, just north of St. Louis, the Lewis and Clark expedition traveled up the Missouri River, crossing what later became the state of Missouri, following the current borders between Kansas and Missouri and Nebraska and Iowa, continuing north through present-day South Dakota and much of North Dakota, and then heading west through what is now Montana. Discovering that the Missouri and Columbia rivers did not in fact connect, the explorers—with the help of the Shoshone (fig. 173), Nez Percé (or "Pierced Noses," a name given to them by the French), and other tribes—

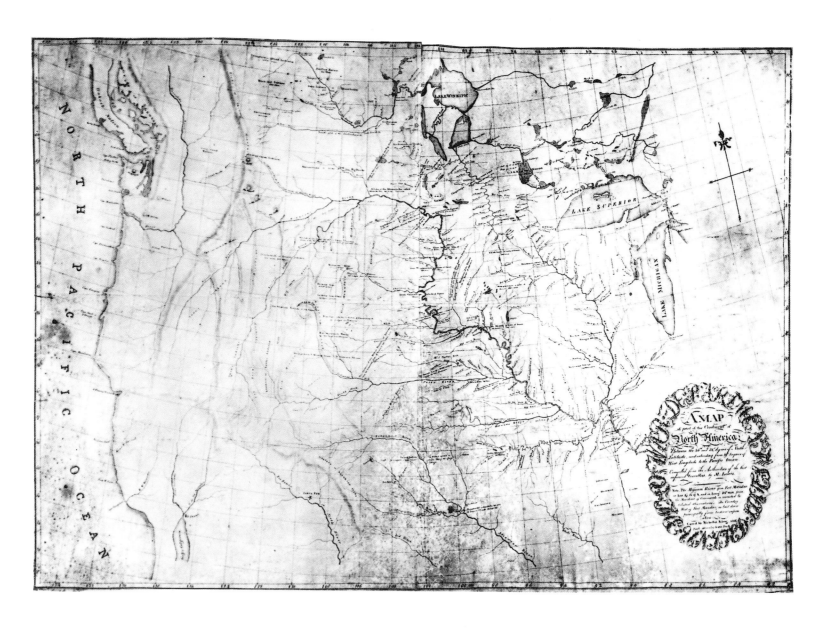

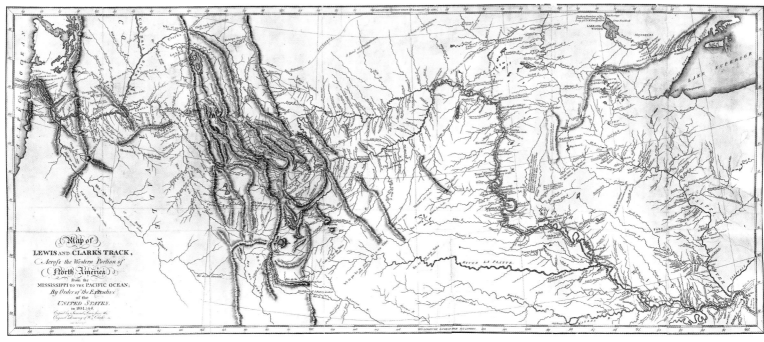

portaged across the Rocky Mountains and the Continental Divide, crossing present-day Idaho and what is now the southeastern part of the state of Washington, until they encountered the Columbia River, which they followed to its outlet into the Pacific Ocean, where they built Fort Clatsop (named after a local tribe) at the end of 1805.

The expedition provided the first map of the trans-Mississippi West, a manuscript by Nicholas King drawn in 1805–6 (fig. 174). William Clark's personal map was not published until it appeared in the journal of 1814 that chronicled the expedition (fig. 175). The journal included information about the region's flora and fauna, geography, and Indian inhabitants. Besides its scientific value, the Lewis and Clark expedition established the claim of the United States to what later became Washington, Oregon, and Idaho, and it opened the Northwest to subsequent exploration and eventual settlement.

The dispute over the land in the Oregon Territory would not be finally resolved until 1846, and dispute over the origin of that name persists to this day. One theory is that what is now the Wisconsin River had originally appeared as "Ouisconsing," and the spelling was changed to "Ouariconsint" on a 1715 map, which, because of space constraints, divided the name into two lines, with "Ouaricon" on top and "sint" below. Referring (through an error) to the unmapped region in the Pacific Northwest, Ouaricon first appeared as "Ouragon" in 1765 in Robert Rogers's *A Concise Account of North America* and reached its current spelling in *Travels through the Interior Parts of North America in the Years 1766, 1767, and 1768*, written by Jonathan Carver and published in London in 1778. Carver's narrative is based on his expedition as the first English-speaking explorer to travel west of the upper Mississippi River.

174. Nicholas King. "A Map of part of the Continent of North America, Between the 35th and 51st degrees of North Latitude, and extending from the 89 degrees of West Longitude to the Pacific Ocean. Compiled from the Authorities of the best informed travelers, by M. Lewis." 1805–6. Manuscript, pen and ink on paper, 80 x 117 cm. Records of the Office of the Chief of Engineers, National Archives, Washington, D.C. The first official map of the trans-Mississippi West, compiled from data furnished by William Clark. The map misrepresents the terrain and drainage patterns west of the Great Bend of the Missouri River.

175. Samuel Lewis. "A Map of Lewis and Clark's Track, Across the Western Portion of North America From the Mississippi to the Pacific Ocean; By Order of the Executive of the United States, in 1804, 5 & 6." 1814. Engraving, 31 x 72 cm. Geography and Map Division, Library of Congress, Washington, D.C. The first published map to incorporate the geographic information obtained from Lewis and Clark's explorations beyond the Mississippi River.

Another significant journey of exploration took place shortly after the Lewis and Clark expedition. In 1806, Lieutenant Zebulon M. Pike, for whom Pikes Peak in Colorado is named, led a small group from St. Louis to explore the southwestern part of the Louisiana Territory. Pike traveled up the Arkansas River into the Rockies and then turned south to the upper Rio Grande, where he was taken prisoner by the Spanish and sent back to the United States. His maps of the journey, published in 1814, offer the first accurate depiction of the southwestern plains.

LOUISIANA

To the south, the Spanish Empire was faltering by 1810, and the inhabitants of the portion of West Florida that was adjacent to the Mississippi River wanted to be part of the United States. They seized Baton Rouge, and the land around it was incorporated into the Territory of Orleans by a proclamation of President James Madison. That territory was defined as the land ceded by France to the United States, lying west of the Mississippi Territory and south of a line beginning on the Mississippi River at 33° north latitude and running along that parallel to the western boundary of the French cession. Two years later, on April 30, 1812, that territory would become the eighteenth state, Louisiana (fig. 176).

The original boundaries of the state of Louisiana began in the southwest at the mouth of the Sabine River and ran northward along the middle of that river to 32° north latitude, then due north to 33° north latitude. The northern boundary proceeded along the thirty-third parallel to the Mississippi River. The eastern boundary ran down the Mississippi to what was then the Iberville River (now Bayou Manchac), and then turned eastward along the middle of the Iberville River, Lake Maurepas, and Lake Pontchartrain to the Gulf of Mexico. The Gulf Coast made up the southern boundary line. In 1812, another five thousand square miles of land was added to the state, bringing the total to almost forty-eight thousand square miles. The southern part of the eastern boundary was shifted from the junction of the Iberville and Mississippi rivers to the eastern mouth of the Pearl River, east of Lake Pontchartrain. From that point, the line proceeded up the Pearl River to 31° north latitude and then west along that parallel to the Mississippi River. That 1812 annexation to Louisiana of the territory between the Mississippi and Pearl rivers, an area still known as the Florida Parishes, gave the United States control of both sides of the Mississippi River Shortly after the state was established, the United States also annexed the region in Spanish West Florida between the Pearl and Perdido (Spanish for "lost") rivers, adding it to the Mississippi Territory. Biloxi and Mobile were included in that annexation.

The capital of Louisiana initially was New Orleans, but it was moved, first to Donaldsonville and then, in 1849, to its current location, Baton Rouge; that name was derived from the French words meaning "red stick," referring to a post that had been placed to mark

176. *Cartographer unknown. "Louisiana." In Mathew Carey's* General History
of the World in Quarters, *Philadelphia, 1814. Engraving, 42 x 52 cm.
Geography and Map Division, Library of Congress, Washington, D.C.
This is the first map of Louisiana after it became a state.*

a boundary between two Indian tribes. Shreveport, located on the Red River, developed in the 1830s and was named for Captain Henry M. Shreve, who cleared the river of a severe logjam and was a major force in bringing commercial river traffic to the area.

The origins of the names of the smaller cities in Louisiana offer evidence of the state's ethnic diversity. Lafayette honored the marquis who fought by George Washington's side in the American Revolution. Chalmette was named for the local plantation owner, I. Martin de Limo de Chalmette. Destrahan took the name of another plantation owner, d'Estrahan. Metairie is the French word for "small farm." Plaquemine means "persimmon" in French and refers to trees that are present in the bayou country. Bastrop was named in 1844 for Baron de Bastrop, who received a land grant in the area during the period of French control. Lake Charles resulted from a translation of the first name of an early Spanish settler, Carlos Salia, into its French equivalent. New Iberia reflects the era of Spanish occupation. Thibodaux was named for its founder, Henry S. Thibodaux, a French Canadian born in Albany, New York, who served Louisiana as president of the state Senate and governor. Other individuals honored by Louisiana place-names include the landowner R. E. Russ, who provided the basis for Ruston; Senator John Slidell; and plantation owner Duncan Kenner. Bossier City was named for Pierre Evariste Bossier, a Creole who served in the state legislature and Congress. Monroe was named indirectly for the fifth president of the United States and directly for the steamboat *James Monroe*, which was the first to reach the town.

Native Americans are represented by several cities bearing tribal names, such as Natchitoches, Opelousas, and Houma, which means "red" and has the same source as the "homa" of Oklahoma. Bogalusa took the Choctaw words meaning "black stream" for its name, and Ponchatoula adopted a Muskogean word meaning "hair hanging," referring to the Spanish moss that hangs from trees. Tallulah, the name of a Cherokee town, was first applied in Georgia and then adopted by the Louisiana city. Two place-names are curious creations. Carencro derives from "carrion crow" and refers to the turkey buzzard, while Westwego merely put the three words *west, we,* and *go* together. Perhaps the most unusual derivation was that of Gretna, which took its name from the Scottish town Gretna Green, where many eloping English couples went to be married. The region where Gretna, Louisiana, evolved was famous for a nineteenth-century justice of the peace who readily married all who so desired. It seemed natural, therefore, to use the Scottish name.

INDIAN LANDS AND THE WAR OF 1812

In the first decade of the nineteenth century, President Jefferson and William Henry Harrison, who as governor of the Indiana Territory was the chief negotiator with the region's Indians, persuaded or forced several tribes to sign treaties divesting them of almost fifty million acres. By 1804, large sectors of Indian lands in western New York, Ohio, Indiana, Illinois, Georgia, and the Carolinas had been ceded to the United States. In 1805 the Michigan Territory was established, followed by the Illinois Territory in 1809, both carved out of the Indiana Territory (what was left of the Northwest Territory after Ohio became a state). Each new territory assumed the name of a local Indian tribe. Territorial status opened more protected land for settlement. Acquiring land from the Indians became an ongoing enterprise, despite occasional resistance. Between 1805 and 1819, land in western New York and Pennsylvania, northern Ohio, eastern Michigan, southern Indiana, Illinois, and Missouri were opened for land purchases and settlement. In the South, pressure for expansion occurred in areas that would allow for the growth of its principal crop, cotton. Large areas in what is now Arkansas and part of Oklahoma continued to be ceded by the native tribes, either to the federal government or to individual land speculators.

By the 1810 census, the population of the United States had grown to 7.25 million. By comparison, there were less than a half-million people in British territories in North America. In 1811, a subsidiary of the American Fur Company of John Jacob Astor developed the first American outpost on the Pacific coast (in present-day Oregon), appropriately named Astoria. Two years later, during the War of 1812 between the United States and Great Britain, the American Fur Company abandoned the Astoria outpost; the British North West Company took it over and changed its name to Fort George. Meanwhile, in 1812, Robert Stuart traveled from Astoria along the Columbia River to the Walla Walla River, then across the Blue Mountains and the Snake River Plain, around several small ranges to the Wyoming Basin, through the South Pass over the Continental Divide to the Platte River, and down the Platte and the Missouri River to St. Louis, thereby establishing an easier trail to the West—the basic route that later became the famous Oregon Trail. That same year, the Missouri Territory, west of the Mississippi River and north of the state of Louisiana, was organized.

As the War of 1812, fought primarily for free trade and American sailors' rights on the high seas, broke out in midyear, several Indian tribes up and down the frontier used the opportunity to try to resist encroachment by American settlers onto their lands. To the north, the Shawnee leader Tecumseh (fig. 177) and his brother Tenskwatawa, also known as "the Prophet," who together had spent years attempting to unite the entire region's tribes against the settlers, allied themselves with the British in Canada. General William Henry Harrison had defeated the Prophet and destroyed the main Shawnee village in the Battle of Tippecanoe (named after the creek there; the name means "buffalo fish") in 1811. Two years later, Harrison decisively defeated the British and Indians at the Battle of the Thames in Upper Canada (now Ontario), east of Detroit; Tecumseh was among the many Indians killed. To the south, General Andrew Jackson led his Tennessee volunteers against the Creek Confederacy in 1813–14, defeating them at Horseshoe Bend, in present-day eastern Alabama, and other battles. As a result, the tribes of the Creek Confederacy were forced to hand over most of their land in the Southeast, including much of what would become the state of Alabama.

Jackson then cemented his fame by forcing the British to abandon a base at Pensacola, in Spanish West Florida, in November 1814 and then by decisively defeating the British at New Orleans on January 8, 1815 (fig. 178). In those days news traveled very slowly, and neither side was aware that the War of 1812 had already formally ended two weeks before the Battle of New Orleans, with the signing of the Treaty of Ghent on Christmas Eve. Jackson's activities in East and West Florida were not quite over; in 1817–18, he set out on a punitive expedition against hostile Seminoles—only the first of a series of wars fought in Florida between Americans and Seminoles during the next twenty-five years.

The treaty ending the War of 1812 restored all prewar boundaries and created boundary commissions to peacefully resolve ongoing and future disputes between the United States and Great Britain over the U.S. border with Canada. In the short term, the commissions were specifically directed to define boundaries related to islands in the Bay of Fundy, off the coast of Maine and the Canadian province of New Brunswick, and to fix the international border all

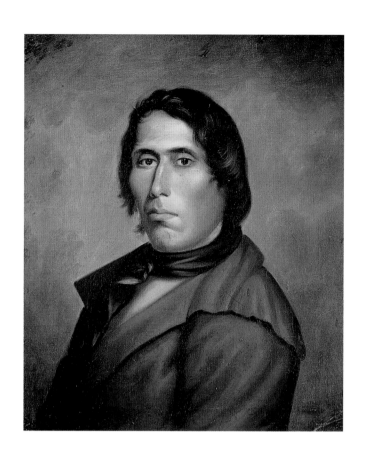

177. *Artist unknown, possibly George Catlin. Believed to be a portrait of Tecumseh. c. 1830. Oil on Masonite board, 63.5 x 76.2 cm. Courtesy the Field Museum, Chicago. Photograph by Ron Testa. The Shawnee chief was one of the most important leaders of Indian resistance to white encroachment.*

178. *Jean Hyacinthe de Laclotte. The Battle of New Orleans. 1815. Oil on canvas, 74.3 x 91.4 cm. Courtesy New Orleans Museum of Art, New Orleans. News that a treaty negotiated in Belgium had ended the War of 1812 did not arrive until after this battle, which confirmed Andrew Jackson's status as a military hero, was fought two weeks later.*

the way from the source of the St. Croix River, between Maine and New Brunswick, to the Lake of the Woods, which is in present-day northern Minnesota, southeastern Manitoba, and southwestern Ontario. In 1818, an agreement between the United States and Great Britain extended the boundary line between the United States and Canada westward from the Lake of the Woods to the Rocky Mountains, and declared that the country west of those mountains should remain open to both countries for ten years. Various commissions, extending over the next thirty years, would deal with the boundary disputes between the two countries that persisted until the current international border from the Atlantic Ocean to the Pacific was settled in 1846.

After the War of 1812, there was an intensification of the move westward from the eastern seaboard. Many roads were proposed and built, but the first major route westward was a waterway. In 1817, construction began on the Erie Canal, extending more than 350 miles from Lake Erie to the Hudson River. The canal, completed in 1825, would lead to the development of the northwestern part of New York State, and it would make New York City the leading eastern seaport. Meanwhile, in 1817, the first steamboat traveled up the Mississippi and Ohio rivers to Cincinnati. Within two years, regular steamboat traffic would be established between New Orleans and Louisville, Kentucky. The first national road was also built by 1819; it ran between Cumberland, Maryland, and Wheeling, in what is now West Virginia. By the 1830s, this road had been extended all the way to Vandalia, Illinois; it is now a segment of U.S. Route 40.

INDIANA

Between 1810 and 1820, the population west of the Appalachian Mountains more than doubled. Four new states were quickly added to the Union in accordance with the rules first set forth in the Northwest Ordinance. On December 11, 1816, Indiana became the nineteenth state, taking the name of the territory that had been established in 1800. The state, which has more than thirty-six thousand square miles, includes some of the land where early Indians known as the Mound Builders (fig. 179) had lived from about the tenth century B.C. until the sixteenth century, and which had subsequently been the home of the Miami, Lenape (Delaware), and Potawatomi tribes.

Indiana, with its defined boundaries, is included on John Melish's 1816 wall map (fig. 169), the first such American-produced map to depict the United States from coast to coast. The state (fig. 180) was bounded on the east by the meridian forming the western boundary of the state of Ohio. On the south, it was separated from Kentucky by the Ohio River, from the mouth of the Great Miami River to the mouth of the Wabash River. The western boundary ran northward along the middle of the Wabash River, from its mouth to a point where a line drawn due north from Vincennes, the oldest settlement in Indiana, would touch the northwestern shore of that river; beyond that,

179. *Artifacts of the Mound Builders, a name given to Indians who lived primarily in the Mississippi and Ohio valleys for millennia, until about the 16th century. In Henry Clyde Shetrone's* The Mound Builders, *Port Washington, N.Y.: Kennekal Press, 1930. Top: The Mainsburg Mound in Montgomery, Ohio, one of the largest conical mounds in the United States. Above: Tobacco pipes found in the Tremper Mound in Scioto County, Ohio.*

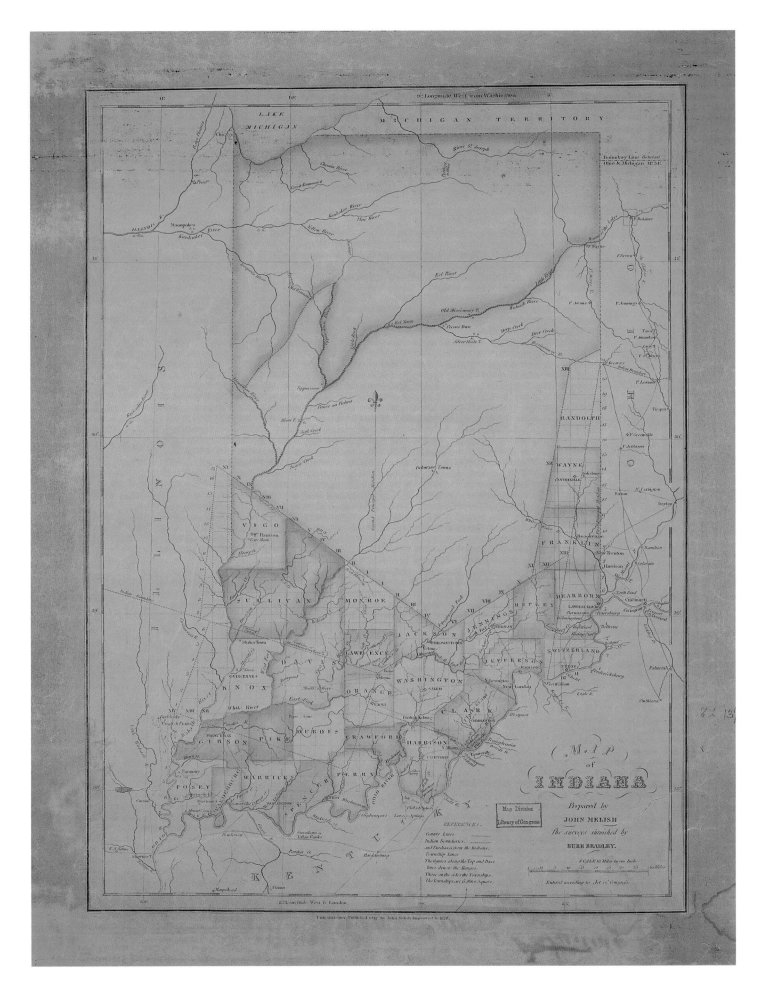

180. John Melish. "Map of
Indiana." Philadelphia,
1817. Engraving,
47 x 33 cm. Geography
and Map Division,
Library of Congress,
Washington, D.C.
The depiction of a frontier
state shortly after it
joined the Union.
The disposition of public
lands is shown on the map,
as are boundary lines
in unsettled areas.

a boundary line ran due north until it intersected with an east–west line drawn through a point ten miles north of the southernmost part of Lake Michigan. From the curve of the lake's southern shore, that east–west line formed the northern border of Indiana, extending to the eastern boundary line just north of Ohio's western border.

Among the state's major cities, Indianapolis, which was settled in 1820 and became the capital five years later, was named merely by adding the Greek word for "city," *polis*, to the state's name. The city of Fort Wayne took its name from the 1794 fort that honored its builder, General Anthony Wayne, the famous Indian fighter; it had replaced a late-seventeenth-century French fur-trading post and fort after Wayne's victory over Indians at the Battle of Fallen Timbers. Evansville, named after its founder, General Robert Evans, was established shortly after statehood as a port on the Ohio River. The future site of the University of Notre Dame, South Bend, was named for the bend of the St. Joseph River that constituted the river's southernmost point. Major cities founded much later include Hammond, named for a meatpacker, George H. Hammond, and Gary, founded by the United States Steel Company (fig. 181) in 1905 and named for E. H. Gary, chairman of the board of directors of the company.

Muncie was named for an Indian tribe that had migrated from Pennsylvania and New Jersey into Indiana. Elkhart took its name from the local river, which had been named by Indians for a heart-shaped island in the stream. Kokomo was given the name of a local Indian, and Mishawaka is a term in the Potawatomi language that

181. *U.S. Steel plant, showing all four blast furnaces, in Gary, Ind., a city founded by the steel company. Courtesy U.S. Steel Group, Pittsburgh*

means "dead tree place." The era of French traders is perpetuated in the name La Porte; the settlement received its name in the eighteenth century because it was a gateway to the frontier. Terre Haute took the French descriptive words meaning "high land," while Valparaiso applied the Spanish for "valley of paradise." Bloomington, the home of the state university, paid homage to the many flowers in the region.

Many other Indiana cities bear the names of individuals. Marion is one of many American cities that honor the Revolutionary War hero known as the "Swamp Fox," Francis Marion. Logansport took the name of a Shawnee who called himself John Logan and was killed in the War of 1812. Munster was named for Jacob Munster, an early settler. Schererville, which was originally known as Crossroads because many Indian trails crossed in the area, was named for its founder, Nicholas Scherer, who began the settlement in 1866. Seymour accepted the name of J. Seymour, a railroad civil engineer who played a role in bringing a railroad to the community in 1852.

MISSISSIPPI

Mississippi was admitted to the rapidly evolving nation on December 10, 1817, as the twentieth state (fig. 182). It took its name from the territory it was previously part of, which in turn had assumed the name of the great river that De Soto had discovered in 1541 and the Algonquin Indians had called Messisipi, meaning "big river." The state, the homeland of the Choctaw, Chickasaw, and Natchez tribes, was created out of the western part of the Mississippi Territory (the boundaries of which had changed considerably since its organization in 1798), and its boundaries were defined in the act enabling statehood. From the northwest corner of the state, the line began on the Mississippi River where the southern border of Tennessee intersected that river, then proceeded east along that border to the Tennessee River, up the Tennessee River a short distance to the mouth of Bear Creek, slightly southwest on a direct line to the northwest corner of Washington County in what later became Alabama, and then slightly southeast to the Gulf of Mexico. The line extended into the gulf to include all islands within six leagues of the shore, ran west to the eastern junction of the Pearl River with Lake Borgne (just east of Lake Pontchartrain, Louisiana), then followed the Pearl River up to 31° north latitude. The southern boundary line then continued along that parallel west to the Mississippi River, which formed the western boundary to the Tennessee border. Almost forty-eight thousand square miles are contained within these boundaries.

As mentioned previously, Biloxi, the oldest settlement, was named for the local Indians by the French fur traders who established a fort there in 1699. That region later came under Spanish control, then British, then Spanish again during the American Revolution, and finally became part of the United States when West Florida was annexed not long before Mississippi became a state. The river city of Natchez (fig. 183) also took its name from the local Indians, and settlers traveling there from Nashville, Tennessee, along the road called

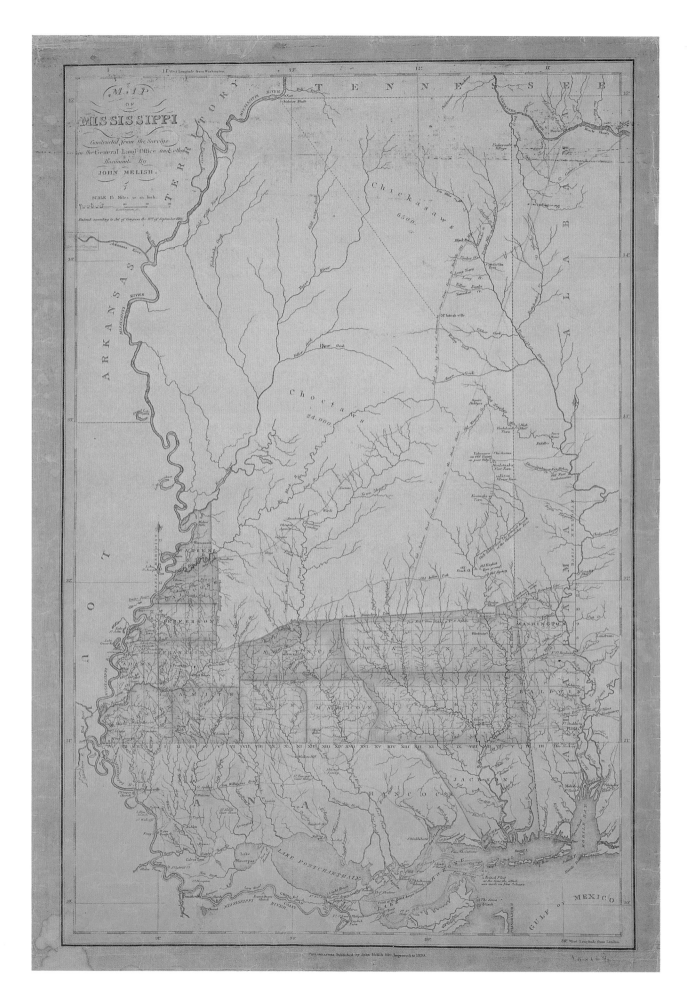

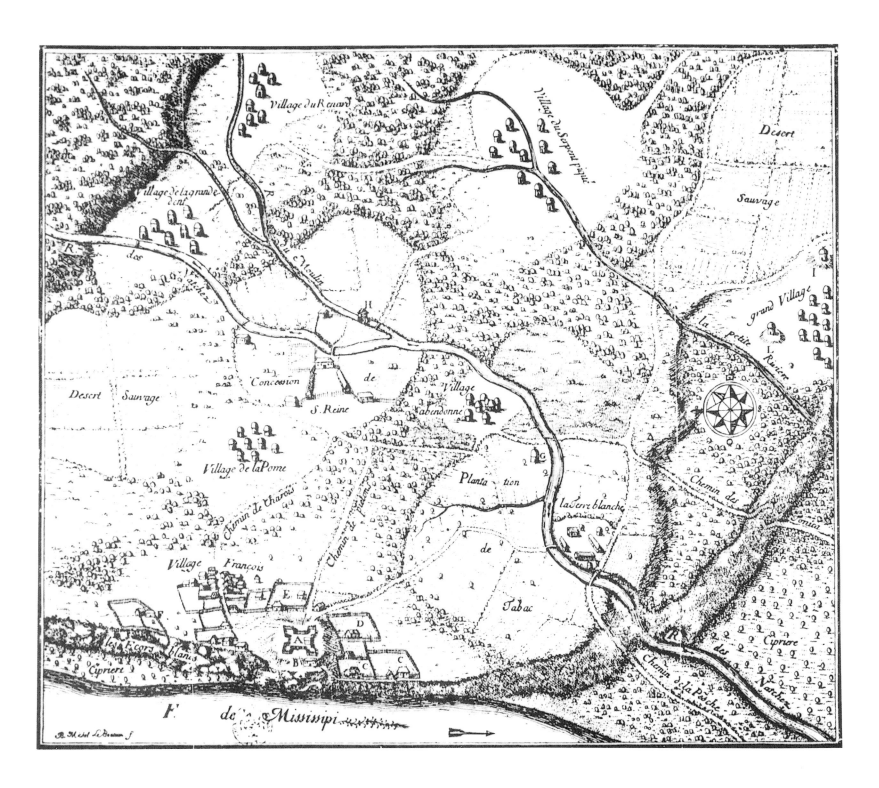

Opposite: 182. *John Melish. "Map of Mississippi." Philadelphia, 1820.*
Engraving, 52 x 37 cm. Geography and Map Division, Library of Congress,
Washington, D.C.

183. *B. Michel le Bouten. "Les Natchez." France, [1728]. Engraving, 21 x 24 cm.*
Private collection. This map accurately shows the position of the French fort
and the area of the bluff south of the settlement.

the Natchez Trace, developed the state's main cotton fields in that region. To the north along the Mississippi River, Vicksburg was named for Newitt Vick, a Methodist minister and early settler. Jackson, which was previously called La Fleur's Bluff, became the capital in 1821, and was named to honor Andrew Jackson, the hero of the nearby wars with the Creeks and Battle of New Orleans.

Meridian was so named because it was erroneously thought the word meant "junction," and a railroad junction was responsible for the town's development. Tupelo, which would gain fame as the birthplace of Elvis Presley, was the Spanish name derived from *ito opelwa*, Creek for "swamp tree." Hattiesburg was named for Hattie Hardy, the wife of the town's founder. Kosciusko honored Thaddeus Kosciusko, the Polish officer who fought in the American Revolution. Pascagoula and Yazoo City took the names of local Indian tribes. Picayune was named for the New Orleans newspaper, because a local inhabitant became editor of that periodical; a Cajun word, *picayune* originally referred to a Spanish-American coin of small denomination, only later becoming a synonym for "petty."

ILLINOIS

The twenty-first state, Illinois (fig. 184), which gained statehood on December 3, 1818, perpetuated the name of the local Indian tribe, which literally means "men." In addition to the Illini, the Sauk (or Sac) and Fox Indians inhabited the land. The state, with more than fifty-six thousand square miles, evolved from the Illinois Territory, which had been created in 1809 from that part of the Indiana Territory lying west of the Wabash River and a meridian drawn through Vincennes and running from a point on the Wabash north to the Canadian line. The state boundaries were defined as beginning at the mouth of the Wabash River and running up that river, following the Indiana boundary line to the northwest corner of that state, and then turning east along the same parallel as the northern boundary of Indiana to the middle of Lake Michigan. The boundary line proceeded north in the middle of the lake to 42°30' north latitude, then west along that parallel to the Mississippi River, down that river—the entire western border—to its confluence with the Ohio River at the southern tip of the state, and up the Ohio to the starting point.

After the opening of the Erie Canal in 1825 connected the Great Lakes and the Atlantic Ocean, the portage point that Jolliet and Marquette had used 150 years earlier on their return from the Mississippi River to Lake Michigan, and which was named for the pungent odor of the wild onions or garlic growing there, evolved into Chicago, one of America's largest and most important cities. Elsewhere in Illinois, as mentioned previously, Peoria, initially spelled Peouarea, was the name of a subtribe of the Illinois Indians. Springfield, the name of the capital city, was first attached to an American town in Massachusetts in 1641, after an English town; here it was simply descriptive. Rockford referred to a river ford marked by a rock. Decatur was named for the naval hero Stephen Decatur. Joliet took

the name (an alternative spelling) of the French explorer Louis Jolliet after being named originally for a girl, Juliet. Moline derived from *molino*, the Spanish word for "mill." The home of the state university, Champaign-Urbana, was the amalgamation of two communities, the first taking the French term for "flat country" and the second meaning "city." Evanston, the home of Northwestern University, was named for Dr. John Evans, who in 1853 participated in the purchase of land on which the university could be built.

Both Indian terms and individuals' names were attached to the developing areas around Chicago. Cicero took its name from a New York town, which in turn was named for the famous Roman orator. Naperville was named for Joseph Naper, who was an early settler in 1831. Wheaton honored Lyon W. Wheaton and Jesse Childs Wheaton, two brothers who settled the area to build a railroad station and a college. The origin of the name Niles is a matter of conjecture, but it is believed that the name comes from an influential newspaper, the *Niles Register*, owned and published by William Ogden Niles in Washington, D.C. Skokie took its name from the Potawatomi word meaning "marsh." Wilmette was named for Archange Ouilmette, the Potawatomi wife of a French trader. Waukegan is Algonquian for "old fort," and Winnetka was a name manufactured by combining the Algonquian *winne*, meaning "beautiful," with a euphonious ending.

Alton was named for Alton Easton, the founder's son. Belleville maintained the earlier French influence in the region with a name meaning "beautiful city." Similarly, Des Plaines took its name from the French name for the local river, meaning "of the flat country." De Kalb honored the self-styled Baron de Kalb (Johann Kalb), the German-born major general who served under General George Washington during the American Revolution and died at the Battle of Camden in South Carolina. Many Illinois cities developed along railroad lines. Rantoul honored Robert Rantoul, a director of the Illinois Central Railroad. Berwyn took its name from that of a Welsh town that had been previously applied in Pennsylvania. Calumet City derived from *calumet*, the French word for the Indian ceremonial peace pipe. Galesburg, birthplace of the poet Carl Sandburg, was named for the New York preacher George Gale, who settled the area in order to build a manual-labor college. Bartlett bears the name of Luther Bartlett, who started the settlement. Similarly, Danville was named for its founder, Dan Beckwith. Elgin first appeared in the United States as a place-name in Illinois and is thought to have come from the title of a hymn. Kankakee took

184. *John Melish. "Map of Illinois." Philadelphia, 1819. Engraving, 64 x 49 cm. Geography and Map Division, Library of Congress, Washington, D.C. This map depicts Illinois shortly after its admission to the Union. The system of land division is shown on the map, as are Indian towns and boundary lines.*

MAP
OF
ILLINOIS

Constructed from the Surveys
in the General Land Office and other
Documents By
JOHN MELISH.

SCALE 15 Miles to an inch.

Entered according to Act of Congress the 16th day of April 1820.

its name from the river in that region, which in turn was from an Indian word meaning "wolf," because the land was inhabited by Mahicans, whose name also means "wolf."

NEW TERRITORIES AND ALABAMA

A few months after Illinois was admitted as a state, the Adams-Onís Treaty formally defined the boundary between the United States and the Spanish possessions in North America, from the Gulf Coast to the Pacific Ocean. Beyond the Louisiana Purchase territory, the boundary line was drawn to skirt the extensive Spanish province of New Mexico and then cross the continent to the Pacific along the forty-second parallel. For five million dollars, Spain ceded to the United States all its remaining land east of the Mississippi River—East Florida and what was left of West Florida, east of the Perdido River, as well as the disputed part west of the Perdido that the United States had already annexed—and gave up all claims within Oregon Country.

After a series of battles with the Creeks and Seminoles, the former Spanish Florida east of the Perdido was organized as a territory in 1822; Andrew Jackson was its first governor. Once the territory was established, the Indians were herded into a reserve, leaving fertile land to the settlers for the growth of cotton. This enticed more settlers from Georgia to move into the region. In 1824, the territorial capital was established at Tallahassee, named for the local Indian tribe and meaning "old town" in Muskogean.

Meanwhile, in 1819, the "Arkansaw" (as it was first spelled) Territory was organized from part of the Missouri Territory. The Arkansaw Territory was defined as the area lying south of a line beginning on the Mississippi River at 36° north latitude, running west to the St. Francis River, then up that river to 36°30' north latitude and west along that parallel to the western Missouri territorial line.

Counterbalancing the two recently admitted northern states of Indiana and Illinois, Alabama joined Mississippi as the second new southern state, on December 14, 1819. The twenty-second state (fig. 185) took its name from both the river and the territory, which had been named for the Alabama, or Alibamu, Indians, part of the Creek Confederacy. The land, home to the Creeks, Cherokees, Choctaws, and Chickasaws, had been traversed by De Soto in 1539–40 and initially settled by French frontiersmen in 1702. The area was opened to American settlement after Andrew Jackson defeated the Creeks at Horseshoe Bend in 1814. The Alabama Territory was formed from the eastern part of the Mississippi Territory in 1817 and set up so that it had some access to the Gulf of Mexico.

The state's boundaries with Tennessee, Mississippi, Georgia, and Spanish Florida (subsequently the Florida Territory) were essentially the same as those defined when the Alabama Territory was established. They were defined as beginning at a point where 31° north latitude intersected the Perdido River and running east to the western boundary line of Georgia, then northward along that line to the southern boundary line of Tennessee, due west along that boundary line to the Tennessee River, up that river to the mouth of Bear Creek, southward by a direct line to the northwest corner of Washington County, Alabama, slightly southeast from that point to the Gulf of Mexico, east along the gulf to the Perdido River, and up that river to the starting point. These boundaries include more than fifty-one thousand square miles.

As noted previously, Alabama's oldest settlement, Mobile, was founded as part of the French effort to establish control of the Gulf Coast, and the name was a variation of Mauvila, the name the Spanish had assigned to the local Indians. Montgomery, the state capital from 1847 and later the first capital of the Confederate States of America, was settled in 1819 and named for the Revolutionary War hero General Richard Montgomery (fig. 186); Montgomery County, however, was named for a Major Montgomery who was killed in the Creek War. Alabama's largest city, Birmingham, did not develop until 1871, and its role in the iron and steel industry led to the natural assumption of the name of an English city with a similar identity. Bessemer's name also had an association with the steel industry; Sir Henry Bessemer of Birmingham, England, was the inventor most responsible for the modern process for manufacturing steel. Huntsville, briefly Alabama's first capital, was named for an early settler, John Hunt. Selma, where Chief Tuskaloosa is said to have met De Soto in the early sixteenth century, developed near the site of Cahaba (also spelled Cahawba), the second capital of Alabama; Selma originally was called Moore's Bluff after a Tennessean, Thomas Moore, who had built a cabin there in 1815; it received its present name, meaning "throne," in 1819 from the future vice president William Rufus King, who selected it from the name of the royal fortress in James Macpherson's *Songs of Ossian*.

The Bible, a European city, a literary village, a political figure, and Native Americans all are also represented by Alabama placenames. Dothan took a name that appears in Genesis, because a minister quoted the passage containing that name at the time the city was being christened. Florence was named by the Italian surveyor of that Alabama community after the famous Italian city. Auburn, like a previously named city in upstate New York, assumed the name of a Yorkshire village described in Oliver Goldsmith's poem "Deserted Village," in which it is called the "loveliest village of the plain." Gadsden was named for James Gadsden, the U.S. minister to Mexico who later negotiated the 1853 federal purchase of Mexican land in what became southern New Mexico and Arizona; he was visiting the Alabama settlement at the time of its naming in 1840, and the citizens seized the opportunity to recognize his accomplishments as the commissioner in charge of resettling the Seminoles in the 1820s, by adopting his name. Cullman was named for Colonel John Cullman, who arrived from Germany and founded the settlement. Eufaula took the name of a regional Creek town, as did Opelika, which means "big swamp." Sylacauga is Muskogean for "buzzard roost." Talladega,

185. John Melish. "Map of Alabama." Philadelphia, 1819. Engraving, 57 x 48 cm. Geography and Map Division, Library of Congress, Washington, D.C. This map shows Alabama at the time it became a state.

186. J. Clemens. "The Death of General Montgomery." 1798. Engraving, after a painting by John Trumbull; 64 x 53.5 cm. Old Print Shop, New York City. Montgomery, Ala., was one of several places named in honor of the general killed in the unsuccessful 1775 assault on Quebec.

which literally means "town on border," was so named because it was on the border between the Creek and Natchez tribes. Tuskegee took the name of the local Indian tribe. The third temporary state capital before the selection of Montgomery was Tuscaloosa, which is Choctaw for "black warrior" and was a variant spelling of the name of the chief who was mentioned in the chronicle from De Soto's 1540 expedition.

MAINE

From the time of the Constitutional Convention in 1787 there had essentially been an equal number of northern free states and southern slave states, divided geographically by the Mason-Dixon Line and the Ohio River. At the beginning of 1820, there were eleven free states and eleven slave states, allowing for equal representation in the U.S. Senate—a balance of power that satisfied those who sought to avoid a political crisis over slavery. Up to then, slavery had been left undisturbed in the territories of the Louisiana Purchase. When Missouri applied for statehood and declared that slavery would be permitted, northerners vehemently objected and sought to impose gradual emancipation on slaves there. The Missouri Compromise of 1820 was designed to allow Missouri to be admitted as a slave state; to maintain an immediate balance, Maine—still part of Massachusetts—would be admitted as a free state. In addition, the compromise prohibited slavery in the remaining territory north of latitude 36°30', Missouri's southern boundary. The Missouri Compromise remained in effect until 1854, when it was repealed by the Kansas-Nebraska Act.

Maine, named after a reference either to the mainland of the continent or to the French province of Maine (the feudal proprietor of which was Queen Henrietta Maria, wife of King Charles I of England), became the twenty-third state on March 15, 1820 (fig. 187). There had been a French settlement on the shore of the St. Croix River in 1604, an English settlement on land in the current state in 1607, and another French settlement on Mount Desert Island that the English destroyed in 1613. After all of these temporary settlements were abandoned, Sir Ferdinando Gorges received the land as a grant from the Council for New England in 1622, and then as a royal charter in 1639. The Massachusetts Bay Colony claimed jurisdiction over Maine in 1652, and Maine formally became part of the royal colony of Massachusetts in 1691. At the end of the American Revolution, the 1783 Treaty of Paris vaguely defined Maine's eastern, northern, and northwestern borders with Canada, from the source of the St. Croix River (which completed the eastern boundary line) to the northeast corner of New Hampshire, as a line drawn north "to the highlands, along the said Highlands which divide those rivers that empty into the river St. Lawrence, from those which fall into the Atlantic Ocean, to the northwesternmost head of Connecticut River. . . ."

Maine's boundaries, encompassing more than thirty-three thousand square miles, were the focus of lengthy contention—other than the previously described border between Maine and New Hampshire, which was settled in 1740. The current boundaries with Canada were not completely settled until 1842, when the Webster-Ashburton Treaty

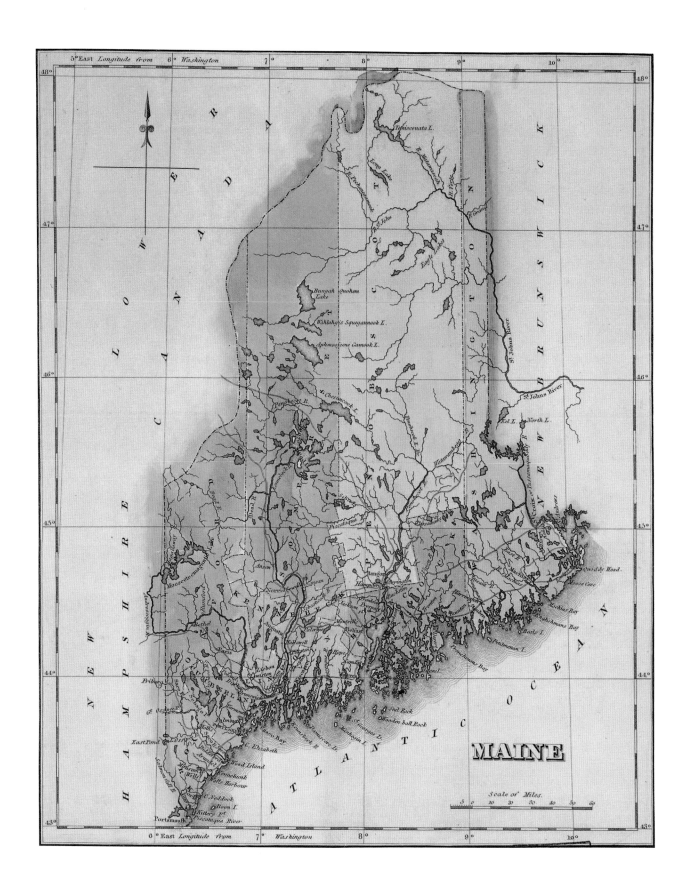

187. Cartographer unknown. "Geographical, Historical, and Statistical Map of Maine." In H. C. Carey and I. Lea's A Complete Historical, Chronological & Geographical American Atlas, *Philadelphia, 1820.* Engraving, 48 x 28 cm. Geography and Map Division, Library of Congress, Washington, D.C. This map shows Maine at the time it became a state.

was signed. In the gradual development of a permanent international border between Maine and Canada, major concern focused on the timberland and fertile soil of the Aroostook, meaning "beautiful river," and St. John river basins in the northern part of the state. Along the potential boundary line stood the Madawaska settlement. This had originally been settled by French Acadians who had found refuge among the Indians. But the state of Maine planned to organize the settlement as a township. According to the finally agreed-on terms, the St. John River became part of the boundary to the north, Madawaska was divided by the boundary line, and the territory to the west was partitioned by an arbitrarily defined line through uninhabited land (fig. 188).

The complexity of the boundary between Maine and Canada is best appreciated by presenting Article I of the Webster-Ashburton Treaty:

It is hereby agreed and declared that the line of boundary shall be as follows: Beginning at the monument at the source of the river St. Croix as designated and agreed to by the Commissioners under the fifth article of the treaty of 1794, between the Governments of the United States and Great Britain; thence north, following the exploring line run and marked by the surveyors of the two Governments in the years 1817 and 1818, under the fifth article of the treaty of Ghent, to its intersection with the river St. John, and to the middle of the channel thereof; thence up the middle of the channel of the said river St. John, to the mouth of the river St. Francis; thence up the middle of the channel of the said river St. Francis, to the mouth of the river St. Francis; thence up the middle of the channel of the said river St. Francis, and of the lakes through which it flows to the outlet of the Lake Pohenagamook; thence southwesterly in a straight line to a point on the northwest branch of the river St. John, which point shall be ten miles distant from the main branch of the St. John, in a straight line, and in the nearest direction; but if the said point shall be found to be less than seven miles from the nearest point of the summit or crest of the highlands that divide those rivers which empty themselves into the river Saint Lawrence from those which fall into the river Saint John, then the said point shall be made to recede down the said northwest branch of the river St. John, to a point seven miles in a straight line from the said summit or crest; thence, in a straight line, in a course about south, eight degrees west, to the point where the parallel of latitude 46°25' north intersects the southwest branch of the St. John's; thence, southerly, by the said branch to the source thereof in the highlands of the Metjarmette portage; thence, down along the said highlands which divide the water which empty themselves into the river Saint Lawrence from those which fall into the Atlantic Ocean, to the head of Hall's Stream; thence down the middle of said stream, till the line thus run intersects the old line of boundary surveyed and marked by Valentine and Collins, previously in the year 1774, as the 45th degree of north latitude, and which has been known and understood to be the line of actual division between the states of New York and Vermont on one side and the British province of Canada on the other; and from said point of intersection, west, along the said dividing line, as heretofore known and understood, to the Iroquois or St. Lawrence River.

Maine's largest city, Portland, took its name from a point on the Maine coast, Portland Head, Maine, which was so named because it reminded the inhabitants of the Portland Bill, the tip of a narrow strip of land jutting out from the southern shore of England. The capital, Augusta, was named in 1797 for Pamela Augusta Dearborn, the daughter of a prominent citizen and Revolutionary War officer, Henry Dearborn. Bangor was named because its slate deposits resembled those in that town in Wales. Orono, the home of the state university, was named for Joseph Orono, an Indian chief of partial French descent who had sided with the Americans during the Revolution. Biddeford, Scarborough, and Yarmouth took the names of English towns; Yarmouth, the oldest of the three, was named in 1680. Windham is the spelling that represents the pronunciation of Wymondham in England. Saco adopted as its name the Algonquian word for "river mouth"; Kennebunk means "long cut at" in the same Indian language; and Skowhegan, which translates as "watching place," was so named because it referred to a location where the Indians searched for Atlantic salmon swimming upriver to spawn.

188. John Mitchell. "The so-called red-line map."
London, 1755. Engraving, hand-colored, 137 x 196 cm.
Courtesy Osher Map Library, University of South Maine,
Portland, Maine. During the 1842 negotiations to define
the boundary between Canada and Maine, Prime Minister
Sir Robert Peel examined a copy of John Mitchell's 1755
map that had been annotated by King George III's
negotiator for the Treaty of Paris in 1783 (see fig. 90).
It agreed with American claims running northward from
the mouth of the St. Croix River almost to the
St. Lawrence River.

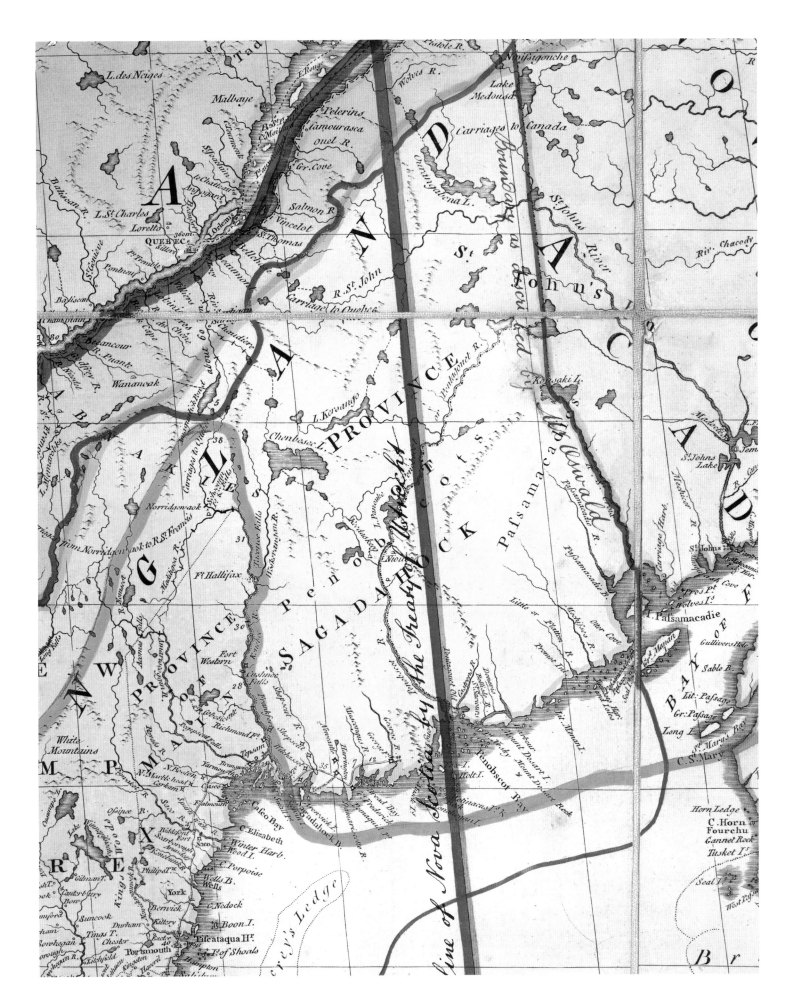

Fulfilling the Missouri Compromise of 1820, Missouri, the native home of the Osage and Missouri tribes, became the twenty-fourth state on August 10, 1821 (fig. 189). In 1812, when Louisiana was admitted to the Union, the name of the District of Louisiana had been changed to the Missouri Territory. Initially that territory included all of the Louisiana Purchase lands except for those within what became the established boundaries of the state of Louisiana. In 1819, as mentioned previously, the Arkansaw Territory had been organized out of the southern portion of the Missouri Territory. After Missouri became a state, the rest of the Louisiana Purchase, to the north and west, remained unorganized until the establishment of the Iowa Territory in 1838, Minnesota Territory in 1849, and Kansas and Nebraska territories in 1854 (in addition to the unorganized Indian Territory, west of Arkansas, which eventually became Oklahoma). Missouri's boundaries were defined with a peculiar irregularity at the southeast corner, to accommodate a landowner who wanted to have his property included in the state.

Therefore, the southeastern boundary began in the Mississippi River at 36° north latitude, then ran west along that parallel to the St. Francis River and up the middle of that river to 36°30' north latitude. The line continued west along that parallel until it was intersected by a meridian passing through the middle of the mouth of the Kansas River at the point where it empties into the Missouri River. The western boundary line originally followed that meridian north all the way to 40°30' north latitude; from there, the northern boundary line ran eastward along that parallel (forming the border with what later became Iowa) until it passed through the rapids of the Des Moines River; then the line ran down along the main channel of that river to its entrance into the Mississippi River, which the line followed back to the starting point. In 1836, the western boundary north of the Kansas River was extended to the Missouri River when Missouri took title to Indian land. Missouri currently contains almost seventy thousand square miles.

The state's name came from the Algonquian name for a tribe living near the mouth of the Missouri River. The name Missouri, which means "place of the big canoes," moved, in an often occurring progression, from river to territory to state. As part of the Louisiana Purchase, it was logical that the state would honor Thomas Jefferson in selecting the name of its capital: Jefferson City. There is another, somewhat aberrant, association with Jefferson that exists in the state. The University of Missouri, located in Columbia, was the first land-grant university to be established on the land acquired through the Louisiana Purchase. One of Jefferson's relatives agreed to a request that Jefferson's original tombstone be moved to the campus. Currently it remains there, much to the dismay of the curators of Jefferson's famous Virginia home, Monticello (fig. 190), where the former president is buried.

Two Missouri cities that were gateways to the West took the names of saints, for distinctly different reasons. As mentioned previously, St. Louis, established as a fur-trading post in 1764, was named for the canonized French king Louis IX, to assert the settlement's allegiance to France (ruled at the time by King Louis XV). St. Joseph was named by its founder, Joseph Robidoux, for his name's saint. St. Charles, St. John, St. Peter, and St. Ann also appear as place-names in Missouri. St. Charles is the oldest city on the Missouri River. It was first settled by the French fur trader Louis Blanchette and originally called Les Petites Côtes (the Little Hills). A stop for the Lewis and Clark expedition, St. Charles was incorporated shortly thereafter, in 1809, and it served as the first capital of Missouri, from 1821 to 1826. Religion also played a role in the naming of Joplin, which took its name from the Reverend H. G. Joplin, who established the first Methodist church in the region.

Kansas City was named because of its location at the confluence of the Kansas (named for an Indian tribe) and Missouri rivers. Independence, which was platted in 1827 on the south bank of the Missouri River and incorporated in 1849, is one of about twenty cities in the United States to take that patriotic name; Fort Osage was built in 1808 on the site that would become Independence. Joseph Smith and his Latter-day Saints, or Mormons, stayed in the region in 1831–33 before eventually moving to Commerce, Illinois, which they renamed Nauvoo. Between 1841 and 1849, Independence was the starting point for wagon trains moving west on the Santa Fe Trail. Creve Coeur—the French *crève-coeur* means "heartbreak"—first appeared on the North American continent as a name that La Salle applied to a fort he built in Illinois in 1680. Cape Girardeau also has a long history. In 1733, Jean Giradot, a French soldier, built a trading post on a promontory overlooking the Mississippi River, and the locale came to be known as Cape Giradot. Sixty years later, Louis Lorimier, under the auspices of the Spanish governor-general who at the time controlled the region, established a military post called Lorimont. A city was incorporated there in 1806, and it adopted the original name, changing the spelling to Cape Girardeau. That city became the busiest port on the Mississippi River between St. Louis and Memphis. Another city with a name derived from the French is Florissant, which means "flourishing."

Arnold, Ballwin, and Chesterfield were all settled early. Arnold began as a French settlement at the junction of the Mississippi and Meramec, meaning "catfish," rivers in 1776. When the area came under Spanish control, a ferry service was established across the Meramec River to provide access to El Camino Real (the Royal Road), the main road from New Orleans to the West. Ballwin, the only city with that spelling in the United States, was founded by John Ball in 1800 and originally called Ballshow; when the city was incorporated in 1837, the name was changed to Ballwin to indicate that it would "win out" in importance over the neighboring city of Manchester. Chesterfield's first settler was Jean Baptist Point du Sable, a Haitian

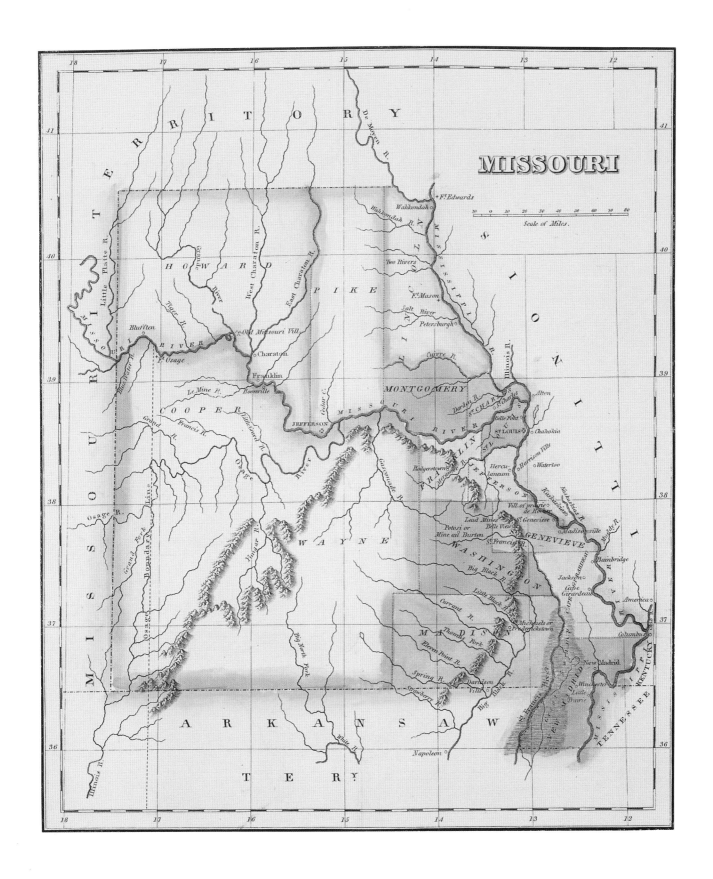

189. *Cartographer unknown. "Geographical, Historical, and Statistical Map of Missouri." In H. C. Carey and I. Lea's* A Complete Historical, Chronological & Geographical American Atlas, *Philadelphia, 1822. Engraving, 48 x 28 cm. Geography and Map Division, Library of Congress, Washington, D.C. This map was published the year after Missouri became a state under the Missouri Compromise.*

190. Thomas Jefferson is buried at his home in Virginia, but his original tombstone is not located there. Top: When Jefferson's heirs replaced his original tombstone, which was in disrepair, it was given in 1883 to the University of Missouri, because it was the first state university developed on Louisiana Purchase land. Courtesy University of Missouri, Columbia. Bottom: Jane Braddick Peticolas. "View of the West Front of Monticello and Garden." 1825. Watercolor on paper, 34 x 46 cm. Courtesy the Thomas Jefferson Memorial Foundation, Inc., Charlottesville, Va.

fur trader, who went on to become the first trader at what would later be Chicago. In 1790, Justus Post laid out the town of Chesterfield and assigned the name, the origin of which is debated; it derives from the English Lord Chesterfield or a breed of hog or a variety of potato.

The origin of the name Lee's Summit, which was established in 1865 and was the highest point on the rail line between Kansas City and St. Louis, is also contested. "Lee" honors either General Robert E. Lee or Dr. Pleasant Lea (with spelling changed), who died in the Civil War. Sedalia derived from adding a Latin ending to "Sed," the nickname of Sarah Smith, daughter of the city's founder, General George R. Smith. Hannibal, which was popularized in Mark Twain's *The Adventures of Huckleberry Finn,* was named for the famous Carthagin-ian general. The name had previously been used by a New York community during the era of assigning classical names. In Missouri, interestingly, nearby is the town of Fabius, named for the Roman general who opposed Hannibal. Afton took the name of Johann George Aff, an early settler.

Among other Missouri cities, Springfield, the state's third-largest city, took a name that appears throughout the United States and suggests a geographic characteristic. O'Fallon took the name of a surgeon in the Continental Army. Moberly was named for a railroad official, Colonel W. E. Moberly, and Kirkwood honored James Pugh Kirkwood, chief engineer of the Pacific Railroad, in 1849. Webster Groves took its name from Daniel Webster, the statesman-orator.

CHAPTER NINE

Continued Population Shifts and State Development

THE ERIE CANAL AND THE RAILROADS

As the United States spread outward, it also demonstrated a new assertiveness. In December 1823, President James Monroe issued what came to be called the Monroe Doctrine, which in part—as a response to the Russian claim of rights to Alaska, extending to 51° north latitude in Oregon Country—declared that the young nation would oppose any future European attempts to colonize additional areas of the North and South American continents. Two years later, the Erie Canal, the first major westward transportation route in the United States, opened up much of the interior of the country to the transatlantic trade by joining Lake Erie, and therefore all of the Great Lakes, to the Hudson River, which flowed south to New York City and emptied into the Atlantic Ocean (fig. 191). This long man-made ditch turned New York City into the leading port and city in the nation, earned for New York State the nickname Empire State (fig. 192), and resulted in the development of western New York. Lockport (fig. 193), Brockport, and Fairport are among the many cities that grew up along the canal, attesting to its importance in the economic growth of the region. The canal passed through Rochester, which was incorporated in 1817; because of its position on the Genesee River, with its falls providing water power, it became the nation's first boomtown and major producer of flour (fig. 194). Incidentally, all but five Rochesters in the United States were named for the city in England; the exceptions are the one in New York, named for its developer, Nathaniel Rochester, and ones in Indiana, Michigan, Minnesota, and Pennsylvania, all named for the town in New York State.

The first so-called railway line in the United States was established in 1826: a horse-drawn conveyance near Quincy, Massachusetts. Two years later, the Baltimore and Ohio Railroad (fig. 195) began as a horse-drawn operation, which would shortly be converted to the first steam railway (fig. 196). As the population spread from the coastal regions across the Appalachian Mountains, it created the stimulus for building railroads. In the 1840s, a group of Georgia businessmen had track laid across the southern end of that mountain

Opposite: 191. *Cartographer unknown. "New York 1825." In Cadwallader D. Colden's* Memoir . . . of the New York Canals, *New York, 1825. Engraving, hand-colored, 29 x 44 cm. Private collection. This map shows the state of New York with its counties in the year the Erie Canal opened for traffic. The route of the canal is depicted, and an inset provides a profile of the canal.*

192. *The Empire State Building, 1981. Located at 350 Fifth Avenue in New York City, the building is 1,250 feet high and was the tallest building in the world from its opening in 1931 until 1972.*

Above: 193. *Artist unknown. Two depictions of Lockport, N.Y., one of many cities that developed along the Erie Canal. In Cadwallader D. Colden's* Memoir . . . of the New York Canals, *New York, 1825. Left: "Process of Excavation, Lockport." Lithograph, 14 x 20 cm. Right: "Deep Cutting, Lockport." Lithograph, 11.5 x 18.5 cm. Private collection*

Opposite, bottom: 194. *G. G. Lange Darmstadt. "Rochester." New York: Charles Magnus. Copperplate engraving, after an 1853 lithograph; 11.5 x 19 cm. Private collection. The nation's first boomtown, as a result of its position along the Erie Canal.*

195. *The Baltimore and Ohio Railroad began in 1828 as a horse-drawn operation for passengers and freight traffic. Right: Herbert Holtham. Sketch of a horse-drawn cart on the Baltimore and Ohio Railroad tracks. In Holtham's "Diary of Travels 1831." Pen and ink on paper, 10 x 18 cm. Private collection. Below: Joshua Barney. "Map of the Country Embracing the Various Routes Surveyed for the Balt. & Ohio Rail Road. . . ." Philadelphia, 1829. Engraving, 27 x 61 cm. Geography and Map Division, Library of Congress, Washington, D.C. Peter Force Map Collection, no. 438. This is the second published survey map of the Baltimore and Ohio Railroad, showing the established tracks as solid lines and surveyed routes as dashed lines.*

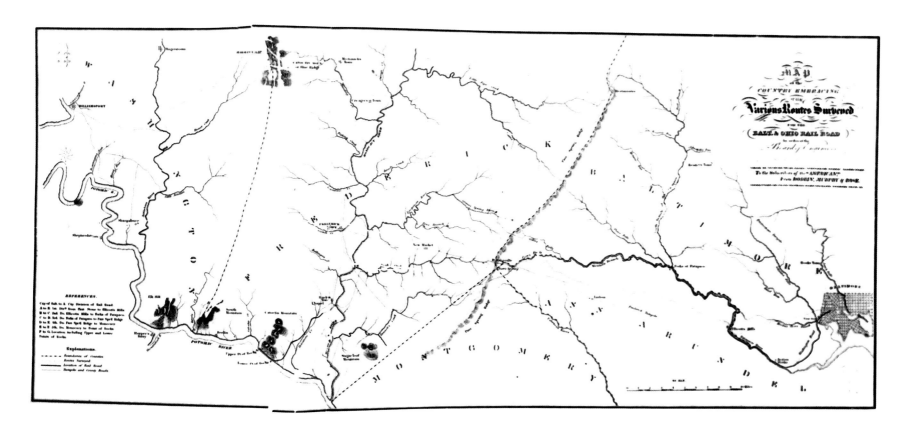

196. *Thomas B. Craig. John Stevens's experimental steam locomotive at Hoboken, N.J. In* Morton Memorial: A History of the Stevens Institute of Technology . . . , *1905. Oil on canvas, 49.5 x 63.5 cm. Courtesy the Library of the Stevens Institute of Technology, Hoboken*

chain. The completion of the railroad led to the expansion of Chattanooga, Tennessee, and the development of the southeastern end of the rail line, which was initially called Terminus. In 1843, when former governor Wilson Lumpkin visited the area accompanied by his sixteen-year-old daughter, Martha, Terminus was officially chartered as Marthasville. Two years later, the name was changed to Atlanta to reflect the terminus of the Western and Atlantic Railroad.

The population of the United States grew rapidly during the first half of the nineteenth century, related mostly to accelerated immigration. About 130,000 immigrants arrived during the 1820s. This figure increased to 540,000 in the 1830s, to 1.5 million in the 1840s, and to 2.8 million in the 1850s. During the first half of the nineteenth century, more than 40 percent of the immigrants were Irish, about 30 percent were German, and only 15 percent were English. The country's population increased from 9.6 million in 1820 to more than 23 million in 1850, an increase of almost 150 percent in thirty years.

REMOVAL OF INDIANS FROM THE EAST

The basic principle that two objects cannot occupy the same place at the same time dominated the movement of settlers as they spread from the established communities to new frontiers. Their displacement of Native Americans persisted and accelerated. Between 1820 and 1850, Americans initiated and intensified a national policy for the removal of Indians. Federal and state officials made plans to move them to lands west of the Mississippi River. During the Monroe administration, the Osage, Quapaw (also called the Arkansas), and Caddo Indians were given the option of becoming citizens or exchanging their properties for new lands in the West. Many large groups migrated west.

During Andrew Jackson's presidency in 1829–37, the removal of Indians from their native lands increased. In 1830, Congress passed the Indian Removal Act, sanctioning Georgia's and Mississippi's disregard of previous federal treaties and permitting the expulsion of Indians. The act gave the president the authority to grant land in the western part of the Louisiana Purchase territory to Indian tribes in exchange for the land they relinquished in the East. That year, the Choctaws signed a treaty calling for their removal from Mississippi within three years. Two years later, the members of the Creek Confederacy yielded and agreed to leave their lands. The Creeks' migration was shortly followed by that of the Chickasaws. Despite resistance, Georgia gradually took over the lands of the Cherokee Nation, and the final curtain for these Native Americans came down in the winter of 1838–39, when General Winfield Scott led the remaining members of the tribe west to the recently designated Indian Territory (present-day Oklahoma); more than four thousand of the approximately fifteen thousand Cherokees died during this "Trail of Tears." Farther south, after a war from 1835 to 1842, most of the Seminoles were rounded up and moved from their Florida homes to the Indian Territory, although a few thousand managed to remain in the Everglades. Already relocated to the Indian Territory by then, the Choctaws and Chickasaws had been settled just north of the Red River, which separated the United States from what was then the Republic of Texas; the Creeks and Cherokees were given land north of the Choctaws and Chickasaws. They and the Seminoles became known as the Five Civilized Tribes.

From what had been the Northwest Territory, the Shawnee, Lenape (Delaware), and Wyandot tribes were deposed from their lands and moved west of the Missouri River. Similarly, the Sauk (Sac) and Fox Indians were moved west of the Mississippi River, where they were constantly threatened by the more powerful and warlike Sioux. In 1832, a twenty-three-year-old clerk in a general store, Abraham Lincoln, served in the Black Hawk War, during which Sauk (Sac) and Fox Indians opposed to removal conducted raids before being pursued from Illinois into the Wisconsin Territory. North of the Indian Territory, some of the Plains tribes—the Osage, Iowa, and Kansa—established settlements between the Arkansas and Platte rivers; to the north of the Platte, the Pawnee and Sioux were located. The United States erected Fort Leavenworth along the Missouri River and Fort Gibson along the Arkansas River as frontier outposts to protect whites from the Indians and at times to intervene in intertribal conflicts. Meanwhile, in the Northeast, the Six Nations of the Iroquois Confederacy, which had been guaranteed safety on their reservations by the New York state government, found their land exploited by land speculators.

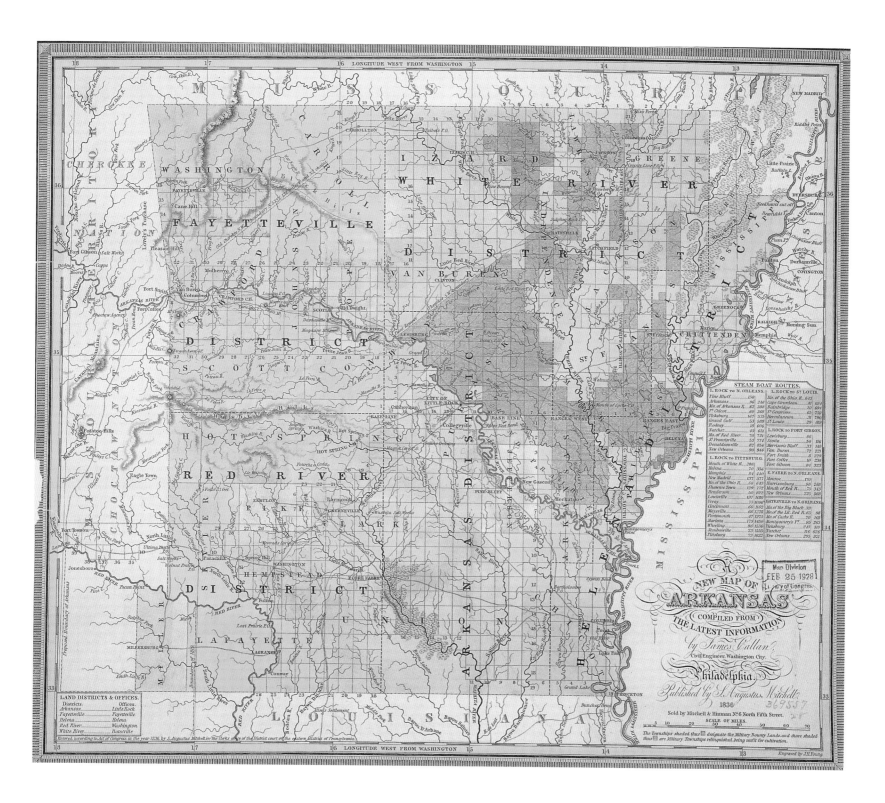

Arkansas, named for the Arkansea tribe (also called the Quapaw) and village that marked the southernmost point of the Mississippi trip of Jolliet and Marquette in 1673, was admitted as the twenty-fifth state on June 15, 1836 (fig. 197). It was the first state to join the Union in nearly fifteen years (the longest such gap until the twentieth century), after a period of less than five years (1816–21) during which six states (Indiana, Mississippi, Illinois, Alabama, Maine, and Missouri) had been admitted. The state's name in the tribe's Siouan language literally means "downstream people." It was once the homelands of the Quapaw, Osage, and Caddo tribes. The French established the first European settlement there, called Arkansas Post, in 1686, along the Arkansas River a few miles from the Mississippi. When the territory was created in 1819 out of the Missouri Territory, it was named Arkansaw. The "w" was changed to an "s" when statehood was achieved.

The state's boundaries, which encompass more than fifty-three thousand square miles, began in the middle of the main channel of the Mississippi River at 36° north latitude, at the southeast corner of Missouri; ran west along that parallel to the middle of the St. Francis River, then up that river to 36°30' north latitude; and followed that parallel, the rest of the southern Missouri boundary, west to the southwest corner of Missouri. The western boundary was defined by a treaty executed with the Cherokee Nation in 1828: a straight line ran southeast until it passed just to the west of Fort Smith, turned almost due south to the south side of the Red River, and followed what was then the Mexican border (soon to become the Texas border) to the northwest corner of Louisiana. From there it ran east along the Louisiana state line to the middle of the Mississippi River, then northward up the river to the starting point at 36° north latitude.

The name of the territorial and then state capital, settled in 1821 and incorporated in 1835, derived from the fact that early voyagers on the Mississippi River had named a rock along the shore Little Rock, because it was smaller than a larger one upstream. In the region of the smaller rock, the future state capital evolved. Texarkana was appropriately named, because it was a city that straddled the two states of Texas and Arkansas. Hot Springs describes its geological characteristic; it is believed that De Soto passed through the area in 1541. In 1832, Hot Springs was designated the first federal reservation for public recreation, a forerunner of the National Park System. Fort Smith was named for General Thomas Smith, who built the fort in 1817 on the shores of the Arkansas and Poteau (the French word for "post" or "pole") rivers to control the Cherokees.

Arkadelphia combines the first syllable of the state's name with the Greek ending meaning "brotherly place." Benton and Bentonville both honor Senator Thomas Hart Benton of Missouri, who was known as "Old Bullion" because he staunchly opposed any easing of the gold standard. Blytheville took its name either from the title of Nathaniel Hawthorne's novel *The Blithedale Romance*, because one of the people responsible for the naming was impressed with the work, or from the Reverend Henry Blythe, a local minister. Conway was named for the pre-Revolutionary British general H. S. Conway, a man who strongly supported the colonies. Jonesboro honored William A. Jones, who was a supporter of establishing the city and its county. Paragould combined the name of two railroad magnates, J. W. Paramore and Jay Gould.

Native Americans are represented by the cities of Pocahontas, named for the Indian princess at Jamestown, and Osceola, named for the famous Seminole chief. Russellville took its name from the local mountain, which was named for the geologist I. C. Russell or an early resident, Dr. Thomas Russell. Hope, the birthplace of President William Jefferson Clinton, was named for Hope Loughborough, daughter of a director of the Cairo and Fulton Railroad.

MICHIGAN

In 1836, the Wisconsin Territory was created, taking its name from the river, originally spelled Ouisconsing or Ouariconsint—the same river that, in a circuitous manner, would provide a derivation for the name Oregon. The territory was formed out of the part of the Michigan Territory that was west of the present state of Michigan.

Michigan became the twenty-sixth state, maintaining the balance between free and slave states after the admission of Arkansas, on January 26, 1837 (fig. 198). The land included within the boundaries of the state, which had been home to the Ojibwa (Ojibway), Ottawa, and Potawatomi Indians, had a relatively long history of settlement, beginning with Étienne Brulé's encampment at Sault Ste. Marie in about 1618, the mission at St. Ignace from which Marquette began his voyage of discovery of the Mississippi River with Jolliet in 1673, and Cadillac's establishment of a fort in 1701 on the shore of the strait joining Lakes Erie and St. Clair.

The Michigan Territory had been established in 1805, comprising that part of the Indiana Territory lying north of a parallel passing through the southernmost bend of Lake Michigan and east of a line drawn from the same point through the middle of Lake Michigan and north to the Canadian border. The boundaries of the state of Michigan were considerably more complex. The southern boundary line began at a point where the northern boundary of the state of Ohio intersected the eastern boundary of the state of Indiana, and it ran east along the Ohio line until it intersected the border between the United States and Canada in Lake Erie. The state line then followed the international boundary line through the Detroit River,

198. *T. G. Bradford. "Michigan." Boston, 1838. Engraving, 36 x 28 cm. Geography and Map Division, Library of Congress, Washington, D.C. This is the earliest map of the new state of Michigan in the collection of the Library of Congress.*

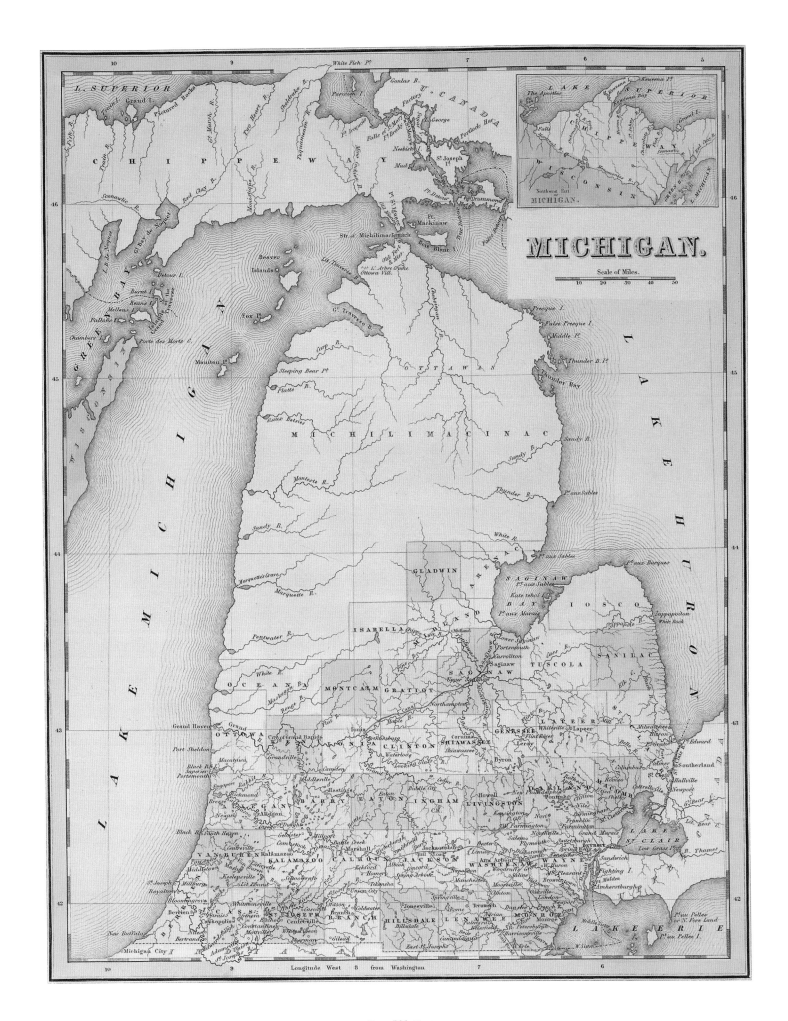

MICHIGAN.

Scale of Miles.

Lake St. Clair, the St. Clair River, Lake Huron, the St. Marys River, and Lake Superior. It continued in that lake to the mouth of the Montreal River (along the border with present-day Wisconsin), through the main channel of that river to the middle of the Lake of the Desert, and then directly southeast to the nearest headwaters of the Menominee River, from an Algonquian term meaning "wild rice"; the line then ran through the middle of the fork and continued down the main channel of that river to the center of the "most usual ship channel" in Green Bay, an inlet of Lake Michigan. The boundary line continued to the middle of Lake Michigan, turned and ran south to the northern boundary of the state of Indiana, then due east along that boundary line to the northeast corner of Indiana, and finally a very short distance south along the eastern boundary of Indiana to the starting point.

When the state of Wisconsin was established in 1848, the boundary between it and the Upper Peninsula of Michigan was redefined. It passed through Lake Superior to the mouth of the Montreal River, through the middle of the main channel of the river to its headwaters, then in a straight line to the center of the channel between the Middle and South islands in the Lake of the Desert; then it ran in a direct line to the southern shore of Lake Brule, along that shore and down the Brule River to the main channel of the Menominee River, and down that channel to the center of the "most usual ship channel" of Green Bay. Michigan currently contains almost fifty-nine thousand square miles.

Michigan's name was taken from that of the lake, which in turn was derived from the Ojibwa tribal name Michiguma, meaning "big waters." The name Detroit, from the French term for "strait," was a logical designation because of the community's location along the short waterway between Lakes Erie and St. Clair. Originally a fort, Detroit was settled in 1701 by a group led by Antoine de La Mothe, sieur de Cadillac, who is appropriately honored with the name of a Michigan city, Cadillac. Detroit was transferred from French to British control toward the end of the French and Indian War and became part of the United States in 1796. Long before it evolved into the center of the automobile industry (fig. 199), Detroit served as the

199. *A five-passenger 1909 Model T; automobile pioneer Henry Ford dominated the industry from 1908 to 1928 with this mass-produced standard model, selling some 15 million cars before replacing it with the Model A. Courtesy Henry Ford Museum and Greenfield Village, Dearborn, Mich.*

territorial capital and from 1837 to 1847 as the state capital, which was then moved to Lansing. That city was named for John Lansing, an eighteenth- and early-nineteenth-century political figure who had been honored with the naming of a village in New York State from which settlers emigrated to Michigan, taking the name with them.

Battle Creek, where an Ottawa village was originally located, became a trading post in 1826; the "Battle" part of the name derived from a dispute between a local Indian and a land surveyor. The area where Inkster—named for Robert Inkster, who built a sawmill there—developed was first settled in 1825 and initially called Moulin Rouge. The location of the University of Michigan was named for the wives of the first two settlers, who arrived in 1824. The two wives, both named Ann, trained the grapevines into an arbor, leading to the designation Anns' Arbor, from which the "s'" was subsequently dropped. Ypsilanti was named for Demetrios Ypsilanti, a Greek who fought for Greek independence in the 1820s. The city of Holland was given its name by the Reverend Albertus Christiaan Van Raalte, who established that settlement of Dutch immigrants in 1847.

Indian names are well represented. Pontiac was named for the great chief of the Ottawas in that region, who terrorized British colonists even after the French and Indian War had come to an end (fig. 200). Owosso was also named for a chief, an Ojibwa named Wasso. Kalamazoo, which was originally called Bronson for the man who platted the area in 1831, took its permanent name from the Potawatomi Kikalamazoo, meaning "rapids at river crossing." Okemos means "little chief," and Muskegon means "swamp at," both in Ojibwa. Wyandotte is the name of an Indian tribe (also spelled Wyandot). Saginaw is Ojibwa for "place where the Sauks live," and Ishpeming also took an Ojibwa term, one that means "high place," because the settlement was located at the watershed between Lake Michigan and Lake Superior.

English words describing physical features also show up in Michigan place-names. Flint took its name from the river, which was called that because it was a source of flint stones. Grand Rapids, which was the site of an Ottawa village, began as a trading post; in 1850, when it was incorporated, it took its name from the area's rapids on the Grand River, which runs through the city. Traverse City denotes a place for portage of canoes across the mouth of the bay off northeastern Lake Michigan. In addition, as mentioned previously, the French word *sault*, meaning "waterfall," was used in the naming of Sault Ste. Marie.

200. *Jerry Farnsworth. Portrait of Pontiac, chief of the Ottawas. 1935. Oil on canvas. Courtesy Museum of the American Indian, Smithsonian Institution, Washington, D.C. Heye Foundation. Pontiac led a major rebellion by allied Indian tribes in the 1760s, besieging Detroit and attacking other British outposts.*

Several other individuals' names have been perpetuated by Michigan cities. Classical times are represented by Romulus, one of the mythical founders of Rome. The period of exploration was remembered by the naming of Marquette; this is particularly appropriate because Father Marquette, the codiscoverer of the Mississippi River, is buried in the state, on the eastern shore of Lake Michigan. Hamtramck took the name of a colonel who fought in the French and Indian War and commanded the garrison at Detroit. Wayne honored General Anthony Wayne, who was victorious over the Indians at the 1794 Battle of Fallen Timbers. Dearborn was named for Henry Dearborn, secretary of war in Thomas Jefferson's cabinet. Jackson, initially called Jacksonborough, took its name in honor of President Andrew Jackson, while Taylor was named for President Zachary Taylor. Ludington, which boasts the site of Father Marquette's grave, was named after James Ludington, an investor who bought most of the timberland in the region and built a sawmill there in the 1860s; the city was incorporated in 1867 and is the last city on this side of Lake Michigan to maintain ferry service to Wisconsin (at Manitowoc). Roseville was named in 1840 by the area's first postmaster, William Rose, to honor his father, Dennison Rose, who fought in the War of 1812.

THE MORMON MIGRATION

During the last two decades of the first half of the nineteenth century, a major incursion was made into the interior of the continent. The trek, which took place over several years, had its origin on a farm (fig. 201) in Palmyra (named for the ancient city in present-day Syria), New York, where Joseph Smith said he received from the angel Moroni gold plates and magic spectacles that permitted him to read the inscriptions on the plates, indicating that the Indians were the lost tribes of Israel and that "saints" were commanded to redeem the pagans. The Book of Mormon was published in 1830. The next year, Smith led his small group of followers to Kirtland, Ohio, to escape neighbors' hostility. The Mormons—officially the Church of Jesus Christ of Latter-day Saints—moved on first to Independence, Missouri, and then to Commerce, Illinois, where they founded a settlement that they called Nauvoo. In 1844, Smith was murdered by a mob; Brigham Young assumed leadership and became known as "the Prophet" (fig. 202). In 1846, the Mormons left Nauvoo, followed the north fork of the Platte River, and continued westward to the Great Basin and Great Salt Lake, which they reached in July 1847 (fig. 203). By 1848, five thousand Mormons had settled in the region, which they named Deseret, a term that appears in the Book of Mormon and means "honeybee." It was organized as the Utah Territory, named for the Ute Indian tribe, in 1850, and Brigham Young was its first governor.

201. *Joseph Smith's cabin, a reconstruction in Palmyra, N.Y.; on the second floor of the original cabin, Smith said, he was visited by the angel Moroni and told where to find the Tablets on the Hill Cumorah. Courtesy Museum of Church History and Art, the Church of Jesus Christ of Latter-day Saints, Salt Lake City, Utah*

202. *Danquart Weggland. Portrait of Brigham Young.
1873. Oil on canvas, 77 x 61 cm. Courtesy Museum of
Church History and Art, the Church of Jesus Christ of
Latter-day Saints, Salt Lake City, Utah*

203. *Minerva Teichert. Madonna 1847. 1936.
Oil on canvas, 183 x 335 cm. Courtesy Museum
of Church History and Art, the Church of Jesus Christ
of Latter-day Saints, Salt Lake City, Utah.
This painting depicts the Mormons' trek westward
to the Great Salt Lake.*

CHAPTER TEN

Closing the Ring

FLORIDA

James K. Polk, who has been dubbed the first "dark horse" nominee in presidential history, was elected the eleventh president on an expansionist platform. After he took office in 1845, he accomplished his aims, effectively establishing the current southwestern, western, and northwestern continental boundaries of the United States during the four years he was in office. Polk also took office the day after the southeastern rim of the nation was completed; Florida was admitted to the Union as the twenty-seventh state (fig. 205) on March 3, 1845, the last day of the administration of President John Tyler. Before statehood, it was suggested that West Florida be separated from East Florida along the line of the Suwanee River, but this concept was discarded.

Florida—which has a state name that is the oldest European place-name on our soil; the oldest European name of a specific location, Cape Canaveral; and the oldest persistent settlement of European origin, St. Augustine—also has a complex geographic history. After the French and Indian War, Great Britain subdivided the Province of Florida, which it had acquired from Spain in exchange for Havana, Cuba, into West Florida and East Florida. The area south of the mouth of the Yazoo River (32°28' north latitude), near what is now Vicksburg, Mississippi, and west of the Apalachicola River became West Florida, and the area east of the Apalachicola and south of that parallel was called East Florida. At the end of the American Revolution, Great Britain ceded the area of West Florida north of 31° north latitude to the United States (which Spain disputed until a 1795 treaty with the United States) and gave the remainder of the two Floridas back to Spain. After the Louisiana Purchase in 1803, the United States claimed the area west of the Perdido River (which became Florida's short western border with southern Alabama) as part of that territory. Another treaty with Spain, in 1819, gave possession of the remainder of Florida to the United States, and in 1822 the Florida Territory was established. The state's boundaries with Alabama and Georgia have been described in the discussion of those states. Florida is made up of more than fifty-eight thousand square miles.

The names of Native Americans who in the past had inhabited the land persist as place-names within the state of Florida. As mentioned previously, the name of the capital, Tallahassee, is from the Muskogean words for "old town" (*talla*, "town," and *hasi*, "old"), and Pensacola was the name of the local Indian tribe. The city of Miami took its name from the river that had been given that Muskogean name, meaning "large." Other Muskogean terms endure in the names of Lake Okeechobee, meaning "big water," and the Okefenokee, meaning "shaking water," Swamp. In the Seminole language, Hialeah means "beautiful prairie," Apopka means "potato eating place," Opa-Locka means "swamp big," and Palatka means "boat crossing." Immokalee is Cherokee for "water trembling."

The early Spanish influence is very evident. Tampa was recorded in Spanish chronicles of the sixteenth century referring to an Indian town; the name was transferred to Tampa Bay, and then to the city in the 1830s. Boca Raton refers to a hidden rock that fretted cables like a gnawing mouse. Delray Beach, settled by a group from

204. *John Disturnell. "Mapa de los Estados Unidos de Méjico." New York, 1847. Engraving, hand-colored, 78 x 108 cm. General Records of the U.S. Government, National Archives, Washington, D.C. This map was attached to the 1848 Treaty of Guadalupe Hidalgo, which ended the Mexican War and added present-day California, Nevada, Utah, and parts of Colorado, New Mexico, Arizona, and Wyoming to the United States.*

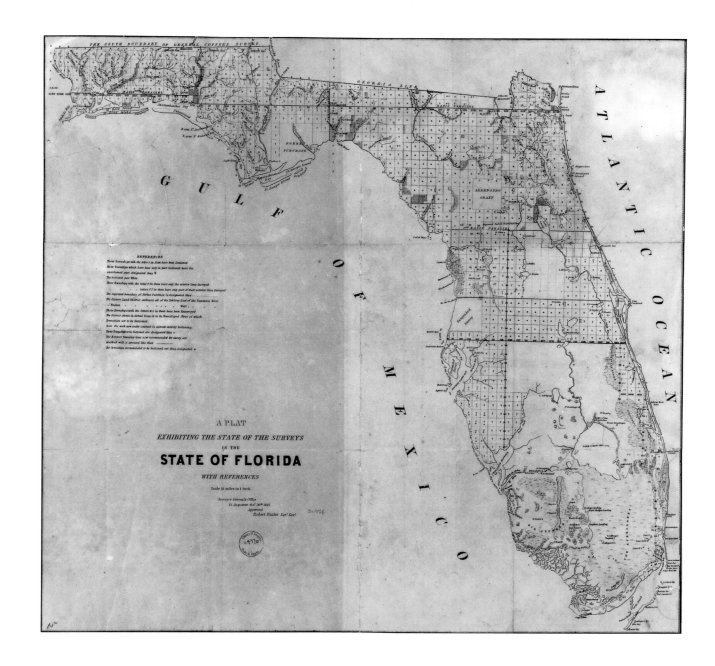

A PLAT

EXHIBITING THE STATE OF THE SURVEYS

IN THE

STATE OF FLORIDA

WITH REFERENCES

Scale 10 miles to 1 Inch

Surveyor General's Office
St. Augustine Oct. 20th 1845.
Approved
Robert Butler Sur. Genl.

Michigan at the end of the nineteenth century, is derived from *del rey*, meaning "of the king." The Keys derive from *cayo*, meaning "small islet," Largo means "long," and Miramar is Spanish for "look at the sea." Biscayne referred to a man known as El Biscaino because he came from the Province of Vizcaya, or Biscaya, in Spain.

Individuals' names were attached to other communities. Jacksonville, which was known as Cowford when it was settled in 1816, was renamed for President Andrew Jackson in 1822, commemorating the role he had played in defeating the regional Indian tribes before becoming the territory's first governor in that year. Gainesville was named for General Edmund Gaines, who commanded troops during the prolonged Seminole Wars (fig. 206). Orlando memorialized Orlando Reeves, who was killed by Indians in 1835 in the area in which the city evolved. Both the city and county of Dade honored Major F. L. Dade, who was killed at the beginning of the Seminole Wars.

205. *Robert Butler. "A Plat Exhibiting the State of the Surveys in the State of Florida with References." St. Augustine, 1845. Engraving, 57 x 63 cm. Geography and Map Division, Library of Congress, Washington, D.C.*

206. *Capt. John Mackay and Lt. Jacob E. Blake, U.S. Topographical Engineers. "Map of the Seat of War in Florida compiled by order of Bvt. Brig. Genl. Z. Taylor, principally from the surveys & reconnaissances of the Officers of the U.S. Army." 1839. Manuscript, pen and ink on paper, 102 x 75 cm. Records of the Office of the Chief of Engineers, National Archives, Washington, D.C. This map depicts the roads, U.S. Army posts, and battle sites during the Second Seminole War, 1835–42.*

MAP
OF THE
SEAT OF WAR
IN
FLORIDA
compiled by order of
BVT. BRIG: GEN: Z. TAYLOR.
principally from the surveys & reconnaissances
of the Officers of the U.S. Army;
BY
CAPT. JOHN MACKAY and LIEUT. J.E. BLAKE
U.S. Topographical Engineers.

Daytona Beach was given its name by Mathias Day, an early citizen, in 1870, and Boynton Beach took the name of Nathan Boynton, who built a hotel in the area in 1894. Bradenton, which developed in the area where De Soto landed in 1539, honored Joseph Braden, who started a sugar plantation in the mid-1800s. St. Petersburg was named in 1888 by Peter Demons, president of the local railroad, who came from that city in Russia. Coral Gables was so named because the first house in the area was built with coral decorating its gables. Panama City was given its name because it was on a southeasterly line drawn

207. *Artist unknown. Portrait of Halpatter-Mico or "Billy Bowlegs," a Seminole chief. In Thomas L. McKenney and James Hall's* The Indian Tribes of North America, *Edinburgh: John Grant, 1934. Lithograph, colored, after 1825–26 painting by Payne King; 17.8 x 9.5 cm.*

from Chicago to the Panama Canal, which was completed at the time the city was settled. Dunedin was named to recognize its settlers' Scottish heritage, and Hallandale derives from Holland-dale, reflecting the origin of its Dutch settlers.

Two forts persist as major communities. Fort Myers, originally built in 1850 after the Third Seminole War, was named for Colonel Abraham Charles Myers, then chief quartermaster in Florida. The Civil War's southernmost battle was fought at Fort Myers on February 20, 1865. Fort Lauderdale also traces its origin to the Seminole Wars (fig. 207), which had begun in 1817–18 and started up again in 1835, after some Seminoles repudiated earlier treaties. Most fighting stopped in 1842 but temporarily flared up again not long afterward, and the Seminoles technically remained at war with the United States until another treaty was signed in 1934. Fort Lauderdale was built by Major William Lauderdale along the New River in 1838, during the Second Seminole War, and moved first downriver and subsequently to the beach. The fort was decommissioned in 1842.

OREGON COUNTRY

At the other geographic extreme of the continental United States stood the region known as Oregon Country. The origin of the name continues to be disputed. As noted previously, the most authoritative suggestion is that it derived from Ouariconsint, a variant spelling of Ouisconsing (the French representation for what came to be called the Wisconsin River); it was divided on a 1715 map into two lines, "Ouaricon" and "sint," for lack of space; and it was converted in later references from "Ouaricon" to "Ouragon" and finally, in a widely read 1778 book by Jonathan Carver, to "Oregon." The name became widely known because of its appearance in William Cullen Bryant's popular 1817 poem "Thanatopsis."

Although the region was first explored by the Lewis and Clark expedition, the United States and British Canada contested ownership for an extended period. In 1818, a few years after the end of the War of 1812, Great Britain and the United States agreed to joint rights to the land that included the current states of Oregon, Washington, and Idaho and the Province of British Columbia. At about the same time, treaty negotiator John Quincy Adams convinced Spain to limit its claims along the Pacific coast to the border of northern California. In addition, Russia agreed to remove its claims to land south of the southern tip of Alaska (fig. 208).

The American Society for Encouraging the Settlement of the Oregon Territory incorporated in 1831, but before 1832, the trappers known as mountain men were the only non-natives inhabiting the region. The British influence was apparent in the naming of the major mountains, Rainier, Hood, and St. Helens, for two members of the British Admiralty and the British ambassador to Spain, respectively. The first major settlement within the Oregon Territory, Fort Vancouver (fig. 209), on the north shore of the Columbia River opposite the entrance of the Willamette River (derived from an Indian name),

208. *Artist unknown. "Russian outpost in California, Ft. Ross." In August-Bernard Duhaut-Cilly's* Voyages autour du Monde, *vol. 2, Paris, 1835. Engraving. Library of Congress, Washington, D.C. In 1812 the Russians set up a supply base at Ft. Rossiya (Russia), 70 miles north of San Francisco Bay. It was eventually abandoned.*

209. *Artist unknown. Ft. Vancouver, c. 1845, as seen from the north, with the Willamette River in the background. Oil on canvas, 60 x 39.5 cm. Courtesy Yale Collection of Western Americana, Beinecke Rare Book and Manuscript Library, Yale University, New Haven, Conn.*

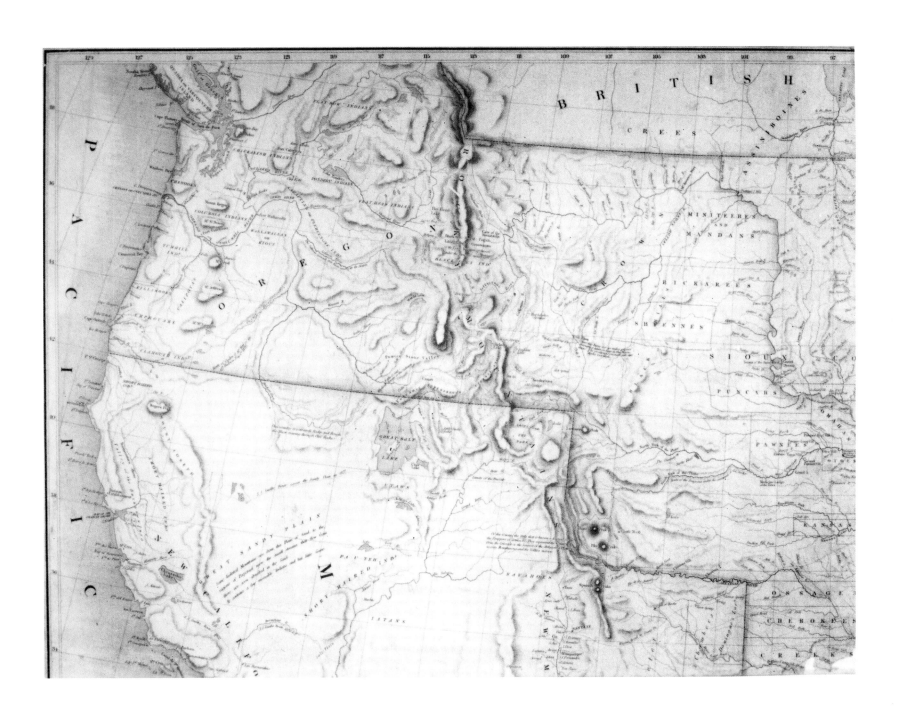

210. *David H. Burr. "Map of the United States of North America With Parts of Adjacent Countries" (detail). In Burr's* The American Atlas Exhibiting the Post Offices, Railroads, Canals, and the Physical and Political Divisions . . . , *London: John Arrowsmith, 1839. Engraving, hand-colored; entire map, 97 x 128 cm. Records of the Post Office Department, National Archives, Washington, D.C. This map depicts routes taken by explorers and fur traders Jedediah Strong Smith and Peter Skene Ogden. Note that the northern boundary line in the Northwest is undefined.*

was established in the mid-1820s and deliberately named by the governor of the Hudson's Bay Company, in order to assert the Canadian trading company's claims, in honor of the British navigator who had conducted a series of explorations of the Pacific Northwest coast about thirty years earlier.

Entrance of American settlers to the Oregon region was facilitated by Jedediah Strong Smith's journey in 1824 across the Rockies through the same South Pass that Robert Stuart had traversed in 1812, in what is now western Wyoming. In 1834, the Reverend Jason Lee and his fellow Methodist missionaries and followers attached themselves to an entrepreneurial expedition led by Massachusetts businessman Nathaniel Wyeth, settled in the Willamette Valley, and raised wheat and cattle. The valley, located between the Coastal and Cascade ranges, afforded woods, fertile land, and a moderate climate.

An emissary acting on behalf of President Andrew Jackson arrived in Oregon in 1836 to determine the potential for settlement. He returned to Washington, D.C., with a most favorable commentary. In the same year, the American Board of Foreign Missions sent Dr. Marcus Whitman and his bride, Narcissa, to Fort Walla Walla in the Willamette Valley; Walla Walla means "small rapid streams" in the language of the Nez Percé. Mrs. Whitman has the distinction of being the first white woman to cross the Rockies. The couple and a small group of settlers were massacred in 1847, probably as a consequence of their poor relationship with the Indians, who were devastated by a measles and scarlet fever epidemic that they attributed to the whites. The massacre served as a stimulus for the Cayuse Wars against the local Indians.

By 1842, Oregon fever had spread throughout Iowa, Missouri, Indiana, and Kentucky, resulting in mass migration to the Pacific Northwest (fig. 210). The six-month journey in Conestoga covered wagons (fig. 211) along the route known as the Oregon Trail usually started out from Independence, Missouri; crossed the Missouri River at Fort Leavenworth, Kansas; moved along the Missouri to the Platte River near the town that was later renamed Council Bluffs, Iowa; followed the Platte and its north fork across the Great Plains; took the South Pass across the Rockies to the Wyoming Basin; and continued along the Snake River and finally the Columbia River. One of the important supply posts on the Oregon Trail was Fort Bridger, in what is now the southwest corner of Wyoming; it was built in 1843 by famed mountain man James Bridger, the first white man to have reported seeing the Great Salt Lake, in 1824.

Amid growing enthusiasm over Oregon, President John Tyler's negotiations with Great Britain to establish a boundary between the United States and British Canada failed in 1844. His successor, James K. Polk, ran for president on the expansionist cry of "Fifty-four Forty or Fight," indicating that he planned to extend the northern border of the United States all the way to 54°40' north latitude—the southern boundary of Russian-held lands, and running across the middle of what is now British Columbia—and he pledged to annex Oregon, as

211. *Scenes of westward migration using the famous Conestoga wagon. Lithograph in Seymour I. Schwartz and Ralph E. Ehrenberg's* The Mapping of America, *New York: Harry N. Abrams, Inc., 1980.*

well as Texas. At the same time, because the fur trade had declined, the Hudson's Bay Company abandoned Fort Vancouver in 1845.

The following year, Polk proved to be more moderate than his campaign rhetoric, and both countries signed a treaty defining the northwestern border at the forty-ninth parallel, passing all the way through Puget Sound but leaving Vancouver Island as British territory. The boundary line ran southward to the west of the San Juan Islands, then westward through the Strait of Juan de Fuca, between Vancouver Island and the Olympic Peninsula of present-day Washington. The strait bears the name of a sixteenth-century captain who passed through those waters and supposedly met a ship coming from the Atlantic—an apocryphal tale of a Northwest Passage. John Melish's 1816 "Map of the United States," the first American-produced wall map depicting the country from coast to coast, pictured that line of division long before it became part of the official border (see fig. 169). Farther east, several earlier boundary disputes between Britain and the United States pertaining to the land between Lake Superior and Rainy Lake, along the northern border of what is now Minnesota, had been settled by the Webster-Ashburton Treaty of 1842. Therefore, by 1846, the east coast and the northern limits of the United States had been permanently defined. Two years later, the Oregon Territory was established, with Oregon City as the capital. Slavery was specifically prohibited within the territory, which consisted of all land west of the crest of the Rocky Mountains and north of 42° north latitude. The territory was reduced by the formation of the Washington Territory in 1853.

TEXAS

The southwestern portion of the United States was completed in a process that took up much of the first half of the nineteenth century. In the Adams-Onís Treaty of 1819, the boundary line between the United States and the Spanish territory to the south of the Louisiana Purchase crossed the southern Plains, skirted the Spanish province of New Mexico, and then passed along the forty-second parallel to the Pacific Ocean. At the time, Secretary of State John Quincy Adams accepted the Sabine River and a linear extension north to the Red River as part of the southeastern boundary line between Mexico and the United States (both the state of Louisiana and part of what was about to become the Arkansaw Territory), in exchange for Spain's cession of Florida to the United States. Facing the United States of America across that border was the United States of Mexico (fig. 204), a republic (from 1824, after a successful revolt against Spain in 1821 and a short-lived independent empire) containing almost 1.7 million square miles, essentially the equivalent of the United States of America. Within about three decades, the United States of America would take control of more than nine hundred thousand of those square miles, including Texas, California, and what was then called New Mexico, a region encompassing part or all of present-day New Mexico, Arizona, Nevada, Utah, Colorado, and Wyoming.

In 1820, Upper California (that portion north of the Baja Peninsula), New Mexico (including Arizona), and Texas were frontier provinces of Mexico (New Spain). Throughout those lands, there were only scattered missions, and the area was sparsely populated with Mexicans. Santa Fe was the capital of the Province of New Mexico. The Province of Texas was about 750 miles in length and width and extended from the Sabine River to El Paso and from the Panhandle to the mouth of the Rio Grande.

During the decade of the 1820s, American settlers from Louisiana and the Mississippi River valley moved into the Mexican territory and settled on the coastal plains of what would become Texas. It began in 1821, when Mexico granted a large segment of land to Moses Austin, a Connecticut native living in western Louisiana. He died shortly thereafter, and the grant passed on to his son, Stephen F. Austin. The grant gave the privilege of initially settling three hundred American families, each receiving 177 acres of farmland plus more than 4,000 acres for grazing stock. Austin was to be given 65,000 acres once two hundred families had come; in effect, until 1828 he ruled the land that had been granted to him. By 1834, because the land was so much cheaper than that available in the United States, Austin's colony had grown to more than twenty thousand colonists, outnumbering the Mexicans in Texas four to one. The colony's Gulf Coast shoreline extended from Galveston Bay to south of Matagorda Bay (fig. 212), and the land included the basins of the Colorado and Brazos rivers.

In 1835, when President Antonio López de Santa Anna assumed dictatorial powers and imposed a uniform constitution for all of Mexico, each Mexican state's individual rights were erased. Texas seceded, expelled the Mexican troops from San Antonio de Bexar, and set up a provisional government. Santa Anna and three thousand Mexican soldiers crossed the Rio Grande, but less than two hundred defenders of the Alamo (fig. 213), San Antonio's fortified mission, held them off for almost two weeks until March 6, 1836, when the mission was taken and the Americans were all killed. Mexican forces also massacred about four hundred Americans after they surrendered near Goliad, to the southeast. On April 21, however, General Sam Houston's army decisively defeated the Mexicans on the shore of the San Jacinto River, named to honor the thirteenth-century Saint Hyacinth, and captured Santa Anna, effectively winning the war for independence. Houston was elected president of the

212. Stephen Fuller Austin. "Map of Texas With Parts of the Adjoining States." Philadelphia, 1830. Engraving, hand-colored, 75 x 62 cm. Records of the Office of the Chief of Engineers, National Archives, Washington, D.C. This map was prepared in order to encourage American immigration to the Mexican province of Texas. It depicts the American colonies of Austin and De Witt along the Gulf Coast, and a grant to Stephen F. Austin in the interior.

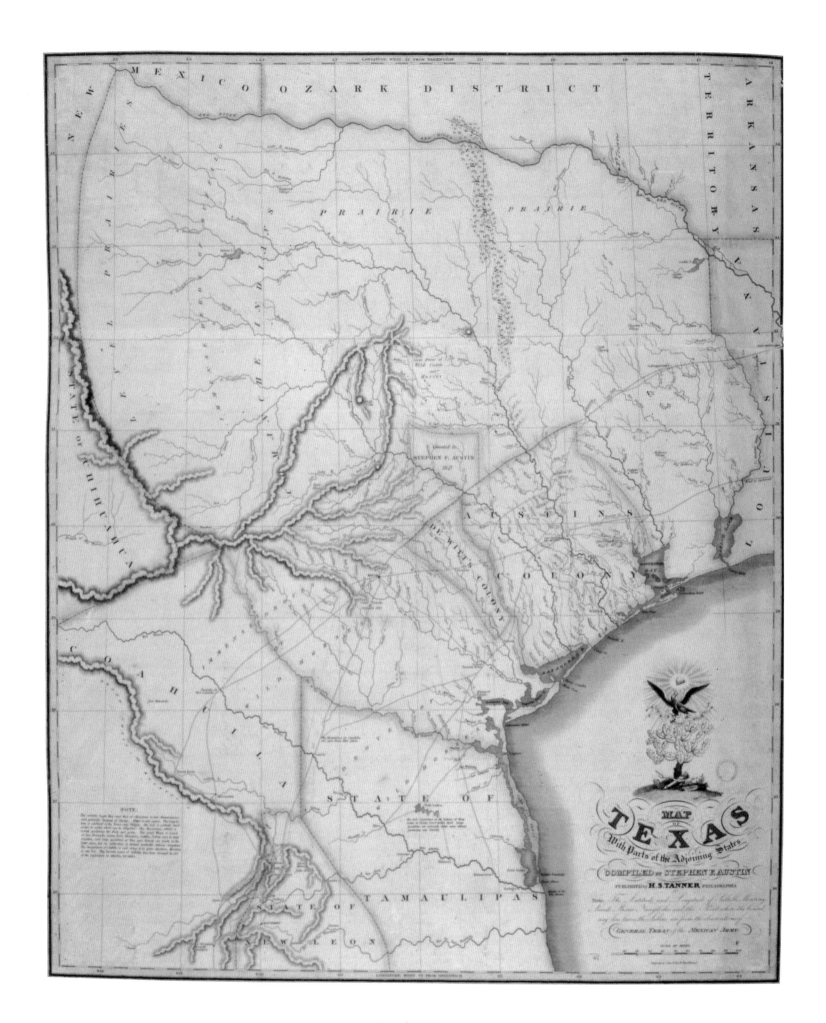

MAP OF TEXAS
With Parts of the Adjoining States
COMPILED BY STEPHEN F. AUSTIN
PUBLISHED BY H.S. TANNER PHILADELPHIA

213. *The Alamo, San Antonio. Courtesy J. Bradley Aust*

Lone Star Republic, which immediately sought recognition and annexation by the United States. The republic claimed the Rio Grande as its southern and western borders (which Mexico vehemently rejected) and in 1839 selected a location for its new capital, named in honor of Stephen F. Austin, who had been defeated by Houston for the presidency, served briefly as secretary of state, and died in 1836. On President Andrew Jackson's last day in office, March 3, 1837, he recognized the Lone Star Republic, which at the time had a population of fifty thousand.

Almost eight years later, President John Tyler, three days before leaving office (and two days before Florida became a state), signed a joint resolution of Congress annexing Texas, and on December 29, 1845, President James K. Polk signed the bill that made Texas the twenty-eighth state (fig. 214). The original boundary lines of the state were defined previously by those of the Republic of Texas, created out of the former Mexican states of Texas and Coahuila. Beginning in the southeast at the mouth of the Sabine River, the line ran southwesterly along the Gulf of Mexico, three leagues from land, to the mouth of the Rio Grande; it continued up that river all the way to its source, in present-day southwestern Colorado; from there, it ran due north to 41°30' north latitude, turned east for one degree of longitude, and then ran south to the headwaters of the Arkansas River (in what is now central Colorado, on the other side of the Rockies from the mouth of the Rio Grande); the boundary line continued east along the Arkansas River to 100° west longitude, ran due south on that meridian (the eastern side of the Texas Panhandle) to the Red River, and followed that river southeastward to the previously estab-

lished western boundaries of Arkansas and Louisiana, which it continued along back to the starting point. As a result of changes in 1850 reducing the western and northern parts of Texas, the second-largest state in today's United States contains about 267,000 square miles.

The state's name first appeared in Spanish chronicles of the mid-sixteenth century; it derived from an Indian word meaning "friends" and was assigned to an Indian tribe. As mentioned previously, the name first appeared on a map in 1718, in the phrase "Mission de los Teijas etablie en 1716" (see fig. 83). The oldest place-name in the state is Corpus Christi, assigned by Alonso Alvarez de Pineda in 1519 to the bay he explored. The community of Corpus Christi was settled as a frontier trading post in 1839. The first formal exploration of what is now Texas was in 1581, by Spanish troops from Mexico crossing the Rio Grande at El Paso del Norte (although the crossing was not given that name until several years later). The first Spanish settlement was established in 1682 near El Paso, on land inhabited by the Tigua Indians; it was called Yselta del Sur, meaning "little island by the sea." In 1780, the Spanish garrison of San Elizaro was built in the region, but the city of El Paso was not settled until 1827, and it was not incorporated until 1873. El Paso is notable as the point from which General John J. "Black Jack" Pershing took off into Mexico in 1916 on his expedition against Pancho Villa, and it was also the site where the horse cavalry of the U.S. Army formally came to an end.

In 1755, on the north bank of the Rio Grande, Captain Tomás Sánchez founded San Augustin de Laredo, a name transposed from a town in Spain, in hopes of colonizing New Mexico; after the Mexican War, the old pueblo, now called Laredo, became a custom station on the Rio Grande. Galveston, the home of the Akokusa and Kanakawa Indians in the 1500s, took its name from the bay, which was named in 1786 to honor Count Bernardo de Gálvez, viceroy of New Spain in 1784–86, who had sent José de Evia to chart the Gulf Coast. In 1817, the region served as home port for the notorious pirate Jean Laffite (often spelled Lafitte). Twenty years later, Michel Menard purchased land from the Austin colony and formed the city of Galveston.

Houston, which began as a riverboat landing on Buffalo Bayou in 1836 and has become one of the nation's leading ports, was named in honor of General Sam Houston, the hero who liberated the Republic of Texas and served as its first president, as well as one of the state's first U.S. senators and then governor. The city was the capital of the republic in 1837–39 and again in 1842–45, during a period of Indian and Mexican raids on Austin, which subsequently became the state capital. The naming of Dallas, which James Neely Bryan settled in 1841, is a matter of some dispute. Bryan specifically indicated that he named Dallas for a friend in 1846, when the land was platted. It is generally held that the name honored George Mifflin Dallas, Polk's vice president just after Texas was annexed and when it became a state—but Bryan had never met Dallas. Alternatively, the city could have been named for Commodore Alexander Dallas, noted for piracy in the Gulf of Mexico, or Walter Dallas, who had fought at San

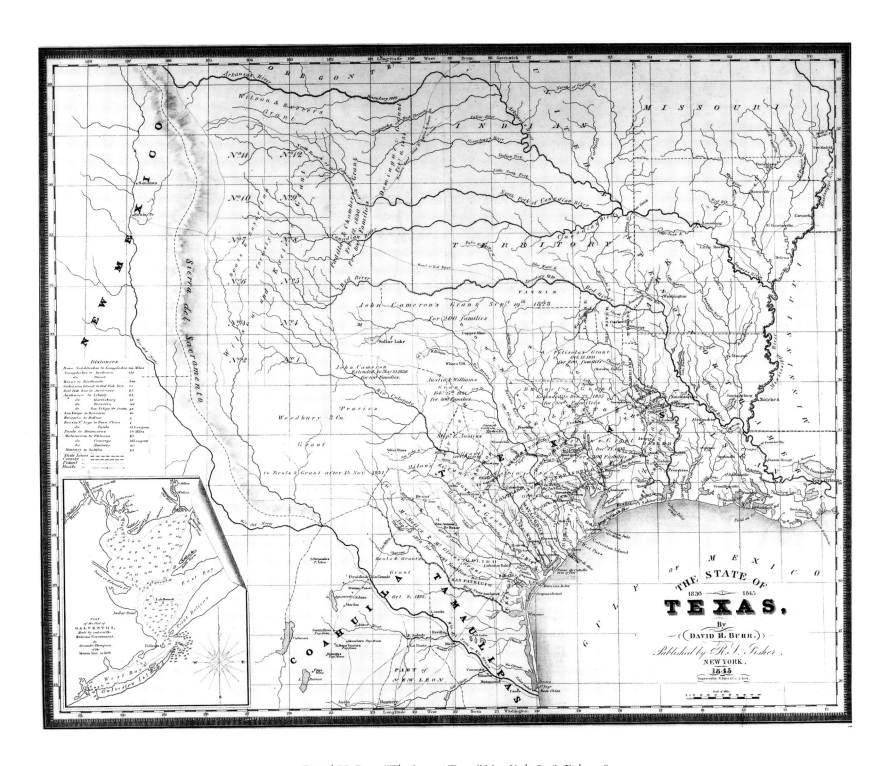

214. *David H. Burr. "The State of Texas." New York: R. S. Fisher, 1845.*
Engraving, 45 x 55 cm. Geography and Map Division, Library of Congress,
Washington, D.C. This map of Texas was published the year in which the
short-lived Republic of Texas became a state in the United States.

Jacinto, or his brother, James, a Texas Ranger, or Joseph Dallas, a friend of Bryan's who had moved to the region from Arkansas. Bryan himself was honored with the naming of a city on the east bank of the Trinity River; the river was given that name, in Spanish, in 1690 by the Alonzo de Léon–Father Damian Massanet expedition, because of its three converging forks. Fort Worth took the name of the fort, built on the fork of the Trinity River not far from Dallas; the fort, the last stop in Texas on the Chisholm Trail, along which cattle were moved from Texas to Kansas, was named for General William J. Worth, who led troops in the Mexican War. Brownsville was also initially a military post, named for Major Jacob Brown, who died during that war; the town developed from Fort Brown after the war confirmed the Rio Grande as the southern boundary of Texas.

Among other cities, Arlington was named for General Robert E. Lee's home in Virginia. Built on land originally belonging to the Caddo Indians, it was first the site of Major Jonathan Bird's fort and was given its current name in 1876, when it became a station on the Texas and Pacific Railroad line. Garland, near Dallas, was part of the vast W. S. Peters Colony real-estate venture before 1846. The settlement, initially known as Duck Creek, joined with neighboring Embree—named for the local physician, Dr. K. H. Embree—in 1887, at which time it adopted the name of the U.S. attorney general, A. H. Garland. Lubbock was named for Tom S. Lubbock, a signer of the Texas Declaration of Independence, Texas Ranger, and Confederate officer.

Marshall elected to honor Chief Justice John Marshall, while Tyler adopted the name of the president who signed the bill that annexed Texas. Temple took the name of Bernard Moore Temple, chief engineer of the Gulf, Colorado and Santa Fe Railroad, who built the tracks through that area. Port Arthur memorialized the given name of Arthur E. Stillwell, who developed the town, and Denton honored Captain John B. Denton, who was killed by the Indians in 1841. Euless, the city where Dallas–Fort Worth Airport was built, took the name of Elisha Adam Euless, who brought the first industry, a cotton gin, to the area.

Abilene and Wichita Falls are names that traveled from Kansas to Texas. Odessa was named by railroad workers from Russia, because the area reminded them of the steppes. Amarillo maintains the region's Spanish imprint; the name is the Spanish word for "yellow," referring to the yellow mud making up the shore of the local stream, which also bore the name. Waco was settled in 1840 on the land of the ancient settlement of Waco Indians.

CALIFORNIA AND THE MEXICAN WAR

In the Pacific Northwest, the first overland settlers from the Midwest branched off the Oregon Trail and settled the Sacramento Valley in 1841. The following year, Commodore Thomas ap Catesby Jones of the U.S. Navy seized Monterey, California. When he found out that war with Mexico had not been declared, as he had believed, he left with apologies. At about this time, a settlement was initiated in the Sacramento Valley that appropriately was named New Helvetia, because its founder, John Sutter, who became a Mexican citizen and received a large land grant in that area, was a native of Switzerland. In 1845, there were only six thousand white settlers in California, but John C. Frémont's report that year on his expedition to Oregon and California, chronicling his travels as he moved south through the Sacramento Valley in central and southern California into Nevada, excited interest in the region (fig. 215).

On taking office in 1845, President Polk immediately attended to the expansionist positions that had gained him the presidency. Oregon and the extensive Mexican province of New Mexico were the northern and southern regions of interest, but California was central to the plan. Polk sent an emissary to Mexico with an offer of twenty million dollars for the land west of New Mexico, including San Francisco, and five million dollars for the Province of New Mexico itself. Mexico, which had already broken off diplomatic relations with the United States to protest the annexation of Texas, and which disputed the claims by Texas to all the land extending south and west to the Rio Grande, spurned the offer. Polk sent troops under General Zachary Taylor to the Nueces River, which the Spanish had named for the nuts (*nueces*) on the pecan trees in the area, and which Mexico claimed was the southern border of Texas. When it became apparent that Mexico was adamantly opposed to recognizing the Rio Grande, well over one hundred miles to the south, as the Texas border, General Taylor (fig. 216) was ordered to cross the Nueces River and occupy the near bank of the Rio Grande.

On April 25, 1846, about a month after Taylor occupied a town at the mouth of the Rio Grande, a small Mexican force crossed the river and skirmished with American troops. This caused the United States to declare war against Mexico. In less than one year, American troops gained control of northern Mexico, including San Diego and San Francisco. A few dozen of the American settlers in California, whom the Mexicans called *osos*, or "bears," staged what is known as the Bear Flag Revolt in 1846, easily seizing poorly defended garrisons and establishing the short-lived Bear Flag Republic; their homemade flag depicted a grizzly bear facing a red star over the words "California Republic" on a field of white. Later that year, Commodore John Sloat, commander of the U.S. Pacific squadron, hoisted the American flag at Monterey and Captain John C. Frémont secured San Francisco Bay.

When Mexico refused to capitulate after the United States gained control of California, General Winfield Scott was sent with an

215. *Charles Preuss. "Map of Oregon and Upper California From the Surveys of John Charles Fremont And other Authorities." Baltimore, 1848. Lithograph, 69 x 87 cm. Records of the U.S. Senate, National Archives, Washington, D.C. The most accurate general map of the West for its time. It depicts information gained by John C. Frémont between 1842 and 1847.*

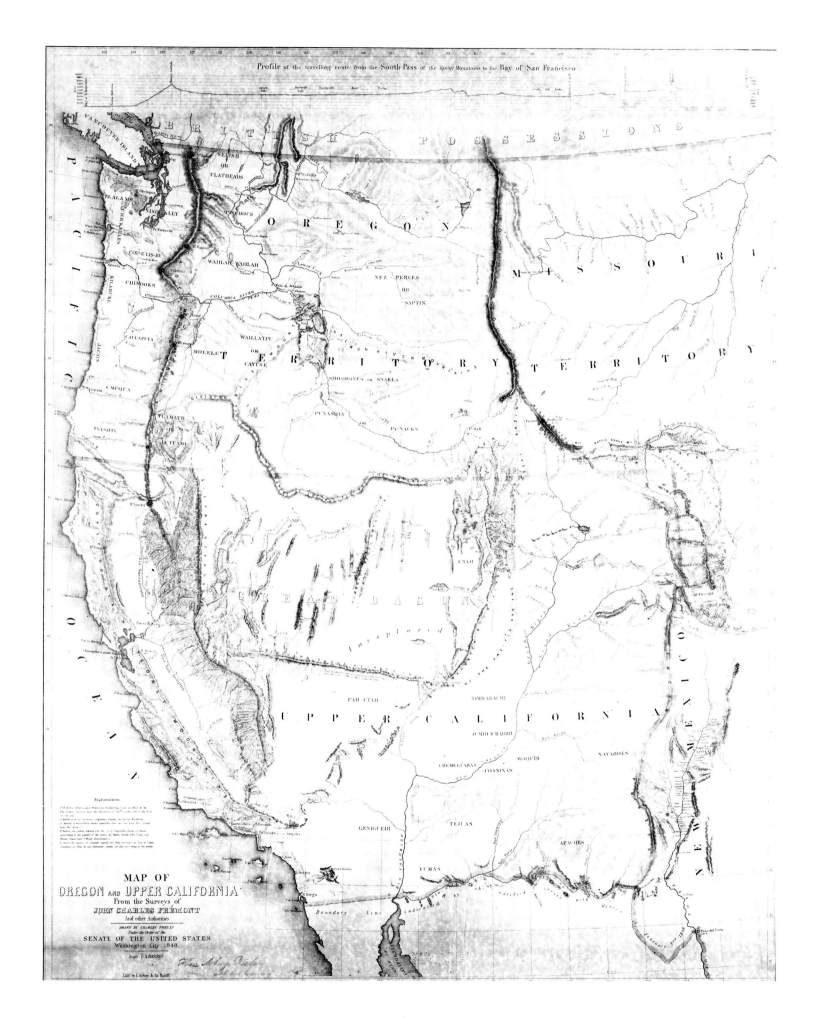

Profile of the travelling route from the South Pass of the Rocky Mountains to the Bay of San Francisco

MAP OF
OREGON AND UPPER CALIFORNIA
From the Surveys of
JOHN CHARLES FRÉMONT
And other Authorities

DRAWN BY CHARLES PREUSS
Under the Order of the
SENATE OF THE UNITED STATES
Washington City 1848.

Scale 1:4000000

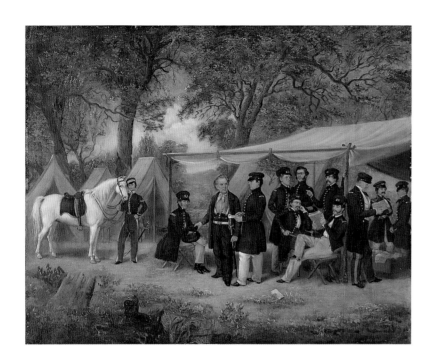

216. *William Carl Brown Jr.* General Zachary Taylor at Walnut Creek. *1847. Oil on canvas, 76.2 x 91.4 cm. Courtesy National Portrait Gallery, Smithsonian Institution, Washington, D.C. This painting depicts Taylor receiving orders from President James K. Polk regarding the U.S. invasion of Mexico. After the Mexican War, in 1848, Taylor was elected to succeed Polk as president.*

tied into the Colorado River, moved across the Colorado River, and followed the division of Upper and Lower California to the Pacific Ocean. The limits of New Mexico were accepted as those that had been laid down on a map of the United States of Mexico, published by John Disturnell in 1847 (see fig. 204). The boundary between Upper and Lower California was specifically drawn as a straight line from the middle of the Gila River, at the point where it joined the Colorado River, to the Pacific Ocean, one league south of the southernmost point of the port of San Diego. The United States thus acquired the Gila River valley as well as San Diego.

The treaty added California, Nevada, Utah, and parts of Colorado, New Mexico, Arizona, and Wyoming to the United States. The cession from Mexico, when added to the previously annexed Texas, totaled about 918,000 square miles, roughly equal in size to the Louisiana Purchase. With the 287,000 square miles of Oregon Territory added to the Texas annexation and the gains from the Mexican War, the United States grew by 64 percent in a period of less than three years. The cost to the United States for all the land acquired through the Treaty of Guadalupe Hidalgo was fifteen million dollars.

In 1853, the government paid Mexico an additional ten million dollars for about thirty thousand square miles of land in the Gila River valley west of El Paso, Texas, in order to provide the territory needed to build a southern rail route between the Gulf States and San Diego. This acquisition, known as the Gadsden Purchase because James Gadsden, the U.S. minister to Mexico, negotiated for the

army of more than ten thousand men, which included among its junior officers Robert E. Lee, George B. McClellan, George G. Meade, Thomas J. (later known as "Stonewall") Jackson, Jefferson Davis, and Ulysses S. Grant, to Veracruz with orders to march on Mexico City. Meanwhile, Santa Anna had come out of exile in Havana, Cuba, and resumed the presidency in September 1846. He led his larger army against Zachary Taylor's forces but was badly beaten at Buena Vista in February 1847, and Winfield Scott's army defeated Santa Anna's in August and September outside Mexico City. The Mexican capital fell on September 14, effectively ending the war (fig. 217).

The Treaty of Guadalupe Hidalgo, signed on February 2, 1848, confirmed the Rio Grande as the southern border of Texas. Under the treaty, the new boundary line between the United States and Mexico began in the Gulf of Mexico, three leagues from land, opposite the mouth of the Rio Grande, and continued up the middle of the river to the point at which the river struck the southern boundary of the Mexican province of New Mexico (north of that current state's southern border), then followed the whole southern boundary of that province to its westernmost point and turned north along the western boundary of the province until it intersected the first branch of the Gila River, named for a regional Indian tribe. The boundary continued westward along the middle of the Gila River until it emp-

217. *Adolphe-Jean-Baptiste Bayot.* "Genl. Scott's Entrance into Mexico City." *1851. Toned lithograph, hand-colored, after a painting by Carl Nebel; 28 x 43 cm. Courtesy Amon Carter Museum, Fort Worth, Tex. The defeat by Gen. Winfield Scott's army of Santa Anna's men and the fall of Mexico City in September 1846 effectively ended the Mexican War.*

federal government, further redefined the border between the United States and Mexico. The new boundary line ran along the Rio Grande from the mouth of that river to 31°37' north latitude, then due west for one hundred miles, south from that point to 31°20' north latitude, and west along that parallel to 111° west longitude. From there, the boundary ran in a straight line northwest to a point on the Colorado River twenty miles below the junction with the Gila River, then continued up the Colorado until it intersected the international border to the Pacific Ocean as previously defined by the Treaty of Guadalupe Hidalgo. With this acquisition, the current boundaries of the forty-eight contiguous states were complete (fig. 218).

218. D. McGowan and George H. Hildt. "Map of the United States West of the Mississippi Showing the Routes to Pike's Peak[,] Overland Mail Route to California[,] and Pacific Rail road Surveys. . . ." St. Louis, 1859. Lithograph, hand-colored, 58 x 72 cm. Geography and Map Division, Library of Congress, Washington, D.C. This map shows the final northern and southern boundaries of the western part of the United States, after the Gadsden Purchase. It also depicts the four major routes of a proposed transcontinental railroad, as determined by the Pacific Railroad Surveys ordered in 1853.

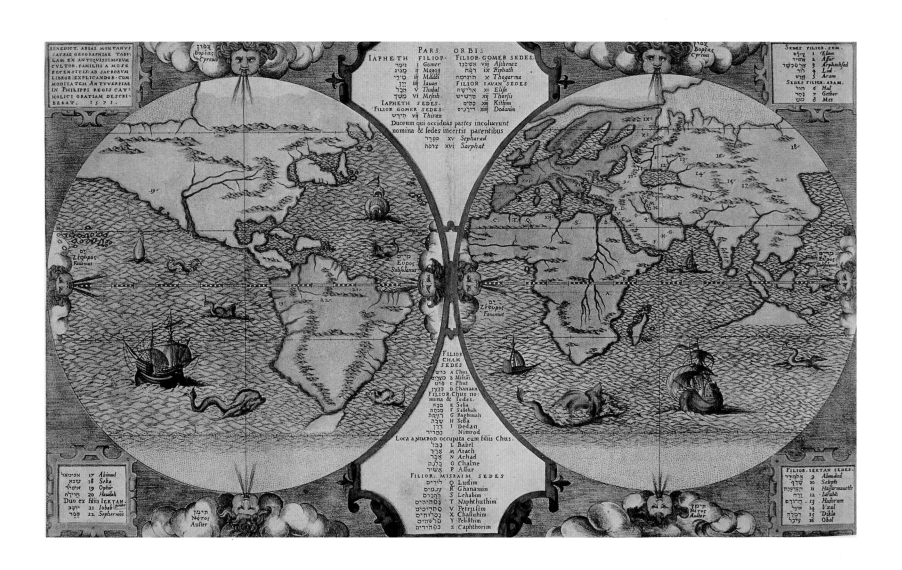

CHAPTER ELEVEN

Development, Disruption, and Reconstruction (1847–67)

IOWA

Within the boundaries of the United States, there was movement of New Englanders into present-day Indiana, Illinois, Michigan, Wisconsin, and Iowa between 1837 and 1841. By 1850, as a consequence of the Erie Canal in New York, Cleveland became a significant port, carrying goods to and from the regions to which the Great Lakes were readily accessible. It was during this period, on December 28, 1846, that Iowa became the twenty-ninth state. A home of the Mound Builders in prehistoric times, it later served as native lands for the Sauk (Sac), Fox, Iowa, and Sioux tribes (fig. 220). Iowa witnessed the passage of La Salle as he approached the Mississippi River in 1682, and the land was incorporated into the United States in 1803 as part of the Louisiana Purchase.

In keeping with the stipulations of the Northwest Ordinance, Iowa progressed from the status of a territory, recognized in 1838, to statehood, in 1846. The Iowa Territory, created out of part of the Louisiana Purchase lands, was north of Missouri, west of the Wisconsin Territory, and south of a line drawn west from the headwaters of the Mississippi River to the Missouri River; after Iowa became a state and its boundaries were established, the northern remainder of what had been the Iowa Territory was organized as the Minnesota Territory.

The state's boundaries (fig. 221), which surrounded about fifty-six thousand square miles, were defined as beginning at the southeast corner in the main channel of the Mississippi River, due east of the mouth of the Des Moines River, then running up the main channel of the Des Moines River to the point of its intersection with the parallel forming the rest of the northern border of the state of Missouri. The line proceeded west along the Missouri border, past Missouri's original western boundary line along its 1836 extension, intersecting the main channel of the Missouri River. From there, Iowa's western boundary line ran up that channel to a point opposite

Opposite: 219. *Benito Arias Montanus. "Sacrae geographiae tabvlam ex antiquissimorvm cvltor."* Antwerp, 1571. Engraving, hand-colored, 32 x 53 cm. Private collection. The only label on the North American continent is "19," keyed to designate "Ophir," the biblical land of gold and plenty—and the number happens to appear in the area of the 19th-century California gold strike.

220. *Karl Bodmer. "Saukie [sic] and Fox Indians."* In Prince Maximilian Alexander Phillip von Wied-Neuwied's Reise in das innere Nord-America in den Jahren 1832 bis 1834, Koblenz: J. Hoelscher, 1839–44. Lithograph, 25.4 x 33 cm. Library of Congress, Washington, D.C. The closely linked but separate Sauk (or Sac) and Fox tribes eventually merged during the 18th century, becoming known jointly as the Sauk and Fox.

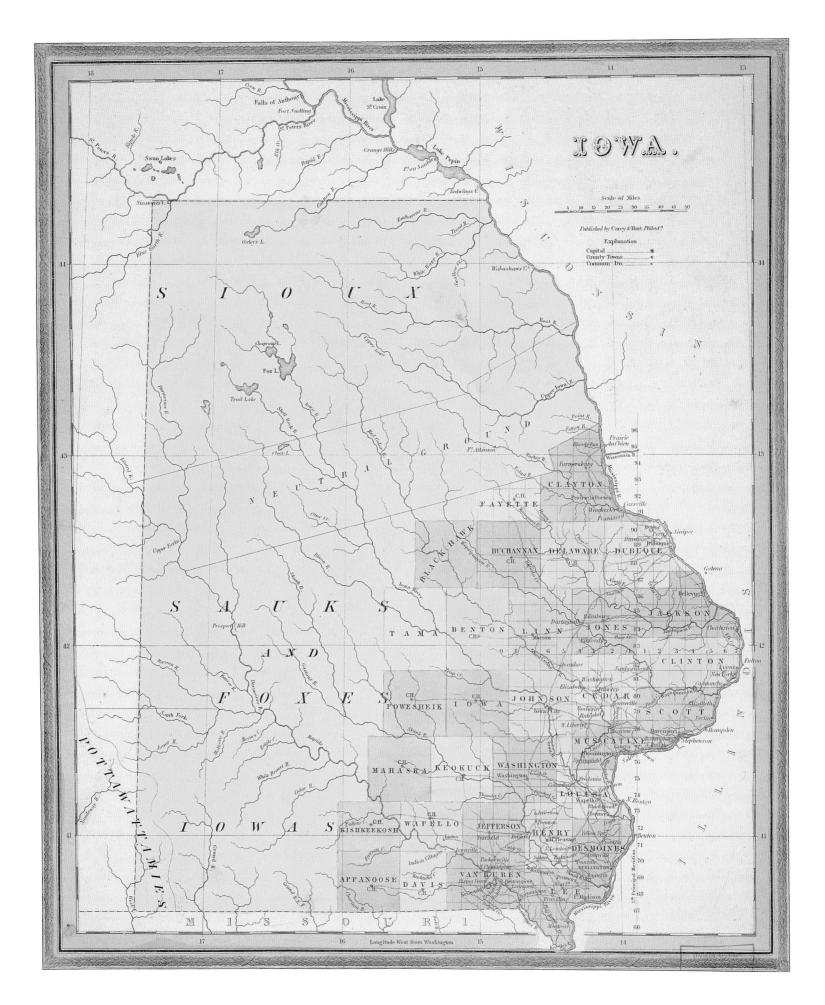

IOWA.

Scale of Miles
5 10 15 20 25 30 35 40 45 50

Published by Carey & Hart Philad.ᵃ

Explanation
Capital
County Towns
Common Do.

the middle of the main channel of the Big Sioux River, then up the main channel of that river to 43°30' north latitude. The northern boundary line ran east along that parallel to the middle of the main channel of the Mississippi River; the eastern boundary line ran down that channel to the starting point.

The state's name, which is thought to mean either "beautiful land" or "sleepy one," and several of the cities' names evolved as contractions of Indian words. It first appeared on a map in the latter half of the seventeenth century as the name "Ouaouiatonon"; it later was shortened to Ouaouia and attached to a river. Dropped and scrambled letters resulted in the name Iowa, which was assigned to the river,

Opposite: 221. S. Augustus Mitchell. "Iowa."
In H. S. Tanner's New Universal Atlas, New York,
1846. Engraving, 40 x 33.5 cm. Geography and
Map Division, Library of Congress, Washington, D.C.
This state map actually appeared before Iowa joined
the Union that year; the publisher desired that it
be included in the contemporary atlas.

222. Titian Ramsay Peale. A depiction of the steamboat
commanded by Maj. Stephen H. Long at Council Bluffs.
1820. Watercolor on paper, 12 x 19 cm. Courtesy
American Philosophical Society, Philadelphia. Council
Bluffs had been the site of a meeting by Lewis and
Clark with Indian tribes in 1804.

the territory, and the state, in that chronological order. The capital and largest city in Iowa began as a fort at the junction of the Raccoon and Des Moines rivers in 1843 and for a short time was named Fort Raccoon before it was changed to Fort Des Moines. The French origin of that river's name is described in chapter 4.

Dubuque, which was founded in 1833, took its name from Julien Dubuque, who in 1785 became the first French settler in the region. Davenport was named for Colonel George Davenport, one of its founders. Ames was named for Oakes Ames, a nineteenth-century politician with railroad interests. Fort Dodge honored Henry Dodge, a governor of the Wisconsin Territory and later a U.S. senator, whose son was the first senator from Iowa. Marshalltown was one of several cities in the United States to adopt the name of John Marshall, the prominent early chief justice of the United States. Mason City is located on the site of a town called Shibboleth (taken from the Bible); when John B. Long developed the city, he changed the name to Masonville to honor his son, who had died on the trip from Illinois to Iowa, and this became Mason City when the Milwaukee System Railroad established a station there, because there was already another town in the state named Masonville. Council Bluffs was a natural site named by Lewis and Clark, who stayed there for five days and met with the Missouri and Oto (or Otoe) Indians in 1804 during their memorable journey of exploration. Between 1846 and 1852, the area was home to the Mormons on their way from Illinois to the Salt Lake Basin. At that time the settlement there was called Kanesville, honoring Thomas Kane, who was sympathetic to the Mormon cause; in 1853 it was renamed Council Bluffs (fig. 222) as a remembrance of the Lewis and Clark expedition.

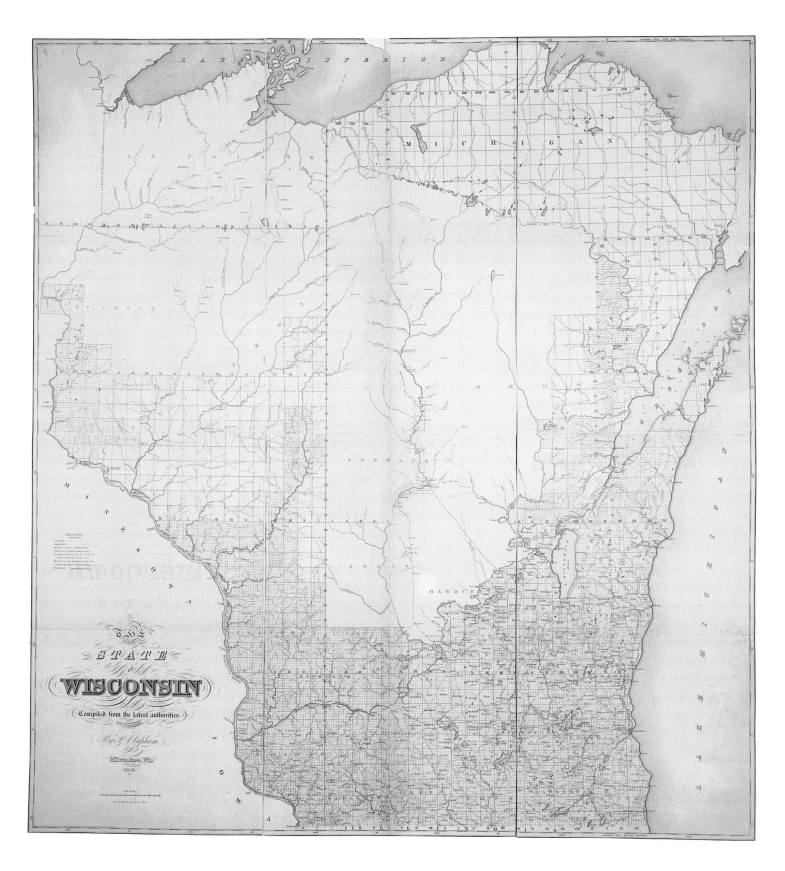

223. *P. A. Lapham. "The State of Wisconsin Compiled from the latest authorities."*
Milwaukee, 1849. Lithograph, 2 sheets joined, 133 x 125 cm. Geography and Map
Division, Library of Congress, Washington, D.C. This large detailed map was
published in the year after Wisconsin achieved statehood.

Sioux City was named for the dominant Indian tribe in the area; Muscatine was a modern spelling of the Mascouten tribe; Algona refers to the Algonquin Indians. Ottumwa is an Indian word meaning "swift water" and referring to the Des Moines River; Maquoketa translates as "bear river." Anamosa adopted the name of a local Indian girl, meaning "white faun"; Keokuk took the name of a Fox chief; and Oskaloosa was named for the wife of the Seminole chief Osceola.

The name of Cedar Rapids described a local geographic characteristic. Amana, which was settled in 1855 by a German communal religious group known as the Amana Society, took the society's name, that of a biblical mountain. One of the most curious of all namings occurred in Le Mars. In 1869, when the railroad completed the tracks to the region, an inaugural excursion was planned. The initials of the first names of the first six women to arrive for the event were joined together, spelling L-E-M-A-R-S.

WISCONSIN

Wisconsin became the thirtieth state on May 29, 1848, taking its name from the river, which previously had been spelled a variety of ways, the most common being Ouisconsing, the French version of an Algonquian term meaning "big long at." When Jean Nicolet arrived on the shore of Green Bay in the seventeenth century to seek the supposed Northwest Passage and trap furs, he encountered Winnebago, Kickapoo, and other Indians, who would later be displaced by Ottawas and Hurons forced into the Wisconsin region after the French and Indian War. Wisconsin was part of the Northwest Territory, and the region fell into British hands for a brief period during the War of 1812.

When the state of Wisconsin was established (fig. 223), its boundaries were set as beginning at the northeast corner of the state of Illinois, which extended into the center of Lake Michigan at 42°30' north latitude; the line followed the boundary of the state of Michigan through Lake Michigan and Green Bay to the mouth of the Menominee River and up the main channel of that river and the Brule River to Lake Brule, continued along the south shore of that lake in a straight line to the channel between the Middle and South islands in the Lake of the Desert, then ran in a direct line to the headwaters of the Montreal River. The boundary line continued down the main channel of the Montreal River to its mouth and then to the middle of Lake Superior, and from there it ran to the mouth of the St. Louis River and up the main channel of that river to the first rapids; then it continued due south to the main branch of the St. Croix River, down the main channel of that river to the Mississippi River, and down the main channel of the Mississippi to the northwest corner of the state of Illinois, from which it ran due east along the northern boundary of that state. A dispute arose involving the line between Michigan and Wisconsin on the northern peninsula, and it was not completely resolved until the U.S. Supreme Court issued a ruling in 1936, defining a precise boundary through Green Bay by bearings and distances. Currently, the state of Wisconsin has more than fifty-six thousand square miles.

The state's capital, which became the first white settlement in that region in 1832, was named for the fourth president, James Madison, after he died in 1836. The name of the largest city, Milwaukee, derives from an Algonquian term meaning "good land"; it had been the site of an Indian trading post in 1674 and became a settlement in 1835. Other Algonquian derivatives include Kenosha, meaning "pickerel"; Menasha, meaning "island"; Menominee, meaning "wild rice," and referring (with variations in spelling) to a river, a county, and a city in western Wisconsin; Oconomowoc, meaning "beaver dam"; Shawano, meaning "south"; Sheboygan, referring to a perforated pipe stem; Waupun, meaning "east"; Wausau, meaning "far away"; and Wauwatosa, meaning "firefly." Oshkosh was the name of a Menominee chief who was active during the first half of the nineteenth century. Lake Winnebago took its name from the local tribe, and Neenah derived from the Winnebago word for "water." The Ojibwa language also contributed to several place-names: Antigo is a shortened form of the original Indian word meaning "evergreen"; Ashwaubenon took its name from the creek and means "lookout place"; Kaukauna refers to a "pike fishing place"; and Manitowoc translates as "spirit spawn," based on the concept that spirits spawn like fish. Waukesha is an adaptation of the Potawatomi word for "fox."

Evidence of the French influence in Wisconsin persists in the names of La Crosse, referring to the French name for the Indian game (fig. 224) played with a crosier-like stick; Eau Claire, meaning

224. *George Catlin. "Ball Players." In* Catlin's North American Indian Portfolio, *London: Day and Haghe, 1844. Lithograph, 29 x 44.5 cm. Library of Congress, Washington, D.C. Indians with lacrosse equipment; the game is Indian, though the name is from the French term for the stick, which resembles a crosier, or staff carried by bishops and abbots.*

"clear water"; Fond du Lac, meaning "foot," or "farther end" (actually, the head), "of the lake," in this case Lake Winnebago; and Racine, meaning "root" and referring to the origin of the waterway that is now named the Root River. Baraboo took its name from the local river, which in turn was derived from the name of the French fur trapper Jean Baribault. Prairie du Chien means "prairie of the dog"; it was, incidentally, one of the locations where Army surgeon William Beaumont conducted his celebrated series of early-nineteenth-century experiments on the stomach of an unusual patient, Alexis St. Martin, to determine the mechanism of digestion. Beloit, located at the confluence of Turtle Creek and the Rock River, was first settled by a French-Canadian fur trapper, Joseph Thibault, who built a cabin there in 1824. The early settlement was called Turtle Creek; after a group from Colebrook, New Hampshire, expanded it, the name New Albany was adopted. Perhaps because the earliest settlers were French, the community in 1827 adopted a name similar to the French Detroit, incorporating "Bel" (suggesting "beautiful").

Appleton, which had been called Grand Chute, honored the wife of Amos A. Lawrence, who had established Lawrence College there in 1847; Sarah Elizabeth Lawrence's maiden name was Appleton. Ripon, the birthplace of the modern Republican Party, took its name from the English town. Stevens Point was named in 1838 for George Stevens, an Illinois lumberman, who established the settlement at a point on the shore of the Wisconsin River. Janesville developed in the region of the Winnebago village called Eneeporoporo, meaning "round rock," referring to a stony outcrop now known as Monteray Point in the Rock River. The settlement was initially known as Black Hawk, but in 1837 it took the name of Henry E. Janes, who started a ferry service across the river and became the first regional postmaster. West Bend developed where rapids provided energy at a western bend of the Milwaukee River. West Allis's name is derived from the community's principal manufacturing plant, Allis-Chalmers. Similarly, Cudahy took its name from the brothers Patrick and John Cudahy, who established a successful meatpacking industry in that city.

CALIFORNIA

On January 24, 1848, gold was discovered in the millrace at Sutter's Mill (fig. 225), one of the properties owned by John Sutter, the founder of New Helvetia. This led to the great migration by tens of thousands of "forty-niners" seeking to gain their fortune. Large numbers of them sailed from the Atlantic coast, all the way around South America, and San Francisco became a city with a population of more than twenty thousand almost overnight. On September 9, 1850, California (fig. 226) was admitted as the thirty-first state, as part of Senator Henry Clay's famous Compromise of 1850, which had four major components: (1) California was to be admitted as a state in which slavery was prohibited; (2) the territories of New Mexico and Utah were to be established with no mention of slavery, leaving that issue up to the people who settled there; (3) new, stronger legis-

lation was passed against fugitive slaves; and (4) the domestic slave trade was abolished in Washington, D.C.

California, also known as Alta, or Upper, California to distinguish it from Baja, or Lower, California (the Baja Peninsula), had been acquired from Mexico by the Treaty of Guadalupe Hidalgo little more than two years earlier, and it never passed through a territorial stage before entering the Union. The state's boundaries were defined as beginning in the northeast at the point of intersection between 42° north latitude and 120° west longitude, then running south along that meridian to 39° north latitude. From there, the boundary continued in a straight line in a southeasterly direction to the Colorado River, where it intersected the parallel of 35° north latitude, then ran down the middle of the river to the boundary line between the United States and Mexico, which it followed on a straight southwesterly line to the Pacific Ocean. The state's western boundary followed the Pacific coastline, three miles west of the shore, all the way to 42° north latitude, and the northern boundary ran east along that parallel to the beginning point. California is the third-largest state and contains almost 159,000 square miles.

The naming of locations and settlements in California has a long history beginning with Sebastián Vizcaíno's voyage at the start of the seventeenth century. In addition to naming Monterey Bay for the viceroy of New Spain, Conde de Monterrey, who sponsored the exploration, Vizcaíno named San Diego Bay on November 12, 1602, for Saint Didacus, the saint on whose day the bay was entered, and he named Santa Barbara on December 4, the day of Santa Barbara, patron saint of the artillery. As indicated previously, the state's name came from the name of a fictitious island and was assigned by the conquistador Hernán Cortés in the 1530s.

Another group of place-names was assigned during the travels of Captain Gaspar de Portolá and Father Junípero Serra in 1769–70. It was during that time that the name Los Angeles was applied to the shore of the river they called La Porciuncula. They established a mission at San Diego, one of several during their trip, and applied the name Santa Ana to a river that they discovered on July 28, 1769; during the Middle Ages, July 28 had been dedicated to Anne (Ana), the mother of the Virgin Mary. They also established a settlement at the end of July 1769 at what was later called Long Beach, and on August 9 they named the Santa Clara River for Saint Clare of Assisi. In addition, they assigned the name Santa Monica to some mountains sighted on May 14, 1770, that saint's day.

The Spanish influence in the region remains evident, and the derivation of the names of many California cities is greatly facilitated by a Spanish dictionary. The name of the capital, Sacramento, Spanish for "Holy Sacrament," was first applied to the valley and river in 1808; the city developed in 1848 under the leadership of John Sutter Jr., whose father owned the millrace where the gold rush began. Considering other selected communities alphabetically: Alameda is a "grove of poplars"; Atascadero is "a miry place or an obstruction"; Cerritos is

225. *Napoleon Sarony and Henry Major. "A View of Sutter's Mill & Cullma Valley."*
New York, 1850. Tinted lithograph, after a painting by William S. Jewett; 43.5 x 63 cm.
Courtesy Yale University Art Gallery, New Haven, Conn. The Mabel Brady Garvan
Collection. The discovery of gold in the millrace here touched off the rapid migration
to California known as the gold rush. Jewett was California's first professional artist.

the diminutive for "hills"; Chico means "small" and was taken from the local Rancho Chico, which in turn derived its name from the stream called Arroyo Chico; Chino means "curly" or "mixed blood" and referred to a local landowner of mixed blood; Chula Vista translates as "pretty view"; Coronado means "crowned"; Costa Mesa combines the words for "coast" and "raised flat land."

El Cajon means "box" and refers to a canyon there; El Centro was so named because it is the "center" of the Imperial Valley; El Monte is a "thicket"; El Segundo means "the second" and was selected for that community's name because a company's second refinery was built there; Encinitas means "oak grove"; Escondido means "hidden" and indicated that sources of water were difficult to find; Fresno translates as "ash tree"; Hermosa Beach applied the adjective meaning "beautiful"; La Brea refers to "pitch or tar"; Laguna Beach took the word meaning "lake"; La Habra is "an opening in the hills." The origin of La Jolla remains disputed, but each of the two possibilities has a Spanish derivation: *hoya* means a "hole" or "pit" and may have referred to one in the area where the Indians stored acorns; *joya*, on the other hand, means a "jewel." Loma Linda translates as "pretty hill"; Los Gatos means "the cats."

In addition, Madera means "wood" and was given its name by the regional lumber company; Manteca means "butter" and was named because of the local butter creamery; Merced is the Spanish word for "mercy" or "grace" and was first applied to the river as Nuestra Señora de la Merced (Our Lady of Mercy); Milpitas means "small field"; Mirada means "view"; Mission Viejo translates as "old village"; Modesto means "modest" and was so named because the financier W. C. Ralston modestly turned down the town's offer to name itself after him; Palo Alto is Spanish for "tall tree," referring to a large redwood tree in the area; Palos Verdes Estates takes its name from the Spanish for "green trees"; Puente means "bridge"; Redondo Beach uses the Spanish for "round"; Salinas refers to "salt pools."

The Spanish propensity for attaching the names of saints to geographic features and settlements, which began with the earliest of discoveries, continued into the eighteenth and nineteenth centuries. More than three dozen California cities bear a saint's name. San Bernardino was named for Saint Bernardino of Siena. San Jose, which began as a pueblo in 1777, was named for Joseph, the Virgin Mary's spouse. San Juan Capistrano, to which the swallows return annually, honored the Franciscan hero of the fifteenth-century siege

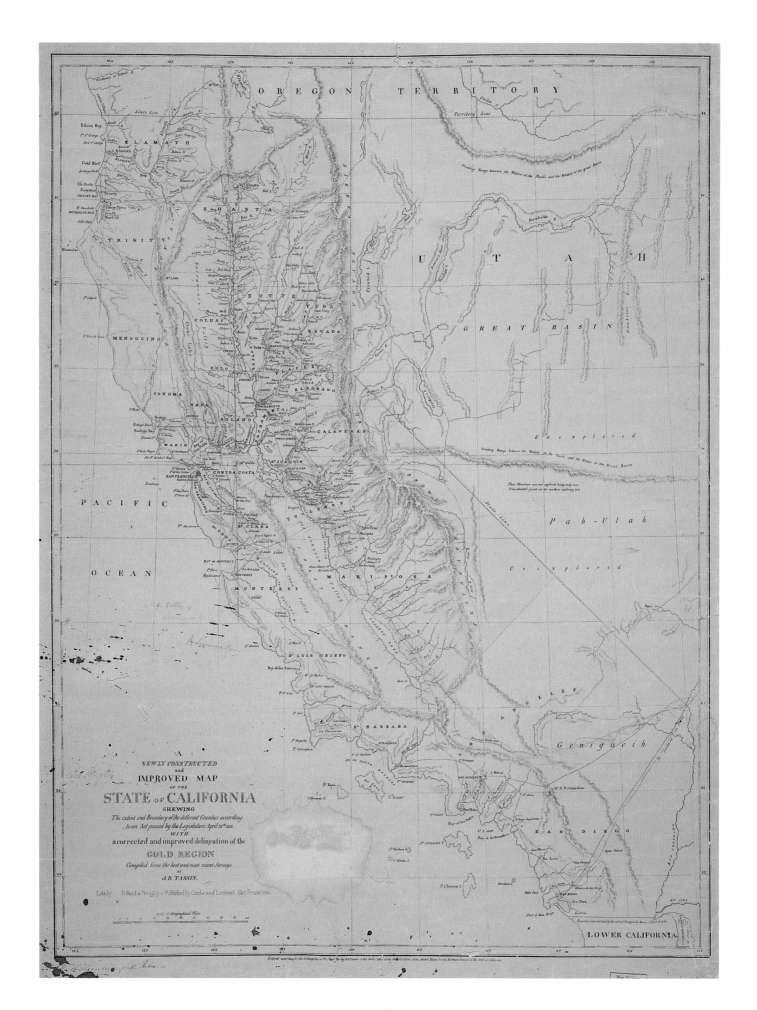

of Vienna. San Luis Obispo began as a mission dedicated to the bishop of Toulouse, who was later canonized. San Mateo was named for the apostle Matthew. Santa Rosa was named for Saint Rose of Lima, Peru, the first person canonized in the New World.

One of the early American settlements in California was located near the end of the peninsula between San Francisco Bay, named for Saint Francis of Assisi, and the ocean. It was originally named Yerba Buena for the mint that grew in the region. As more settlers entered the area, a local entrepreneur, M. G. Vallejo, planned a new town on the bay, which he wanted to name San Francisco for the bay and also for his wife, Francisca Benicia. The populace of Yerba Buena, in order to maintain its identity as the principal settlement on the bay (fig. 227), changed their town's name to San Francisco in 1847, blocking Vallejo's bid to use that name himself and thus to link his own development with the bay. Instead, he named his development Benicia, after the second name of his wife; his own name

228. *Golden Gate Bridge, from the San Francisco side.*
Courtesy Golden Gate Bridge Highway and Transportation
District, San Francisco

Opposite: 229. *Thomas Gainsborough.* The Blue Boy.
c. 1770. Oil on canvas, 178 x 122 cm. Courtesy
the Huntington Library, Art Collection, and Botanical
Gardens, San Marino, Calif.

became attached to another town nearby. The explorer, and later presidential candidate and general, John C. Frémont, whose name identifies another California city, named the opening of San Francisco Bay into the Pacific Ocean the Golden Gate (fig. 228), because of its resemblance to Constantinople's harbor, which was known as the Golden Horn. The adjacent coastal community, Daly City, was named for John Daly, who ran a dairy and was a prominent citizen. Oakland, across the bay, took its name from the local oak groves.

The name Ophir, which appears in the Old Testament as "a land rich in gold," was adopted by several mining towns during the gold rush. On a 1571 world map (fig. 219), the only designated location on the North American continent bears the number "19," which is keyed to the word "Ophir"; serendipitously, the number is located in the region of the gold strikes that would take place almost three centuries later.

In 1857, a group of German immigrants settled an area along the Santa Ana River and joined the river's name to the German word for "home," *heim*, to form the name Anaheim. In 1875, when a settlement that would become the site of the Rose Bowl and Parade was established near Los Angeles, its founding fathers commissioned a missionary to provide them with an Indian term that would connote "Crown of the Valley." The four long names that were submitted ended with *pa, sa, de,* and *na*, thought to mean "valley." The endings were joined to form Pasadena as the name for the locale. Authentic Native American words and names are also notable in California place-names. Azusa means "skunk"; Napa is an Indian term of unknown meaning; Novato was the name of an Indian chief; Petaluma is a tribal name; Poway was the name of a local Indian village, as was Temecula; Cucamonga is Shoshone for "sandy place," and Yucaipa means "wetland" in the same tongue; Simi Valley is from the Chumash for "village"; and Lake Tahoe is from the Washo for "lake."

Several individuals of diverse influence were memorialized by California cities. Bakersfield honored one of its early settlers, Colonel Thomas Baker. Stockton's name came from Commodore Robert F. Stockton, who took possession of Los Angeles and San Diego for the United States during the Mexican War. Berkeley was named for the eighteenth-century philosopher Bishop Berkeley, who was responsible for the statement "Westward the course of empire takes its way." Huntington Beach took the name of Henry E. Huntington, the railroad magnate who also built a streetcar line in Los Angeles and established a museum that, among its many treasures, houses Thomas Gainsborough's painting *The Blue Boy* (fig. 229). Burbank was named for David Burbank, a sheep rancher on whose land the city grew. Davis was named for its early settler Jerome C. Davis. Barstow used the middle name of the developer William Barstow Strong; the surname had already been assigned to another locale.

Torrance took its name from the real-estate developer Jared S. Torrance, who founded the city in 1911. Clovis was named for the rancher Clovis Cole; Vacaville was also named for a local rancher, J. M. Vaca. Visalia was named for the Vise family, and Yorba Linda combined the name of an early settler, Antonio Yorba, with that of the adjacent town of Olinda when the two joined to become incorporated. Fullerton was named for George H. Fullerton, president of the Pacific Land and Improvement Company, which developed the area. La Verne was also named for the local real-estate developer, as was Monrovia, which incorporated the surname of William Monroe.

Livermore took its name from Robert Livermore, an English sailor who settled the area in 1839. Irvine was named for the Irvine family, which owned most of the land on which that city eventually developed. James Irvine, whose name was attached to the southern California city, was a prosperous sheep rancher who in 1878 owned 110,000 acres stretching twenty-three miles from the Pacific Ocean to the Santa Ana River; forty-eight thousand acres of the land had been owned by Don José Adres Sepulveda and had been known as Rancho San Joachin. Redding was named for a land agent, B. B. Redding. Santee was named for the region's first postmaster. Lynnwood took the name of Lynn Wood Sessions, the wife of the dairyman. Ontario was named by an early settler, G. M. Chaffer, for his former home in that Canadian province. The city of Moreno Valley used the Spanish word for "dark-skinned" to honor its founder, F. E. Brown. Beverly Hills was initially called Beverly in 1907, at which time it adopted the name of Beverly Farms, where the soon-to-be president William Howard Taft had recently stayed; in 1911, the name was changed to Beverly Hills.

Whittier honored the poet John Greenleaf Whittier. Other California place-names honoring writers include Hawthorne, named for Nathaniel Hawthorne, and Richard Dana, the author of *Two Years Before the Mast,* whose name was attached to the city of Dana Point because

the novel included a scene in which a character swings on a rope over a cliff. Mythology is represented in the names of Ceres, the goddess of the harvest; Hesperia, the name of the Evening Star; and Pomona, the goddess of fruit. More down-to-earth, Fontana assumed the name of the Fontana Land Development Company, while Folsom's name came from that of the Folsom Development Company, and Norco is a contraction of the North Corona Land Company. Menlo Park was named in 1854 by two brothers from Menlough, Ireland. Oxnard, incorporated in 1903, took its name from the Oxnard brothers, who built a sugar-beet factory in the area in 1897. Orange was named for its dominant crop. And Eureka adopted the expression, from the ancient Greek, meaning "I have found it!"—the exclamation of fortunate gold miners.

THE 1850S

By 1850, the population of the United States had grown to more than 23 million, from 17 million ten years earlier. The land that had been opened to settlement in the first half of the nineteenth century was already home to more than 40 percent of the people in the country. In 1851, a wide-ranging peace treaty was signed with the Plains Indians at Fort Laramie—located in what is now southeastern Wyoming, and named for a trapper, Jacques Laramie, who had been killed in the area by Indians in about 1821. During the 1850s, the introduction of Cyrus McCormick's reaper spurred growth in farming throughout what would become the Plains states. This in turn provided stimulus for expansion of the railroad system. Lines extended west from St. Louis, Milwaukee, and Chicago. The latter was the point of origin of the Illinois Central, which reached Cairo, Illinois, by 1856. Chicago was also connected by rail to New York City, and the population of Chicago grew from only about 350 in 1830 to almost 100,000 by 1860.

The territories of New Mexico and Utah were established by acts of Congress on September 9, 1850, as part of the Compromise of 1850, which also admitted California into the Union. The land that originally constituted the New Mexico Territory was taken in part from the area that Mexico ceded directly to the United States in accordance with the Treaty of Guadalupe Hidalgo, as well as from some of the area that the treaty had recognized as being part of the state of Texas. Before the proclamation of New Mexico's territorial status, the Texas border west of 103° west longitude was modified, and Texas received ten million dollars for ceding that land, as far south as 32° north latitude, to the proposed New Mexico Territory. At the same time, Texas sold to the United States a strip of land north of 36°30' north latitude—the 1820 Missouri Compromise line, which was still in effect then, dividing slave states like Texas from free states to the north—between 100° west longitude and 103° west longitude.

The original territorial boundaries for New Mexico began in the southwest corner at a point in the Colorado River where that river intersected the border between the United States and Mexico. The southern boundary line ran eastward along what was then the

230. *Sidney Edwards Morse and Samuel N. Gaston. "Kansas & Nebraska."*
New York, 1856. Lithograph, hand-colored, 57.8 x 58.4 cm. Geography and Map
Division, Library of Congress, Washington, D.C. Fillmore Collection.
This map shows the two new territories created by an act of Congress that put
an end to the Missouri Compromise of 1820.

international border to the Rio Grande (mostly along the Gila River), followed the Rio Grande a short distance to 32° north latitude, then continued east to 103° west longitude. From there, the eastern boundary line ran north all the way to 38° north latitude. The northern boundary line ran west along that parallel to the summits of the Rocky Mountains, followed the crest of the mountains down to 37° north latitude, and then continued west along that parallel to intersect the California border, which the western boundary line ran along back to the starting point. In 1853, the territory's southern boundary was extended to incorporate the land acquired in the Gadsden Purchase, as previously described; the territory was subsequently reduced by the establishment of the Colorado Territory to the north in 1861 and the Arizona Territory to the west in 1863 (including a roughly triangular portion that subsequently became part of the state of Nevada).

The Utah Territory, established on the same day in 1850, also included land acquired from Mexico through the Treaty of Guadalupe Hidalgo. The territory was originally bounded on the west by the state of California; on the north by the Oregon Territory, along the forty-second parallel; on the east by the crest of the Rocky Mountains; and on the south by the New Mexico Territory, almost entirely along the thirty-seventh parallel. It included parts of what eventually became the states of Colorado, Nevada, and Wyoming, following the establishment of additional territories that reduced the size of Utah.

In the Pacific Northwest, the Washington Territory, formed out of the northern part of the Oregon Territory, was established in 1853, with Olympia as its capital. The name initially proposed for the territory was Columbia, but because the nation's capital was in the District of Columbia, the name of the first president was adopted instead. The territorial capital's name dates back to 1788, when John Meares, a British naval officer and explorer, named a peak in that area Mount Olympus. The name was then assigned to the peninsula on which the mountain was located, and finally to the city. The territory's southern boundary was the Columbia River from the Pacific Ocean to the forty-sixth parallel, then east along that parallel. The eastern boundary was the crest of the Rocky Mountains along this parallel.

After thirty-four years, the Missouri Compromise came to an end on May 30, 1854, replaced by the Kansas-Nebraska Act, a new attempt to resolve controversies about slavery, as well as over the future route of a transcontinental railroad, resulting from the rapid westward expansion of the country. Much of the remaining territory, and the likeliest rail routes, were north of the 1820 line intended to separate future slave states from free states. The act established two new territories out of the rest of the land of the Louisiana Purchase: Kansas and Nebraska (fig. 230), both of them north of the Missouri Compromise line; the act effectively repealed the prohibition of slavery set forth in the Missouri Compromise, however, by permitting the settlers of each territory the right to decide for themselves whether to have a free or slave state. In 1844, John C. Frémont had

suggested that the name for a single territory be Nebraska, adapted from a Siouan term that means "flat river without high banks," referring to the Platte River. Kansas, as previously noted, took its name from the local Indian tribe and had been cited as early as the Marquette map drawn in 1673–74.

MINNESOTA

Minnesota (fig. 231) became the thirty-second state on May 11, 1858, taking its name—initially applied to a river across the southern part of the state, and then to the Minnesota Territory—from the Siouan word meaning "cloudy or sky-tinted water." The land of the Ojibwa and Sioux was first explored by Father Louis Hennepin in the early 1680s, at which time he named the local Falls of St. Anthony, at the site of what later became Minneapolis. After 1820, the presence of Fort Snelling, built by Colonel Josiah Snelling as Fort St. Anthony and renamed for him five years later, allowed settlements to develop with relative safety in the vicinity of the entrance of the Minnesota River into the Mississippi. Larger numbers of settlers moved westward into the region from the Wisconsin Territory during the 1840s.

The Minnesota Territory was established in 1849, created from the northern portion of what had been the Iowa Territory, outside the limits of the state of Iowa. Minnesota's original boundaries essentially followed the U.S. border with Canada to the north, the Wisconsin border to the east, and the Iowa border to the south. To the west, the territory initially also included the large region extending to the Missouri River, starting partway along the western boundary of Iowa and running northwest all the way to the mouth of the White Earth River, in present-day North Dakota; from there it was a short distance north along that river to the international boundary line.

When statehood was achieved, the boundaries, surrounding about eighty-four thousand square miles, were set as beginning at the new northwest corner, far to the east of the original one, in the center of the main channel of the Red River of the North where it intersected with the boundary between the United States and Canada. The western boundary line proceeded south along that river to the Bois de Sioux River, up that river to Lake Traverse, and up the center of that lake to its southernmost point. It continued to the head of Big Stone Lake and through the center of that lake to its outlet, then ran due south to the previously established Iowa border. The southern border of Minnesota was the northern border of Iowa, extending east to the Mississippi River. The eastern Minnesota border followed the previously established western border of Wisconsin: up the main channel of the Mississippi River until it intersected the St. Croix River, up the main channel of that river to a point intersecting a line drawn to the first rapids of the St. Louis River, then down that river to and into the middle of Lake Superior, on the boundary line of Wisconsin and Michigan, until it intersected the international border between the United States and British Canada. The northern boundary line followed the international border that had been finally

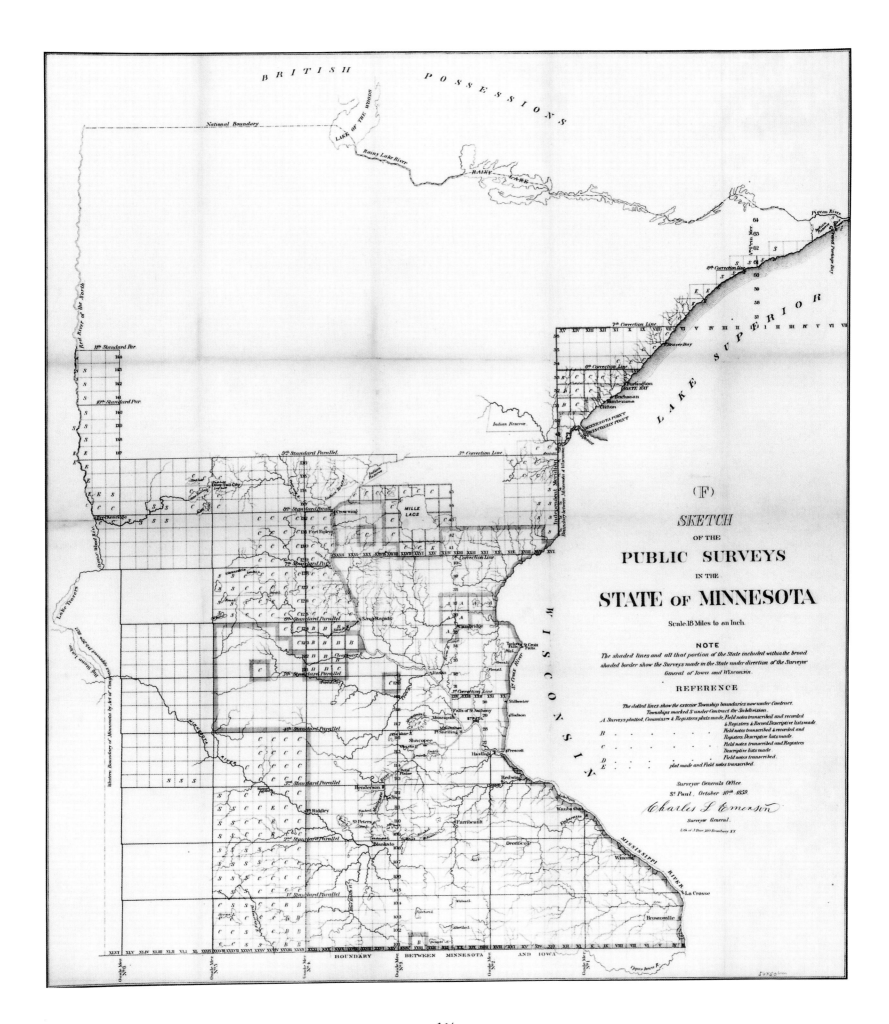

SKETCH
OF THE
PUBLIC SURVEYS
IN THE
STATE of MINNESOTA

Scale 18 Miles to an Inch.

NOTE

The shaded lines and all that portion of the State included within the broad
shaded border show the Surveys made in the State under direction of the Surveyor
General of Iowa and Wisconsin.

REFERENCE

The dotted lines show the exterior Township boundaries now under Contract.
Townships marked S under Contract for Subdivision.
A Surveys platted, Commiss[r]s & Registers plats made, Field notes transcribed and recorded
& Registers & Record Descriptive lists made.
B . . . . Field notes transcribed & recorded and
Registers Descriptive lists made.
C . . . . Field notes transcribed and Registers
Descriptive lists made.
D . . . . Field notes transcribed.
E . . . . . . plat made and Field notes transcribed.

Surveyor Generals Office
St Paul, October 10th 1859.

Charles L. Emerson
Surveyor General.

Lith of J. Bien 180 Broadway N.Y.

settled, after many disputes, by the Webster-Ashburton Treaty of 1842, from the Pigeon River through a series of specified lakes, rivers, and points of land to the Lake of the Woods; there it extended northward and westward to include part of that lake, ran due south to 49° north latitude, and continued west along that parallel to the starting point.

The name Minneapolis combines the Siouan term *minnehaha,* meaning "waterfalls," and *polis,* the Greek word for "city"; it began as a military post in 1819 and was incorporated in 1867. St. Paul, which at one time was referred to as Pig's Eye Landing, was the capital of the territory and became the state's capital. It assumed the name of a mission that had been founded in 1841 by a French priest, Lucien Galtier. It is said he chose the name because Saint Paul was the apostle to the gentiles, and the Indians were regarded as being in the same category.

Many Indian words and names have been retained as place-names in Minnesota. Bemidji was the name of an Ojibwa chief, Chaska is an Ojibwa name used for a firstborn child, and Winona was the name reserved for the firstborn daughter of a prominent member of that tribe. Also in the language of the Ojibwa, Chanhassen literally translates as "tree sweet juice," referring to maple syrup; Mankato describes "earth bluish green," a term that the Indians used for painting; Minnetonka means "big water"; and Owatonna is the word for "straight," which was also first applied to what is now called the Straight River. Anoka is Siouan for "on both sides."

Albert Lea took its name from Lake Albert Lea, which in turn was named for a U.S. Army lieutenant who came from Fort Raccoon, later called Fort Des Moines, in 1835 to map the area. He named the lake Fox Lake for a white fox he saw during the survey, but the name was later changed officially. Blaine honored James G. Blaine, the senator from Maine who later ran for president, while Ramsey took the name of the territory's first governor. Fridley had been called Manomin, meaning "wild rice," in 1879; it took its current name from Abram Fridley, who had immigrated to the region from upstate

231. *Charles L. Emerson. "Sketch of the Public Surveys of the State of Minnesota." St. Paul, 1859. Lithograph, 56 x 49 cm. Geography and Map Division, Library of Congress, Washington, D.C. This map shows Minnesota the year after it became a state.*

New York and then became the first representative to the territorial legislature and later the state legislature. Hibbing was named for its founder, Frank Hibbing. Austin took the first name of its first settler, Austin R. Nichols. Fergus Falls was named for James Fergus, who financed the trip to settle the area, even though he never set foot in the town. Faribault honored the fur trapper Alexander Faribault; it was founded and named in 1826. Brainerd's name came from the maiden name of Anne Eliza Brainerd Smith, the wife of J. Gregory Smith, president of the Northern Pacific Railway at the time of the town's founding; Mrs. Smith was a direct descendent of John Alden of the Plymouth Colony, and she worked so actively for the Union cause during the Civil War that she was commissioned a lieutenant colonel.

Rochester, the home of the Mayo Clinic, was named in 1854 by George Head, who moved to the region from Rochester, New York. Edina was first used as the name of the local flour mill; the Scottish immigrants who ran the mill subsequently elected to form a compact and honor Edinburgh in the name of the village as well. Similarly, Inver Grove Heights was named by its Irish settlers for a place in their homeland. International Falls, which frequently has the coldest temperature in the forty-eight contiguous states, is so named because of its location on the border with Canada. St. Cloud took its name from a French palace, because the person designating the name was reading at the time about that palace during the Napoleonic era.

OREGON

On February 14, 1859, Oregon (fig. 232) entered the Union as the thirty-third state, bringing the total number of free states to eighteen; there were fifteen slave states. (In fact, after the slave states of Florida and Texas joined the Union in 1845, all of the next five states, beginning with Iowa at the end of 1846, prohibited slavery.) At the time that Captain Cook sailed along the Oregon coast, in 1778, the land was populated by Bannock, Chinook, Klamath, and Nez Percé tribes. John Jacob Astor opened an American Fur Company post at Astoria in 1811, forming the first settlement in the Northwest. Larger groups of settlers began arriving by way of the Oregon Trail in the early 1840s. Eleven years passed between the creation of the Oregon Territory and statehood.

The state boundaries of Oregon began in the southwest corner one league into the Pacific Ocean west of the coastline at 42° north latitude and continued north, at the same distance from the coast, to a point opposite the middle of the north channel of the Columbia River; the northern boundary line ran in an easterly direction up the middle channel of that river to 46° north latitude and continued along that parallel to the middle channel of the Snake River; the eastern boundary line followed the middle channel of that river south to the mouth of the Owyhee River, then ran in a straight line due south to 42° north latitude; and the southern boundary line ran west along that parallel to the starting point. A total of ninety-seven thousand square miles are included within these boundaries.

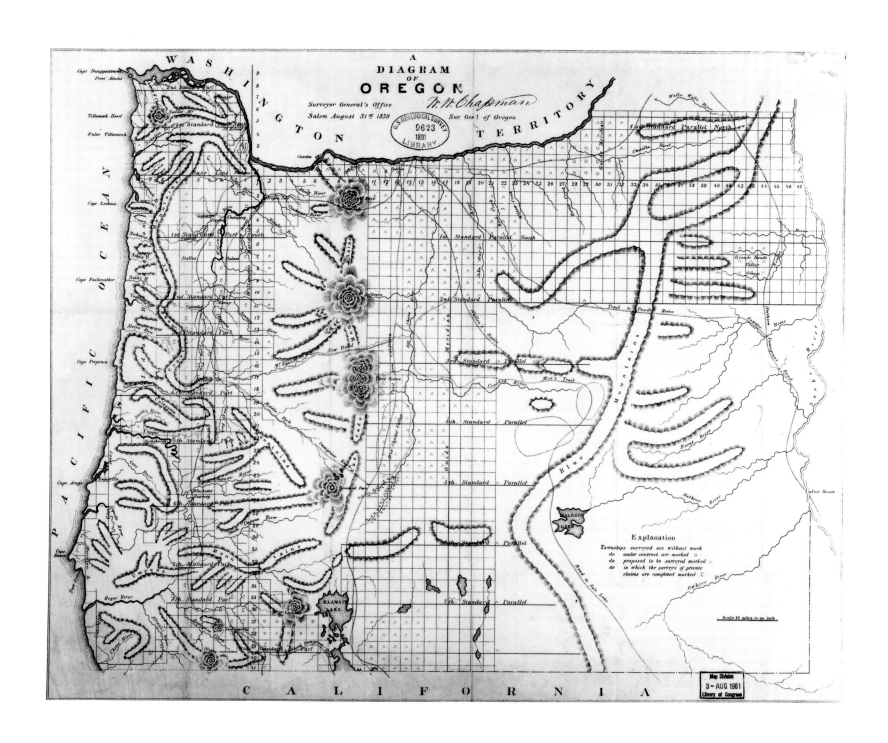

232. *W. W. Chapman. "A Diagram of Oregon." Salem, 1859. Lithograph, 44 x 55 cm. Geography and Map Division, Library of Congress, Washington, D.C. This is the earliest map of the new state of Oregon to be published in the state capital.*

Salem, the capital, like its Massachusetts counterpart, adopted the anglicized form of the Hebrew word for peace, *shalom*, as in Jerusalem (the Holy City of Peace); the city developed on the site of an Indian village called Chemeketa, meaning "meeting or resting place." Medford, meaning "middle ford," also transported its name from New England. Portland's name was determined by the toss of a coin to settle an argument between settlers from Portland, Maine, and Boston. Eugene was named for Eugene Skinner, who had settled Skinner's Butte and established a community that was first called Eugene City. Corvallis derives from the Latin term meaning "heart of the valley"; it was settled in 1845 and initially called Marysville after an early settler, Mary Lloyd.

Albany was given its name in 1848 by two brothers from Albany, New York, who were among the early settlers. Aloha was named at a time when the Hawaiian song "Aloha Oe" was popular. Beaverton, which developed as a shipping point on the Oregon Central Railroad, was named to reflect the abundance of beaver dams in the region. Bend, Oregon's largest city east of the Cascade Mountains, was named for the turn in the river on which it is located. Coos Bay, originally called Marshfield, was renamed in 1944 for the bay, which in turn bears an Indian tribal name.

Springfield is a name that was liberally applied to many communities throughout the United States, usually with no specific reason. In the case of Springfield, Oregon, however, the name was adopted because in 1848 the first settlers, Elias and Mary Briggs, called their homestead "the spring field." The name Grants Pass honored President Ulysses S. Grant and was first applied to a newly developed road, then later to the city that evolved in the area. Pendleton was named for George H. Pendleton, the 1864 Democratic candidate for vice president and later a U.S. senator from Ohio. Hillsboro was founded by and named for David Hill, who arrived in 1842 by way of the Oregon Trail. The post office was called Columbia at first; the name was changed in the 1850s to Hillsborough, and subsequently its current spelling was adopted.

The town of Oswego was founded in 1847 on Clackamas Indian land by Albert Alonzo Durham, who named it after his birthplace in upstate New York; in 1960, when the community annexed Lake Grove, that name was adopted. Gresham was settled in 1852 by pioneers who came from the coast to the Willamette River valley; it was named for the U.S. postmaster general in the early 1880s, Walter Quintin Gresham, in the hopes that he would then favor the community with its own post office. McMinnville was named in 1843 by William Newby, a founder, who came from the town of that name in Tennessee. Roseburg's name was an expression of appreciation to Aaron Rose, an early settler who donated land to the community. Tualatin is an Indian word, the meaning of which is unknown, that was first used to designate a river and later applied to the city. Tigard, a community that developed on the shore of the Tualatin River, was named for an early settler, Wilson M. Tigard.

On January 29, 1861, Kansas (fig. 233) became the thirty-fourth state, and the last to achieve statehood before the onset of the Civil War. When Coronado traversed the land in 1541, it was home to the Kansa, Wichita, and Pawnee Indians. The Kansa village that appeared on Marquette's 1673–74 map of the Mississippi River was the central location for that tribe, whose name means "south wind people" in the Siouan language. When the Kansas Territory was formed in 1854 by the same act that created the Nebraska Territory to its immediate north, it extended westward from Missouri to the borders of the New Mexico and Utah territories; its southern boundary was the thirty-seventh parallel except for the western section, which met the northern border of the New Mexico Territory at the thirty-eighth parallel. The act declared that Kansas (and Nebraska) could become a free or slave state based on the territorial citizens' vote. Proslavery settlers from neighboring Missouri and antislavery settlers from as far away as Massachusetts streamed into the territory to try to control the outcome, sparking confrontations that soon gave it the nickname "bleeding Kansas" (some of the fighting involving a radical abolitionist named John Brown). After repeated votes, the establishment of rival territorial governments, and the rejection by Congress of a proslavery constitution, Kansas was admitted to the Union as a free state. Kansas remained in the Union during the Civil War, and it sustained the greatest number of lives lost among all Northern states.

The state boundaries, which encompassed about eighty-two thousand square miles, were defined as beginning at the southeast corner at a point on the western border of the state of Missouri where it intersected 37° north latitude; the southern boundary line ran west along that parallel to the twenty-fifth meridian west from Washington, D.C. (which meant just west of 102° west longitude); the western boundary line ran north along that meridian to 40° north latitude; the northern boundary line ran east along that parallel to the previously established western border of Missouri; most of that border now constituted the eastern boundary line of Kansas, south along the Missouri River to the mouth of the Kansas River, and then due south from there to the starting point at the thirty-seventh parallel. The part of the Kansas Territory west of this area became part of the Colorado Territory in 1861.

Kansas City (across the state line from Kansas City, Missouri) was settled by the Wyandot Indians in 1843, sold to the federal government in 1855, and incorporated as a city in 1859. Topeka, the capital, took its name from a Siouan word meaning "place to dig potatoes." Wichita and Shawnee were Indian tribal names, and Salina was named for the nearby Saline River, on which it was originally staked out by William A. Phillips in 1858; it derives from the Spanish word meaning "salt." Lawrence was specifically settled by abolitionists to prevent the new territory from becoming a slave state, and it was

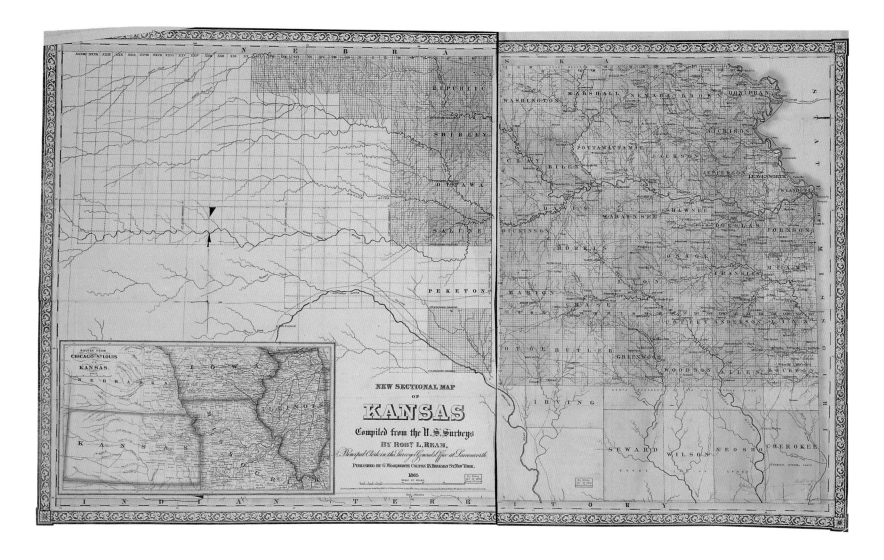

233. *Robert L. Ream. "New Sectional Map of Kansas compiled from the U.S. Surveys." New York: G. Woolworth Colton, 1865. Lithograph, 72 x 120 cm. Geography and Map Division, Library of Congress, Washington, D.C. This early map of the state, published four years after Kansas joined the Union, shows internal boundaries.*

named for the project's main financier, Amos A. Lawrence. Leavenworth was named for Colonel Henry Leavenworth, who established a fort there in 1827. Similarly, Dodge City honored Colonel Henry Dodge, who had established Fort Dodge at that site; the city became widely known as a frontier town that served as the backdrop for the escapades of Bat Masterson and Wyatt Earp. Hutchinson was named for C. C. Hutchinson, who founded the community in 1871. Both Dodge City and Hutchinson were stations on the Atchison, Topeka and Santa Fe Railroad. Coffeyville, which was initially called Cow Town, took the name of Colonel James A. Coffey, who established a trading post in the region in 1869. Overland Park received its name because of its role as a stagecoach station.

The point of origin of the Atchison, Topeka and Santa Fe Railroad, a town founded by proslavery forces from Missouri, was named for David R. Atchison, a U.S. senator from Missouri who then became a leader of the violent proslavery groups known as the "border ruffians." Abilene's name derived from the Hebrew word *abel*, meaning "meadow." Abilene was the end of the Chisholm Trail, established by Jesse Chisholm, along which herds of cattle were driven from Texas to the Kansas Union Pacific Railroad terminus between 1867 and 1872. At the time of its naming, Sylvia Hershey, the wife of Abilene's founder, Timothy Hershey, quoted Luke 3:1, which refers to Abilene as the region controlled by Lysanias. Hays honored the Union general Alexander Hays, who died during the Civil War. Before the settlement was incorporated, Hays's name replaced the name of the fort in the area, Fort Fletcher. Lenexa was named for a Shawnee woman, Len-ag-see. Olathe means "beautiful" in the Shawnee language. The town of Liberal was so named because of the attitude of its settlers, who liberally shared their water supply with those less fortunate during a drought. The town of Manhattan was given its name by the Cincinnati Company of Ohio, which hoped to establish a metropolis in the Midwest like the one in the East. Initially, the two small communities of Canton and Poleska had adopted the name Boston when they joined together, but the name eventually became Manhattan, and today, in a nod to New York's nickname "the Big Apple," its inhabitants occasionally refer to it as "the Little Apple."

Statehood for Kansas was just one more indication of westward expansion. By 1860, most of the major rivers in the United States were trafficked by steamboats. Goods were carried on the Mississippi River to and from New Orleans. There were links between New Orleans, St. Louis, Louisville, Cincinnati (fig. 234), and Pittsburgh serviced by more than five hundred commercial vessels. The Erie Canal's success had stimulated the development of an extensive canal system in the

East. A railroad system also had expanded rapidly in the East. By 1860, tracks had been laid between the eastern seaboard cities of Boston, New York, Philadelphia, Baltimore, Charleston, and Savannah, as well as cities in the Midwest such as Detroit, Chicago, St. Louis, and Memphis (fig. 235). The rail line linking Atlanta to Chattanooga opened to traffic in 1850. The waterways, railroads, and improved roadways all facilitated westward expansion.

DISUNION— AND THREE NEW TERRITORIES

And then came the Civil War, the bloodiest and worst period of disruption in the history of the United States. Not quite eighty-five years after its birth, the Union was torn apart by the secession of Southern states and the formation of the Confederate States of America. On December 20, 1860, six weeks after Abraham Lincoln

234. *Charles Fontayne and William S. Porter. "The Cincinnati Panorama of 1848" (panel 3). Daguerreotype, one of 8 plates, each 16.5 x 21.5 cm. Courtesy Public Library of Cincinnati and Hamilton County*

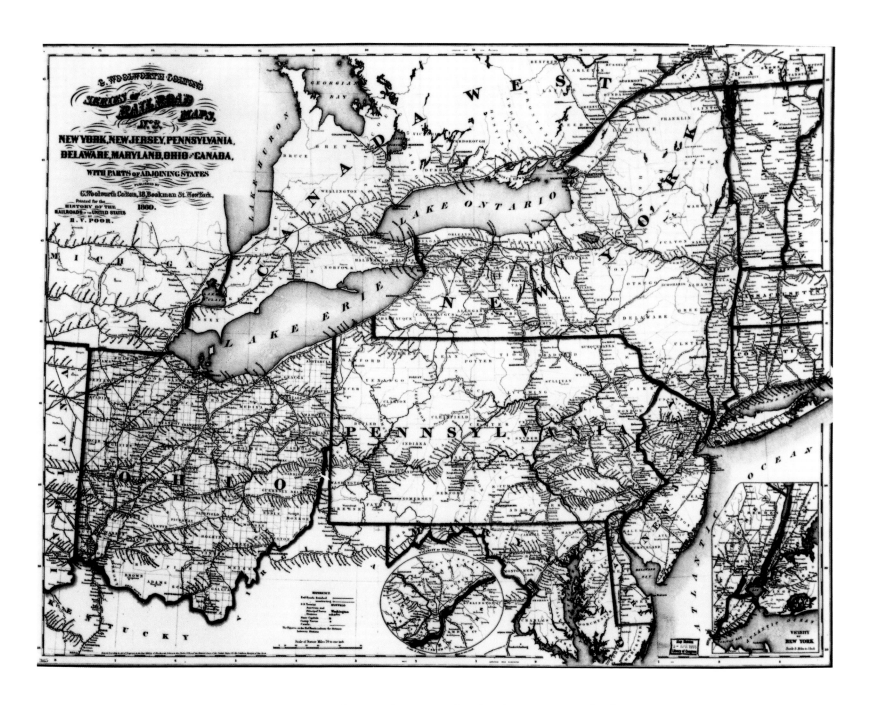

235. *George Woolworth Colton. "G. Woolworth Colton's Series of Railroad Maps N.3. . . ." New York, 1860. Lithograph, with outline in color, 68 x 90 cm. Geography and Map Division, Library of Congress, Washington, D.C. This map shows state, county, and town boundaries and indicates mileage between train stations. Completed rail lines are shown as solid lines; those under construction appear as dashed lines.*

was elected president, South Carolina seceded from the Union. During the ensuing forty-two days, Mississippi, Florida, and Alabama also left the Union, in quick succession in early January, followed in turn by Georgia, Louisiana, and, on February 1, Texas. By the time Kansas became the thirty-fourth state on January 29, six of the other thirty-three states had left the Union. On February 8, 1861, in Montgomery, which had previously succeeded Tuscaloosa as the capital of Alabama, the Confederate States of America was created, and two days later, Jefferson Davis, a U.S. senator from Mississippi until he resigned after the secession of his state, received word that he had been elected its president.

Before the first battle of the Civil War took place in 1861, three new territories, Colorado, Dakota, and Nevada, were formally recognized. Previously, an attempt had been made to establish what was called the state of Jefferson, including present-day Colorado and parts of Nebraska, Wyoming, and Utah, but the voters in 1859 had expressed their preference for a territorial government. Congress turned them down, however, at that time. On February 28, 1861, Colorado, with the same boundaries as the current state, received designation as a territory of the United States. It was created out of parts of the territories of Utah (the irregularly shaped area of present-day Colorado west of the crest of the Rockies), New Mexico (a small southern portion of Colorado, between 103° west longitude and the Rockies, south of 38° north latitude), Kansas (the rest of the eastern portion of Colorado that is south of 40° north latitude, west of the Kansas state border), and Nebraska (the northeastern portion of Colorado, east of the Rockies and south of 41° north latitude). As previously noted, the name, meaning "colored red" in Spanish, was first assigned to the river by Don Juan de Oñate during expeditions that extended from 1598 to 1602. Among the many names that had been considered for the newly formed territory were Arizona, a Papago term meaning "a place with a small stream," and Idaho, which erroneously was thought to mean "gem of the mountains" in the local Indian language. Within the Colorado Territory, the most notable discovery had been Pikes Peak, which Lieutenant Zebulon M. Pike saw and initially named Grand Peak during his 1806 expedition through the southwestern part of the Louisiana Purchase; it was subsequently renamed to honor its discoverer.

The Dakota and Nevada territories were recognized on March 2, 1861. Dakota took its name from that of the western division of the Sioux Nation; the Siouan word *dakota* means "ally." The Dakota Territory not only included what would later become the states of North Dakota and South Dakota, but it extended farther westward to the summits of the Rocky Mountains, including present-day Montana and a large part of what is now Wyoming. The Nevada Territory was taken from the western part of the Utah Territory. Its eastern boundary as a territory was the thirty-ninth meridian west of Washington, D.C., or just west of 116° west longitude, and the southern boundary was the thirty-seventh parallel; both were changed when Nevada achieved statehood. The name of the Washo tribe had been associated with the lands of Nevada, but the Congressional Committee on Names selected Nevada, Spanish for "snowcapped," because of the proximity to the Sierra Nevada range; these mountains had been named on maps as early as 1566. The irony is that very little of the famous mountain chain is located within Nevada's territorial boundaries.

THE CIVIL WAR, 1861–62

The Civil War began on April 12, 1861, with the bombardment of Fort Sumter (fig. 236) in the harbor of Charleston, South Carolina; the Union troops inside surrendered the next day. In the ensuing four years of bloody battles, the names of established cities and barely recognized locales appeared in the bold print of newspaper headlines. The first name on this long list, Fort Sumter, honored a Revolutionary War hero, General Thomas Sumter. The confrontation and surrender touched off a call for volunteers on both sides, and additional acts of secession: on May 6, the Arkansas and Tennessee state legislatures voted to secede, followed two weeks later by convention delegates in North Carolina and three days after that by the voters of Virginia, despite determined opposition to secession in the western counties of that state. On June 8, Tennessee voters approved their legislature's secession vote, despite heavy opposition in the eastern part of the state. The four other slave states—Missouri, Kentucky, Maryland, and Delaware—were kept in the Union, with varying amounts of difficulty.

After a number of skirmishes, the first important land battle took place on July 21, 1861, at a Virginia creek known as Bull Run, near Manassas Junction—named after an Indian word of unknown meaning, or perhaps for Manasseh, eldest son of Joseph and founder of one of the twelve tribes of Israel. In what became a common pattern, the Union side referred to the battle by the name of the waterway, while the Confederates referred to the nearest town; thus, the first major Union defeat is known as both First Bull Run and First Manassas. Several months of organization and relative inaction by both sides followed, other than a tug-of-war over control of Kentucky. Then, in February 1862, an obscure Union general named Ulysses S. Grant took the strategic Forts Henry and Donelson in northwestern Tennessee, opening up the Tennessee and Cumberland rivers and much of the western part of the state. On March 7–8, the most significant battle of the trans-Mississippi West was fought at Pea Ridge, Arkansas. The day after the Union victory there, the first naval confrontation between ironclad ships—the Confederate *Merrimack*, renamed CSS *Virginia*, and the Union *Monitor*—took place at Hampton Roads. This Virginia waterway, flanked by Newport News, Portsmouth, and Norfolk, and the nearby city of Hampton took their names from a shortening of Southampton, in honor of the seventeenth-century earl of Southampton who had endorsed early English colonization of America. Later that month, the Peninsular

236. Currier & Ives. "Bombardment of Fort Sumter, Charleston Harbor 12th & 13th of April 1861." New York. Lithograph, 23 x 30.5 cm. Prints and Photographs Division, Library of Congress, Washington, D.C. This attack started the Civil War.

campaign of General George B. McClellan's Army of the Potomac, aimed at the Confederate capital of Richmond, finally got under way in eastern Virginia, while in the state's Shenandoah Valley to the west, named after an Algonquian term meaning "spruce stream," General Thomas J. "Stonewall" Jackson and a small Confederate force outmaneuvered a series of larger Union armies for more than three months.

On April 6–7, a battle that resulted in more than thirteen thousand troops killed, wounded, or missing for the North and more than ten thousand casualties for the South—the bloodiest battle in the Western Hemisphere up to that point, ending in a relatively small Union victory—took place at a church called Shiloh (the Union name for the battle, from a biblical place-name) and nearby Pittsburg Landing, along the Tennessee River in southern Tennessee. On April

25, Admiral David Farragut's Union naval forces seized New Orleans, opening up the mouth of the Mississippi. McClellan's indecisive campaign toward Richmond ended in failure and withdrawal by early July; in late August, another Union army was defeated in a second battle at Bull Run and Manassas. On September 17, Antietam, a creek in Maryland with another Algonquian name, made the headlines as the site of a major battle (which Confederates called Sharpsburg, after the nearby town), with a combined total of more than twenty-six thousand casualties—making it the bloodiest single day of the war. Though costly and not followed up, it was enough of a Union victory for President Lincoln to announce his Emancipation Proclamation, to take effect on January 1, 1863. On November 5, however, frustrated by McClellan's inaction after Antietam (and perhaps by major Democratic gains in the previous day's elections), Lincoln finally decided to replace the popular but cautious Union general. In December, the Union troops withdrew after sustaining major losses—more than twelve thousand casualties—at Fredericksburg, the Virginia city that had been named in early colonial days for Frederick Louis, Prince of Wales and son of King George II of England.

TWO NEW TERRITORIES AND WEST VIRGINIA

Toward the beginning of 1863, the United States recognized two new territories in the West. The territorial status of Arizona (though with much different boundaries) was first designated in January 1862 by the Confederate States of America, nearly a year after settlers there declared that the area was no longer in the Union; on February 24, 1863, the reorganized territory received formal recognition by the Union. It included that part of the New Mexico Territory lying west of the thirty-second meridian west of Washington, D.C., or just beyond 109° west longitude. An attempt had been made to assign James Gadsden's name to the region, because his negotiations for the purchase of a large southern strip of land had completed the acquisition of much of the land in the United States. When the congressional selection of a name was finished, however, the choice was Arizona, "a place with a small stream," in part as a consequence of the urging of an influential delegate who had been a major investor in the Arizona Mining and Trading Company.

The Idaho Territory, recognized on March 3, 1863, derived its name from the word that the Kiowas and Apaches applied to the Comanches. In the Comanche language, phonetically, the word means "good morning." It had been thought that Idaho means "gem of the mountains," but this was untrue. The territory was assembled from parts of the territories of Washington (to the east of the portion directly north of Oregon, which later became the state of Washington), Nebraska (present-day southeastern Wyoming), Dakota (the western part of that territory, which later became Montana and northern Wyoming), and a small piece of the Utah Territory west of the Rocky Mountains (to just west of the northern border of the Colorado Territory). The northern boundary line of the Idaho Territory initially extended east all the way to the twenty-seventh meridian west of Washington, D.C., or just west of 104° west longitude; from there, its eastern boundary line ran due south to the northern border of the Colorado Territory, at 41° north latitude; its southern boundary line ran along the northern boundary of the Colorado Territory and one degree of longitude beyond it, to the thirty-third meridian west of Washington, D.C., or just west of 110° west longitude, before turning north to 42° north latitude, which it then followed west to the southeast corner of Oregon. The Idaho Territory eventually produced the states of Idaho, Montana, and Wyoming (except for the small southwest corner, which came from the Utah Territory).

Midway through the Civil War, on June 20, 1863, West Virginia—with its twenty-four thousand square miles and a strongly pro-Union population that refused to secede when the rest of Virginia did—became the thirty-fifth state (fig. 237). The first name that was proposed for the state was Kanawha, the name of a local Indian tribe and river. The boundary lines of West Virginia as they relate to Maryland, Pennsylvania, Ohio, and Kentucky were defined when its lands were part of Virginia. West Virginia originally consisted of forty-eight counties in 1863; Berkeley and Jefferson counties were transferred from Virginia to the northeast corner in 1866. The existing borders between McDowell, Mercer, Monroe, Greenbrier, Pocahontas, Pendleton, Hardy, Hampshire, Morgan, Berkeley, and Jefferson counties in West Virginia and the adjacent counties in western Virginia constituted the new boundary between the two states.

In the state of West Virginia, the remains of the ancient Mound Builders are preserved at Moundsville. The early explorers entered the area in the 1670s, and the first European settlements were founded by Germans in the 1730s. The state's capital, Charleston, initially called Charlestown, was founded in 1794 and named by its founder, George Clendenin, for his father, Charles. Huntington took the name of the railway magnate C. P. Huntington. Wheeling derives from the Lenape (Delaware) language; *wih-link* translates as "place of head" and referred to a place where a decapitation had occurred. Morgantown, the home of the state university, was named for Zackquill Morgan, son of the first permanent settler in West Virginia.

The town of Beckley, founded in 1838, is located in an area that had been first traversed in 1750 by Dr. Thomas Walker, the discoverer of the Cumberland Gap. The town was named for its founder, Alfred Beckley, son of John James Beckley, whom Thomas Jefferson appointed as the first clerk of the House of Representatives. Clarksburg, which received its charter from the Commonwealth of Virginia in 1785 and was the birthplace of the Confederate hero Stonewall Jackson, was so named to honor the Revolutionary War general George Rogers Clark. Martinsburg became the county seat in 1778 and was named for Colonel Thomas Bryan Martin, nephew of the Virginia landowner Lord Fairfax. Close by is Harpers Ferry (named for Robert Harper, who settled the area in 1734), where abolitionist John Brown tried to seize the federal arsenal in 1859. Parkersburg was named for Revolutionary War captain Alexander Parker, who purchased the land in 1783; it was originally called Neal's Station and developed on the Little Kanawha River, named for the Indian tribe, as a port for the shipment of oil. Weirton developed in the early twentieth century when Ernest Weir founded the regional steel company.

THE CIVIL WAR, 1863–64

Amid the formation of a new state and two new territories, the war was approaching its turning point, in mid-1863. On May 1–3, 1863, the Army of the Potomac engaged Confederate troops at Chancellorsville, Virginia. The North suffered defeat, but the South lost one

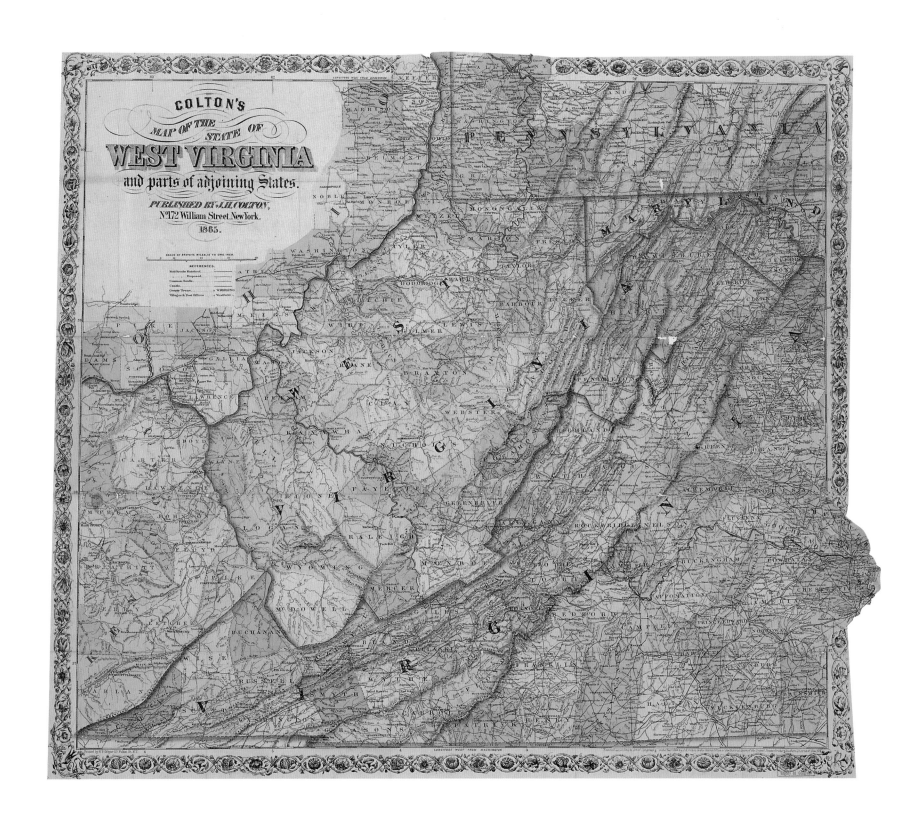

237. *J. H. Colton. "Colton's Map of the State of West Virginia and parts of adjoining States." New York, 1865. Lithograph, 61 x 73 cm. Geography and Map Division, Library of Congress, Washington, D.C. This map, published in the year the Civil War ended, shows West Virginia, which refused to secede along with the rest of Virginia at the start of the war, and which was admitted as a separate state two years later.*

of its most brilliant generals, Stonewall Jackson, who was accidentally wounded by his own men at night; he died a week later. On May 18, Grant began his long siege of Vicksburg, the key to the entire Mississippi River. After constant bombardment from land and ships on the Mississippi, as well as several failed assaults by Union troops, the Confederates formally surrendered the city on Independence Day, July 4. At the same time, General Robert E. Lee's Confederate troops were invading the North, and on July 1, 1863, near Gettysburg, Pennsylvania, a town that had been laid out by James Gettys, a three-day battle began (fig. 238). Each side sustained more than twenty thousand casualties, but Lee's troops were defeated and forced to withdraw. As a result of those two crucial defeats, the Confederates were almost entirely on the defensive for the rest of the war, and its final outcome was almost inevitable.

The rest of the year featured the Chickamauga and Chattanooga campaigns. In Tennessee, the Union army moved southeast from Tullahoma, meaning "red town," into Chattanooga, named by the Creeks to designate Lookout Mountain. The two-day battle just across the Georgia line at Chickamauga Creek—prophetically named by the Cherokees, meaning "river of death"—began on September 19 and resulted in more than sixteen thousand killed, wounded, or missing Union troops and more than eighteen thousand Confederate casualties. The victorious Confederate army then laid siege to Chattanooga. While Ulysses S. Grant, who had become the Union commander in the region, was making preparations for a major offensive, President Lincoln dedicated the military cemetery at Gettysburg on November 19 with his famous address of ten memorable sentences. On November 23–25, the Battle of Chattanooga resulted in a major defeat for the Confederacy.

On February 14, 1864, General William Tecumseh Sherman entered Meridian, Mississippi, and dismantled the railroad lines in the area before withdrawing across the state to Vicksburg. In Florida

238. John B. Bachelder. "Gettysburg Battle-Field." New York, 1863. Lithograph, colored. Geography and Map Division, Library of Congress, Washington, D.C. This map shows troop positions at various times during the three-day battle, the largest battle ever fought on U.S. soil.

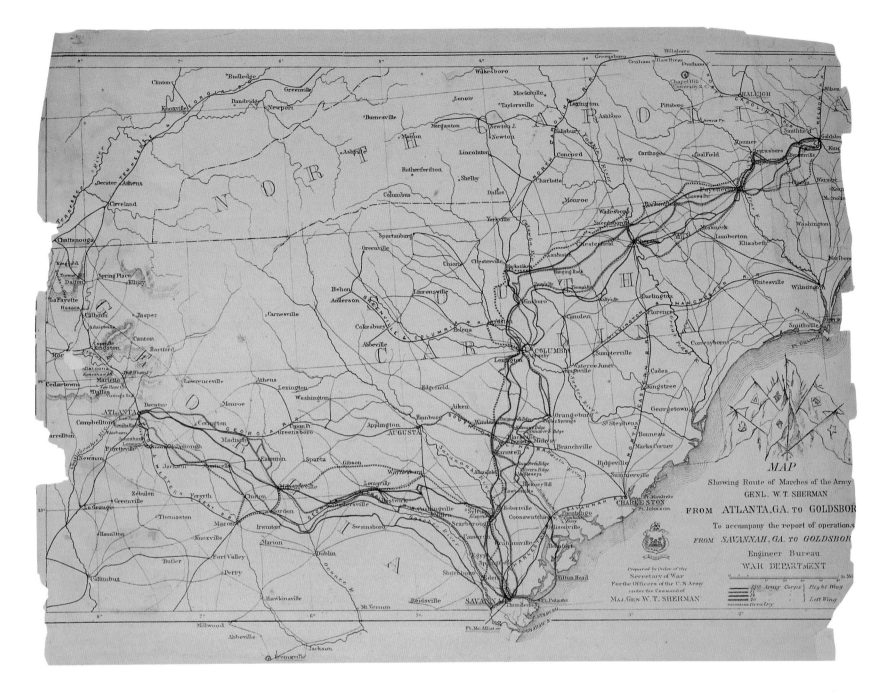

239. Cartographer unknown. "Map Showing Route of Marches [of] the Army of Genl. W. T. Sherman from Atlanta, Georgia to Goldsboro, N.C." [Washington, D.C.]: U. S. Department of War, 1864. Lithograph, 28.5 x 38 cm. Geography and Map Division, Library of Congress, Washington, D.C.

240. Las Vegas, from the Stratosphere Tower. 1996. Courtesy Stratosphere Tower, Las Vegas

that month, Union troops occupied Jacksonville and Gainesville. Lincoln wanted control of the state so that it could be represented at the Republican convention. This led to the Battle of Olustee, meaning "black water" in Seminole, on February 20. The Union troops were defeated.

On May 4, 1864, the Army of the Potomac, now under the direct command of Grant (who had been made a lieutenant general in March), entered the Wilderness, an area in northern Virginia that took its name from the dense forest. During the following two days, both sides suffered a large number of casualties. The two armies moved south to Spotsylvania, which had been named in 1720 by combining a portion of Governor Alexander Spotswood's name with the Latin for "woods." Near that small Virginia community, nearly two weeks of fighting took place, and May 12 became one of the bloodiest days of the war, with combined casualty estimates totaling nearly twelve thousand. More clashes, along the North Anna River on May 23–26, were followed by the Battle of Cold Harbor, Virginia, on June 1–3. Oddly, that locale, only a few miles from Richmond, had taken its name from a location in England where a shelter had been built to protect travelers from the cold. Unable to generate a decisive victory, the Union troops moved on to Petersburg, Virginia, beyond the James River. After a series of poorly conducted and costly assaults on the city, Grant began a siege of Petersburg, which would last from June 18 until almost the end of the war ten months later.

At the same time, in the spring of 1864, General Sherman was conducting a march south, with Atlanta (fig. 239) as the goal. Beginning from Chattanooga on May 7, he reached that strategic city in Georgia, and after a series of battles and a loose four-week siege, the Confederates evacuated Atlanta on September 1.

ANOTHER NEW TERRITORY AND NEVADA

On May 26, 1864, while Grant and Sherman were on the march, Montana Territory was recognized, just twenty-two years after the first group of settlers, led by Thomas Fitzpatrick, passed through the northwestern part of that region on their way to Fort Walla Walla. Montana was created out of the Idaho Territory, taking land east of the summits of the Rocky Mountains. Montana, meaning "mountain" in Spanish, adopted the name that had previously been considered for the naming of the Idaho Territory.

On October 31, 1864, Nevada entered the Union as the thirty-sixth state. The state was regarded as a Republican stronghold, and this was an important consideration in granting statehood before the upcoming presidential election. When the Nevada Territory was organized from the western part of the Utah Territory in 1861, its eastern

boundary was along the thirty-ninth meridian west of Washington, D.C., or just west of 116° west longitude, and its southern boundary was at 37° north latitude. When it was admitted as a state (fig. 241), the eastern boundary was moved to the thirty-eighth meridian west of the nation's capital, and in 1866 it shifted to the thirty-seventh meridian west of Washington, D.C., or just west of 114° west longitude. At the same time, the roughly triangular portion between the southern boundary, the boundary of California, the Colorado River, and the thirty-seventh meridian west of Washington, D.C., was added from the Arizona Territory, giving the state its present limits. The current state, containing about 110,500 square miles, is bounded on the east by the thirty-seventh meridian of longitude west of Washington, D.C., on the south by the Colorado River to the thirty-fifth parallel, on the southwest by the California line, on the west by 120° west longitude, and on the north by 42° north latitude.

Nevada had been explored by Jedediah Strong Smith in 1827 and by John C. Frémont in 1843–46. Mormons established the first permanent settlement there in 1851; it was initially referred to as Mormon Station, when it was in the Utah Territory, and it subsequently became Genoa, near current Carson City. About ten years later, with the discovery of silver—the famous Comstock Lode—at what soon became Virginia City, named for a miner nicknamed Virginia, the population rapidly increased. Soon after that, the state took its name, meaning "snowcapped," from the Sierra Nevada range, even though those mountains are located almost entirely in California. Carson City, the capital of the territory and later the state capital, was named for Christopher "Kit" Carson, the frontiersman, who rode throughout the area; the city was established in 1861, not long after the discovery of the Comstock Lode. Las Vegas was first settled by Mormons in the mid-1850s. The land was purchased by a railroad in 1903 and took its name from the Spanish word *vega*, meaning "meadow," referring to the meadows used for camping during travels and cattle drives. The city was incorporated in 1911, and gambling was declared legal in 1931. It is currently the most rapidly growing large city in the United States (fig. 240).

Reno was named for the Union general Jesse L. Reno, killed at the Battle of South Mountain, Maryland, in 1862; the city developed in 1868 when the Union Pacific Railroad came to the area. The locale had the geographic advantage of providing a place to ford the Truckee River, near the notorious Donner Pass to California. That river was named in 1844 to honor an Indian by that name who aided a wagon train headed to the West. Elko, like Reno, grew from a Union Pacific Railroad station in 1868. Henderson, named for Senator Charles B. Henderson, was established when the communities of Pittman and Basic joined; Pittman, initially called Midway City, was a product of the 1931–36 construction of Boulder Dam (renamed Hoover Dam, after former president Herbert Hoover, in 1947). Sunrise Manor was named for the nearby Sunrise Mountain, even though that mountain is dwarfed by the neighboring Frenchmans Mountain.

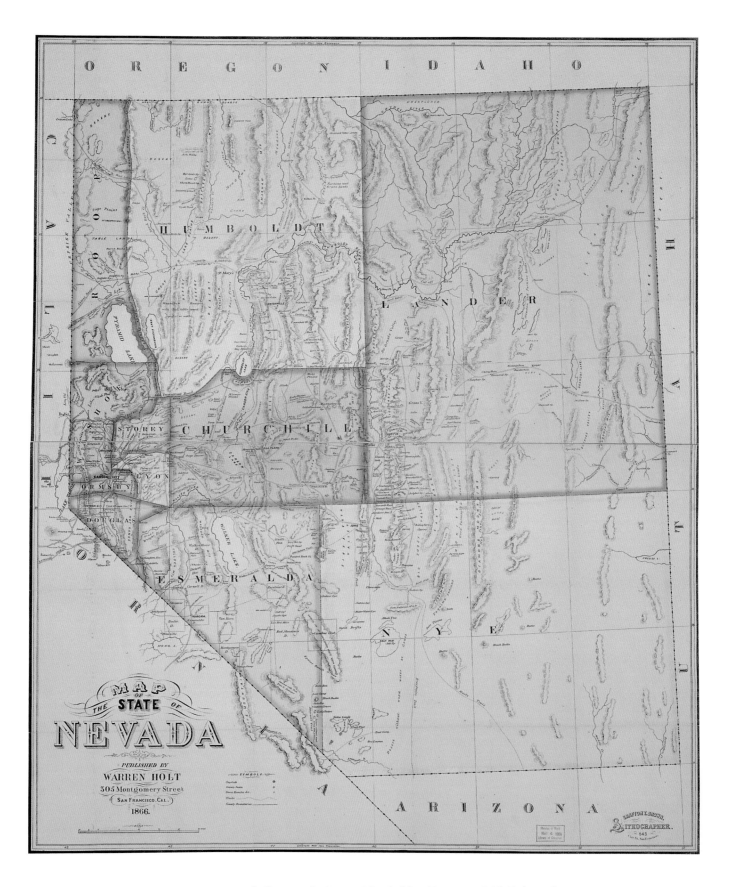

241. *Warren Holt. "Map of the State of Nevada." San Francisco, 1866. Lithograph,*
85 x 72 cm. Geography and Map Division, Library of Congress, Washington, D.C.
This map shows Nevada, the second state to join the Union during the Civil War,
two years after it was granted admission. Publication of a state map in
San Francisco was uncommon at that time.

On November 16, 1864, eight days after President Lincoln was reelected in a landslide over General George B. McClellan, General Sherman left Atlanta and began his March to the Sea, which ended in Savannah on December 10; eleven days later, Union troops occupied that city. In 1865, Sherman advanced through the Carolinas, where fighting continued. In Virginia, on March 2, General George Armstrong Custer routed Jubal Early's Confederate forces at Waynesboro, named for General Anthony Wayne, who had been victorious over the Indians at the Battle of Fallen Timbers in 1794; it was originally called Waynesburg and was renamed Waynesboro in 1831. The Battle of Waynesboro finally brought an end to the fighting in the Shenandoah Valley. On March 29, the Appomattox campaign in southern Virginia began. It was directed at cutting off the Confederacy's rail supplies to Petersburg. Jefferson Davis evacuated the Confederate capital of Richmond, which was also important as a manufacturing center, on April 2. Seven days later, General Lee surrendered to General Grant at the tiny village of Appomattox Court House (fig. 242), named for the nearby river; it was initially referred to as Apumetec's River, the name of an Indian queen recorded in the English chronicles of Virginia, which were written in 1607.

And so the Civil War came to an end, although the harshest blow of the war—the assassination of President Lincoln—came on April 14, five days after Lee's surrender, and some skirmishes, as well as the surrender of all remaining Confederate forces, continued for another two months or so. There followed a period of Reconstruction, extending from 1865 to 1877, during which time all the former Confederate states rejoined the Union and were eventually put in charge of their own affairs again, subject to the constitutional amendments prohibiting slavery and stating that blacks had equal rights of citizenship.

242. *The Civil War effectively ended on April 9, 1865, when Gen. Robert E. Lee surrendered the largest Confederate army to Gen. Ulysses S. Grant. Library of Congress, Washington, D.C. Above: This lithograph by Thomas Nast shows the surrender of Gen. Lee and his army to Lt. Gen. Grant. Left: This uncredited photograph shows Union troops outside Appomattox Court House after the meeting of Grant and Lee had taken place.*

CHAPTER TWELVE

Completing the Nineteenth Century

NEBRASKA

Nebraska was the first state to be admitted to the Union after the Civil War. Statehood for the thirty-seventh state, which took effect on March 1, 1867, after Congress overrode a presidential veto, marked the culmination of a long history beginning with a land that was home to the Pawnee, Arapaho, Cheyenne, and Sioux Indians and was first visited by a European in 1541, when Francisco Vásquez de Coronado reached it during his inland explorations. The Louisiana Purchase brought the land into the United States, and the Nebraska Territory was established in 1854 as part of the Kansas-Nebraska Act. The boundaries for the state were established as a result of the organization of the Colorado and Dakota territories in 1861 and the Idaho Territory in 1863. Both the Homestead Act of 1862, which made 160 acres available for a nominal fee to anyone who lived on the land for five years, and the arrival of the railroad led to the influx of a large number of settlers.

The boundaries of the state (fig. 244), as adopted from those of the reduced Nebraska Territory, were as follows: beginning at the point of intersection of the western boundary of the state of Missouri with 40° north latitude, the line ran due west along that parallel (the northern border of Kansas) to the twenty-fifth meridian west of Washington, D.C., or just west of 102° west longitude, then north along that meridian to 41° north latitude, then west to the twenty-seventh meridian west of the nation's capital, or just west of 104° west longitude, and then north again to 43° north latitude; from there, the northern boundary line ran east along that parallel to the Keya Paha River (from the Siouan for "turtle hill"), down the middle of the channel of that river to the Niobrara River (from the Omaha for "spreading river"), and down the Niobrara to its junction with the Missouri River; from there, the northern and eastern boundaries followed the middle of the channel of the Missouri to the starting point. In 1882, the northern boundary was changed by adding the small portion of the Dakota Territory lying south of 43° north latitude, east of the Keya Paha River, and west of the main channel of the Missouri River. Approximately seventy-seven thousand square miles are contained within these present lines.

In the 1730s, the Mallet brothers, French frontiersmen traveling up the Missouri River, came upon a broad, shallow river that joins it. The Indians called it Nibthaska, *ni* meaning "river" and *bthaska* "flat." The river was assigned the French equivalent of "flat," Platte, while the territory and eventually the state were given the Indian name, altered to Nebraska. The largest city, Omaha, was founded in 1854, the year the local Indians ceded their lands, and it was incorporated in 1857. The capital of the Nebraska Territory, it took its name, which means "upstream people," from that of the local Indian tribe. The state capital was named to honor the recently assassinated Abraham Lincoln, who joined Jefferson, Madison, and Jackson as presidents with names memorialized as state capitals; the settlement originally was named Lancaster, but it was renamed in 1867 when it became the capital.

Scotts Bluff was named for the trapper Hiram Scott, who died in the area and whose bones were later found and identified. Kearney (an alternative spelling) was a name initially attached to the fort in the area, in honor of General Stephen W. Kearny. Beatrice honored

243. *Kicking Bear. "Battle of Little Big Horn." c. 1898. Watercolor on muslin,*
91 x 180 cm. Courtesy the Southwest Museum, Los Angeles, Calif.
Two decades after the event, this old subchief of the Sioux presented his version
of the battle, commonly known to whites as "Custer's Last Stand." The resident
Indian agent wrote in the names of the Indian leaders and warriors.

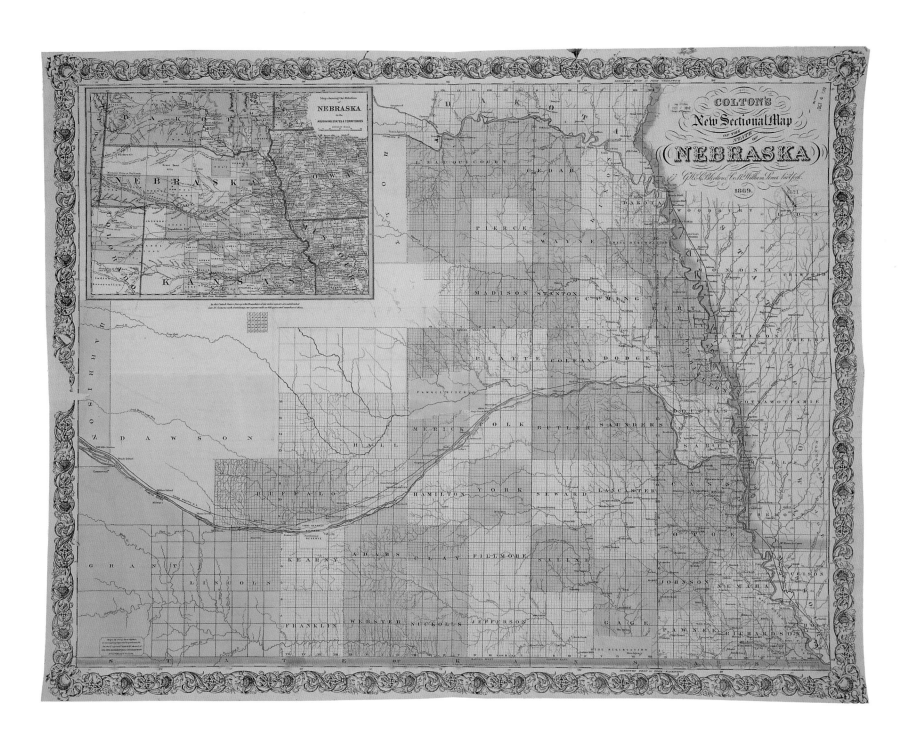

244. G. W. and C. B. Colton. "Colton's New Sectional Map of the State of Nebraska." New York, 1869. Lithograph, 73 x 95 cm. Geography and Map Division, Library of Congress, Washington, D.C. This map of the first state to enter the Union after the Civil War was published two years after Nebraska became a state. The map includes internal boundaries.

Julia Beatrice Kinney, the oldest daughter of Judge J. F. Kinney, one of the early settlers. North Platte developed at the north and south forks of the Platte River after the Union Pacific Railroad laid tracks in the area in 1886. Similarly, McCook grew out of a railroad station on the Chicago, Burlington and Quincy line in 1883. Ironically, the name honors Brigadier General Alexander M. McCook, whose troops conducted raids on railroads during the Civil War.

THE TRANSCONTINENTAL RAILROAD

Railroads were a major factor in the development of the West. The transcontinental railroad, the most important link in the nationwide network, resulted from a directive issued in 1853, under the provisions of the Army Appropriation Act, to survey railroad routes to the Pacific Ocean. Four routes were authorized: a northern route from the upper Mississippi River to the Columbia River, a central route from St. Louis to San Francisco, a route along the thirty-fifth parallel from Memphis to Los Angeles, and a southern route from New Orleans to San Diego. The last proposed route led to the Gadsden Purchase of the southern parts of present-day Arizona and New Mexico from Mexico. The wartime Railroad Act of 1862 provided governmental support for the first transcontinental rail line, between Omaha and Sacramento, to be built westward by the Union Pacific and eastward by the Central Pacific. Working at a feverish pace, the two railroads joined at Promontory, Utah, near the Great Salt Lake, on May 10, 1869 (fig. 245).

Boosted by construction of the Union Pacific Railroad across the southern part of the region, the Wyoming Territory was recognized in 1868. It was created out of the southeastern portion of the Idaho Territory (previously part of the Dakota and Nebraska territories) and a very small section—one degree of longitude and one of latitude—of the Utah Territory (which formed the southwest corner of Wyoming). The name Wyoming was taken from an Algonquian word meaning "large prairie" or "great plains." The appearance of the name of an eastern Indian tribe in the West was the result of a

245. Transcontinental railroad tracks are joined at Promontory, Utah, May 10, 1869. The two chief engineers, Montague (left) and Dodge, are seen shaking hands. The engine called Jupiter is at left, and No. 119 is at right. Courtesy Union Pacific Railroad, Omaha. Photograph by Col. Savage

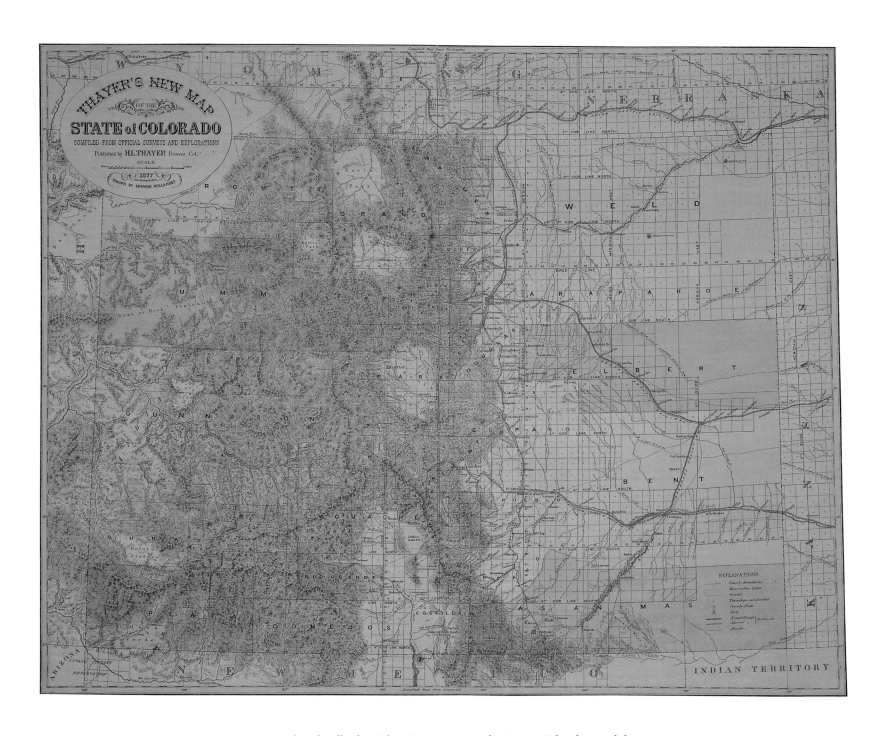

246. *Edward Rollandet. "Thayer's New Map of the State of Colorado compiled from official surveys and explorations." Denver: H. L. Thayer, 1877. Lithograph, 62 x 78.5 cm. Geography and Map Division, Library of Congress, Washington, D.C. This is the first map of Colorado published in that state, a year after it joined the Union.*

translocation of the name of the Wyoming Valley in eastern Pennsylvania. In 1778, settlers in that Pennsylvania valley were massacred by Indians and Tory troops during the American Revolution, and the name of the valley was later popularized in Thomas Campbell's widely read 1809 poem "Gertrude of Wyoming."

COLORADO

On August 1, 1876, almost three hundred years after Spanish explorers first set foot on that land, Colorado became the thirty-eighth state. Spain laid claim to the land in 1706, but the United States acquired a portion of the area as part of the Louisiana Purchase in 1803; Mexico ceded the rest to the United States in 1848. The state assumed the boundary lines of the Colorado Territory as defined in 1861, comprising parts of the territories of Utah, New Mexico, Kansas, and Nebraska. The state is a perfect rectangle, with borders running along major parallels (fig. 246). The boundary line began in the southeast corner at the point of intersection of 37° north latitude and the twenty-fifth meridian west of Washington, D.C., or just west of 102° west longitude; from there, it extended west along that parallel to the thirty-second meridian west of Washington, D.C., or just west of 109° west longitude—the point, now called Four Corners, marking the unique junction of four states: Colorado, Utah, New Mexico, and Arizona (fig. 247). The western boundary line ran north along that meridian to 41° north latitude, and the northern boundary line ran east along that parallel to the previously described twenty-fifth meridian west of the nation's capital, from which the eastern boundary line ran south to the starting point. There are about 104,100 square miles within the state.

The capital city of Colorado was named to honor James William Denver, who had a diversified and extraordinary career. A native Virginian, Denver moved west and served as a schoolteacher, surveyor, newspaper editor, and lawyer. As a captain, he led troops from Veracruz to Mexico City during the Mexican War and later brought under control the guerrilla warfare in the Kansas Territory, which initially extended west to the Rocky Mountains. Denver's additional accomplishments included his roles as commissioner of Indian affairs and as a general in the Civil War. Denver was governor of the Kansas Territory, much of which later became part of Colorado, and a settlement of miners named its developing community after him.

The adjacent city of Aurora took its name from the Latin word meaning "dawn." The home of the University of Colorado, Boulder, was so named in 1858 because of the large boulders left after the gold-mining activity in that area. Pueblo is the Spanish word for "town," and that city first appeared as a trading post, Fort Pueblo, in 1842 along the Arkansas River; the post was abandoned in 1854, but the area was rejuvenated by the arrival of the Denver and Rio Grande Railroad in the 1880s. Fort Collins was named for Lieutenant Colonel William Oliver Collins, who was commander of the Eleventh Ohio Regiment of Volunteer Cavalry and was stationed at Fort Laramie.

Greeley honored Horace Greeley, founder and editor of the *New York Tribune* and the man who popularized the inspiring phrase "Go west, young man"; the expression was actually introduced by John B. Soule in the *Terre Haute (Indiana) Express* in 1851. Greeley had stimulated the formation in the Colorado Territory of what was initially named Union Colony and later renamed for him. Greeley ran against Ulysses S. Grant in the 1872 presidential election, as the nominee of both the new, reformist Liberal Republican Party and the Democratic Party. After a resounding defeat, Greeley suffered serious mental problems and died before the end of the month.

Colorado Springs was founded in 1871 at the foot of Pikes Peak as a consequence of the discovery of gold in 1859. At the time of the Pikes Peak gold rush, Richard Sullivan Little arrived in the area as an engineer. He remained and built a flour mill just south of Denver, and when a village was established there in 1872, the settlers elected to bestow Little's name on it, resulting in Littleton. Arvada was named for Hiram Arvada Hoskins, whose family had founded the town, and Loveland honored W. A. H. Loveland, a railroad official. Durango was named in 1880 for the city in Mexico; that name was selected by a former governor of the state because he had recently visited the Mexican city. Golden was named not for the precious metal that was mined there but for Thomas Golden, who could not get his wagon up the canyon and therefore sold his goods to the prospectors.

247. *The junction of four states (the only such site in the United States): Arizona, Utah, Colorado, and New Mexico. In Franklin K. Van Zandt's* Boundaries of the United States and the Several States, *Geological Survey Professional Paper 909, Washington, D.C.: U.S. Government Printing Office, 1976.*

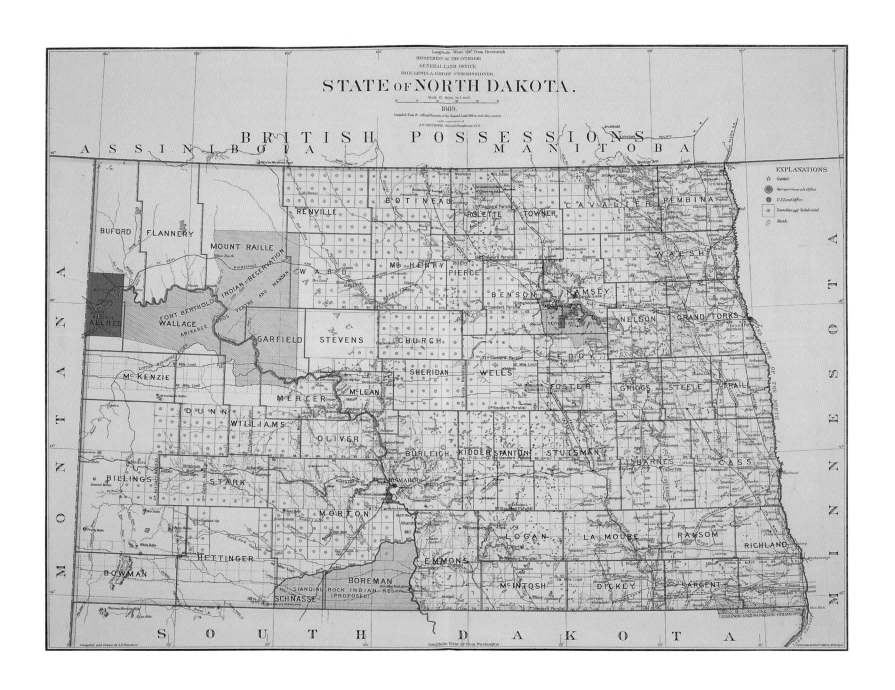

248. *A. F. Dinsmore. "State of North Dakota." New York, 1889. Lithograph,
62 x 84 cm. Geography and Map Division, Library of Congress, Washington, D.C.
This map was published almost immediately after North Dakota became a state.*

Three communities worth noting developed in the twentieth century. In 1908, Westminster University of Colorado was built and advertised as the Princeton of the West. Three years later the surrounding town was incorporated and called Harris, but the name was subsequently changed to Westminster to honor the college. The school closed in 1917. In the 1950s, a planned community was built and named for Governor Dan Thornton. In 1969, Wheat Ridge was incorporated and so named because it was originally a farming community. The first permanent settler arrived in the area in 1870, and the community's growth was caused by its carnation crop.

NORTH DAKOTA

Thirteen years elapsed between Colorado's statehood and the admission of the next state. Then, in just a ten-day period in November 1889, the number of states was increased to forty-two by the addition of North Dakota, South Dakota, Montana, and Washington.

After the Dakota Territory, which took its name from a Siouan word meaning "ally," was formed in 1861, land was taken from that territory to contribute to the creation of the territories of Idaho and, subsequently, Montana and Wyoming. At the time the Dakotas were admitted to the Union, the western boundary of both states was set at the twenty-seventh meridian west of Washington, D.C., or just west of 104° west longitude. The northern boundary line, which separated North Dakota from Canada, was along the parallel of 49° north latitude. The southern boundary line of South Dakota began at the intersection between 104° west longitude and 43° north latitude and ran east to intersect with the Missouri River; from there, the line followed that river southeasterly to its junction with the Big Sioux River, at the southeast corner of the state. The eastern boundary line began in the north at the Canadian border and followed the Red River of the North along the Minnesota border to the Bois de Sioux River, Lake Traverse, and Big Stone Lake; continued due south along that state's border to the Iowa line; and then followed the Iowa border a short distance west to the Big Sioux River and then southward to the junction of the Big Sioux and the Missouri.

On November 2, 1889, North Dakota was set off from South Dakota, with the parallel of 45°56' as the dividing line, and it became the thirty-ninth state (fig. 248). It contains approximately 70,700 square miles. In 1738, Pierre Gaultier de Varennes, sieur de La Vérendrye, became the first European to set foot on land in what would become the state. The southwestern part of the state was acquired as part of the 1803 Louisiana Purchase, and the northern and eastern parts became United States property in 1818 as part of a treaty with Great Britain. There was a short-lived settlement on the shore of the Red River of the North in 1812, but the first permanent settlement of old Selkirk, near Pembina, was not established until 1851. Wahpeton, which is the name of a tribe meaning "dwellers among leaves" in the Siouan language, is the second-oldest white settlement; located on the Red River of the North near the southeast corner of the state, it was initially called Chahinkapa, meaning "top of trees," when it was founded in 1869, and it was subsequently called Richville before assuming its current name in 1873.

In 1873, Bismarck, later a territorial capital and then the capital of North Dakota, was named for the German chancellor by a railroad official, because German bondholders provided financial support for the building of that railroad. Mandan, across the Missouri River from Bismarck, was named for the Indian tribe. Lewis and Clark stayed with the Mandans over the winter of 1804 during their memorable expedition. The state's most populous city, Fargo, took its name from William George Fargo, a director of the Northern Pacific Railway and cofounder of the Wells, Fargo express. The influence of the railroads also affected the naming of other cities: Minot was named after H. D. Minot, a director of the Great Northern Railroad; Dickinson took the name of Wells S. Dickinson, a railroad land agent who founded the town on a site he owned; and Williston incorporated the name of S. Willis James, a railroad stockholder. Jamestown was so named because it developed along the James River, where the Pipestem River flowed into it. The home of the University of North Dakota, Grand Forks, was given its name because the community developed at the point where the Red Lake River joined with the Red River of the North.

SOUTH DAKOTA

Also on November 2, 1889, in the only instance in which statehood was granted twice on the same day, South Dakota became the fortieth state (fig. 249), consisting of about seventy-seven thousand square miles. Before the Louisiana Purchase brought the land that constitutes the state within the boundaries of the United States, the region had been explored by La Vérendrye's two sons in 1742–43. In 1913, some children discovered an eight-by-six-inch inscribed lead plate that those explorers had buried on a hill on the west bank of the Missouri River, which was accordingly given the name Verendrye Hill. The Sioux who lived in the region were granted land by the U.S. government in 1868, and they refused to sell it to settlers. Nevertheless, when Lieutenant Colonel George Armstrong Custer reported in 1874 that there was gold in the Black Hills, a rush of settlers followed. After years of conflict, the Sioux were defeated and moved into reservations, losing the rest of their land. Their final defeat was the massacre at Wounded Knee in 1890, marking an end to the Indian wars of the nineteenth century.

The capital of South Dakota, Pierre, was named for Fort Pierre, which in turn had been named for Pierre Chouteau Jr. of the American Fur Company, which built the fort in 1832. The name of the state's largest city, Sioux Falls, is a reminder of the Indians who once owned most of the land. Rapid City took its name from the local Rapid Creek, roughly translating the French reference to it as "l'eau que court." Aberdeen, settled one year after the railroad line through the region was completed, was named for the birthplace in Scotland of Alexander Mitchell, the president of the Chicago,

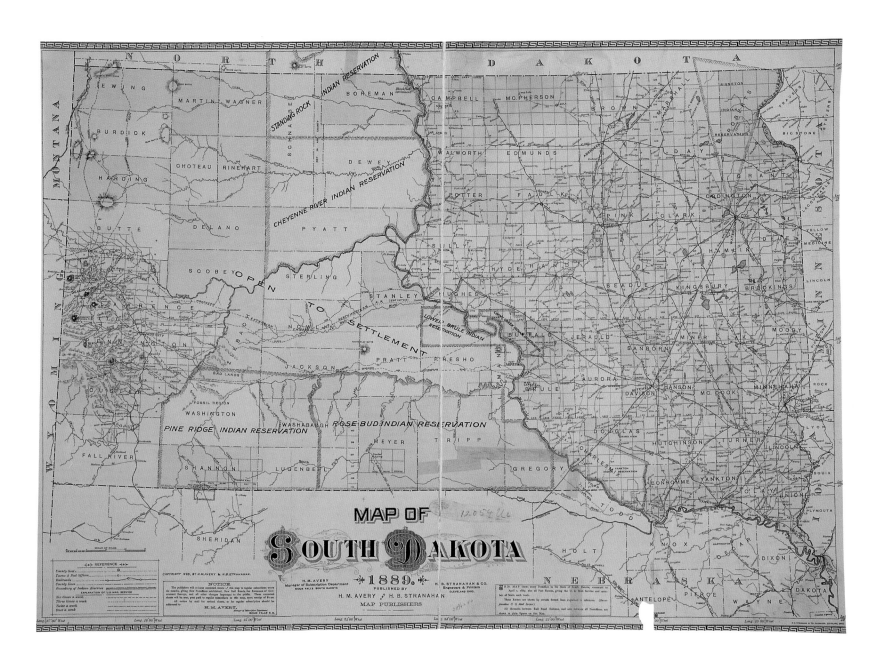

249. H. M. Avery and H. B. Stranahan. "Map of South Dakota." Cleveland,
1889. Lithograph, 73 x 102 cm. Geography and Map Division,
Library of Congress, Washington, D.C. This map was published almost
immediately after South Dakota joined the Union. Publication of the map in
Cleveland was unusual at that time.

250. Arthur W. Ide. "Ide's Map of Montana Compiled and Drawn by Reeder
and Helmick." Helena, Mont., 1890. Lithograph, 63 x 101 cm. Geography
and Map Division, Library of Congress, Washington, D.C. This is the first map
of Montana to be published in the state capital.

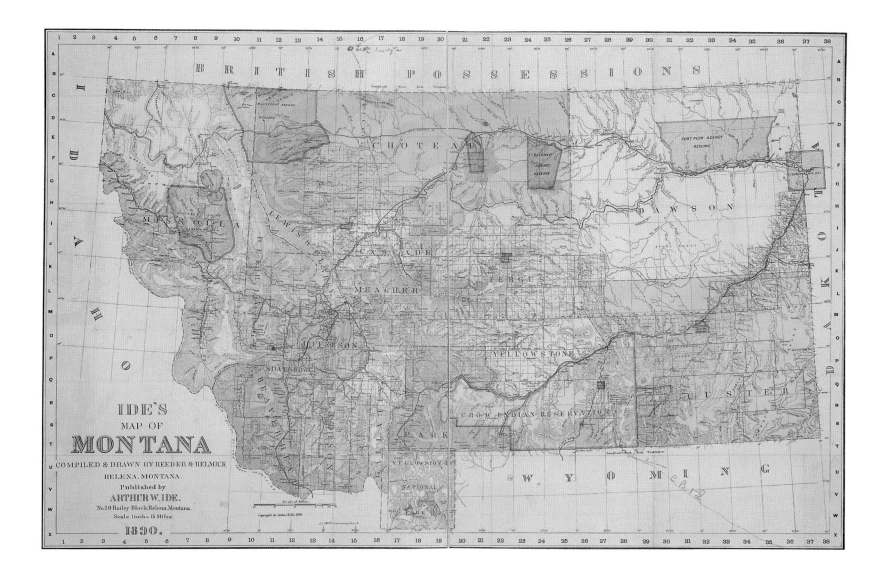

Milwaukee and St. Paul Railroad, who was honored by the city in South Dakota that bears his name.

Brookings was named for Wilmot W. Brookings, a manager of the Western Town Company of Dubuque, Iowa, who moved to the area of the new settlement, served as a justice and as territorial governor, and was a member of the constitutional convention of 1889 that led to statehood for South Dakota. Vermillion, the home of the University of South Dakota, took its name from the local river, which in turn was named because its dirt provided the red pigment that the area's Indians used as war paint. Yankton is the name of one of the three subdivisions of the Dakota, or western Sioux.

MONTANA

Montana, meaning "mountain" in Spanish, became the forty-first state on November 8, 1889 (fig. 250). Most of its land was also included in the Louisiana Purchase, and Lewis and Clark traversed a portion of its land. Significant settlement did not take place until 1858, after gold was discovered in the region. Two years later, ranching began to flourish. In 1876, a famous battle (fig. 243) took place at the

Little Bighorn River, named for the area's sheep. Lieutenant Colonel George Armstrong Custer and his detachment of more than two hundred troops of the Seventh Cavalry were all killed by a much larger force of Sioux and allied tribes; the sole survivor on the American side, ironically, was Custer's horse, Comanche—an Indian tribal name. The Montana Territory was carved out of the Idaho Territory in 1864, and Montana's territorial boundaries were almost identical with those of the state. They began in the southeast corner at the intersection of the twenty-seventh meridian west of Washington, D.C., or just west of 104° west longitude, and 45° north latitude. The southern boundary line ran west along the forty-fifth parallel until it intersected with the thirty-fourth meridian west of Washington, D.C., or just west of 111° west longitude; from there, it ran due south to 44°30' north latitude, then west to a point at which that parallel intersected with the crest of the Rocky Mountains. From the crest, the line ran northward and westward until it intersected with the Bitterroot Range. The western boundary line followed the crest of the Bitterroot Range to the thirty-ninth meridian west of Washington, D.C., or just west of 116° west longitude, then ran due north to 49°

north latitude, the boundary between the United States and Canada. The northern boundary line ran east along that parallel to the twenty-seventh meridian west of Washington, D.C., and the eastern boundary line ran south along that meridian—the western border of the Dakotas—to the starting point. Montana is the fourth-largest state, consisting of 147,000 square miles.

The capital, Helena, took its name from a town in Minnesota, from which one of the influential founders had come. The largest city, Billings, appropriately was named for Frederick Billings, president of the Northern Pacific Railway, because the city's development in 1882 was specifically due to that railroad. Anaconda was named for the large copper mine there, which took the name of the large snake because of a Civil War report that General Ulysses S. Grant had encircled General Robert E. Lee "like an anaconda." Bozeman honored John M. Bozeman, who initiated that settlement in 1864 along the westward route known as the Bozeman Trail. Great Falls describes a local geographic feature, as does Butte, meaning "a hill rising abruptly with sloping sides and a flat top." Missoula is a Flathead Indian term meaning "by very cold water," with the word *cold* connoting "dread" rather than the temperature. Kalispell is a variation of a tribal name. Havre took the name of the French city Le Havre.

WASHINGTON

On November 11, 1889, three days after Montana attained statehood, Washington became the forty-second state (fig. 251). It was the only territory and is the only state to bear a president's name. When Mississippi became a territory, an attempt was made to name it in honor of George Washington, but the river's name won out. When it came time to name the Washington Territory, the name Columbia was considered first. The land, which originally was home to the Nez Percé, Chinook, Yakima, and other tribes, was explored along its coast by Captain Cook in 1778, and George Vancouver of the Royal Navy entered Puget Sound in 1792. In 1846, a treaty with Great Britain set the northern U.S. border in that region at 49° north latitude, finishing the map of territorial rights for the continental United States. The completion of the Northern Pacific Railway expedited the great influx of settlers that took place in the 1880s.

When the Washington Territory was formed in 1853, the land was taken from the northern part of the Oregon Territory (see fig. 215); in 1863, the territory was reduced by the organization of the Idaho Territory to the east. The state's boundaries, which encompass sixty-eight thousand square miles, began one league west of a point at the mouth of the Columbia River and ran east through the main channel of that river to the intersection with 46° north latitude, then due east along that parallel to the Snake River. The eastern boundary line (the western border of the Idaho Territory) ran northward down the main channel of the Snake River to the mouth of the Clearwater River, then due north on the meridian that passes through the mouth of the Clearwater River—just west of 117° west longitude—to the

Canadian border at 49° northern latitude, which is the northern boundary line, extending west to Puget Sound; from there, it followed the 1846 treaty line for the U.S. border with Canada—southward west of the San Juan Islands and east of Vancouver Island, then westward through the Strait of Juan de Fuca, between Vancouver Island and the Olympic Peninsula, to the Pacific Ocean.

Vancouver, the oldest city in the state, traces its beginnings to 1792, when Captain Robert Gray first entered the mouth of the Columbia River. Later that year, Lieutenant William Broughton, serving under George Vancouver, explored one hundred miles up that river and named a point for his leader. In 1806, Lewis and Clark reported that the point afforded the most favorable site for settlement west of the Rockies. In 1825, the Hudson's Bay Company moved its headquarters in the Northwest from Astoria and named the site Fort Vancouver. The region became part of the United States in 1846, and the site was renamed the city of Columbia. In 1857, when the city was incorporated, the name was changed to Vancouver.

Olympia, the territorial and then state capital, took its name—given to it by settler Isaac Ebey in 1846—from the Olympic Peninsula, which in turn received its name from Mount Olympus, a regional peak so designated by British naval officer and explorer John Meares during his travels in 1788. The region, known to the local Indians as "the black bear place," was explored first by the British lieutenant Peter Puget in 1792 and then by the American lieutenant Charles Wilkes in 1841, at which time Budd Inlet was named for Midshipman Thomas Budd. Seattle (fig. 252), the state's most populous city, was settled in 1851 and incorporated in 1869. The name comes from a local Indian chief commonly called Seattle or Seatlh (also sometimes spelled See-yat). Nearby Tacoma was given the Siwash name meaning "snowy peak," and previously applied by the Indians to the mountain that George Vancouver dubbed Mount Rainier; attempts were made on several occasions to restore the Indian name to that majestic mountain. Tacoma is on Commencement Bay, named that by the Wilkes expedition of 1841 because it was the first bay at the foot of Puget Sound. The region was originally colonized by the Hudson's Bay Company at Fort Nisqually (from an Indian tribal name) in 1833, and the city of Tacoma was incorporated in 1884.

Spokane, which comes from the name of an Indian tribe and river, a Siwash word meaning "children of the sun," began as the village of Spokane Falls in 1872; it was destroyed by fire in 1889 and reincorporated in 1891, at which time it became Spokane. Anacortes was named in 1876 by its planner, Amos Bowman, for his wife, Anna Curtis, whose name was given a Spanish twist. The founders of Bellevue chose a name to stress the "beautiful view." Bellingham's name came from a bay that Vancouver named in 1792 for Sir William Bellingham, who had assisted in the preparation for that voyage. Bothell was named for David C. Bothell and his wife, Mary Ann, who filed the first claim for a piece of land in that town in 1909. Bremerton was named for its founder, William Bremer, in 1891.

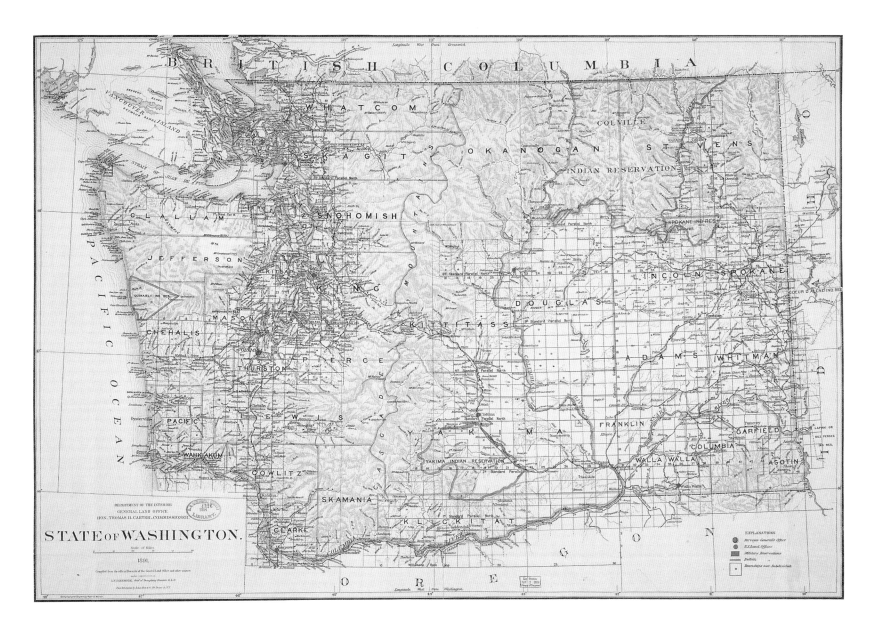

251. *A. F. Dinsmore. "State of Washington." New York,*
1891. Lithograph, 66.5 x 97.5 cm. Geography and
Map Division, Library of Congress, Washington, D.C.
This map shows Washington as it was about
two years after it became a state.

252. *Seattle, from Kerry Park, including the Space*
Needle and a view of Mt. Rainier.
Photograph by Brian Huntoon

The city of Cascade-Fairwood recognized the Cascade Range, named because of the cascades of the Columbia River that course through those mountains. The name of Des Moines can be traced back to the Iowa city, and it was adopted by the Des Moines City Improvement Company when it began its building activities in Washington in 1867. The city of Edmonds planned to honor Senator George F. Edmunds of Vermont, but unfortunately the name was misspelled during transmission. Enumclaw Mountain's name was adopted by the city; the mountain's name was designated by an Indian word meaning "home of evil spirits," because the Indian who gave it that name was said to have been caught by a lightning storm in the area. Ephrata, which appears in the Bible as another name for Bethlehem or to identify an orchard in the desert, was given its name by the Great Northern Railroad staff. Kennewick, which was the homeland of the Chemnapam Indians, is their word for "winter haven" or "grassy place." Because Kent County in England was noted for its production of hops and a city in Washington also specialized in the growing of hops, it was logical for that American city to adopt the English county's name.

Kirkland honored the British-born steel tycoon Peter Kirk, who built the Moss Bay Iron and Steel Works on the eastern shore of Lake Washington in 1880. In that lake, Mercer Island was named for one of the three pioneer brothers who were early settlers. Marysville was named by the town's founder, Samuel Hill, for his wife and mother, both named Mary. Pullman selected its name from that of George M. Pullman, the railroad car manufacturer, in hopes that he would act as a benefactor. The ploy failed. When Ezra Meeker arrived at a site that he developed, he gave it the name of the local Puyallup tribe, a name meaning "generous people."

Other Native American contributions to city names in the state of Washington include Snohomish, Steilacoom, Tukwila, Walla Walla, Wenatchee, and Yakima. Snohomish was the name of a tribe, adopted by the settlement that developed at the confluence of the Snohomish and Pilchuck rivers; the latter name means "red water." Steilacoom was the name of a local chief, although the name usually appeared as Tail-a-coom. Tukwila means "land of hazelnuts" in the language of the Duwamish tribe. Walla Walla, as mentioned previously, is a Nez Percé term that translates as "small rapid streams." Wenatchee is the name of an Indian tribe, which translates as "river flowing from canyon." Yakima, which was first settled on the site of Fort Simcoe—named for the late-eighteenth-century Canadian leader John Graves Simcoe—was named North Yakima in 1886, taking the tribal name; when the city was incorporated in 1918, "North" was dropped.

On July 3, 1890, Idaho was admitted as the forty-third state (fig. 253). The land was traversed by Lewis and Clark, who stayed with the Nez Percé Indians in 1804 and 1805, during their exploration of the extent of the Louisiana Purchase. In 1810, the Missouri Fur Company built Fort Henry as the first American trading post in the region. Between 1818 and 1846, when a convention with Great Britain extended the boundary line between the British and American possessions westward along the forty-ninth parallel, the land was held jointly by Great Britain and the United States; then it became the sole possession of the United States. Early settlement in the 1860s was stimulated by the prospect of finding gold, and ranching followed shortly thereafter. In 1860, Franklin was established as the first town.

The Idaho Territory, which was formed in 1863 out of parts of the Washington, Dakota, Nebraska, and Utah territories, was subsequently reduced to its present state size by the contribution of its eastern portion for the establishment of the territories of Montana and Wyoming. The boundaries of the state began in the northeast corner at the intersection of the thirty-ninth meridian west of Washington, D.C., or just west of 116° west longitude, with 49° north latitude (the U.S. border with Canada). The eastern boundary line—mostly along the western border of Montana—followed that meridian south until it reached the summits of the Bitterroot Range, from which it continued southeastward along the crest of the Bitterroot Range and the Continental Divide until it reached the thirty-fourth meridian west of Washington, D.C., or just west of 111° west longitude. From there, the eastern boundary line ran due south along that meridian to 42° north latitude. The southern boundary line extended due west along that parallel to the intersection with a meridian drawn through the mouth of the Owyhee River. The western boundary line—along the Oregon and Washington borders—ran due north along that meridian to the mouth of the Owyhee, then down the Snake River to the mouth of the Clearwater River, and finally due north along the meridian passing through the mouth of the Clearwater River to the Canadian border, which forms the short distance of Idaho's northern boundary line east to the starting point. Approximately 83,500 square miles are included within these lines.

Idaho was the first name suggested for what then became Colorado, and Montana was the first name suggested for Idaho when it became a territory. The name Idaho was first applied in this country at Idaho Springs, Colorado. In 1861, the name was used for a city in the Washington Territory, before it became part of the Idaho Territory.

253. A. F. Dinsmore. "State of Idaho." New York, 1891.
Lithograph, 101 x 67 cm. Geography and Map Division,
Library of Congress, Washington, D.C. This map shows
the 43rd state one year after it joined the Union.

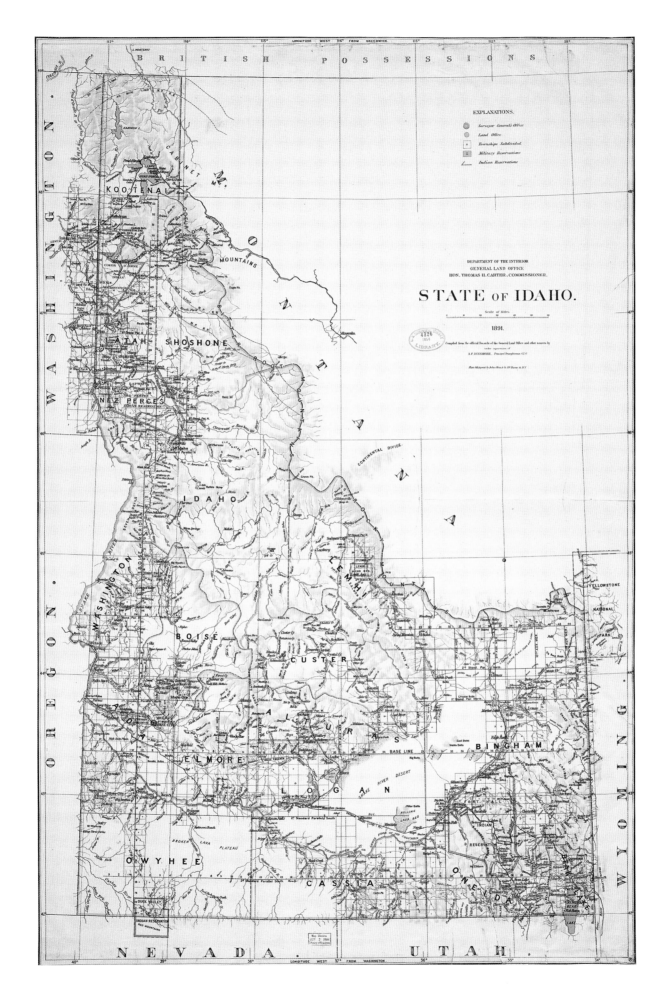

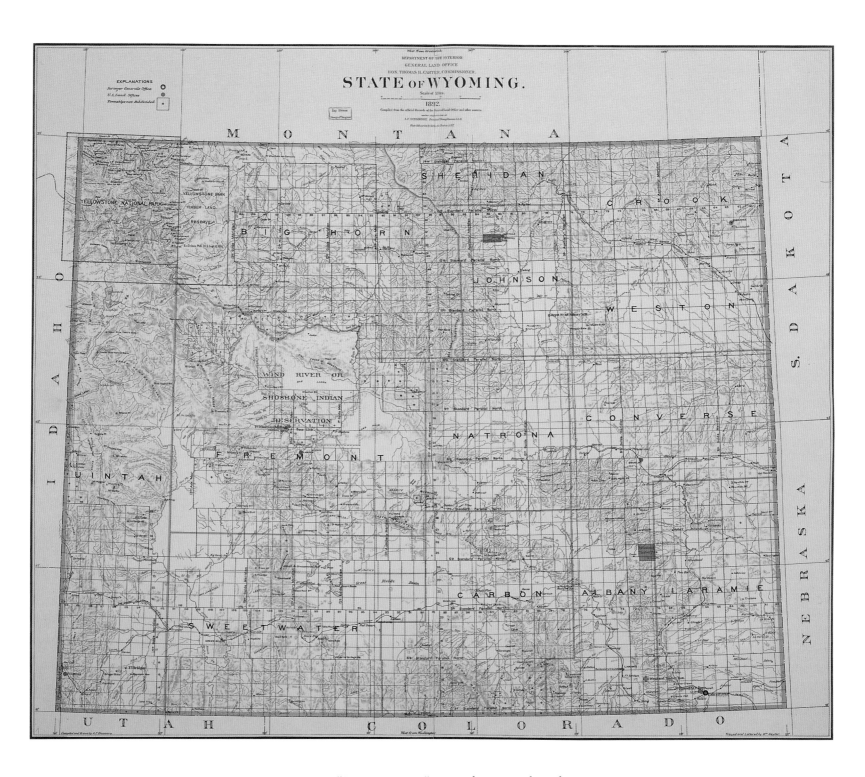

254. *A. F. Dinsmore. "State of Wyoming." New York, 1892. Lithograph, 76 x 90 cm.*
Geography and Map Division, Library of Congress, Washington, D.C. This map
was published within two years of Wyoming's becoming a state.

Boise, the state's capital and its largest city, took its name from the French *rivière boisée*, meaning "wooded river." Blackfoot is located at the confluence of the Blackfoot and Snake rivers and was named for the former, which in turn was derived from the name of an Indian tribe, a western extension of the Algonquins; it is believed that the tribal name came from the blackened moccasins that the men wore, and it has been suggested that the blackening came from the ashes of prairie fires. In 1818, the Hudson's Bay Company built a post at that site, and initially the settlement was called Grove City.

The city of Coeur d'Alene, from the French for "heart of awl," took its name from the local river and lake, which in turn were designated with the name the French gave to the area's Salish-speaking Indians, known for their trading skills. Idaho Falls identified the local falls within the city of that name. Moscow, the home of the University of Idaho, was named after the Russian capital, and the name of the home of Idaho State University, Pocatello, honored a Bannock chief who lived in the area. Nampa was the name of a Shoshone chief. Lewiston, the first territorial capital, took its name from Meriwether Lewis, who passed through the region during his expedition's journey of discovery westward and also on the return trip; the state's oldest city, Lewiston developed in 1861 as a supply center for gold miners. Rexburg was named, with altered spelling, by and for T. E. Ricks, the leader of that settlement. Twin Falls took its name from the falls of the Snake River—named for an Indian tribe—along which the community is located.

WYOMING

Wyoming, which had been organized as a territory in 1868 from areas that at one time or another had been part of the territories of Nebraska, Dakota, Idaho, and Utah, followed Idaho into the ranks of states by one week, becoming the forty-fourth state on July 10, 1890 (fig. 254). The land, the homeland of the Crow, Shoshone, Cheyenne, Arapaho, and Sioux, was acquired as part of the Louisiana Purchase, except for the southwest corner. It became a ranching center in 1868 after the advent of the Union Pacific Railroad. There are almost ninety-eight thousand square miles within the state. The boundary lines formed a rectangle, beginning in the northeast corner at the intersection of the twenty-seventh meridian west of Washington, D.C., or just west of 104° west longitude, and 45° north latitude; from that point, the northern boundary line—along Montana's southern border—proceeded west to the thirty-fourth meridian west of Washington, D.C., or just west of 111° west longitude; the western boundary line ran due south along that meridian to 41° north latitude; the southern boundary line ran due east along that parallel to the meridian just west of 104° west longitude; and the eastern boundary line ran due north along that meridian—part of the western borders of South Dakota and Nebraska—to the starting point.

The capital's name, Cheyenne, recognized the tribe in the area, while the state's two other large cities commemorated men who died in the vicinity. Casper was named for Lieutenant Caspar W. Collins, who was killed in a battle with the Indians in 1865; his name first was given to Fort Caspar. The "a" was changed by a clerical error to an "e" in the 1880s when the railroad arrived. The city, which became the second largest in the state, initially was settled on the shore of the Platte River at the convergence of the Oregon, Bozeman, Mormon, and Pony Express trails. Laramie, originally a fort where two famous treaties—the first in 1851 and the second, with Red Cloud and the Sioux Nation, in 1868—were signed, took its name from the river, which in turn bore the name of the trapper Jacques Laramie, who had been killed by the Indians in the region in about 1821. Cody was founded by William "Buffalo Bill" Cody (fig. 255), the famous scout, buffalo hunter, and showman, who arranged to have the Chicago, Burlington and Quincy Railroad run tracks to his land on the south fork of the Shoshone River. Rawlins was named for John A. Rawlins, a Union general in the Civil War who camped there in 1867. The famous Union general Philip H. Sheridan was honored with the naming of a city after him, by a founder who had served under him.

255. *Photographer unknown. Portrait of Buffalo Bill. New York, 1909. 23 x 18.5 cm. Courtesy Buffalo Bill Museum and Grave, Lookout Mountain, Golden, Colo.*

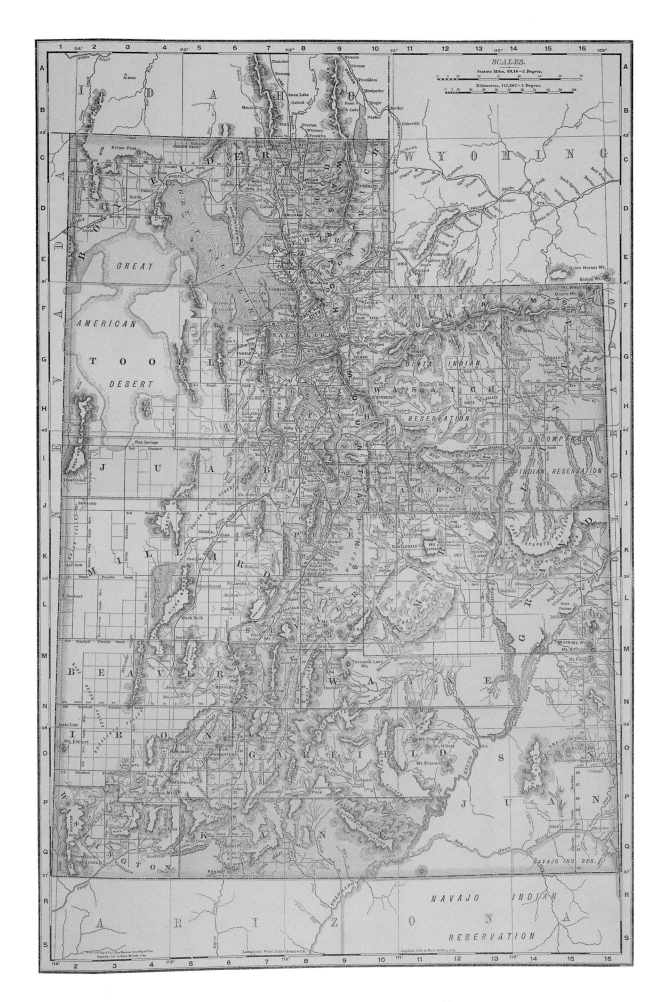

256. *Cartographer unknown.
"Utah." In* Indexed Atlas of
the World, *Chicago:
R. McNally & Co., 1898.
Lithograph, 48 x 32 cm.
Geography and Map Division,
Library of Congress,
Washington, D.C. The earliest
map of the state of Utah in
the Library of Congress,
published two years after Utah
was admitted into the Union.*

On January 4, 1896, Utah became the forty-fifth state—the twenty-ninth and last state added during the nineteenth century (fig. 256). The land, which was initially the home of the Ute, Paiute, and Navaho (also spelled Navajo) Indians, was first explored in the 1770s by Spaniards from Mexico, led by Father Francisco Garcés, and it witnessed the establishment of Spanish missions beginning in 1776. The region became part of the United States in 1848 as a result of the cession from Mexico after the Mexican War. The Mormons who started settling the area in 1847 formed what they called the state of Deseret in 1849, but the Mormon name was not accepted when the U.S. government established the Utah Territory in 1850, because of strenuous objections by Senator Thomas Hart Benton of Missouri. The name Utah, referring to the native Ute tribe, appeared as the names of a river and lake in the 1845 report of explorer John C. Frémont, Benton's son-in-law; it had also appeared in Spanish writings as early as 1720, as "yutta." In the Navaho language, the name means "upper or higher." For all these reasons, the name Utah won congressional approval.

When the Utah Territory was established, its limits were the state of California to the west, the Oregon Territory to the north, the summits of the Rocky Mountains to the east, and 37° north latitude to the south. The area was subsequently reduced by contributions to the territories of Nevada and Colorado, as well as two small portions that eventually became part of the Wyoming Territory, bringing the size of the state of Utah to approximately eighty-five thousand square miles. The present boundaries began in the northeast corner at the intersection of 42° north latitude and the thirty-fourth meridian west of Washington, D.C., or just west of 111° west longitude. The boundary line ran due south to 41° north latitude, then east to the thirty-second meridian west of the nation's capital, or just west of 109° west longitude; these two boundary lines were along the southwestern border of Wyoming. The rest of the eastern boundary line—the western border of Colorado—proceeded south along that meridian until it intersected 37° north latitude. The southern boundary line extended west along the thirty-seventh parallel to the thirty-seventh meridian west of Washington, D.C., or just west of 114° west longitude. The western boundary line, along most of Nevada's eastern border, ran due north along that meridian to its intersection with 42° north latitude. Finally, the northern boundary line ran east along the forty-second parallel to the starting point.

The Wasatch Range was named for a Ute Indian chief, whom the Spaniards referred to as Guasache. The state capital, Salt Lake City, took its name from the Great Salt Lake, which was given a role of prominence as early as the 1703 writings of Baron de La Hontan, describing his earlier travels around the interior of the continent. Bountiful was the second community to be settled. Only three days after Brigham Young and his followers arrived at the Great Salt Lake, Perrigene Sessions led a group to the area where Bountiful developed. It was first called Sessions Settlement, and then North Mill Creek Canyon; in 1855, Bountiful became the settlement's permanent name, taken from that of an ancient city in the Book of Mormon.

Ogden was named for the local river, which in turn was named for Peter Skene Ogden of the Hudson's Bay Company, who explored the area in the 1820s. Ogden is not far east of Promontory Point, the end of a peninsula jutting into the northern end of the Great Salt Lake; it was at the similarly named Promontory, about thirty miles to the north, that the famous golden spike was hammered down in 1869, completing the first coast-to-coast railroad line. Orem honored Walter C. Orem, the president of the Salt Lake and Utah Railroad. Provo was named for the French-Canadian trapper Étienne Provot, who lived in the region in the 1820s.

Kaysville was named for William Kay, an early settler who became the first Mormon bishop in the region. Nearby Layton, on the road from Salt Lake City to Ogden, was first settled in 1857 and was part of Kaysville until 1902, when the separated community was named for Christopher Layton, a leader in the Church of Jesus Christ of Latter-day Saints. Logan was a name initially assigned to a regional fort, in honor of an early trapper. Kearns grew out of a World War II U.S. Army base that subsequently closed but provided the nucleus for a modern city named for Thomas F. Kearns, a mining leader and U.S. senator.

OTHER DEVELOPMENTS

The nineteenth century was also marked by the first U.S. acquisitions of land outside the borders of the contiguous forty-eight states, as the country began to look outward for new resources and markets. Not long after missionaries began visiting the Hawaiian Islands in 1820, American companies arrived there to develop the sugar and pineapple industries. In 1859, an American ship sailing from Hawaii discovered the Midway Islands more than a thousand miles to the northwest, near the international date line; eight years later, the United States took possession of that isolated island group. That same year, the United States purchased Alaska, which most people considered worthless, from Russia. Hawaii was annexed in 1898, and Puerto Rico was ceded by Spain that same year, after the Spanish-American War (which also brought the Philippines, and in effect Cuba, under American control for decades). At the turn of the century, an international treaty gave the United States control over Eastern Samoa, the islands now known as American Samoa, lying east of 171° west longitude, far to the south of Hawaii.

CHAPTER THIRTEEN

The Twentieth Century

OKLAHOMA

Oklahoma was originally the home of the Osage, Kiowa, Comanche, and Apache tribes, and the land was included in the Louisiana Purchase. It was formalized as the Indian Territory in the 1830s, providing the United States with the opportunity to move the so-called Five Civilized Tribes—the Cherokees, Chickasaws, Choctaws, Creeks, and Seminoles—out of the southeastern states and across the Mississippi River. After the Civil War, the Five Civilized Tribes (some of which had supported the Confederate States of America) were forced to cede land to the federal government to establish a new territory. When it came time to name the area, the Reverend Allen Wright, chief of the Choctaws, suggested Oklahoma, because *okla* means "people" and *homa* means "red" in his native language.

The Oklahoma Territory was organized in 1890, a year after it was officially opened up to white settlement in a famous "land rush." It was made up of the western part of the Indian Territory, as well as a narrow strip of unorganized public land north of the Texas Panhandle (and of the 1820 Missouri Compromise line dividing free and slave states) that Texas had sold to the United States in 1850. When Oklahoma (fig. 257) was admitted as a state in 1907, its land also incorporated an area called Cherokee Outlet in Greer County and the Indian Territory to the east, which by then had been broken up by congressional action into individual allotments and often acquired by white settlers. The congressional act to admit Oklahoma into the Union also included provisions for the later admission of New Mexico and Arizona.

On November 16, 1907, Oklahoma became the forty-sixth state, keeping its territorial name (fig. 258); the capital, Oklahoma City, incorporated in 1890, further perpetuated the Choctaw term. The state's boundaries encompassed about seventy thousand square miles. The northern boundary line, between Oklahoma and Kansas (as well as the southeast corner of Colorado), ran along the parallel of 37° north latitude to 103° west longitude. The short western border on the Panhandle ran south along that meridian from 37° north latitude

Opposite: 257. *A. F. Dinsmore and M. Hendges. "State of Oklahoma." Washington, D.C., 1907. Lithograph, 54.5 x 107.5 cm. Geography and Map Division, Library of Congress, Washington, D.C. This map was published within weeks of Oklahoma statehood.*

258. *The cast of Oklahoma!—the 1943 Rodgers and Hammerstein musical set around the time the territory became a state. Costars Alfred Drake, as Curly, and Joan Roberts, as Laurey, are in the "surrey with the fringe on top"; Celeste Holm, as Ado Annie, stands to the right of Lee Dixon, as Will Parker. Theater Guild, New York*

to 36°30'. The long border between Oklahoma and Texas began at that point, extended east along 36°30' north latitude to 100° west longitude, then south along that meridian to the intersection with the south fork of the Red River; the line then followed the winding Red River eastward to the Arkansas border, at 94°37' west longitude. The eastern boundary line, along the Arkansas border, ran due north from that point to the Arkansas River, then northwest to the starting point, just beyond the southwest corner of Missouri.

The Indian origin of place-names is more pervasive in Oklahoma than in any other state. Tulsa, which was incorporated a year before statehood, took its name from that of a local Creek settlement, meaning "old town." The genesis of that name was a similarly named town in the original Creek land in the Southeast; when the forced westward migration occurred, the Creeks carried ashes of their ancestors and the name from the original Tulsa to their new settlement. Anadarko derives from the Na-da-ka Indian tribe. Chickasha (from Chickasaw), Choctaw, Muskogee, and Ponca City are all taken from tribal names. Sapulpa was named for James Sapulpa, an early Creek settler in the area. Okmulgee, a place-name meaning "water bubbles" in Muskogean and first used in Georgia (where Ocmulgee is still the name of a river, as well as a national monument at the site of ancient Indian villages), was assigned by the settlers of that Oklahoma city because of a nearby stream. Tahlequah, the Cherokee capital in the Indian Territory, was also a place-name, meaning "old town," that was moved from an earlier Cherokee settlement in the southeastern part of the United States. Owasso, meaning "end" in the Osage language, was selected because of that settlement's role as a railroad terminus. As a city name, Broken Arrow reminds us of the ceremony in which an arrow is broken to symbolize the reunion of disagreeing factions within North American Indian tribes.

Norman, the name of the hometown of the University of Oklahoma, came from the railroad station there. Laborers working for a young surveyor and supervisor, Abner E. Norman, burned his name into the trunk of an elm tree to taunt the boss, who was not present; when the station was completed, it took its name from the tree. A settlement developed in the area in 1889. A similar situation pertained to the naming of the city of Moore. It was the name of a conductor on the Atchison, Topeka and Santa Fe Railroad; the name was placed on a sign at the train stop, which later became the nucleus of the community. Bartlesville took the name of Jacob Bartles, a Civil War veteran who built a gristmill in that locale in 1873. Enid also adopted an individual's name, that of a woman who had been romanticized in Alfred Lord Tennyson's popular poem "Geraint and Enid."

259. A. F. Dinsmore. "State of New Mexico." Washington, D.C.: The Eckert Lithographing Co., 1912. Lithograph, 93.5 x 79 cm. Geography and Map Division, Library of Congress, Washington, D.C. This map was published several months after New Mexico joined the Union.

The year 1912 marked the admission of two new states, and with that the completion of the contiguous forty-eight states, encompassing all the land between Canada and Mexico, from the Atlantic Ocean to the Pacific. On January 6, New Mexico became the forty-seventh state (fig. 259). That area, in which Spanish explorers discovered pueblos in the sixteenth century, and which was ceded by Mexico at the end of the Mexican War in 1848, was the stopping point for many of the settlers heading to the West along the old Santa Fe Trail. The New Mexico Territory was established in 1850, consisting of land acquired by the Treaty of Guadalupe Hidalgo and also some land ceded by Texas. The territory was enlarged in 1853, by the Gadsden Purchase and reduced in 1861 and 1863 by the cession of land to the Colorado and Arizona territories, respectively. In addition, when New Mexico became a state, its eastern border with Texas was adjusted slightly, based on an 1874 survey; as a result, that boundary line was shifted to just a few miles west of 103° west longitude, rather than right on that meridian, as is the very short eastern border with the end of the Oklahoma Panhandle. As a state, New Mexico's northern boundary line was at 37° north latitude; its western boundary line was the thirty-second meridian west of Washington, D.C., or just west of 109° west longitude; and the southern boundary line with Texas began at the eastern corner at 32° north latitude and continued west along the boundary with Texas until it jogged south to include the land acquired by the Gadsden Purchase.

New Mexico's state boundaries began in the northeast corner at the intersection of 103° west longitude and 37° north latitude—the northwest corner of Oklahoma—and from there ran south to 32° north latitude. The southern boundary line ran west along the thirty-second parallel to the intersection with the Rio Grande, from which point it proceeded down the main channel of that river to its point of intersection with the boundary line between the United States and Mexico, established by the 1848 Treaty of Guadalupe Hidalgo; then it followed that international border west, south, and west again to its intersection with the thirty-second meridian west of Washington, D.C., or just west of 109° west longitude. The western boundary line ran due north along this meridian to the thirty-seventh parallel, which formed the northern boundary line—almost all of the southern border of Colorado—east back to the starting point.

The state of New Mexico, which encompasses approximately 122,000 square miles, took its name from Mexico, which was a name that the Spanish conquistadores adopted in the early sixteenth century. The original inhabitants of Mexico called themselves Mexicas, and the word *mexico* in Nahuatl, the language of the Aztecs and Mexicas, is a combination of three words: *metx(tli)*, meaning "moon"; *xic(tli)*, meaning "navel"; and *co*, meaning "in." Thus, this aggregation of words results in a term meaning "in the navel of the moon." It may also mean "place of the [Aztec] war god," referring to Mexitel.

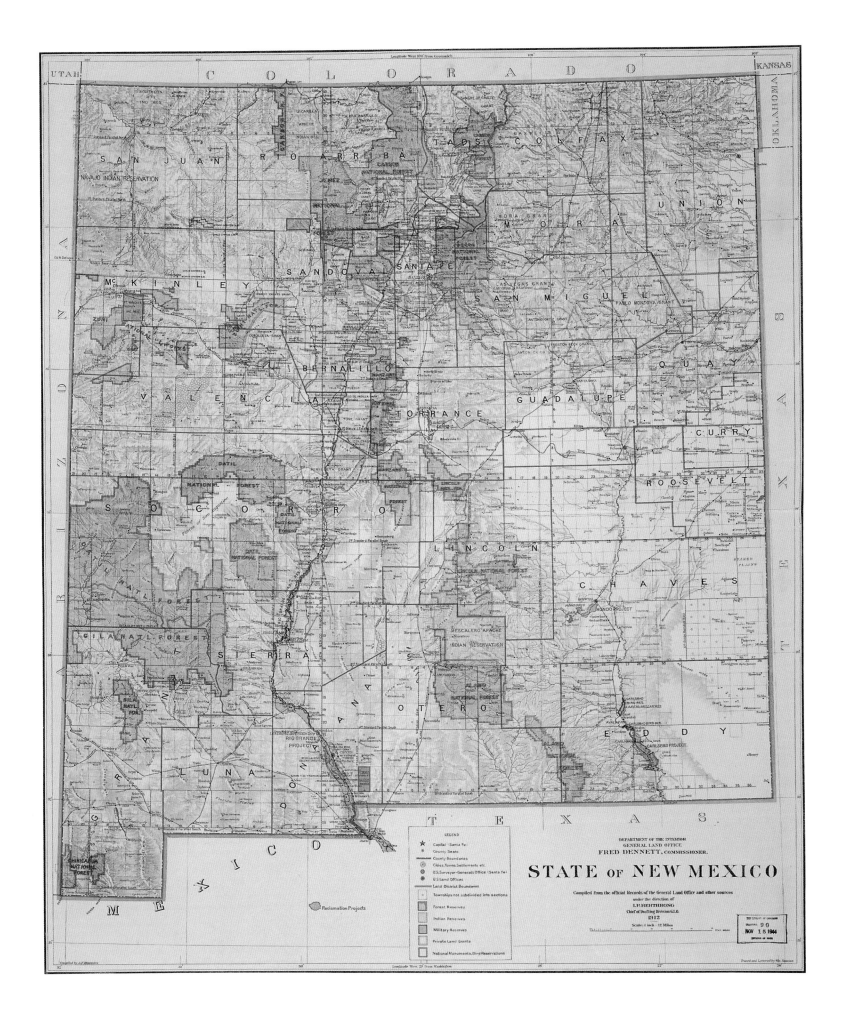

STATE of NEW MEXICO

DEPARTMENT OF THE INTERIOR
GENERAL LAND OFFICE
FRED DENNETT, COMMISSIONER.

Compiled from the official Records of the General Land Office and other sources
under the direction of
I.P. BERTHRONG
Chief of Drafting Division G.L.O.
1912
Scale: 1 inch = 12 Miles

LEGEND
★ Capital (Santa Fe)
• County Seats
County Boundaries
⊙ Cities, Towns, Settlements, etc.
⊙ U.S. Surveyor-Generals Office (Santa Fe)
● U.S. Land Offices
Land District Boundaries
Townships not subdivided into sections
Forest Reserves
Indian Reserves
Military Reserves
Private Land Grants
National Monuments, Bird Reservations

Reclamation Projects

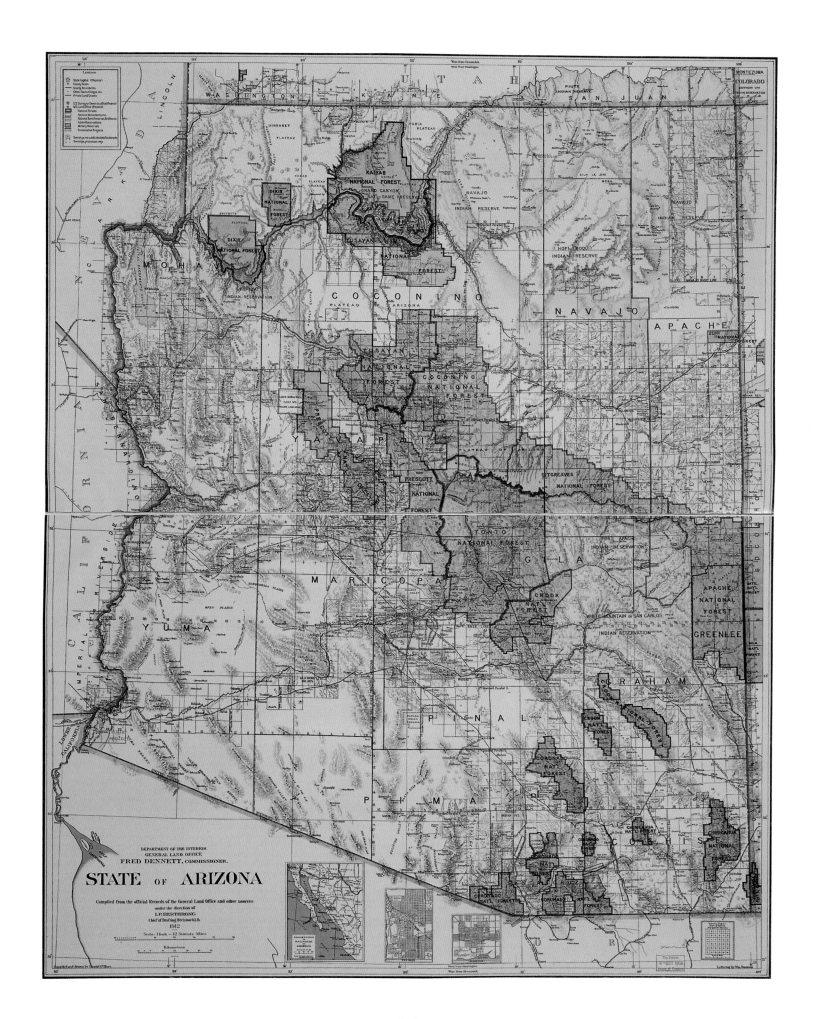

It was appropriate that the second-oldest continually functioning community in what is now the United States should be maintained as the state capital. Santa Fe, meaning "holy faith," is what remains of the original settlement, La Villa Real de las Santa Fe de San Francisco. Albuquerque was settled in 1706, when it took the name of the duque de Alburquerque, the viceroy of New Spain, dropping the first "r" in much the same way that Cleveland dropped an "a" from the name of the man it was honoring. The Spanish influence persisted in the naming of Los Alamos, for the poplar trees there, and Las Cruces, for the crosses over buried settlers killed by Indians in the region. Alamogordo also incorporates *alamo*; *gordo* means "big."

Carlsbad, with its medicinal springs, imported its name from the German spa of Karlsbad. The largest Indian center in the Southwest is Gallup, which was named in 1881 for David Gallup, an Atchison, Topeka and Santa Fe Railroad paymaster, who set up a small company office in that locale. Tucumcari took the Indian name of a regional mountain, meaning "ambush." Clovis has an obscure origin, supposedly having been given the name of a fifth-century Frankish king by the daughter of a railroad magnate. The city of Hot Springs changed its name to Truth or Consequences in 1950 with the promise that the popular radio and television show would broadcast from that locale as the center of an annual celebration; the name remains, long after the show has vanished.

ARIZONA

On February 14, 1912, Arizona, meaning "a place with a small stream" in the Papago language, became a state, completing the "forty-eight" (fig. 260). The land of the last of the contiguous states to be admitted into the Union was actually one of the first to be traversed by Europeans, when Álvar Núñez Cabeza de Vaca made his historic trek in 1536, when Fray Marcos de Niza explored the area in 1539, and when Francisco Vásquez de Coronado arrived in 1540. Most of the territory was ceded to the United States by the Treaty of Guadalupe Hidalgo in 1848. The final segment, south of the Gila River (named for an Indian tribe), was added by the Gadsden Purchase of 1853. The homeland of the Navaho, Papago, Hopi, and Apache tribes was formally organized as a territory in 1863, comprising land from the western part of the New Mexico Territory. Settlement in the area increased in 1886 after the final surrender of Geronimo (fig. 261), thereby ending twenty-five years of Apache wars.

The state of Arizona consists of about 114,000 square miles. The boundaries were described as beginning in the northeast corner (known as Four Corners, the only spot where four states meet) at the intersection of 37° north latitude and the thirty-second meridian west of Washington, D.C., or just west of 109° west longitude; the eastern boundary line proceeded south along this meridian, the western border of New Mexico, to the international border between the United States and Mexico, which the southern boundary line followed west and then northwest to the Colorado River; the western

Opposite: 260. *I. P. Berthrong. "State of Arizona." Washington, D.C.: The Eckert Lithographing Co., 1912. Lithograph, 95 x 77.5 cm. Geography and Map Division, Library of Congress, Washington, D.C. This map, published shortly after Arizona became a state, shows the last of the 48 contiguous states to join the Union.*

261. *Geronimo in 1884; the earliest known photograph of the Apache leader, then about 55 years old. Courtesy National Archives and Records Service, Washington, D.C. Photograph by A. Frank Randall*

boundary line ran up the main channel of that river, along part of the eastern borders of California and Nevada, to the point of intersection with the thirty-seventh meridian west of Washington, D.C., or just west of 114° west longitude, and from there due north to 37° north latitude; finally, the northern boundary line ran eastward along that parallel, the southern border of Utah, back to the starting point.

Phoenix, the state's capital and largest city, was settled in 1870 and incorporated in 1881, and it took its name—from the mythological bird that arose from the ashes—because relics from an ancient Indian culture had been discovered in the area. Tucson was the site of a Spanish presidio, or fortified settlement, in the mid-eighteenth century and was included in the Gadsden Purchase; the city took its name from the mission there, which was so named by the Papago Indians because the word means "black base," referring to the base of a nearby mountain. Mesa, which adopted the Spanish word meaning a "flat hill with steep sides," was founded by a group of Mormons. Sierra Vista is Spanish for "mountain view." Nogales derives from the Spanish *nogal*, meaning "walnut"; the plural was used because there were two such trees, one on each side of a local boundary. And there are two cities of Nogales, one on each side of the U.S.–Mexican border.

Flagstaff originally was the name of a local spring, called that because a flag was flown from a tall tree alongside it. Tempe was named for the ancient Greek Vale of Tempe, a valley near the home of the gods, Mount Olympus. Yuma was named after a local Indian tribe. The Indian heritage throughout Arizona is also evidenced by the naming of Apache Junction and Lake Havasu City; Havasu means "blue" in the Mohave language.

In 1891, Dr. Alexander J. Chandler arrived as the first veterinarian in the Arizona Territory. He eventually accumulated eighteen thousand acres, and in 1912 he established the township that became a city named for its founder. Scottsdale, which was incorporated in 1951, is built on the site of an old Hohokam village and is named for Chaplain Winfield Scott, who arrived in the area in 1881. Sedona was named for an early woman settler, Sedona N. Schnebly.

ALASKA

Nearly forty-seven years later, Alaska, the largest state and the one with the second-fewest inhabitants (exceeding only Wyoming), achieved statehood on January 3, 1959, thereby becoming the forty-ninth state (fig. 264). Its history dates to its discovery in 1741 by the Danish explorer Vitus Bering, who sailed under the Russian flag. In 1778, Captain Cook explored and described the Alaskan coast. In 1793, Russian fur traders led by Alexander Baranov established the first permanent settlement, at St. Paul's harbor on Kodiak Island. In 1867, Russia sold all of the nearly 590,000 square miles of its Alaskan territory to the United States for 7.2 million dollars, the equivalent of 1.9 cents per acre. At the time, the seemingly useless acquisition was mocked as "Seward's Folly," called that because the negotiations were conducted by William H. Seward, secretary of state (fig. 262).

In 1885–87, Lieutenant Henry Allen explored and mapped the area around the Yukon, Tanana, and Koyukuk rivers. The first of these rivers was initially named Yukonna, the Athapaskan (or Athabascan) word for "big river." Tanana is a shortening of *tananatana*, meaning "mountain people river." Koyukuk derives from an Eskimo tribal name. The initial population spurt occurred during the Alaskan gold rush in the 1890s and early 1900s. In 1912, Alaska was made a territory.

The chain of islands belonging to Alaska extends westward beyond the halfway point around the world from Greenwich, England, to 172°30' east longitude, although the international date line bends to the west of Attu so that all of the Aleutian Islands observe the same calendar day. The boundary between Alaska and Canada from the northern coast to the so-called southeastern panhandle, at 60° north latitude, runs along 141° west longitude. Disputed since the 1896 Yukon gold strike, the boundary of the southeastern panhandle was fixed in 1903 by a United States–Canada Alaskan boundary tribunal. The agreed-on boundary passed in a straight line from Cape Muzon to the southern end of Tongass Passage, then through the passage up the Portland Canal to 56° north latitude. The line then ran from one specified mountain summit to another until it reached the head of the Lynn Canal, from which point it traversed the White and Chilkoot passes. From there it took a southwesterly course to Mount Fairweather, then continued northwesterly to the higher mountains around Yakutat Bay and finally to Mount St. Elias, where it intersected the 141st meridian. It has been pointed out that if Alaska and the Aleutian Islands were superimposed on the contiguous forty-eight states in a true north–south position, touching the Canadian border just west of the Lake of the Woods, the state's boundaries would reach the Atlantic Ocean between South Carolina and Georgia, cross the Mexican border from southwestern New Mexico, and touch the Pacific Ocean in southern California (fig. 263).

Alaska is an Aleut word meaning "part of the mainland." Juneau, the state capital, was settled during the gold rush and took the name of one of the early successful miners, Joe Juneau. Juneau and Richard Harris, after leaving the Alaskan town of Sitka, made the first major discovery of gold in Alaska in 1880. A town site that was named Harrisburgh was established, and the federal government sent Lieutenant Commander Charles Rockwell to maintain order. When the town was incorporated, because Harrisburgh was used to designate other places in the United States, the name Rockwell was accepted instead; aggressive lobbying by Juneau, however, resulted in the change to its permanent name.

Fairbanks also grew up around mining camps. In 1902, E. T. Barnette established the first trading post in the area, and when it was incorporated in 1903, he induced the settlers to honor Charles W. Fairbanks, an Indiana senator who headed the 1903 boundary commission and the following year was elected vice president under Theodore Roosevelt. The state's most populous city, Anchorage, was founded in 1914 as an outgrowth of a railroad construction camp;

262. *Emanuel Leutze.* Signing of the Alaska Treaty. *1867. Oil on canvas,*
102 x 153 cm. Courtesy the Seward House, Auburn, N.Y. This major
U.S. acquisition was widely regarded as "Seward's Folly" at the time.

263. *The relative size of Alaska and the contiguous United States. In Franklin K. Van Zandt's* Boundaries of the United States and the Several States, *Geological Survey Professional Paper 909, Washington, D.C.: U.S. Government Printing Office, 1976.*

264. *"State of Alaska" (atlas plate 18). July 1959. Lithograph, 48 x 63 cm. Courtesy National Geographic Society, Washington, D.C. This modern map was published the year Alaska became the 49th state.*

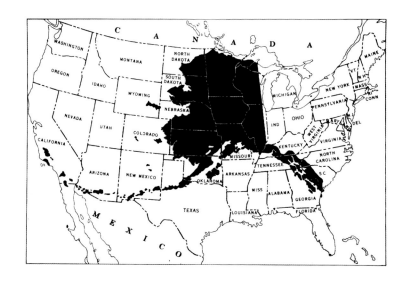

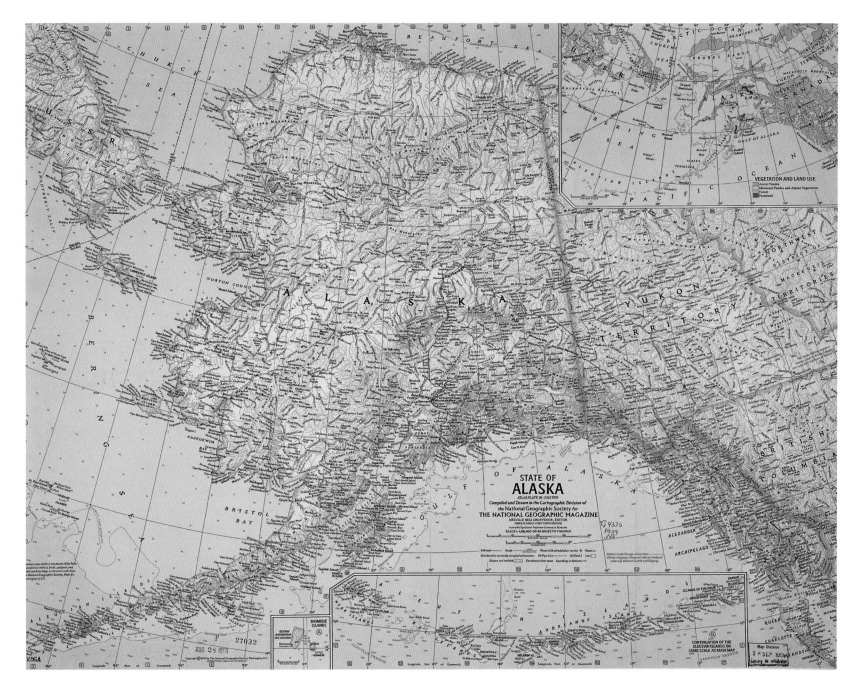

an old postal drop-off point along the coast had been called Knik Anchorage, and when the city was incorporated in 1920, it assumed part of that place-name.

The city of Ketchikan, which began as a salmon factory in 1883 and was incorporated in 1900, took as its name a Tlingit description *katch konna,* meaning "spread wings of prostrate eagle," referring to a local waterfall in which a central rock creates a winglike flume. Kenai adopted a modification of an Eskimo word, *kakny,* in which *ny* means "river." The island city of Sitka is a compaction of the Tlingit *shee atika; shee* means "seaward," and *shee atika* translates as "people on the outside of seaward." Kodiak was the name appropriately assigned to the largest of the Aleutian Islands, because the word means "island" in the Eskimo language.

HAWAII

On August 21, 1959, Hawaii achieved statehood, completing the current fifty-state United States of America. The islands of Hawaii were first settled between A.D. 300 and 600 by Polynesians from the Marquesas Islands or Tahiti, far to the south. On January 18, 1778, Captain James Cook became the first European to discover the islands, and on January 21 he set foot on land, at Waimea on the island of Kauai. On February 13, 1779, he was killed by natives on the island of Hawaii. By 1810, King Kamehameha I had united all the islands under his sovereignty. Ten years later, the Reverend Hiram Bingham established a native Congregational Church. King Kamehameha III created a constitutional monarchy in 1840 (fig. 265). In 1893, dissatisfied Hawaiians and Americans in the sugar industry overthrew Queen Liliuokalani (who also composed the famous song "Aloha Oe"). The following year, Sanford B. Dole, the American sugar and pineapple magnate, took charge of the new republic, which the United States annexed in 1898. Hawaii was granted territorial status in 1900.

Hawaii is made up of eight larger islands and more than one hundred minor ones, scattered over an area in the Pacific Ocean that occupies about 2,000 miles in a northwest to southeast direction, with a width of about 150 miles (fig. 266). The major islands are located between 19° and 22°15' north latitude and between 155° and 162° west longitude. They have a total area of about 6,400 square miles and a total coastline of 957 miles. The eight main islands, in decreasing size, are Hawaii, Maui, Oahu, Kauai, Molokai, Lanai, Niihau, and Kahoolawe.

The state of Hawaii takes its name from the island of Hawaii, which is the largest and southernmost island. The name, which derives from *hawaihi* or *owhyhee,* meaning "homeland," also means "big island" in Polynesian. In addition, the word *hawaii* refers to an aqueduct or flume. Some individuals have suggested that Hawaii means "burning Java" or "little Java." Most linguists, however, suggest the Hawaiian place-names are so ancient that the precise etymology cannot be determined. Tourists are told that the name of the most populated island, Oahu, means "gathering place," and that the name of

265. *James Dwight Dana. "Honolulu, Oahu, Nov. 1840 Drawn from shipboard. Wilkes Exploring Expedition." Sketch, pen and ink on paper, 33 x 106.7 cm. Courtesy Hawaiian Mission Children's Society Library, Honolulu. This scene was drawn the same year King Kamehameha III created a constitutional monarchy.*

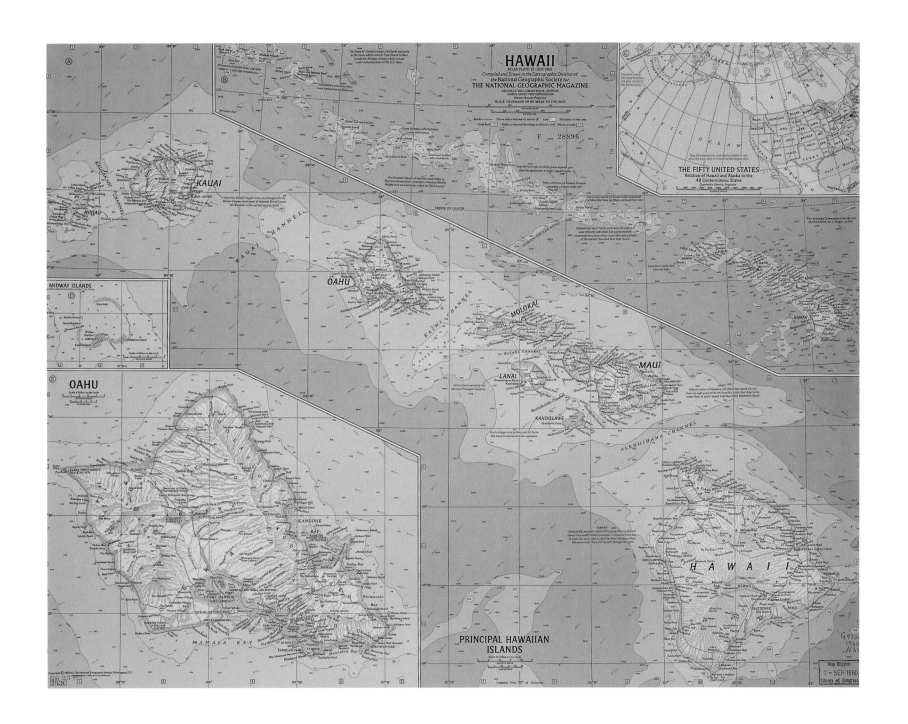

266. *"Hawaii" (atlas plate 15). July 1960. Lithograph, 48 x 63 cm.
Courtesy National Geographic Society, Washington, D.C. This map shows
Hawaii shortly after it became the 50th and most recent state.*

267. Honolulu, with Waikiki Beach and Diamond Head in the background.
Courtesy Jose B. Lee, Honolulu

the state capital, Honolulu, derives from Polynesian for "safe harbor."
Honolulu's harbor (fig. 267) was first entered by Europeans in 1794,
and that city was designated as the capital of the kingdom in 1850. The
island of Maui was supposedly named for a mischievous demigod.
Kauai, the oldest of the islands, is called the "garden island." Molokai
is a former leper colony that is now known as the "friendly island";
the name Molokai is said to translate as "calm waters." Lanai formerly
was the island with the largest pineapple plantations, and it is the one
island name that linguists suggest has a known meaning, "conquest
day." The name Kahoolawe has been presumed to refer to the "island
of death"; it is uninhabited and was used as a practice bombing target
for the U.S. Navy during World War II.

PUERTO RICO

Puerto Rico (fig. 268), comprising that island's almost thirty-five
hundred square miles and the nearby West Indian islands of Vieques,
Culebra, Mona Island, Muertos, and Desecheo, were ceded to the
United States by Spain in 1898 at the end of the Spanish-American
War (fig. 269) as part of a treaty that also included the cession of
Guam in the western Pacific Ocean. The history of Puerto Rico as it
relates to the United States dates to the second voyage of Christopher Columbus, in 1493. The explorers arrived at an island that the
native Taino and other Arawak Indians called Boriquén or Borinquén,
which translates as "the great land of the valiant and noble Lord."

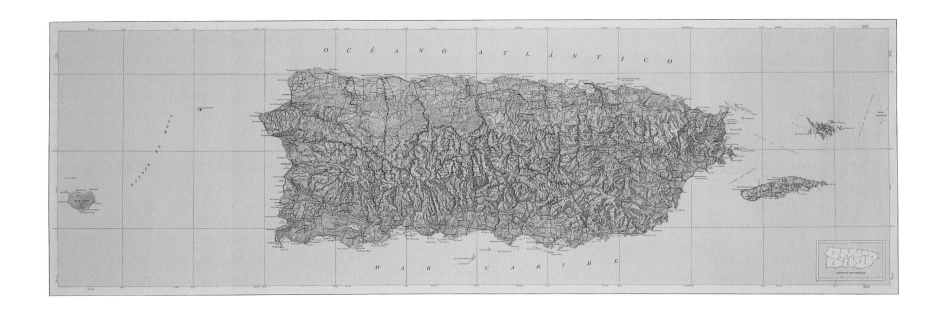

268. *Cartographer unknown. "Puerto Rico E Islas Limitropes." Washington, D.C., 1952. Lithograph, 131.5 x 41 cm. U.S. Department of the Interior Geological Survey, Washington, D.C. This map of Puerto Rico and adjacent islands was published the year Congress granted it commonwealth status.*

269. *W. G. Read. Teddy Roosevelt's "Rough Riders" in battle. Philadelphia: George H. Harris & Sons, 1898. Lithograph, 37 x 51 cm. Library of Congress, Washington, D.C. Col. Theodore Roosevelt leads his "Rough Riders" up Kettle Hill, near Santiago, Cuba, on July 1, 1898, during the Spanish-American War. The overall battle, commonly known as San Juan Hill, made Roosevelt a war hero and resulted in his becoming President William McKinley's running mate in the election of 1900—and president when McKinley was assassinated the following year.*

In 1508, Juan Ponce de León, who had been on that second voyage, began the conquest and colonization of the island, which Columbus named San Juan Bautista for Saint John the Baptist; Puerto Rico, or "rich port," was originally the name of the port. In a brief time, the roles of the two names were reversed.

Ponce de León founded the island's first settlement in 1508 and called it Caparra. Across the bay from that site, San Juan originated in 1521. The village called La Ribera de Arecibo was settled in 1566, taking its name from a local Indian chief, Jamaica Aracibo; the city of Arecibo was founded in 1616. Bayamón also took the name of an indigenous chief, called Bahamon or Bayamongo. The first sugar mill was built in the area in 1548, and the city, which initially had been known as El Pueblo del Chicharrón, was founded in 1770.

Mayagüez, from the Taino Indian name for the regional river, translates as "place of great waters." At its founding in 1760, the settlement called itself Nuestra Señora de la Candeleria, but the Indian term persists. Fajardo, known as La Metropoles del Sol Nacienta (meaning "the city that guards the sun"), was settled in 1772. A year later Cayey, first called Cayey de Muesas, was founded. Caguas, which was settled in 1775, derives its name from a local chief, an early Christian convert; the settlement's original name was San Sebastian de Pinal de Caguax. The city of Carolina, which was incorporated in 1857, was originally named Trujillo Bajo. The city developed in a region known as La Tierra de Gigantes (meaning "the land of giants"), because a resident was supposedly seven feet eleven inches tall.

In 1952, Congress granted the island of Puerto Rico commonwealth status, with local autonomy. A local referendum and congressional approval are both required for it to become the fifty-first state. In 1998, however, a referendum indicated that the inhabitants preferred that Puerto Rico be maintained as a commonwealth.

OTHER U.S. POSSESSIONS

A few other islands besides Puerto Rico remain under the control of the United States. The U.S. Virgin Islands, located in the northwestern part of the Lesser Antilles a short distance east of Puerto Rico, were ceded by Denmark in 1917 for twenty-five million dollars. The territory, which has a popularly elected governor but is administered by the U.S. Department of the Interior, consists of 133 square miles of land on dozens of islands and islets, the main ones being St. Croix, St. Thomas, and St. John. There are about one hundred thousand permanent residents, and the capital is Charlotte Amalie on St. Thomas.

Guam is a territory located in the Mariana Islands in the western Pacific Ocean, about six thousand miles southwest of San Francisco. (The rest of the Northern Mariana Islands, taken from Japan during World War II, constitutes a U.S. commonwealth, similar to that of Puerto Rico.) Part of the Spanish cession after the Spanish-American War, Guam is under the jurisdiction of the Interior Department, and its current government was established in 1950. The capital is Agaña. The island is about thirty miles long and varies between four and a half and eight miles wide. The population is approximately one hundred thousand.

American Samoa, which became part of the United States in 1900 and is also administered by the Interior Department, is located about twenty-two hundred miles southwest of Hawaii in the South Pacific. For several years toward the end of the nineteenth century, the Samoan Islands were a joint protectorate of the United States, Great Britain, and Germany. In 1900, Britain withdrew and the United States received the islands in the group that were east of 171° west longitude. (Western Samoa remained in German hands and eventually became independent.) The seven islands that constitute American Samoa encompass about eighty square miles of land. The capital is Pago Pago, located on the largest island, Tutuila. The population is about sixty thousand.

Wake, Midway, and Johnston islands also belong to the United States. Wake Island, which consists of about three square miles of land on three islets (Wake, Wilkes, and Peale) around a lagoon, is located in the western Pacific Ocean about two thousand miles west of Honolulu, Hawaii. The United States acquired it in 1898; it was in Japanese hands for nearly all of World War II. It is administered by the U.S. Air Force. Midway comprises an atoll and two islands (totaling about two square miles) located twelve hundred miles west of Honolulu, and it became a U.S. possession in 1867. It is now a naval installation, with a population of less than five hundred military personnel, as well as a National Wildlife Refuge. Johnston Atoll, located a few degrees of latitude due south of the western Hawaiian Islands and claimed by Hawaii during the mid-nineteenth century, consists of Johnston Island, Sand Island, and other small islands. Together, the two larger islands have two hundred acres and a few hundred inhabitants, all government personnel and contractors; it is administered by the federal Defense Nuclear Agency and is managed as a National Wildlife Refuge. Elsewhere in the Pacific, more than one thousand miles from Hawaii, the United States also has control over the tiny and mostly uninhabited Baker and Howland islands to the southwest and Jarvis Island, Kingman Reef, and Palmyra Atoll to the south; in the Caribbean, between Jamaica and Haiti, only a lighthouse marks U.S. control of the tiny island of Navassa.

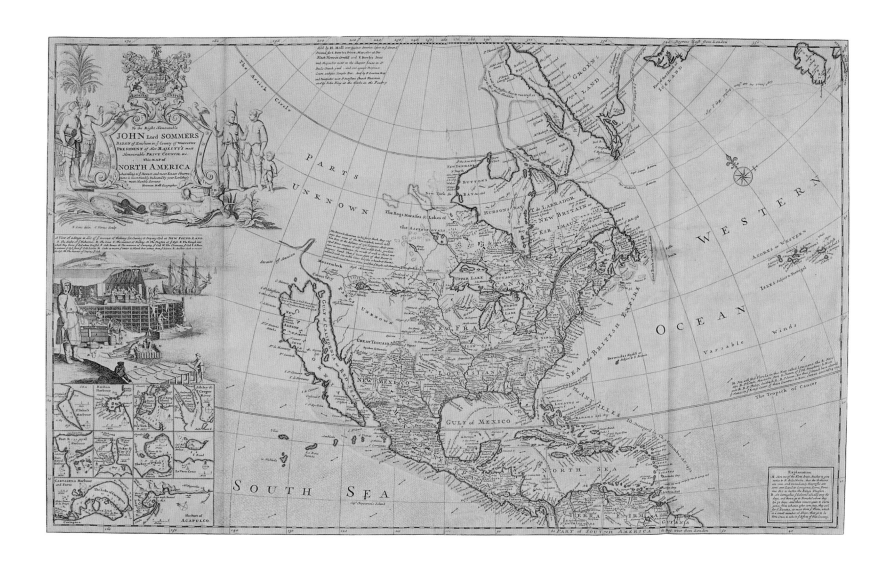

CHAPTER FOURTEEN

Condensing the Chronological Circle

It can be said that the evolution of "this land" began in Puerto Rico, where a brief landing in 1493, during Columbus's second voyage, was followed twenty years later by Juan Ponce de León's use of that island as a base from which he launched the first European explorations of the mainland that eventually became the United States of America. Four centuries later, the geographic evolution of the United States came full circle with the acquisition of Puerto Rico, and at the beginning of the twenty-first century, that island has been considering whether to become the fifty-first state. During the past five hundred years, the arcs of that chronological circle defining this land have included a panoply of discovery, settlement, growth, acquisition, expansion, political power shifts, aggrandizement, disruption, reconstruction, and division of territory—all gradually resulting in the current fifty states.

Various European powers participated in completing those arcs by extending their territories into what turned out to be a vast continent, already inhabited by natives whom the Europeans called Indians (because of lingering confusion with the East Indies), living in hundreds of nations. The Spanish made the initial incursions into what is now the United States, from their vantage points in the Caribbean and Mexico, during the sixteenth century (fig. 271). Their major contributions in the realm of discovery were in the peninsula they called Florida, along the west coast, and in the southwestern region. The French approached the continent from the north and were the major explorers of the Great Lakes and the Mississippi River Basin. The Dutch settled in New York and other northeastern areas in the early and mid-seventeenth century, but their control was short-lived. The English, who eventually displaced the Dutch, colonized the entire east coast, starting in what later became North Carolina and Virginia to the south (fig. 272) and in two Massachusetts colonies to the north; in a little more than a century, they had established the thirteen colonies—most as commercial ventures, but some as refuges for religious dissidents—that later became the first states of the new nation. Toward the end of the 1700s, Russian traders began to leave a minuscule imprint on the extreme northwestern part of the continent.

Opposite: 270. *Herman Moll. "Map of North America According to ye Newest and most Exact observations." 1720. Engraving, hand-colored, 57 x 97 cm. Private collection. A late map still showing California as an island. A vignette depicts codfish processing, and Eskimos and Indians are portrayed on the cartouche. There are also insets of Boston, New York City, and Charleston.*

271. *Sebastian Münster. "Novae Insulae, XVII Nova Tabvla." 1540. Woodcut, 24 x 34 cm. Private collection. The first map (titled "New Islands, New Tables") depicting the New World as an insular landmass. It shows continuity between North and South America, and it also depicts the imagined "Sea of Verrazano."*

During the eighteenth century (fig. 270), England, an expanding empire that now called itself Great Britain, gained control of almost all the French lands at the end of a long war—only to lose its own colonies (except for Canada) just two decades later, after another war. That War for Independence, the American Revolution (1775–83), established the United States of America. While delegates to the Constitutional Convention in 1787 were still in the midst of establishing a new system of federal government to unite the thirteen states more effectively, and years before a federal district was selected to be the seat of that government (fig. 273), the young but rapidly growing nation made provisions to allow expansion westward from the settlements of the original colonies, which clung to the eastern seaboard, into the public lands stretching to the Mississippi River.

Westward expansion suddenly took on new dimensions with the doubling of the size of the country because of the 1803 Louisiana Purchase from the French, who had obtained that territory again after a short period of control by the Spanish (fig. 274). Within twenty-five years, access to the interior of the continent, and from the rich interior to the coastal trading ports, had been facilitated by the appearance of commercially viable steamboats plying the Mississippi and other rivers, by the construction of the first national roads, by the completion of the Erie Canal in upstate New York, and by the beginnings of a rapidly developing network of railroads. In the course of the American push westward, one Indian tribe after another was displaced from its lands, by treaty or conquest—and often displaced again as settlers moved into an agreed-upon new tribal homeland.

The acquisition of land—by treaty, as in the case of Spanish-held Florida in the Southeast and the Oregon Country in the Pacific Northwest, which the British had claimed; by secession, in the case of Texas, which fought for independence from Mexico before joining the United States; by conquest, as in the case of California and most

272. Theodore de Bry. The village of Secoton, Va. c. 1585. Engraving, after a 1585 drawing by John White. Private collection. An Indian village, showing living quarters, planted fields, and a council. John White landed in Virginia but later returned to England, leaving behind his daughter. In 1587 she gave birth to Virginia Dare—the first child born of English parents in the New World.

273. Charles Burton. The U.S. Capitol. 1824. Watercolor, gum arabic, and graphite on off-white wove paper, 40.5 x 63 cm. Courtesy the Metropolitan Museum of Art. Purchase, Joseph Pulitzer Bequest, 1942 (42.138) Copyright 1989. The domed Capitol building, shown here with its tree-lined approach, was greatly enlarged in the mid-1800s.

274. *Abraham Bradley Jr. "Map of the United States, Exhibiting the Post-Roads, the situations, connections & distances of the Post-Offices, Stage Roads, Counties, & Principal Rivers" (detail). 1804. Engraving, hand-colored; entire map, 97 x 134 cm. Geography and Map Division, Library of Congress, Washington, D.C. This map was published before information was gained from the Lewis and Clark expedition. Land west of the Mississippi River is almost completely devoid of place-names.*

of the Southwest, acquired as a consequence of the Mexican War (fig. 275); and by payment, as in the case of the Gadsden Purchase from Mexico of what later became southern Arizona and New Mexico, as well as the vast, neglected Russian possession of Alaska—all contributed to the establishment of the current extent of the United States. A succession of well-worn trails, railway tracks, and roads joined the territories to one another (fig. 276). And filling the expanding frontiers of the country was an ever-growing stream of migrants, fed in turn by increasing numbers of immigrants, drawn from foreign shores by the promise of economic opportunity and liberty (fig. 277).

In a steady progression from the late eighteenth century to the early twentieth century, areas were obtained, settled, organized as

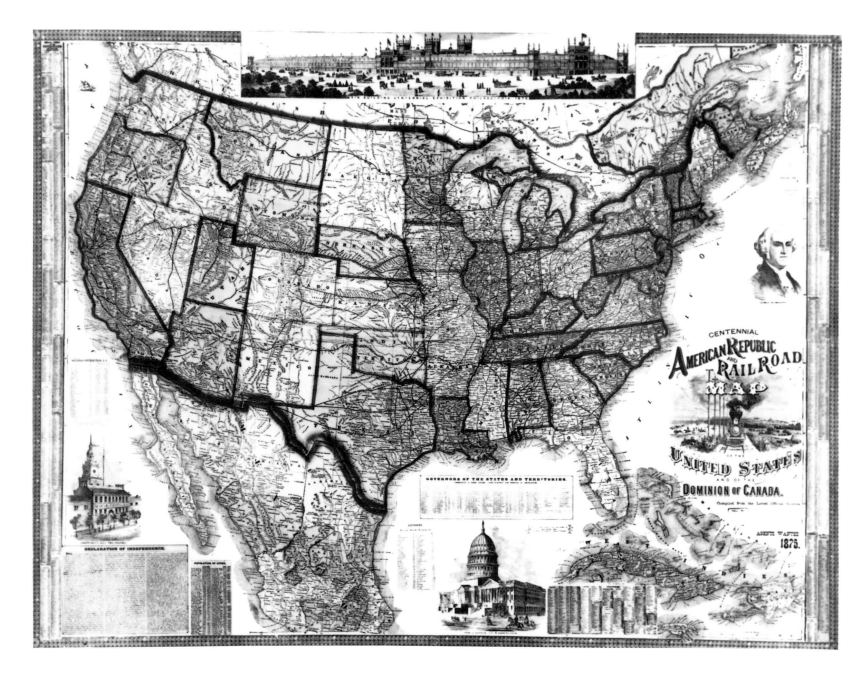

Opposite, top: 275. *C. B. Graham. "Mouth of Night Creek." In William H. Emory's* Notes of a Military Reconnaissance . . . , *Washington, D.C.: Wendell and Van Benthuysen, 1848. Lithograph, after a drawing by John Mix Stanley; 10 x 17 cm. The earliest view of the Southwest.*

Opposite, bottom: 276. *Gaylord Watson. "Centennial American Republic and Railroad Map of the United States and of the Dominion of Canada. Compiled from Latest Official Sources." New York, 1875. Lithograph, hand-colored, 94 x 129.5 cm. Geography and Map Division, Library of Congress, Washington, D.C. The map, actually published a year before the centennial, is decorated with pictures of the Capitol building, Independence Hall, George Washington, and the main building of the 1876 Centennial Exhibition in Philadelphia.*

277. *Edward Moran. The Statue of Liberty Enlightening the World. 1886. Oil on canvas, 100 x 126 cm. Courtesy the Museum of the City of New York. This was painted in the same year that the famous gift from France was dedicated.*

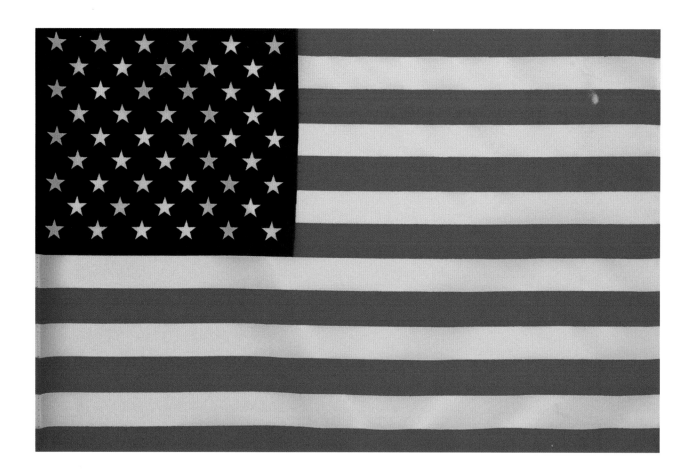

278. *Current flag of the United States of America, with 50 stars.*
Photograph by Martha Smith

territories, and admitted as states. Within the country's continental confines, this partitioning into states and territories, which in turn contributed to more states, created the internal mosaic pattern of the United States. In the second half of the twentieth century, with the addition of the distant states of Alaska and Hawaii, as well as the establishment of commonwealth status for Puerto Rico, the current pattern was completed (fig. 278).

During the two hundred years from 1790 to 1990, the area that constitutes this land more than quadrupled, from 891,364 square miles to 3,787,428 square miles, including land and water; in the same period, the population of the United States soared from about 3.9 million to 248.7 million. The land within the continental United States abuts two oceans, the Atlantic and Pacific, as well as the Gulf of Mexico. The length of the northern border between the forty-eight contiguous states and Canada is 3,987 miles long, while the border between Alaska and Canada totals 1,538 miles. The southern border with Mexico is 1,433 miles long.

The northernmost city is Barrow, Alaska, and the northernmost landmass is Point Barrow, named in 1826 for Sir John Barrow, the English geographer and promoter of the expedition that discovered the point. The southernmost city is Hilo, Hawaii, and the southernmost land is South Cape on the Hawaiian island of Ka Lae. Because of the international date line, both the easternmost and westernmost points are in Alaska; the former is Point Semisopochnoi Island, and the latter is Amatignak Island. The westernmost city is Atka, Alaska; because the western Aleutian Islands are too sparsely populated, the easternmost city is Eastport, Maine. If only the contiguous forty-eight states are considered, the northernmost point is the northwest angle of Minnesota, and the northernmost city is Bellingham, Washington, which took its name from the bay that English explorer George Vancouver named in 1792 for Sir William Bellingham, who aided in preparing for that voyage; the southernmost point and city are Key West, Florida; the easternmost point is West Quoddy Head, Maine; and the westernmost point is Cape Alava, Washington.

The geography of the United States is also marked by a high point of 20,320 feet at Mount McKinley (fig. 279), Alaska, and a low point in Death Valley (fig. 280), California, of 282 feet below sea level—the lowest point in the Western Hemisphere. The settlement with the highest elevation is Climax, Colorado, and the one with the lowest is Calipatria, California.

279. *Mt. McKinley, the highest peak in the United States. In Franklin K. Van Zandt's* Boundaries of the United States and the Several States, *Geological Survey Professional Paper 909, Washington, D.C.: U.S. Government Printing Office, 1976.*

280. *Death Valley, Calif.: Badwater, the lowest point in the valley—and the country—at 282 feet below sea level. In Franklin K. Van Zandt's* Boundaries of the United States and the Several States, *Geological Survey Professional Paper 909, Washington, D.C.: U.S. Government Printing Office, 1976. Photograph by Josef Muench*

281. *"The United States. Produced by the Cartographic Division of the National Geographic Society." Washington, D.C., 1988. Lithograph, 58 x 84 cm. Courtesy National Geographic Society, Washington, D.C.*

All over this land, the pieces of the mosaic that constitutes the United States, and the locales within those pieces, have been anointed by names drawn from the history of the land and the people who participated in its evolution (fig. 281). During the past five centuries, the names and descriptive words of Native Americans have been affixed to maps, juxtaposed with Spanish, English, French, Dutch, German, Swedish, Swiss, Italian, and Polynesian place-names and terms. Saints, kings, aristocrats, heroes, settlers, developers, entrepreneurs, and the relatives of founders have been memorialized in the names that persist.

The romance of the discovery and evolution of the country has been augmented by the selection of terms used to identify all the places,

both natural and of human origin, that exist in the United States. In his poem "American Names," Stephen Vincent Benét focuses on the intrigue and infatuation associated with the variety and origin of place-names that dot this land. Many people share his sentiment: "I have fallen in love with American names."

The seventeenth-century explorer John Smith wrote the truth when he stated that "History without Geography wandereth as vagrant without certaine habitation." But his introductory remark, "As Geography without History seemeth as carkasse without motion," is incorrect; as we have seen, geography incorporates history, and, as such, it propels itself along with an intrinsic vitality (figs. 282 and 283).

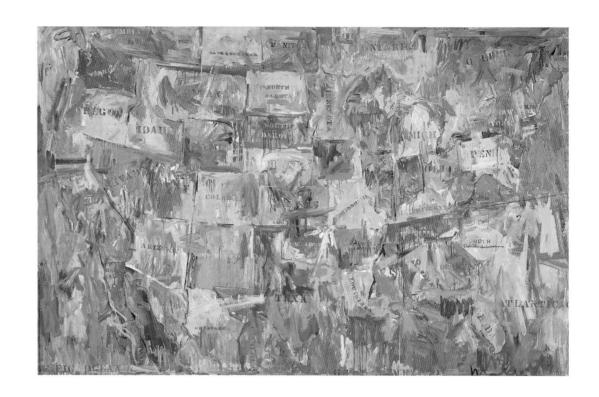

282. *Jasper Johns. Map. 1961. Oil on canvas,*
198 x 315 cm. Courtesy the Museum of
Modern Art, New York City.
Gift of Mr. and Mrs. Robert C. Scull.
© Jasper Johns / Licensed by VAGA,
New York City

283. *Jasper Johns. Flag. 1954. Encaustic, oil,*
and collage on fabric mounted on plywood,
103 x 154 cm. Courtesy the Museum of
Modern Art, New York City. Gift of Philip
Johnson in honor of Albert J. Barr, Jr.
© Jasper Johns / Licensed by VAGA,
New York City

Bibliography

Allen, John Logan. *Passage Through the Garden: Lewis and Clark and the Image of the American Northwest.* Urbana: University of Illinois Press, 1975.

Ambrose, Stephen E. *Undaunted Courage.* New York: Simon & Schuster, 1996.

Andrews, Charles M. *The Colonial Period of American History.* 4 vols. New Haven, Conn.: Yale University Press, 1934–37.

Bailyn, Bernard. *Voyagers to the West.* New York: Alfred A. Knopf, 1986.

Bancroft, George. *The History of the United States of America from the Discovery of the Continent.* Abridged and edited by Russell B. Nye. Chicago: University of Chicago Press, 1966.

Berkhofer, Robert F., Jr. *The White Man's Indian: Images of the American Indian from Columbus to the Present.* New York: Random House, 1978.

Billington, Ray Allen. *Westward Expansion: A History of the American Frontier.* 4th ed. New York: Macmillan, 1974.

Bolton, Herbert E., and Thomas M. Marshall. *The Colonization of North America, 1492–1783.* New York: Macmillan, 1920.

Boorstin, Daniel J. *The Americans: The National Experience.* New York: Random House, 1965.

Bowman, John S., ed. *The Civil War: Day by Day.* Greenwich, Conn.: Brompton Books, 1989.

Brown, Lloyd A. *Early Maps of the Ohio Valley: A Selection of Maps, Plans, and Views Made by Indians and Colonials from 1673 to 1783.* Pittsburgh: University of Pittsburgh Press, 1959.

Brown, Ralph H. *Historical Geography of the United States.* New York: Harcourt, Brace, 1948.

Burrus, Ernest J. *Kino and the Cartography of Northwestern New Spain.* Tucson: Arizona Pioneers Historical Society, 1965.

Calhoun, Milburn, and Jeanne Frois, eds. *Louisiana Almanac.* Gretna, La.: Pelican Publishing Company, 1997.

Clark, Charles E. *The Eastern Frontier: The Settlement of Northern New England, 1610–1763.* New York: Alfred A. Knopf, 1970.

Cleland, Hugh. *George Washington in the Ohio Valley.* Pittsburgh: University of Pittsburgh Press, 1955.

Cumming, William P. *British Maps of Colonial America.* Chicago: University of Chicago Press, 1976.

————. *The Southeast in Early Maps: With an Annotated Check List of Printed and Manuscript Regional and Local Maps of Southeastern North America During the Colonial Period.* Princeton, N.J.: Princeton University Press, 1958.

Cumming, W. P., S. E. Hillier, D. B. Quinn, and G. Williams. *The Exploration of North America.* New York: American Heritage Press, 1972.

Cumming, W. P., R. A. Skelton, and D. B. Quinn. *The Discovery of North America.* New York: American Heritage Press, 1972.

DeVorsey, Louis, Jr. *The Indian Boundary in the Southern Colonies, 1763–1775.* Chapel Hill: University of North Carolina Press, 1966.

DeVoto, Bernard. *The Course of Empire.* Lincoln and London: University of Nebraska Press, 1952.

Ehrenberg, Ralph E. *Geographical Exploration and Mapping of the 19th Century: A Survey of the Records in the National Archives.* Reference Information Paper No. 66. Washington, D.C.: U.S. Government Printing Office, 1973.

Espenshade, Abraham H. *Pennsylvania State Names.* State College, Pa.: Pennsylvania State College Press, 1925.

Fortier, Alcee, ed. *Louisiana: Comprising Sketches of Parishes, Towns, Events, Institutions, and Persons, Arranged in Cyclopedic Form.* Vols. 1 and 2. Madison, Wis.: Century Historical Association, 1914.

Friis, Herman R. "Highlights in the First Hundred Years of Surveying and Mapping and Geographical Exploration of the United States by the Federal Government 1775–1880." *Surveying and Mapping* 18 (1958): 186–206.

Gard, Robert E., and L. G. Sorden. *The Romance of Wisconsin Placenames.* Minoqua, Wis.: Heartland Press, 1988.

Garrett, Wilbur E., ed. *Historical Atlas of the United States.* Washington, D.C.: National Geographic Society, 1988.

Gipson, Lawrence Henry. *The British Empire Before the American Revolution.* Vols. 5–8. New York: Alfred A. Knopf, 1930–61.

Gould, Charles N. *Oklahoma Place Names.* Norman: University of Oklahoma Press, 1933.

Graebner, Norman A. *Empire on the Pacific: A Study in American Continental Expansion.* New York: Ronald Press, 1955.

Gudde, Erwin G. *California Place Names: The Origin and Etymology of Current Geographical Terms.* Berkeley: University of California Press, 1969.

————. "Fremont-Preuss and Western Names." *Names: Journal of the American Name Society* 5 (1957): 159–81.

Haring, C. H. *The Spanish Empire in America.* New York: Harcourt, Brace & World, 1947.

Harrisse, Henry. *The Discovery of North America: A Critical, Documentary, and Historic Investigation, with an Essay on the Early Cartography of the New World.* London: H. Stevens, 1892.

Johansen, Dorothy O., and Charles M. Gates. *Empire of the Columbia: A History of the Pacific Northwest.* 2nd ed. New York: Harper & Row, 1967.

Lancaster, Bruce, and J. H. Plumb. *The American Heritage Book of the Revolution.* New York: American Heritage Publishing Company, 1932.

Marshall, Thomas M. *A History of the Western Boundaries of the Louisiana Purchase, 1819–1841.* Berkeley: University of California Press, 1914.

McArthur, Lewis L. *Oregon Geographic Names.* Salem: Oregon Historical Press, 1952.

Meany, Edmond S. *Origin of Washington Geographic Names.* Seattle: University of Washington Press, 1923.

Meinig, D. W. *The Shaping of America: A Geographical Perspective on 500 Years of History.* Vol. 1, *Atlantic America, 1492–1800.* New Haven, Conn., and London: Yale University Press, 1986.

————. *The Shaping of America: A Geographical Perspective on 500 Years of History.* Vol. 2, *Continental America, 1800–1867.* New Haven, Conn., and London: Yale University Press, 1993.

Mitchell, Robert D., and Paul A. Groves, eds. *North America: The Historical Geography of a Changing Continent.* Totowa, N.J.: Rowman & Littlefield, 1987.

Modelski, Andrew M., comp. *Railroad Maps of the United States: A Selective Annotated Bibliography of Original 19th-Century Maps in the Geography and Map Division of the Library of Congress.* Washington, D.C.: Library of Congress, 1975.

Morison, Samuel Eliot. *The European Discovery of America.* Vol. 1, *The Northern Voyages, A.D. 500–1600.* New York: Oxford University Press, 1971.

————. *The European Discovery of America.* Vol. 2: *The Southern Voyages, A.D. 1492–1616.* New York: Oxford University Press, 1974.

————. *The Oxford History of the American People.* New York: Oxford University Press, 1965.

Morison, Samuel Eliot, and Henry Steele Commager. *The Growth of the American Republic.* 3rd ed. New York: Oxford University Press, 1942.

Morris, John W., and Edwin C. McReynolds. *Historical Atlas of Oklahoma.* Norman: University of Oklahoma Press, 1965.

Nebenzahl, Kenneth. *Atlas of the American Revolution.* Chicago: Rand McNally and Company, 1974.

Onuf, Peter S. *Statehood and Union: A History of the Northwest Ordinance.* Bloomington: Indiana University Press, 1987.

Paullin, Charles O. *Atlas of the Historical Geography of the United States.* Edited by John K. Wright. New York: American Geographical Society, 1932.

Pearce, Thomas M. *New Mexico Place Names: A Geographical Dictionary.* Albuquerque: University of New Mexico Press, 1965.

Pukui, Mary K., Samuel Elbert, and Esther T. Mookni. *Place Names of Hawaii.* Honolulu: University of Hawaii Press, 1974.

Read, William A. *Florida Place-Names of Indian Origin and Seminole Personal Names.* Baton Rouge: Louisiana State University Press, 1934.

Ristow, Walter W. *Maps for an Emerging Nation: Commercial Cartography in Nineteenth-Century America.* Washington, D.C.: Library of Congress, 1977.

Schwartz, Seymour I.: *The French and Indian War 1754–1763: The Imperial Struggle for North America.* New York: Simon & Schuster, 1994.

Schwartz, Seymour I., and Ralph E. Ehrenberg. *The Mapping of America.* New York: Harry N. Abrams, Inc., 1980.

Shirk, George H. *Oklahoma Place Names.* Norman: University of Oklahoma Press, 1965.

Smith, Bradley. *The U.S.A.: A History in Art.* New York: Thomas Y. Crowell, 1982.

Socolofsky, Homer E., and Huber Self. *Historical Atlas of Kansas.* Norman: University of Oklahoma Press, 1972.

Stewart, George R. *American Place-Names: A Concise and Selective Dictionary for the Continental United States of America.* New York: Oxford University Press, 1970.

————. *Names on the Land.* New York: Random House, 1945.

Van Zandt, Franklin K. *Boundaries of the United States and the Several States.* Geological Survey Professional Paper No. 909. Washington, D.C.: U.S. Government Printing Office, 1976.

Vogel, Virgil J. *Indian Place Names in Illinois.* Springfield: n.p., 1963.

Wagner, Henry R. *The Cartography of the Northwest Coast of America to the Year 1800.* Berkeley: University of California Press, 1937.

Wheat, Carl I. *Mapping the Transmississippi West 1540–1861.* Vols. 2–5. San Francisco: Institute of Historical Cartography, 1958–63.

Wheat, James C., and Christian F. Brun. *Maps and Charts Published in America Before 1800: A Bibliography.* New Haven, Conn.: Yale University Press, 1969.

Winsor, Justin, ed. *Narrative and Critical History of America.* 8 vols. Boston: Houghton, Miflin and Company, 1884–89.

Acknowledgments

As was true of many of my past writings, Wendy Cowles Husser contributed significantly. Richard Slovak's careful editing and in-depth research were essential ingredients of the scholarship of the final product. Ron Grim, Specialist in Cartographic History at the Library of Congress, and his staff expedited the research and reproduction of many of the maps. Martha Smith and Royal Chamberlain produced most of the photographic material. Maria Miller's artistry was responsible for the elegant design and presentation. I am particularly appreciative of the comments of Senator Daniel Patrick Moynihan and the foreword by the Honorable Barber Conable Jr., a former member of Congress. The knowledge, love, and endorsement of the promulgation of American history by these congressional leaders have been exemplary.

Index